Eschatology ι
Shape of Christian Belief

Robert C. Doyle

In honour of
David Broughton Knox and James B. Torrance
my best teachers.

paternoster press

First published in 1999 by Paternoster Press

05 04 03 02 01 00 99   7 6 5 4 3 2 1

Paternoster Press is an imprint of Paternoster Publishing,
PO Box 300, Carlisle, Cumbria, CA3 0QS, UK
http://www.paternoster-publishing.com

British Library Cataloguing in Publication Data
A catalogue record for this book is available from the British Library

ISBN 0-85364-818-2

Cover Design by Mainstream, Lancaster
Typeset by WestKey Ltd, Falmouth, Cornwall
Printed in Great Britain by
Caledonian International Book Manufacturing Ltd, Glasgow

Contents

Preface

This book has come out of two ongoing and related experiences. The first is rooted in theology, especially as it concerns the promises of God for the future. Towards the end of the Scriptures we have a promise which focuses a history of promise stretching back to Abraham, and further back to Eden. The promise is that God has given us his divine power, so that we may have everything necessary in order to escape our present corruption, and 'become participants in the divine nature' (2 Peter 1:1–4). That is, by an amazing act of sheer grace we are becoming sharers of God's glory, partners together in that most holy communion of God's inner life. Our experience of that communion is faith in 'the One he has sent', and the transformation of life and being which accompanies our faith union with this Christ, and through and in him with the Father and the Spirit. The wonder of it is that God has promised to do this for us whose existence is characterized by 'corruption'.

Flowing from this promise is the simple observation that knowl‐ edge of the last things, 'eschatology', must have its foundation in its end point, namely the being of God, his nature, who he is and how he acts. To ask questions and find answers about 'the last things' is not merely to acquire knowledge of future events, but is to be led into the whole of theology, to the very heart of the matter, where God *is*. Which brings me to the second experience. This book has come out of long dialogue in the theology classroom. In my own circumstances here in *Terra Australis* I have tried to teach in a way that introduces the foundational aspects of a topic, and then leads students on into grasping some of the deeper interconnecting structures of Christian thought. I hope to arouse genuine and reverent curiosity, and thus a deeper appreciation and assurance of the 'breadth and length and height and depth' of the grace and the love of the God who has drawn us to himself.

I hope this helps account for the nature of the book and makes it useful in the classroom. In the language of the trade, it is offered as an 'advanced textbook'. It contains introductory descriptions of the particulars of eschatological belief as they have surfaced in the church's historical experience and attempts to place them within the overall theological outlook of various Christian writers. Finally, each position is assessed in terms of the normative teaching about God's being and action contained in Holy Scripture.

Although my aim is to foster a systematic theology in the reader, the method I have followed is structured by historical theology. At a public lecture in Sydney on the 500th anniversary of Martin Luther's birth, Heiko Oberman gave a telling apologetic for the value of historical theology. We historians of theology are like porters on a railway platform. As the great systematicians slowly engage their new and powerful locomotives of Christian thought, with the refurbished and realigned carriages of theological topics lined up behind in regular and impressive order, we poor historians run along the platform pushing a wheelbarrow, shouting, as the great engines come up to full power: 'Stop! Stop! Here are things you have left behind!' Historical theology has the benefit of raising questions that we may be ignorant of or have forgotten, and raising them in the context of a real human struggle to remain faithful to God's self-disclosure. To do this in a such a way as to raise the wider issues and offer a critique has meant that I have had to make choices. These have been dictated by my assessment of the contribution an individual or movement has made to the development of eschato-logical thinking and wider theological thought. In the end, they are personal choices based on a necessarily limited experience; and while your own situation may lead you to consider other theological figures, I hope the style and content of this book will prove stimulating.

Many acknowledgements and expressions of gratitude are due. My students and the faculty at Moore Theological College have been keen conversation partners, and at times it is hard to know whether it is I who speak, or they. No endeavour to cover nearly 2000 years of Christian theological construction could be effec-tively done alone. My own modest research interests have tended to be in and around John Calvin, a love I have had the honour of sharing for nearly two decades with my former teacher, James Torrance of the University of Aberdeen. I am also deeply indebted to the many scholars who have laboured before me in various areas of eschatological thought, and whom I have sought to fully acknowledge in the appropriate places. David Steinmetz very kindly read earlier versions of the two chapters on Luther and Calvin while I was on sabbatical leave at Duke University, North Carolina, and made several helpful criticisms. The libraries of both Moore College and the Divinity School at Duke University have been invaluable. My wife, Roslyn, and my four children have been patient and supportive to a degree that I too often have not fully reciprocated. This is their book too. If others are to be rightly credited with whatever strengths there may be in the following exposition, the faults are mine alone.

Where I have expressed criticism of the eschatological thinking of our theological forebears, it is in the knowledge that they have endeavoured to serve the church and Christ's cause in the world as vigorous and faithful teachers, and for our benefit still speak.

Soli Deo gloria

Abbreviations

ANF	The Ante Nicene Fathers
CD	Karl Barth, *Church Dogmatics*
Com	commentary
CR	*Corpus Reformatorum*
FOC	The Fathers of the Church
FOCn	The Fathers of the Church, a new translation
Ins	John Calvin, *Institutes of the Christian Religion*
LCC	Library of Christian Classics
LW	Luther's Works, American Edition
LXX	Septuagint
NIV	New International Version
NPNF (1)	The Nicene and Post-Nicene Fathers, First Series
NPNF (2)	The Nicene and Post-Nicene Fathers, Second Series
NRSV	New Revised Standard Version
OS	*Ioannis Calvini Opera Selecta*
RSV	Revised Standard Version
RV	Revised Version
SC	Sources Chretiénnes
SCG	Thomas Aquinas, *On the Truth of the Catholic Faith: Summa Contra Gentiles*
Serm	sermon
ST	Thomas Aquinas, *Summa Theologiae*

1

Why Eschatology?

Eschatology and the Shape of our Theology

For most of us, and indeed for many theologians, theology is in 'small bits', or topics. Theology textbooks will have, say, a chapter on conversion, another on the doctrine of revelation, yet another on sanctification. No doubt because of the great depth and range of the subject, we tend to think and speak not so much in terms of an overall theology, but in terms of topics. The same often occurs with our knowledge of the Bible. We may have detailed knowledge of the Book of Acts, but not quite see how it fits into the ebb and flow of the entire history of God's dealings with us as unfolded from Genesis to Revelation.

However, somewhat paradoxically, anyone who has spent time trying to think seriously about Christian issues will have an overall shape to their theology. The human mind works to make sense of individual items which come to its attention by constructing a framework which allows it to see where the individual pieces of knowledge should fit, and therefore their significance in the total scheme of things. Our minds inevitably construct this framework, even if they have to fill in what they do not know by guesswork. The point for theology is this: even if there are vast gaps in our knowledge of God, and even if we have guessed wrongly, all of us are likely to have a framework, a shape to our theology. When we face questions raised by new information, whether from the Bible or from experience, this shape enables us to find answers.

It is not hard to show that the shape of one's theology is determined by the way one understands several main ideas: crea-tion, the nature of humanity, the cross, and eschatology. If one has these major areas right, then the rest of one's theological reflection is more likely to be true to the teaching of Holy Scripture. If not, then the reverse.

The meaning of the cross is explored in systematic theology under several titles, but most especially 'atonement' and 'justification'. So, for example, if we believe, as the medieval church tended to believe, that the righteousness Christ won on the cross is in fact stored as merits in a treasury of merits which God only opens and distributes to offset our sins or demerits in response to an appropriately contrite approach, then forgiveness only comes to the ordinary sinner with great difficulty. For the ordinary sinner, when honest with himself, knows that his contrition or sorrow at sin falls far short of what it should be when seen with God's eyes. So, the medieval Christian committed him or herself to a rigorous sacra - ment of penance, while, for all that effort, never having the assur - ance that enough had been done to gain full forgiveness and escape the fires of purgatory, or even of hell itself. But view the cross through a different doctrine of justification, as the sixteenth-century Reformation did, and life changes dramatically. As Calvin put it, when we see that because of the death of Christ we have in heaven a loving Father, instead of an angry judge, we repent with gratitude, assurance, even joy.[1]

Consider another example, drawn from the medieval period, but also thoroughly contemporary. In the Middle Ages the Christian church in the West almost exclusively understood the atonement in terms of the satisfaction theory of Anselm, whereby the death of Christ rendered satisfaction for the dishonour we have done God in our rebellion against him as our rightful Lord. For all the problems associated with the medieval presentation of the satisfac - tion theory, it was a powerful and helpful picture of the meaning of the cross. But, as Gustav Aulén pointed out so many years ago, it so dominated their thinking that an older theory of the atonement was all but ignored, the *Christus Victor* (Christ is Conqueror).[2] This 'classical theory' stressed the fact that on the cross our Lord was victorious over the satan and all his domain, and had smashed all the powers of darkness. We may put it this way. The church had stressed the text, 'he himself bore our sins in his body on the tree'

---

[1] 'We mean to show that a man cannot apply himself seriously to repentance without knowing himself to belong to God. But no one is truly persuaded that he belongs to God unless he has first recognized God's grace.' *Institutes of the Christian Religion* (tr. F.L. Battles; London: SCM, 1961) 3.3.2. The whole of chapter three deserves close study.
[2] Gustav Aulen, *Christus Victor: An Historical Study of the Three Main Types of the Idea of the Atonement* (London: SPCK, 1931).

(1 Pet. 2:24), but not sufficiently understood the importance of, 'having disarmed the powers and authorities, he made a public spectacle of them, triumphing over them by the cross' (Col. 2:15). It is no surprise then that the theological writings and the religious culture of the period showed sustained fear and preoccupation with demons and the demonic. Much of popular Christian culture was little better than a sort of magic to ward off the ever-present, all-pervasive, and almost all-powerful satan.

The Protestant Reformation not only saw further developments in the satisfaction theory, but also a recovery of *Christus Victor*, especially by Martin Luther. Having once again grasped the complete once-for-all-ness of the cross over not only our sin but also the demonic, the Reformers were once again able to appreciate the significance of Paul's dictum, 'be wise about what is good, and remain innocent about what is evil' (Rom. 16:19). With evil crushed on the first Good Friday and Easter Sunday, and made a silly captive in Christ's triumphant parade, demonologies (and their 'white' counterpart in popular thought, angelologies), disappeared from the writings of the main Reformation theologians, and eventually over the next two centuries, almost completely from popular Protestant culture. So it is not a surprising 'new trend' when the present resurgence amongst some Christians of books and conferences on how to deal with the demonic, how to exorcize, etc., evinces ignorance of the significance the Bible gives to the cross. In John Wimber's book on evangelism, *Power Evangelism*, not only is the gospel not clearly defined, but forgiveness is only spoken of in passing.[3] The emphasis is on the present miraculous power Christians need for maturity. Wimber's understanding of Jesus and his kingdom, and the outlook he urges his readers to adopt, is essentially that of the ministry of Christ before Golgotha, before his victorious resurrection and present heavenly session.

Therefore, one of my aims in this book is to show how eschatology, like our knowledge of the cross, is foundational in shaping our theological thought, and to encourage you in serious study of it. To contend that eschatology is basic to and powerful in determining our Christian world-view and behaviour is not to

---

[3] *Power Evangelism: Signs and Wonders Today* (London: Hodder & Stoughton, 1985). Cf. Robert Doyle (ed.), *Signs and Wonders and Evangelicals: A Response to the Teaching of John Wimber* (Sydney: Lancer, 1987).

deny that it in turn is shaped by other, 'external' and 'internal', factors. Externally, the pressures of various social circumstances and philosophical outlooks on Christians do, and have, influenced their eschatology. It is a truism of church history that during times of persecution, expectations of an immediate, apocalyptic end to the world grow strong. Internally, in a very real sense eschatology is an articulation of hope that grows from faith, 'a projection on to an unknown future of the understanding of God and God's workings with which believers presently live'.[4] Our doctrines of God, salvation, humankind, and even of the church, all help shape eschatology. However, as I hope to show, eschatology in turn presses upon and shapes these four doctrines. Often it is a two-way process. Further, especially in Chapter 2 which deals with the particulars of the eschatological teaching of Holy Scripture, I hope to show that eschatology is not just a secondary doctrine, a by-product of more fundamental convictions about God, the world and human existence,[5] but a primary one, built into the very fabric of Christian thought. Eschatology, I will contend, is an integral and most basic part of the substance of biblical theology.

Eschatology and the Shape of the Present

> Christianity that is not entirely and altogether eschatology has entirely and altogether nothing to do with Christ.
>
> Karl Barth[6]

> There is therefore only one real problem in Christian theology, which its own object forces upon it and which in turn forces on mankind and on human thought: the problem of the future.
>
> Jürgen Moltmann[7]

Eschatology is a word with many meanings. Essentially, as religious doctrine about 'last things', it is faith in final solutions. It is the hope of believing people that the incompleteness of their present experience

---

[4] Brian E. Daley, *The Hope of the Early Church* (Cambridge University Press, 1991) 2.

[5] Daley, *Early Church*, 2.

[6] *Epistle to the Romans* (Oxford University Press, [6]1933) 314.

[7] *Theology of Hope: On the Ground and the Implications of a Christian Eschatology* (London: SCM, 1967) 16.

of God will be resolved, their present thirst for God fulfilled, their present need for release and salvation realized. It is faith in the resolution of the unresolved, in the tying-up of all the loose ends that mar the life of the believer in the world.

Brian E. Daley[8]

'Eschatology' as a word first occurs in 1844 and literally means 'knowledge of the last things'. In systematic theologies it has tradi-tionally been placed at the end of the work. Further, in the nineteenth century it suffered much disparagement at the hands of many Chris-tian writers, being termed 'a baseless science'. Last, then, in word and in deed. But as the quotations from Karl Barth and Jürgen Moltmann indicate, it has benefited from a resurgence of interest in the twentieth century.

One does not have to read too far into the New Testament, or the history of the Christian church's reflection on the last things, to see that the main concern of eschatology is 'hope': 'What can a Christian hope for, now and in the future?' It is immediately apparent from Scripture that this 'hope' has a lot to do with the future, and yet is to determine our Christian lives now. Hoping for the full incoming of the new creation, which we do not yet see, says Paul, should produce patience in the believer (Rom. 8:24–5). In a direct address to his readers, Peter states as a matter of plain fact, as well as exhortation, that the realization that their hope is living because it is tied to the resurrection and heavenly session of Jesus Christ produces rejoicing 'with an indescribable and glorious joy' in his readers, even under conditions of persecution (1 Pet. 1:3–9).

What is involved in investigating the Bible's teaching on eschatology?

We look for ideas and themes which speak of the final state of things – the kingdom of God, resurrection, consummation, heaven, the return of Christ, etc. So, for example, exploring the theme of the 'kingdom of God' we see that eschatology has to do with the nature of God's rule now in the light of his final rule. Further, 'resurrection' and 'consummation' raise questions about the nature of our present hope. A close reading of Romans 8 bears this out.

Perhaps the burning question which has driven much eschatology is, 'How does God work *now* in the light of his final rule?' We shall see a very interesting answer, which is still determinative for how many Christians behave today, when we look at the Ptolemaic

---

[8] Daley, *Early Church*, 1.

eschatology of the medieval period. To take another example, in examining the biblical material we will come to the conclusion that 'heaven' is not a metaphor for fixed eternal principles, but a metaphor for the untrammelled rule of God. The witness of the New Testament inexorably ties 'church' and 'heaven' together (Eph. 1:3–23; 2:6; Heb. 12:18–24). A little reflection on ecclesiology in the light of eschatology shows that our understanding of 'heaven', and how it relates to 'church', strongly influences our practical church activities. And, by way of a final example, as we explore the 'kingdom of God' we will see that God works in the world through his word of promise which produces faith, and that the characteristic contemporary context of this faith under God's rule is suffering!

Thus, eschatology has to do with how and why God, who has revealed himself as Father in Jesus Christ, relates past and present and future, all of which are under his sovereign control, to us *now*. And how, as a consequence, we are to relate ourselves to *him*.

In our present-day context we must be careful not to underestimate the relevance of this. The future which contains the last things is entirely in the hands of the sovereign or free Lord who transcends time and who therefore transcends our present and our future. Yet we know from the Bible that this *future*, these last things which God promises to do, impacts our *present*:

> The creation awaits in eager expectation for the sons of God to be revealed (Rom. 8:19).

What is to come throws light on what *is*:

> I consider that our present sufferings are not worth comparing with the glory that will be revealed to us (Rom. 8:18).

Søren Kierkegaard points out that most people take an absolute view of the relative and a relative view of the absolute, so that their values are confused. A correction of orientation comes when the final and definitive victory of God's kingdom is perceived. We no longer assign eternal value to what is temporal and transitory.

What is to come also has the power to shape secular politics. If we are to believe the media, three former leaders of English-speaking countries bordering the Pacific basin – Ronald Reagan (United States), David Longe (New Zealand), and Bob Hawke (Australia) – all had three things in common:

- They came from profoundly Christian backgrounds; being respectively endorsed by the Moral Majority, a Methodist lay
  preacher, and the child of a Congregationalist minister.
- Consciously or otherwise, they had eschatologies which we may
  categorize as ethnocentric millennialism, religious utopianism
  and secular utopianism.
- They had the power to make far-reaching political and military
  decisions at a time when the Soviet empire formed a bloc of
  enmity to western democratic values.

Throughout his presidency, Mr Reagan was interested in the political ramifications of millennialism. Larry Jones and Gerald Sheppard have drawn the evidence together and highlighted its main
features. 'More than any other American president in recent history,
Ronald Reagan has displayed a keen interest in biblical prophecy.
His interest is evidently more than academic, for he has linked a
number of political decisions to biblical prophetic scenarios familiar
to fundamentalist dispensationalism.'[9] They pointed out that the
sort of advice the President received concerned foreign policy. His
theological advisers pulled no punches, they painted a scenario
whereby 'America as a nation could tempt Jesus to return by
offering him the burnt sacrifice of a world-in-nuclear-flames'.[10]
Reflecting a Methodist rejection of the 'total depravity' of humanity
before God due to original sin, and the affirmation of human moral
progress, Mr Longe removed his country from the U.S. nuclear
umbrella, hoping for a peace based on sweet reason instead of brute
force.

If bad eschatology has the potential to place us in violent and
hopeless confrontation with our neighbour, it has the more horren-
dous consequence of a direct assault on God. Bad eschatology can
engage us in a Promethean or Babel-like repudiation of God by
attempting to drag him down from heaven and make him serve our
ends on our terms. On the other hand, a true understanding of
eschatology can leave us with the perspective of Augustine of Hippo:

> There are some things which are to be enjoyed, some which are to be
> used, and some whose function is both to enjoy and use. Those which

---

[9] L. Jones and G.T. Sheppard, 'The Politics of Biblical Eschatology:
Ronald Reagan and the Impending Nuclear Armageddon', *TSF Bulletin*
8:1 (1984) 16.
[10] Jones and Sheppard, 'Politics of Eschatology', 19.

are to be enjoyed make us happy; those which are to be used assist us and give us a boost, so to speak, as we press on towards our happiness . . . So in this mortal life we are like travellers away from our Lord: if we wish to return to the homeland where we can be happy we must use this world, not enjoy it, in order to discern 'the invisible attributes of God, which are understood through what has been made' [Rom. 1:20] . . . To enlighten us and enable us, the whole temporal dispensation was set up by a divine providence for our salvation. We must make use of this, not with a permanent love and enjoyment of it, but with a transient love and enjoyment of our journey, or of our conveyances (so to speak) or any other expedients whatsoever (there may be a more appropriate word), so that we love the means of transport only because of our destination.[11]

True eschatology will help safeguard us from making God an object of mere use and the world an idol. God, and life with God, will be viewed not only in terms of the present moment, but also in terms of a gloriously different and wonderful future. Eschatology drives out utopianism, the false belief in heaven on earth now, wrought by human activity, even religious activity. Instead, the God who created the heavens and the earth, and inhabits heaven, will become for us both the subject and object of our fellowship. In his freedom he will act to make us his children, and we will delight to be heirs of the kingdom of heaven, citizens of a heavenly commonwealth. To not be limited by the harsh realities of our earthly existence and to have a sure hope of the better world to come in the sweet company of the God who so loves us that he is known as Father is a truly liberating, joyful aspect of Christian existence.

Structure of this Book

In order to more truly reflect the full scope of Christian eschatology many writers deal with it under three headings – personal (e.g. bodily resurrection, God's final judgment of individuals), corporate (the role and hope of the church in the light of the eschaton) and universal (the new heavens and the new earth). These distinctions

---

[11] R.P.H. Green trans. and ed., *Augustine: De Doctrina Christiana*, Oxford Early Christian Texts (Oxford: Clarendon, 1995) book 1.7–8.85; pp. 17–18, 49.

are well worth keeping in mind, but taken in isolation they are somewhat artificial and liable to distortion. So I propose to follow a different course.

The next chapter seeks to outline the main features of the Bible's teaching on eschatology. That is, it exposes the 'raw data' that the church has had to work with in thinking about the last things. The chapters which follow examine the Bible's teaching on eschatology from the twin vantage points of historical and systematic theology. After exploring the distinctive features of Christian eschatology as it occurs in one historical period or in a theologian of historical importance, I have sought to pose critical questions which come from the broader framework of systematic theology, questions from the viewpoint of the person of God and his work in the world. This should bring out how eschatology helps shape the rest of Christian theology, and *vice versa*. At the end of each chapter are a number of 'questions over coffee', or discussion questions. These are intended not only to act as points of review, but also to raise wider concerns relating to both theology and pastoral practice. I hope that they will encourage 'theological thinking'.

In all this I have three main aims: to highlight certain issues which have been and remain especially important for Christian thought and activity; to see if there is one common centre or key to the Bible's rich assortment of eschatological themes; and to leave you with 'the big picture'. This should illustrate the interdependent nature and unique significance of individual, corporate and universal eschatology, as well as eschatology's productive relationship with the rest of Christian thought. My ultimate goal is to offer a cohesive picture of how we may hope for God to act in the world for our redemption.

Issues

As we move through the historical and systematic material we will critically examine several contemporary and related issues in eschatological studies. This list is not meant to be exhaustive, but serves to highlight major questions which determine how we think and act as Christians.

1. Time, eternity and history
What is the relationship between the past, the present and the future, and how do they affect each other? This is the problem of the relationship between our present earthly history and the final

revelation of God. What is the relevance of something which happened over 2000 years ago, and is said to be of eternal significance, to the present moment? What is the cash value of our 'hope' now? What is the relationship between the end (the object of our hope) and present-day reality? Christianity is often accused of espousing, 'pie in the sky by and by when we die', or, con- versely, of being nothing more than the quaint curator of an ancient Semitic and Hellenistic museum. In the nineteenth century Kierkegaard gave one of Christianity's most profound responses to this problem in the face of the self-satisfied formality of his contemporaries. His book, *Philosophical Fragments*, roots the problem and the solution in the gracious nature of the eternal God who became incarnate, and the existential response he elicits from an ignorant and frightened humanity.[12] But that gloomy Dane's epoch-making reply is limited by the philosophical and theological framework within which it works, and a too narrow concentra- tion on the individual, to do full justice to the biblical material. Jürgen Moltmann, who seeks to work from within the biblical material and a credal trinitarianism, will be more helpful on this issue.

2. Hermeneutics and language

The differences evident between the prophetic and apocalyptic literature of the Bible as they speak of the last things focuses an important problem in eschatology. How can we in theological discourse, in the pulpit, speak coherently and truly about Christian hope? This involves both the question of how we are to interpret the Bible, and laying down touchstones for a language appropriate to our audience and the object or our inquiry.

Apocalyptic is said to be characterized by the belief in two totally distinct and different ages, one under the control of the prince of darkness, the other characterized by eternal and perfect righteous- ness. Apocalyptic tends to show the future things as coming down out of heaven without involving itself in the connection that these future things have to the present. Prophecy, on the other hand, shows future things as coming forth from what already exists on earth.[13]

---

[12] Søren Kierkegaard, *Philosophical Fragments*, trans. H.V. Hong et al. (Princeton: Princeton University Press, 1962) 30–35.
[13] G.C. Berkower, *The Return of Christ* (Grand Rapids: Eerdmans, 1972) 308, using Abraham Kuyper's definitions.

There has been much work done on this in biblical studies[14] as well as in theology. From theology's point of view, it is the problem of the language of eschatology. At one level there is the obvious problem of distinguishing form and content. In a perceptive essay, Karl Rahner points out that these are not easily distinguished in the eschatological assertions of the biblical tradition.[15] It is not only that there is never any concept without imagination, an image to convey it, but that there are special problems in trying to separate form and content in the biblical material. They are very much interwoven and dependent on each other, if for no other reason than that the Scriptures seek to speak of a future reality which far transcends our present experience and is contingent only on the sovereign will of God who creates out of nothing and will, he promises, re-create out of an all-consuming judgment (2 Pet. 3:7–13; Heb. 12:25–9). At the very least, our eschatological language needs to be seen to be anchored to the content of that ancient assertion, which is coloured as much as conveyed by its unique form. Any modern discourse which strays from this must be suspect of saying something quite different to Scripture.

3. God and creation

What is the relationship between God and his creation, between God's immanence and his transcendence, between a God who is above the heavens and yet is present to his people, between heaven and earth? This is very much related to that of the relationship between history and eternity. It concerns the relationship between the historical, immanent future, and the future which is spoken of by Holy Scripture as transcending time, and therefore, history because God is directly present there. The focus in this issue is on the nature of God and his activity in the world.

---

[14] A. T. Lincoln, *Paradise Now and Not Yet* (Cambridge University Press, 1981), has a very stimulating analysis of the problem as it occurs in Paul's writings. In his magisterial analysis of the biblical material, P.D. Hanson distinguishes between prophetic eschatology and apocalyptic eschatology and explores the connection between them (*The Dawn of Apocalyptic: The Historical and Sociological Roots of Jewish Apocalyptic Eschatology* [Philadelphia: Fortress, 1979] 1–31, 427–44).

[15] Karl Rahner, 'The Hermeneutics of Eschatological Assertions', in *Theological Investigations*, vol. 4 (Baltimore: Helicon, 1966) 344–6.

The Key Theme

Often eschatology has been dealt with under separate topics like 'the kingdom of God', 'resurrection of the dead', and 'final judgment'. We might well ask whether there is one great central theme running through the biblical material, not only integrating separate components, but in fact very much determining their content and meaning. The importance of this to our own under-standing is obvious, as it will provide a key to organizing material and answering questions raised by the Bible's often different and seemingly confusing portrayal of future events and realities. The chapters which follow will illustrate how Christian writers have sought such a central focus to eschatological thought and will also seek to critically evaluate the organizing principles they have proposed.

The Big Picture

If we arrive at a biblically coherent eschatological 'schema', then it will inform our attitudes, actions, and, especially, our preaching. If we grasp the big picture the Bible offers, we will understand the place of eschatology in the knowledge of God, and therefore in knowledge of ourselves.

I hope that the following treatment of historical developments in Christian eschatology will not only begin to fulfil the three aims of this book, but will also sharply demonstrate how eschatology shapes all theology. Yet as we do this we need to keep in mind that our Christian forebears, like us, struggled to be faithful to Christ, Christ as he is revealed in the Scriptures, Christ clothed with his promises. Empathy, and humility, are appropriate. Fur-ther, most of them did not write treatises dealing with eschatology as such. That is a modern, and helpful, phenomenon dating from the nineteenth century. Therefore, except for the odd work or section here and there on points of special interest to the writer, like 'heaven' or 'soul sleep', we have to undertake the irksome task of scanning a wide range of writings to cull the relevant data. Yet, because most great thinkers tend to work within a consistent framework of logic, the results are, more often than not a trust-worthy representation of the content and interrelations of the author's thought-world.

All the historical material is interrogated, or engaged with, through firm but friendly discourse. This examination comes from within the broader theological understanding of the writers them-selves, or from systematic theology as a whole, or from both. The aim is to expose the theological meaning of the Bible's leading concepts concerning eschatology, and thus to expose and highlight concepts that may credibly be thought of as significant for 'the big picture'.

Finally I will attempt to draw a conclusion as to what the big picture actually is.

OVER COFFEE

- How should we seek to exorcize demons?
- Is there one key theme or idea which determines the content and meaning of the Bible's teaching on the 'last things'?
- How appropriate is it to sing the chorus:
  'Turn your eyes upon Jesus
  look full in his wonderful face,
  and the things of earth will grow strangely dim
  in the light of his glory and grace'?
- What is the relation between God and the future?

2

Eschatology in the Bible

The statements of systematic theology are recognition statements. They are our recognition, confession and preaching of the meaning of the story of the Bible, as we take what the Bible says and examine it in the light of the character of the One who spoke these words, and who has acted in the world in Jesus Christ. The Bible informs us that miraculously this speaking or proclamation is not ours alone, but also the Holy Spirit's (compare 1 Pet. 1:23 with 1:12; see also 1 Thess. 1:4–6; 2:13).

What then, at the beginning of the task of recognition and confession, are the main components of the Bible's specific teach-ing about the last things, and how does the Bible itself organize them? First, the themes of judgment and consummation strongly suggest themselves as the basic lenses which focus the meaning of other components. Secondly, the Bible also clearly emphasizes that knowledge of the last things is not just about future events and realities, but that eschatology is and always has been grounded in pivotal events in our earthly, human history, at the centre of which is Jesus Christ. Christian eschatology has an irreducibly historical face. Thirdly, there is a pastoral concern in the New Testament about the question of the time between our Lord's ascension into heaven and his promised return again in power and glory, a concern about death and the intermediate state. Finally, the New Testament portrays the resurrection of Jesus Christ as the one event, above all else, which determines Christian eschatological reality.

Grammar of Eschatology: Judgment and Consummation

The New Testament has a number of recurrent ways of talking about 'the end', about eschatology. Expressions such as 'heaven',

'hell', 'the kingdom of God', 'the return of Christ', and 'resurrection' command our attention, shaping and giving content to biblical
eschatology. To some extent then, to start with 'judgment and
consummation' and to class these as the 'grammar' of eschatology
is a little arbitrary. But perhaps not. Because of its pervasive and
controlling character, eschatology is not just a topic in Holy Scripture, it is also a 'language' of Holy Scripture, that is, it is the way
in which God reveals himself to us in the pages of his written
revelation. A grammar gives us not only the basic forms and
inflexions of a language, but also the rules governing the use of the
language, in this case, 'eschatology'.

Now, it could be argued that the scriptural themes of promise,
the kingdom of God, mediatorial kingship, parousia and resurrection also qualify as 'grammar'. But, given that eschatology deals
especially with the things of the end, judgment and consummation
(fairly obviously) constitute its 'basic grammar'. This grammar not
only sets out the basic structures within which the Bible talks of the
last things, but also defines what is ungrammatical, that is, it sets
the limits beyond which we cannot go. Why we cannot go beyond
certain limits in regard to, say, the doctrine of hell will, I hope, be
clearer by the end of this section.

The Bible is clear that history will have a twofold outcome:
judgment and consummation. Thus questions about judgment and
consummation are questions about our expectations for concrete
reality as Jesus returns to usher in the last phase of his kingdom.

The question of judgment, expressed as heaven and hell, in many
ways focuses our minds as we stand on the edge of an unchangeable
eternity watching our theological birds, so to speak, come home to
roost. Our understanding of bliss and perdition accurately reflects
the content and direction of the rest of our theology; as Richard
Niebuhr shows in his description of nineteenth-century liberalism:

> A god without wrath brought men without sin into a kingdom without
> judgment through the ministrations of a Christ without a cross.[1]

What then does the Bible say about the concept of judgment itself,
and what are the major theological themes flowing from a consideration of 'judgment'? Behind these questions is the observation
that the central theme underlying the particulars used by the Bible

---

[1] H.R. Niebuhr, *The Kingdom of God in America* (New York: Harper &
Row, 1956) 193.

writers to describe the eschaton's final and definitive impingement into human and cosmic affairs is *judgment*.

Judgment

In the Old Testament 'to judge' also means 'to rule' (Exod. 2:14; 1 Sam. 8:6–7; 2 Sam. 15:4, 6). As a judge, God brings salvation, peace and deliverance, especially to the persecuted and oppressed (Deut. 10:18). The hope of Psalm 72:1 f. is characteristic: 'Give the king thy justice, O God, and thy righteousness unto the royal son. May he judge the people with righteousness, and thy poor with justice.'

Although men and women may act as 'judges', in the end, all justice is ascribed to God. Yahweh is Lord and Judge (Deut. 1:17). As judge he helps his people (Jdg. 11:27; 2 Sam. 18:31). He never deviates from justice (Ps. 7:21), and will not suffer his honour to be brought into disrepute. He judges the nations (Gen. 11:1 ff.; Ps. 67:5; Amos 1:2; Joel 4:2; Mal. 3:2 ff.), especially on the 'day of Yahweh', when he will destroy all ungodliness (Isa. 2:12–18; 13:9; Jer. 46:10; Ezek. 30:3 ff.; Zeph. 1:7–18). He comes to the aid of anyone suffering violence and injustice. His judgments are just, i.e. they are in harmony with the faithfulness whereby he espouses the cause of his chosen people, guides them and ensures their safety. God's judgment is motivated by love, grace and mercy, and its outcome is salvation, (Isa. 30:18; Ps. 25:6–9; 33:5; 103:6 ff.; 146:7).

In the New Testament these themes continue but the central focus falls on the person and work of Jesus Christ. Developing the focus of the Old Testament, it is God and Jesus who judge (Jn. 5:22, 29 f). They are called *kritēs*, judge (2 Tim. 4:8; Heb. 12:23; Jas. 4:12; 5:9; Acts 10:42), and God's word is called *kritikos*, a discerner (Heb. 4:12). Jesus has come to bring judgment (Jn. 9:39); God's judgments are unsearchable (Rom. 11:33), his activity as judge begins with the church (1 Pet. 4:17); future and eternal judgment is in his hands (Acts 24:25; Heb. 6:2). Divine judgment often includes punishment (Jn. 3:17 f.; Rom. 2:5–12; 3:6; 1 Cor. 11:13 f.; 2 Thess. 2:12; Heb. 10:30; 13:4; Jas. 5:9). God's condemnation is just (Rom. 2:2 f.; 3:8) and swift (2 Pet. 2:3). The prince of this world is judged.

The central focus of this is the words and works of Jesus, which judge and bring salvation or destruction. God condemned sin in the flesh (Rom. 8:3). God has turned Sodom and Gomorrah into ashes and condemned them (2 Pet. 2:6). When we are judged, we are chastened so that we may not be condemned along with the world

(1 Cor. 11:32). We bring condemnation on ourselves through unbelief (Mk. 16:16; Rom. 14:23). Divine judgment brings separa - tion (Jn. 3:19) and destruction (Heb. 10:27). Those who hear Jesus' word and believe him do not come into judgment (Jn. 5:24). The dead who have done evil will arise to judgment. Thus, the word of the gospel judges as it saves and separates (Mt. 10:34 ff.; Rom. 2:16). The fact of coming judgment means that all of humanity is advancing towards God's final verdict on themselves and their works.

For Paul and the early church, Jesus is the judge of all the world, as God the Father is. Divine patience still gives men time to repent and believe in Christ who has been made 'to be sin, who knew no sin, so that in him we might become the righteousness of God' (2 Cor. 5:21; cf. Rom. 3:23 ff.; Gal. 3:13; Col. 2:13 ff.). The Judge is the Saviour. Judgment already rests upon unbelievers because they refuse the Saviour, while believers escape condemnation (Jn. 3:16 ff.; 11:25 f.)

In this way the principles of judgment in the New Testament are a development of those found in Old Testament prophecy. It is the Elect One, God's Beloved, his Chosen who is judged, for divine judgment falls upon Christ crucified. Yet this is God's saving work, for in judging Christ he remains faithful to his elect people and to his own honour. The wrath of God is fully revealed only by the gospel (Rom. 1–3), as the 'word of the cross' is preached. Christ 'is set for the fall and rising of many' (Lk. 2:34).

Christ, two outcomes of history, and universalism

The Scriptures are clear that history will have a dual outcome at the last judgment. The later writings of the Old Testament reveal the expectation of a final, universal judgment (Isa. 66:15; Joel 3:1) with a twofold outcome: 'Many of those who sleep in the dust of the earth shall awake, some to everlasting life, and some to shame and everlasting contempt' (Dan. 12:2).

Stubborn rebellion against God spells spiritual doom: 'They who are far from thee are lost . . . thou dost destroy all who wantonly forsake thee' (Ps. 73:27).

Further, the New Testament affirms the supernatural realities of heaven and hell, not as mere states of mind, but as space–time dimensions beyond our space and time (Jn. 14:2–3; Rev. 20–22). The twofold destiny of humankind is a constantly recurring theme: 'Go through the narrow gate' (Mt. 7:13); those who die without

faith in Christ as the promised Messiah die in a state of condemnation (Jn. 3:18; 8:24); Paul draws a sharp distinction between the
two species of humanity, the elect and the reprobate (Rom. 2:7–8);
only the unrighteous will be thrown into the lake of fire.

Yet alongside of this stress on two outcomes, there is also a
universalism which sees God's gracious rule as everywhere triumphant: 'All the ends of the earth shall see the salvation of our God'
(Isa. 52:10). The whole world is destined to come to Mount Zion
(Pss. 47; 48). Both the Old and New Testaments assert: 'It is not
his will for any to be lost, but for all to come to repentance' (2 Pet.
3:9; cf. Ezek. 18:23). Even God's action in hardening hearts (Rom.
9:18) is said to be directed towards God's ultimate purpose that all
should receive mercy (Rom. 11:30–2; cf. Jas. 2:13).

But, as we have noted above, some reject this mercy and thereby
doom themselves. The parables of the talents (Mt. 25:14–30), the
faithful and wicked servants (Mt. 24:45–51), the wise and foolish
maidens (Mt. 25:1–13), all show the seriousness of repentance and
faith. The New Testament stresses that we can fall from grace
through our negligence and stubbornness (2 Pet. 1:9–11; Gal. 5:4).

Jesus Christ, in his person and work, is seen as the foundation
for both the dual outcome and universalism. The advent of Christ,
the mediatorial King, opens the door not only to heaven but also
to hell. Those who reject his offer of salvation are confirmed in their
sins as self-judgment (Heb. 3:18–19; Jn. 3:16–18).

The universal atonement wrought by the cross is the basis of
universalism (Col. 1:20; 2:15; cf. 1 Tim. 4:10). This atonement
has not only seen sin judged in the flesh (Rom. 8:3), it also stands
as the foundation for hell. It is the denial of the Lord who bought
them that brings perdition on the false teachers (2 Pet. 2:1). As
the representative of the new humanity Jesus Christ includes in his
body only believers, but as the representative of a fallen race, he
encompasses all humanity, both saved and lost.

Vocabulary of the two outcomes: hell and heaven

Hell
Affirming the existence of hell in a biblical way needs care. One
of the most powerful biblical statements on hell is found in
2 Thessalonians 2:7–10:

> When the Lord Jesus is revealed from heaven in blazing fire with his
> powerful angels, he will punish those who do not know God and do

not obey the gospel of our Lord Jesus Christ. They will be punished with everlasting destruction and shut out from the presence of the Lord and from the majesty of his power on the day he comes to be glorified in his holy people and to be marvelled at among all those who have believed.

Hell, then, is reserved for unbelievers, 'those who do not know God and do not obey the gospel of our Lord Jesus Christ'. How are we to understand this teaching, especially in the face of the fact that the vast majority of humankind die without the opportunity of hearing the gospel at all, let alone clearly?

While we must distinguish between God's justice and his love we must avoid separating them in the ways older theologians some-times did. Thus John Owen (1616–83) makes God's justice a natural or 'essential' attribute, and love only an 'arbitrary' one, the effect of his will. But the Bible affirms that being and doing are one in God, for God is love (1 John 4:8, 16). Owen's view was that whereas God relates to all humankind through justice, he only loves the elect.

But by holding love and justice together, it can be said that God's rejection takes place, not just in spite of his love, but at the hands of his love. God's holy love is inexorable towards man's sins, for a holy love cannot tolerate sin though it embraces the sinner. Thus it is, not because God's love is limited but because it is unlimited, that hell as well as heaven is necessary.[2]

If, when discussing hell, you place the final focus of God's revelation on *humankind*, hell may slide into purgation. For God in his love punishes on earth for the sake of the sinner. If, however, the final focus is on God's relationship to *himself*, then hell stands as a testimony to God's faithfulness to his promises and to his being:

Faithful is the saying, 'For if we died with him, we shall also live with him, if we endure, we shall also reign with him, if we shall deny him, he also will deny us, if we are faithless, he abides faithful; for he cannot deny himself' (2 Tim. 2:11–13).

Whatever our stress, several things are clear about hell in its relationship to God. First, God is present in hell. Hell is exclusion from fellowship with God, not exclusion from his presence. Indeed,

---

[2] Donald G. Bloesch, *Essentials of Evangelical Theology*, vol. 2: *Life, Ministry, and Hope* (New York: Harper & Row, 1982) 224–5.

it is the presence of God which makes hell, hell – because by God's presence man is continually reminded of his guilt (2 Thess. 1:9 [*apo* as 'the point at which something begins', see RV] and Rev. 14:10; cf. the parable of Lazarus and Dives in Lk. 16:19–31; Ps. 139:7–8).

Secondly, Jesus is Lord and King over both heaven and hell (Rev. 1:18; 20:1). Hell is within the sphere of the kingdom of God, although it represents an aberration from it, not membership of it (Phil. 2:9–11; Rom. 14:11). Heaven encompasses hell; hell is in-cluded in the dominion of heaven. The grace and kingship of Jesus embrace even hell, as can be seen from references to the resurrection from the dead (Isa. 26:19; Jn. 5:25–9), and Jesus' descent to hell (Eph. 4:8,9; 1 Pet. 3:19–20; 4:6).

Therefore, thirdly, grace extends even to hell. How to express this is the difficulty. Thomas Aquinas assumed that the sufferings in hell are mitigated because Christ is present. Clearly, not all punishments are equal, and we would expect all punishments to be just. That is, although hell as separation is eternal, punishment or the fires would not necessarily be so. God punishes by desert. Donald Bloesch advances the idea that God's grace acts in hell not in purification, but in preservation. 'God's love destroys the false self-esteem of the sinner, but it upholds the sinner even in his misery.'[3] But, the difficulty in this position is that grace in the Bible is primarily effective in saving believers and in the conquest of our enemies.

Is the punishment in hell for unbelievers, especially those who have not heard the gospel, eternal, or can we, on the grounds of justice (Lk. 12:47–48; Rom. 2:1–16), expect an end to the pain of separation, even eventual annihilation? In a poignant and sensitive written debate with David Edwards, John Stott, while not moving from the eternal nature of the unbeliever's separation from God, has tentatively come out on the side of an eventual annihilation. Stott considers four grounds which suggest that annihilationism may be scripturally based, if not stated directly by the text itself: language, imagery, justice and the universal scope of the work of Christ.[4] For example, Stott points out that the 'torment' of Revela-tion 14:10, because it will be experienced 'in the presence of the holy angels and of the Lamb', seems to refer to the moment of judgment, not to the eternal state. It is not the torment itself but its

---

[3] Bloesch, *Essentials of Evangelical Theology*, 225.
[4] In the sense of the universal scope of Christ's work, not the eventual salvation of all.

'smoke' (symbol of the completed burning) which will be 'for ever and ever'.[5] The whole debate is worthy of close study.[6]

Overall, four things need to be said. First, as 2 Thessalonians 2:7–10 shows, unbelievers are in immanent danger of hell, and hell is eternal separation from God. Secondly, the texts (Mt. 18:8; 2 Thess. 1:9; Rev. 14:10–11; 20:10) traditionally offered to support the notion of eternal suffering for unbelievers, although weighty, do not fully support this idea. Thirdly, justice is said to operate in the punishment of the wicked at judgment; 'but the one who does not know and does things deserving punishment will be beaten with few blows' (Lk. 12:48); 'God will give to each person according to what he has done' (Rom. 2:6). Fourthly, the Bible's teaching on hell is in the context of its teaching on the wrath and judgment of God, which is both the *context* and the *content* of the gospel (Rom. 1:1–3:31, especially 2:16). Anything extra to the Bible which in any way diminishes the Bible's overwhelming emphasis on the all-encompassing nature and the imminence of the outpouring of God's wrath and judgment is irresponsible, and has no place in gospel preaching. As Romans 1 to 3 so carefully highlights, we as rebellious humanity are in a very bad way, and rescue lies solely in the hands of the good God who sent his Son to be a sacrifice of atonement. We must flee from the wrath to come, through faith and repentance. As Albert Schweitzer pointed out, Jesus preached like a man going up the side of a volcano. The situation is urgent.

Faced with the prospect of God's terrible wrath on his rebellious creation, the appeal to 'will be beaten with fewer blows' speaks of justice, not comfort. For those in distress at the death of non-Christian friends and relatives, the comfort the Bible offers is eschatological. For it promises that there will be a day when things now seen with tears and distress will be seen only as joy. How this can be, we cannot say, but that it will be, we can be certain:

> Then I saw a new heaven and a new earth; for the first heaven and the first earth had passed away, and the sea was no more. And I saw the holy city, new Jerusalem, coming down out of heaven from God, prepared as a bride adorned for her husband; and I hear a loud cry from the throne saying, 'Behold, the dwelling place of God is with men. He will dwell with them, and they shall be his people, and God himself will

---

[5] D.L. Edwards and J.R.W. Stott, *Essentials: A Liberal–Evangelical Dialogue* (London: Hodder & Stoughton, 1988) 318.

[6] Edwards and Stott, *Essentials*, 273–331.

be with them; he will wipe away every tear from their eyes, and death shall be no more, neither shall there be mourning nor crying nor pain any more, for the former things have passed away.' (Rev. 21:1–4).

Heaven

As to heaven, by way of summary we can say several things. First, heaven is not only a free gift, it is also a reward or prize procured by the merits of Christ (Rom. 6:23). Secondly, heaven is both a state and a place – a paradisal transformation and real relationships are the metaphors used to describe it (Rev. 21:22; Lk. 20:35–6; Rev. 21:4). It entails not simply spiritual existence, but also bodily existence. Heaven also includes both a restored earth and a renewed heaven, and is therefore more accurately spoken of as a new heaven and a new earth. There we feast on spiritual food and drink the water of eternal life (Lk. 14:14; Mt. 26:29; Rev. 21:6; 22:1–2). The goal of all this activity is fellowship.

Thirdly, there are real treasures and rewards in heaven on the basis of the fruits of faith (Mt. 6:6, 18–20; Lk. 6:35; 1 Cor. 3:8). But no distinction or discrimination in fellowship is envisaged. Finally, heaven is eternal, i.e. 'age-long', a quality of time which will see no terminus (Rom. 8:38–9), a quality characterized by joy and peace (Mt. 8:12; 24:51; 25:30; Lk. 13:28; Rev. 21:1–7).

Vocabulary of universalism: palingenesia, apokatastasis, anakephalaiosis

In describing the universal scope of Christ's work, particularly as it impinges on eschatology, three words or concepts emerge as important in the Bible and the history of theology. Despite a tendency in the history of theology to give them separate meanings, biblical revelation treats the first two as synonyms, and its treatment of the third reveals the true, defining foundation of eschatology, and thus the glorious 'limits' of thinking.

The first word is 'palingenesia'. It can be translated new birth, renewal, restoration, regeneration. In the Greek New Testament, the noun *palingenesia* occurs twice: in Matthew 19:28 it refers to the eschatological restoration of all things under the Messiah for which Israel was waiting; in Titus 3:5 the word refers to the renewing of the individual. But, although the word *palingenesia* occurs only twice, cognates and notional occurrences are more widespread.

In the Old Testament regeneration is individual, national, and cosmic on a continuum which runs from renovation of Israelite hearts (Deut. 30:6; Jer. 31:31–4) through God's new messianic administration of his covenant with his people (Jer. 31:32, 39:40) to a new creation (Isa. 65:17–25). In the New Testament, not only is there stress on individual regeneration, but there is a closer tying of it to the cosmic such that one participates in the ultimate cosmic regeneration by personal regeneration now, by the Spirit. Christ's life and work and the gospel are central to these notions. For example, 2 Corinthians 5:17, Ephesians 2:10 and Galatians 6:15, speak of a work of new creation in Christ; and in I Peter. 1:23 and 1:3, James 1:18 and Acts 16:14–15, *anagennaō* is used with respect to the resurrection – God begets anew by means of the gospel which leads to faith.

The second word is 'apokatastasis'. The only occurrence of the word apokatastasis is in Acts 3:21: *achri chrōnon apokatastaseōs pantōn* (until the time of restoration of all things). Restoration implies a return to a previous state of well-being. The general expectation as it appears in biblical theology is attached to the re-appearance of past great leaders, such as Elijah (Mk. 9:12; Mt. 17:11). It is Jesus, of course, who is the Elijah figure, who comes to restore the kingdom (Acts 1:6).

Strictly speaking then, the idea of *apokatastasis* in the Bible is the same as *palingensesia* or regeneration, involving cosmic and individual restoration with the re-assertion of God's kingship, a new heaven and a new earth with new individuals in it. In this regard, the Septuagint describes the activity of the returned Elijah in terms of the individualistic 'turning of the hearts of the fathers to the children, and the hearts of the children to their fathers' (Mal. 4:6), as '*hos apokatastēsei kardian patros pros hyion kai kardian anthrōpou pros ton plēsion autou*' (LXX Mal. 3:23).

However, although apokatastasis is only another word to de-scribe the universal denouement of history and a re-integration of humanity to life with God, it has gained a special use in historical theology through Origen (185–254, an Alexandrian exegete). Origen attempted to unite the notion of salvation as radically discontinuous from present life and the notion of salvation being by gradual stages as the individual soul is lifted until it is finally incorporated in the divine life itself.

Thus in the history of dogma, apokatastasis is the doctrine that ultimately all free moral creatures – angels, men, and devils – will share in the grace of salvation. In the early church Clement of Alexandria and Gregory of Nyssa were also proponents of this position. Later support comes from certain of the Anabaptists,

Moravians and Christadelphians, and from individuals like F. Schleiermacher. Such teaching is also known as 'universalism', but needs to be distinguished from the universal scope of Christ's work.

The third metaphor to describe the universal scope of Christ's work is 'anakephalaiosis' (*anakephalaiōsis*) from Eph. 1:10, which focuses on Christ as both the ground and final encompass-ing point for universal reconciliation. Ephesians 1:10 can be translated: 'God summed up all things in Christ' (RV), or, 'to bring all things in heaven and on earth under one head, even Christ' (NIV). That is, Christ is the head over all things, and as the head he gathers all things up into himself. This is sometimes known as 'recapitulation'. It is especially associated with Irenaeus (130–200). Irenaeus gives two meanings to recapitulation. First, Christ retraced the steps of Adam and humanity. Christ passed through all the stages of life – infant, child, youth, adult – in order to sanctify all who are born again to God through him. He became what we are in order to make us what he is. As a result of his life, death and resurrection, all that was lost in Adam was regained in Christ. Christ thus comprehended or brought to a head in himself the whole of fallen humanity and restored us to communion with God. Secondly, Christ is the summing up and completion of the entire history of salvation. 'Recapitulation' denotes the total work of God for man's redemption. In Christ is summed up the 'sure word of prophecy', which had always looked for a new messiah, a new redemption, a new Exodus, a new covenant, a new inheri-tance, etc. This salvific and revelational summing-up means that Christ encompasses all God's redemptive purposes in two ages which are centred on himself, the present age and the eternal age to come, and provides a hermeneutic for understanding the rela-tionship between the Old and New Testaments. No salvific idea can be properly understood unless interpreted 'backwards from Christ'.

John Calvin (1509–64) understood *anakephalaiōsis* not only along general Irenaean lines, but especially in terms of fellowship or union with God. Anakephalaiosis or recapitulation (Lat. *recapi-tulatio*) is not a word that John Calvin uses often, but he has a great deal to say about Christ our head (Lat. *capitus*) and the headship he exercises. In this headship Christ is both our Brother and our Lord (*Com* Hebrews 3:2, CR 83.36). Calvin stresses that Christ's headship must be actualized in our union with or fellowship with

God. Christ as head is joined to his members. If Christ's mediatorial role, and consequently his headship, are not to prove fruitless and useless, its power must be diffused through the whole body of believers (*Com* Jn. 17:21). That is, Christ's headship must not be a mere theoretical possibility, or a raw, despotic overlordship, but an actuality involving communion or fellowship between Christ and his new creation. Thus, since the goal of headship and the all-head-ship-in-Christ (anakephalaiosis) is fellowship, the stress falls on faith in Christ as the bond of our union with him.

It is this emphasis on faith effecting union with Christ (Rom. 6:1–11; Eph. 1:3–6) that moves anakephalaiosis from a metaphorical principle to fellowship; that is, away from universalism in the sense of every rational soul being saved to the reality of the obedience of faith which is nourished in Christ. Here, the Bible gives us not just a 'limit', but a glorious, wonderful truth which points us to the 'end' being a real sharing in the life of God.

Historical Face of Eschatology

A closer look at the unfolding of the Bible's flow of events from creation to new creation, from Genesis to Revelation, shows that God's end-time purposes are neither restricted to the New Testament nor hinge on the occurrence of special words like 'heaven' or 'hell', but are deeply embedded in the matrix of the Bible's progressive revelation. God's end-time purposes and activities operate from creation onward, and find expression at key points in the history of Israel and the world. Three themes run throughout: promise, the kingdom of God, and mediatorial kingship. These find their embryonic form in Genesis 1 and 2, then develop as the story of Israel unfolds before a world which will eventually be swept up into God's eschatological activities. This gathering up of the nations is both past and present. It happens through the coming of Jesus Christ, his death, resurrection, ascension and heavenly session, and the preaching of the gospel as the church expands across the Jew–Gentile barrier and Christianity finds its true expression not as a sect of Judaism, but as the religion God wants for all the nations. Eschatology does not just concern a 'transcendent future', but is concerned with the thoroughly historical realities in which God works to bring in this future. That is, eschatological realities are deeply implanted in history, revealed in history, and shape history.

Eschatology as promise: from creation to new creation

It is clear from the contents of Genesis 1 to 3, and the way the rest of Scripture uses these chapters, that the foundation for knowledge of the last things is in the knowledge of the first things.[7]

The beginning of the Bible – the beginning of time, the world, humankind, and humankind's relationship to God and the world – is pregnant with purpose. The purpose, the end, the eschaton is implicit in the beginning: 'In the *beginning, God created*'. Formlessness and emptiness is replaced by order and existence. The creation is architectonic – light, sky, land and seas, vegetation . . . moon and sun, animals and fish – with its penultimate goal in humanity, and its ultimate goal in God's rest in Genesis 2:1–3. Humankind is not the consummation. Humans are the agents through whom the aims of creation will be realized. Gen. 2:1–4a forms the conclusion to the first account of creation.

The six days of creation find their significance in the seventh. The divine rest on the seventh day indicates the goal of creation. This is a goal which will be maintained, despite our rebellious efforts to vitiate it. Further, there is great promise implicit in this description, as well as an explicit warning that God will judge: 'You are free to eat from any tree in the garden; but you must not eat from the tree of the knowledge of good and evil, for when you eat of it you will surely die' (Gen. 2:16–17).

The events of chapter 3, the first sin and its punishment, see God keeping his promise to judge, and also his purpose to have a creation imaging itself in obedient and trusting fellowship. For the promise to judge now has alongside it the promise to redeem. The possibility or redemption is hinted at in Genesis 3:1–24, where the punishment is mitigated, and it is said that the offspring of the woman will strike the snake's head. That God will redeem his lost creation is given clear expression in the rescue of Noah, his family, and representative creatures as a terrible judgment is poured out on all the rest of a thoroughly dissolute and godless humankind. At the end

---

[7] For example, see Gen. 9:1 ff.; 15:18; Deut. 26:9; 11:11–12; Ps. 8; Ezek. 47:1–12; Isa. 54–55; 65:13–25; 66; Lk. 3:38; 4:1–13; 2:52; Jn. 1:1–18; Rom. 5:12–21; 8: 19–23; 1 Cor. 11:1–16; 15:35–49; 2 Cor. 3:18; Heb. 2; 4:7–13; 2 Pet. 3:8–13; Rev. 4; 22. With respect to the Old Testament's use of motifs from Genesis 1 and 2, I am indebted to W.J. Dumbrell, *Covenant and Creation: An Old Testament Covenantal Theology* (Exeter: Paternoster Press, 1984).

of the cycle of punishment and mitigation, spread of sin and spread of grace, which typifies Genesis 1 to 11, we find Genesis 12:1–3 as the climax of the previous chapters. As we move from the prehis-torical into a world history which we can recognize as ours from its historical markers, we meet Abraham and, most importantly, God's promise to Abraham. It is a promise of redemption, not only for Abraham and a nation which will come from Abraham, but ultimately for all the nations. This promise to Abraham, which is explicitly ratified in chapters 15 and 17 and recognizably fulfilled in Jesus Christ, is the reiteration of God's first intentions and existing relationship to humankind in Genesis 1 and 2. Abraham stands as the re-creation counterpart to the un-creation event of the Babel dispersion. Paul in Romans 4:17 makes the promise of redemption to Abraham even more explicitly the reiteration of God's purposes in creation. Here, the language of election, as it applies to Abraham, is conceptually similar to the language of creation in Genesis 1: *kalountos ta mē onta hōs onta*, '(God) who calls into existence the non-existent'.

Kingdom of God

If the form of God's eschatological purpose to bring in the new creation is the promise of redemption, then the content which guarantees that it is and will be a reality in historical experience is expressed, especially in the New Testament, in terms of the 'king-dom of God'. There will be a new creation, and it will have the shape it has both now and in the future because God in Christ is king.

Again, the biblical theme that God is king has its roots in Genesis 1–3. Here we see that God is king and that his goal is humankind's fellowship with himself. God creates by royal fiat, 'Let there be light'. The goal of this kingly activity is the sabbath rest, the open communion of God with his creatures in the 'cool of the day', without guilt. To that end, Adam is chosen as vice-regent and given a command to keep him in life-giving and dependent fellowship with God. But Adam and Eve actively and subversively seek to assert their own kingship against God's by themselves becoming determiners of what is good and evil. This breaks the paradisal fellowship, and subsequently humanity loses both control and any possibility of rest.

Genesis 12:1–3 is the divine response to Genesis 3 to 11. The kingdom of God established in global terms is the goal of the

Abrahamic promise, the blessing of all the families of the earth. This begins with a series of separations – Abraham from the world, Isaac from the wider Abrahamic family, Jacob from his brothers, etc. Israel becomes a 'great nation' amongst, but separate from, 'the nations'. Pointedly, in the context of the renewal of the promise at Sinai in Exodus 19:4–6, after the eloquent restatement of Yahweh's kingship in verse 5, Israel as a covenant people, the 'holy nation', is given the task of functioning as a priestly royalty: 'You will be for me a kingdom of priests and a holy nation.' In history, Israel mirrors and activates God's kingship over his creation, a redemptive kingship.

With Israel's unbelieving call for a specific king, and God's gracious provision of his own king, David, the redemptive kingship of God in Israel and the world becomes focused in one man.

Mediatorial kingship of Christ

The Old Testament leaves us with the messianic promise that a shoot from the stump of Jesse, a true and consummate descendant of David, will bring a Spirit-directed reign of God not only to Israel but to all the nations and all of creation. There is also the obscurer figure of the Suffering Servant whose atoning sacrifice will bring peace and justification (Isa. 53).

In line with the priestly kingship seen in David, and the institutions of the kingdom and priesthood seen in the Sinaic covenant, there are other clues in the Old Testament that priesthood and kingdom have a structural and organic unity which is the substantial foundation of the messianic promise. For example, in Psalm 2:6 God's king reigns from the place of the sacred: 'I have installed my King on Zion, my holy hill' (see also, Jer. 33:15–18; Zech. 6:9–11 and Dan. 9:25).

In the New Testament it is Jesus Christ who is put forward as the fulfilment of these expectations, who alone is called 'the only Son, who is in the bosom of the Father', who has made the Father known (Jn. 1:18). It is Jesus who brings in the kingdom of God, who fulfils God's promises for the future (2 Cor. 1:20). Therefore, ineluctably the New Testament throws up for its readers the question of how Jesus Christ determines eschatology, how does he confirm our future? Three recurrent themes describe in rich detail the eschatological nature of Christ's mediatorial kingship: Christ is our king, our priest, and the one who is both Ruler and Ruled.

Christ is our king: victor, ruler, judge

The New Testament message is the gospel of the Kingdom. Jesus does not just herald its coming, he is its coming. The kingdom of God is also the kingdom of Christ, as is widely attested in New Testament references to the kingdom of the Son of Man (Mt. 13:41; 16:27); 'my kingdom' (Lk. 22:30; Jn. 18:36); 'the kingdom of his beloved Son' (Col. 1:13; 2 Tim. 4:18); 'the eternal kingdom of our Lord and Saviour Jesus Christ' (2 Pet. 1:11). God has given the kingdom to Christ (Lk. 22:29), and when he has subjected all things to himself, he will restore the kingdom to the Father (1 Cor. 15:24). Therefore, it is 'the kingdom of Christ and of God' (Eph. 5:5). There is no tension between 'the power and the kingdom of our God and the authority of his Christ' (Rev. 12:10; see also 11:15).

Christ is lord over us as God's messianic king who rules for God and unto God, and in that his kingship is mediatorial.

Jesus Christ is king, he does not become king. The resurrection and ascension, the exaltation, is the public manifestation of Christ's reign, such that it is after this that the New Testament starts to especially call Jesus 'Lord'. Three names or descriptions fill-out the content of Christ's kingship: Christ our Victor, Christ our Ruler, Christ our Judge.

First, the cross is not only a sacrifice for sin, it is also a royal victory – the regal conquest of Christ over the devil, death and sin. In Colossians 2:15 the triumphal chariot is a metaphor for the cross: 'And having disarmed the powers and authorities, he made a public spectacle of them, triumphing over them by the cross.'

The cross then, is the final victory over and conquest of satan. When George Eldon Ladd[8] defers the final victory over satan to the consummation, when he is 'thrown into the lake of burning sulphur' (Rev. 20:10), Ladd does not do justice to the finality of the cross. John Wimber's 'Signs and Wonders Movement' develops the notion of a two-stage victory to the point where the power of the message of the cross is all but vitiated without the concurrence of modern day miracles.[9] But the New Testament does not state that the proclamation of the gospel needs to be assisted by further defeats of satan on his way to the lake of sulphur.[10] Ladd's

---

[8] George Eldon Ladd, *A Theology of the New Testament* (London: Lutterworth Press, 1974) 64–9.

[9] John Wimber, *Power Evangelism: Signs and Wonders Today* (London: Hodder & Stoughton, 1985) 18–21.

[10] Cf. Wimber, *Power Evangelism*, 44–60.

statement that 'the resurrection of Christ is the first stage' in the victory of God,[11] needs modifying in the light of the fact that the resurrection of Jesus is the expression or result of the victory already won on the cross, and we are included in it now (Rom. 6:1–11; 1 Pet. 1:3–5). For those reasons, we have to assert that in a real way the victory of the kingdom of God has been completed. In Romans, Paul states quite plainly that God's great act of saving righteousness and justification has already occurred at Golgotha, although it continues to call for a present response of faith, and looks forward to a future moment when Jesus will return to make publicly visible what he has done and what it has accomplished in the world (see Rom. 2:16; 3:21–2; 5:1–11; 8:33; Gal. 5:4–5; 1 Cor. 4:4–5). What awaits is not so much an equivalent second stage in a two-stage process, but a consummation which is the unveiling of what already is: 'Jesus our Lord, who was put to death because of our trespasses and raised because of our justification' (Rom. 4:25).[12]

Secondly, Christ is our ruler. The conquest of the cross is only the beginning of Christ's triumphal reign, for he continues as our kingly protector (Rev. 12:10; Rom. 8:31–39), whose continuous rule tramples down his enemies (1 Cor. 15:25). However, Christ's protective rule is usually spoken of using the metaphor of a

---

[11] Ladd, *Theology*, 558.

[12] *dia* + ACC can be taken retrospectively or prospectively. Most commentators opt for translating the second dia prospectively, despite the parallelism of the clause, without giving grammatical or contextual reasons; e.g. W. Sanday and A.C. Headlam, *A Critical and Exegetical Commentary on the Epistle to the Romans* (Edinburgh: T. & T. Clark, 1902) 116; C.K. Barrett, *The Epistle to the Romans* (London: A. & C. Black, 1973) 100; E. Käsemann, *Commentary on Romans* (London: SCM, 1980) 129. C.E.B. Cranfield, while acknowledging the force of the grammatical parallelism, asserts that the second *dia* must be final but, for all that, does not want to rigidly separate the death and resurrection of Jesus Christ: 'For what was necessitated by our sins was, in the first place, Christ's atoning death, and yet, had His death not been followed by His resurrection, it would not have been God's mighty deed for our justification' (*The Epistle to the Romans* [Edinburgh: T. & T. Clark, 1975] 252 and f.n. 1). In the end, context and grammar must decide. Paul's argument thus far has revolved around the double justification of God by the faithfulness of Jesus Christ which ended in his death on the cross, in which justification we are justified by faith (cf. Rom. 3:1–26).

shepherd (Jn. 10:7–16, cf. the description of David in Ezek. 34:23–24), or fellow sufferer (1 Pet. 4:13; 5:10–11), which indicates our present experience of this last age.

Thirdly, Christ is our judge. While Christ's rule is a dominion of holy love, he is also the judge. It is a judgment which delivers us both from our sins and our enemies. Three New Testament statements make this clear: the gospel is the gospel of judgment (Mt. 3:11–12; Rom. 2:16; 2 Pet. 3:7); judgment has started now with the household of faith (1 Pet. 4:17–18); final judgment will come with the consummation of the kingdom (Mt. 25:31–46; 2 Pet. 3; Rev. 20:11–15).

It is one's response to the Word of the King that determines all (2 Cor. 2:14–16; Mk. 1:15; etc.).

Christ is our priest
Redemption, the restoration of all things, means reconciliation to God as well as the dominion of God. The goal of God's kingship is a people who find their rest, the centre of their existence in him, that is, who are in communion with him and each other, who worship him. Therefore Christ's priestly work, involving both his atoning self-offering to the Father on our behalf and his present heavenly intercession, is inseparable from his kingly rule. As can be seen in the Old Testament depiction of the end times as that time when all the nations, including Israel, will worship God aright, the notion of Christ as a kingly priest is a thoroughly eschatological concept (Zech. 8:20–3; 14:1–21; Heb. 8; Rev. 4 and 5; Phil. 2:9–11).

The writer of the epistle to the Hebrews describes our Lord as the *leitourgos* (Heb. 8:2), *the* Minister of the sanctuary; the One True Worshipper, the leader of our worship, who has gone ahead to lead us in our prayers and intercessions. As such the *leitourgia* or worship of Jesus is contrasted with the *leitourgia* or worship of men. This is the worship and offering which God has provided for men and which alone is acceptable to God. 'Now the point in what we are saying is this: we have such a priest, one who is seated at the right hand of the throne of the Majesty in heaven (the) minister in the sanctuary and the true tabernacle set up by God' (Heb. 8:2).

Thus Christ is the Royal Priest, the Man for others, our representative, our head and substitute. Further, we see that in this royal priesthood, this mediatorial kingship, Christ is both the ruler and the ruled.

Christ is both ruler and ruled

We are often used to thinking of Jesus' mediatorial kingship in terms of '*both* priest *and* sacrifice'. Further, the New Testament's description of Jesus as mediator makes it clear that he is both God to us and our man to God (1 Tim. 2:5; Gal. 3:19–20), and God's man for us and *the* one man for God.

It is at this point we can start to appreciate how Jesus really does fulfil Old Testament eschatological hopes of a humanity which is in perfect submission and fellowship with its Creator, whom in the creeds we confess as 'God the Father'. Three powerful images in the New Testament highlight this fulfilment: the last Adam (Rom. 5:12,21), the elect one (Lk. 9:35; 23:35; also Acts 2:23; 4:27 f.; 1 Pet. 1:20; Rev. 13:8), and the ruler who hands his kingdom over to another (1 Cor. 15: 20–8).

Christ's obedient submission to the Father is widely attested (Phil. 2:8; Heb. 5:8), but perhaps never more eloquently than in the context of kingship and the end times. 1 Corinthians 15:20–28 has this train of events:

- everything *has been* subjected to Christ
- everything *will be* subjected to Christ
- Christ is subject to the Father (cf. Jn. 8:28; 5:19; etc.)
- Christ will subject his kingdom to the Father.

Will Christ's reign then end? No, it is an 'eternal reign and kingdom' (Lk. 1:33; 2 Pet. 1:11). How then are we to understand these two pieces of data (1 Cor. 15:20–8 and 2 Pet. 1:11)? By thinking them into each other. What result do we get? John Calvin, along with Hilary of Poitiers and several other church fathers,[13] becomes confused at this point, and asserts what the text does *not* assert by conceiving of 'handing over' in terms of Christ no longer being ruler

---

[13] Hilary writes: 'The end of the subjection is then simply that God may be all in all, that no trace of the nature of [Christ's] earthly body may remain in Him. Although before this time the two were combined within Him, He must now become God only; not, however, by casting off the body, but by translating it through subjection; not by losing it through dissolution, by transforming it in glory: adding humanity to His divinity, not divesting Himself of divinity by His humanity. And He is subjected, not that He may cease to be, but that God may be all in all, having, in the mystery of the subjection, to continue to be that which He no longer is, not having by dissolution to be robbed of Himself, that is, to be deprived of his being' *On the Trinity* 11.40 (NPNF (2) 9.214–5).

in his humanity but in his divinity. 'Then the veil will fall and we shall see the glory of God without hindrance, as he reigns in his kingdom. Christ's humanity will no longer stand in the middle, keeping us from the final view of God.'[14] It is possible to rescue Calvin from the baldness of this unfortunate statement,[15] but it is better to interrogate the biblical material ourselves.

'Kingdom' can be conceived of as 'rule' or 'dominion' – the abstract meaning, and 'realm' – the concrete meaning. The concrete 'realm' is not much spoken of in the New Testament, but it is mentioned in Matthew 4:8 (= Lk. 4:5); Matthew 24:7; Mark 6:23 and Revelation 16:10; and all the references are secular. 'Realm' as a metaphor for the people over whom Christ rules is found in Colossians 1:13; Luke 16:16; and Matthew 11:11; 21:31; 23:13. It may be helpful for us to see this handing over to the Father at the end of the age (1 Cor. 15:24) in terms of realm – the handing over of the redeemed to the Father, the consummation of the kingship wielded by the Elect One, the true Adam, who is the Son of God. What then is the nature and goal of this kingship? That we too might be in a filial relationship to God, 'children of God . . . not born of the will of the flesh, but of God' (Jn. 1:13). The significance of the subordination of the Son to the Father and the transference of the kingdom to the Father lies ultimately in the 'consummation of the Fatherhood of the Father'.[16]

It is through this rule by the Ruled One that we are presented to the Father (Jn. 6:37–40; 5:19–27; 14:6–11, 23; 17:20, 21, 24, etc.); 'through him we both have access in one Spirit to the Father' (Eph. 2:18).

Sharers of Christ's kingdom

All we have said so far can be expressed in terms of Christ's mediatorial kingship having a twofold purpose – for us, for God. The object of the divine rule is the redemption of humankind and their deliverance from the powers of evil (1 Cor. 15:23, 28 is definitive). Christ's reign means the destruction of all hostile powers, the last of which is death. The kingdom of God is the reign of

---

[14]　Calvin, *Com* 1 Cor. 15:27.
[15]　R.C. Doyle, 'The Context of Moral Decision Making in the Writings of John Calvin' (unpublished PhD thesis, University of Aberdeen, 1981) 317–22.
[16]　Jürgen Moltmann, *The Crucified God* (London: SCM, 1974) 266.

God in Christ destroying all that is hostile to divine rule. Further, in the exercise of his kingship, Christ reveals the Father and brings all of creation to the point where God's filial purposes are complete and all creation sees that God is all in all, the Father of his domain.

The sharers in this filial kingdom are those who respond to the word of the Kingdom in repentance and faith (Mt. 13:18–23). Forgiveness of sins is the characteristic of kingdom-sharers (Col. 1:12–14). This repentance is so radical that it can only be described as 'self-denial' (Mk. 8:34–9:1). In this we are like the Lord of the Kingdom 'who did not account equality with God a thing to be grasped, but taking the form of a servant . . .' (Phil. 2:6–11). This is never described as anything less than painful. *Suffering* in fellowship with the King is thus also a necessary characteristic of a sharer (Phil. 1:29; 1 Pet. 2:21; Rom. 8:17–18; 2 Cor. 1:5–7; Phil. 3:10: 'I want to know Christ and the power of his resurrection and the fellowship of sharing in his sufferings, becoming like him in his death, and so, somehow to attain to the resurrection from the dead.' 'Rejoice that you participate in the sufferings of Christ so that you may be overjoyed when his glory is revealed' (1 Pet. 4:13).

This denial of self, this suffering with Christ is entirely positive however, because it is like Christ's self-denial. It is not an inward movement of the soul in on itself, but entirely outward to God and our neighbour and is to bring about the restoration of righteous kingdom relationships (2 Cor. 1:5–7; 4:10–12): 'We always carry around in our body the death of Jesus, so that the life of Jesus may also be revealed in our body' (cf. Col. 1:24).

The theological import of this view of the purpose of Christ's kingdom can be illustrated by its impact on theological anthropology. To a large degree, our vision of hope determines our view of humanity. Thus in Marxism the end point is a communistic material world, brought about by the operation of the dialectical laws of materialism in the context of class and economic warfare. Here, the truly human person is the *Material Person*, the product of social engineering. In the hedonistic west, the goal is the fully satisfied senses, gained through the sensate personalities search for sensual experience. Here, the truly human person is the *Sexual Person*, the product of sensual libertarianism. But the Christian view of humanity is radically different due to a radically different starting point, and the end point which is inherent in that starting point: the *Fellowship Person*, whose self, or centre of being is found in his relationship to God and his neighbours.

Return of the King: parousia

A number of terms are used to describe the second advent of Christ, including *hēmera* (the day), *apokalypsis* (revelation), *epiphaneia* (appearance, coming). But one of the most prominent of the New Testament's descriptions of the kingship of Christ is the notion of 'advent' or 'parousia'. The word parousia, used as the verb *pareimi* and the noun *parousia* in the New Testament (translated *adventum* in Latin), generally means presence and arrival. Its most striking usage is eschatological and refers to an event. Jesus proclaimed the kingdom of God as imminent and the parousia as having a decisive effect upon the present in that people are to live now in the light of this coming event, for this final appearance will usher in the consummation of God's end time purposes.

The New Testament makes a number of points when describing Christ's final advent. For convenience, we can number them:

1. Jesus has come, but he is coming again: 'So Christ also, having been once offered to bear the sins of many should appear a second time apart from sin, to them that wait for him, unto salvation' (Heb. 9:28; see also Acts 3:20 f.).
2. Christ came as the suffering servant, he shall come again as the conquering king and judge (Mk. 13:26; Mt. 26:64; Jude 14,15; Rev. 19:11 ff.).
3. The parousia is unexpected (1 Thess. 5:2–3; Mt. 24:42–4; Lk. 12:39–40; Rev. 3:3; 16:15; the parables of Mt. 24 and 25).
4. Christ's coming will be 'visible and bodily': Jesus said that all the tribes of the earth would see the Son of Man coming in his glory (Mt. 24:30, 26:64; see also Acts 1:11). The angels made a similar announcement on Mt. Olivet (Acts 1:11; Rev. 1:7; Heb. 9:28). Jesus will appear in bodily form, in his glorified humanity (Acts 1:11; 3:20–1; Heb. 9:28; Rev. 1:7). This, of course, is a corollary of his resurrection.
5. The purpose of the second coming of Jesus Christ is to introduce two mighty events: the resurrection of the dead and the last judgment. Both the righteous and the unrighteous will be resurrected to appear before the judgment throne of Christ (Mt. 12:36–7; 25:32; Rom. 14:10; 2 Cor. 5:10).
6. Christ's coming marks the end of the old age and the beginning of a new heavens and a new earth (2 Pet. 3:10). Matthew 19:28 speaks of the regeneration of the cosmos.

7. The parousia has practical consequences: In the light of the coming victory, Christians should show steadfast devotion to the work of the Lord (1 Cor. 15:58). The stress is on gospel preaching and gospel living (esp. 1 Tim. 4; 2 Tim. 4:1–8).
8. Cosmic, earthly and personal disturbances have been caused, are caused and will be caused by gospel's breaking into a rebellious world. These disturbances, or signs, include:
   * the appearance of Antichrists (1 Jn. 4:3; 2 Jn. 7; Mt. 24:24; Rev. 13:7).
   * wholesale destruction of peoples and nations by fire (Joel 2:3; Rev. 8:7–8).
   * great earthquakes and famines (Rev. 6:12; 18:8; Lk. 21:10–11).
   * apostasy under the influence of false prophets (Mt. 24: 10–11, 24; 1 Tim. 4:1; 2 Tim. 4:3–4; 2 Thess. 2:3, 9).
   * widespread persecution (Mt. 24:9–10; Mk. 13:9,12–13; Lk. 21:12–17).
   * eclipses of heavenly bodies (Isa. 13:10; Joel 2:30; Mt. 24:29; Rev. 8:12).
9. The parousia offers hope. This is perhaps the apical biblical motif, not only because it is the attitude that is to characterize Christians as they look forward to the final advent with its cosmic sweep, but also because the content of that hope is grounded in the person and work of Christ, notably his resurrection (Tit. 2:13; Rom. 8:18–39; 1 Pet. 1:3–5; Col. 1:22–3).

How both systematic and biblical studies have interpreted these ideas has by and large depended on decisions made about two background issues: the nature of the kingdom of God, and the relationship between eschatology and 'futurology', knowledge of the future. (Most western societies have an interest in futurology, Australia even having had a Commission for the Future.) Closely allied to one's view of the nature of the kingdom of God is the formal relationship you strike between knowledge of the goal at the end of history, and knowledge of the future of history before its 'end' or goal. Hendrikus Berkhof argues that the relationship between our history, both now and in the future, and the 'end' is one of 'extrapolation'.[17] Helpfully, Jürgen Moltmann makes a distinction between *futurum*, which grows out of the present, and

---

[17] Hendrikus Berkhof, *Christian Faith: An Introduction to the Study of the Faith* (Grand Rapids: Eerdmans, 1979) 522–5.

parousia, that which comes from the other side.[18] That seems to keep the tension where the Bible does, because if on the one hand the promises made through the prophets relate to future changes occurring through the usual historical processes, like Cyrus liberating Israel from exile (Isa. 45:1), the New Testament notion of *parousia* speaks of a dramatic intervention from God's side which transcends present historical experience. That is why the straight-line extrapolation from where we are now to the future which God promises as *parousia*, that we see in certain forms of postmillennialism, is untenable.[19] Although, as seen in the promise of resurrection, there is continuity, there is also a distinctive discontinuity, such that the 'new' is a quantum leap from the 'present' of Christian experience (1 Cor. 15:35–56).

With respect to the question of the nature of the kingdom of God, it may be asked, did Jesus preach an in-breaking of a supernatural kingdom in the imminent or close future, or did he see the kingdom realized in his own ministry and teachings? Should the church preach an eschatological kingdom or one that is present now in the fellowship of believers? Several current answers can be sketched out to these questions in terms of realized eschatology, historical eschatology, futurist eschatology and transcendent eschatology, although to some extent these categories overlap.

The notion that the kingdom of God is already 'realized' has had its most formative expression in the biblical studies of C. H. Dodd,[20] but has also been developed by Rudolph Bultmann, Ernst Käsemann, and in a more mystical or spiritual direction, Paul Tillich. In Dodd's view the kingdom came to be known as an experienced reality in the life of Jesus and in his resurrection. Jesus' eschatological imagery only symbolizes the abiding truths of an ongoing universe – whether conceived of morally, religiously, or existentially. Eternal life is a present reality for the community of faith. The kingdom is not a future time when the world will be re-created, but a timeless eternity, a state of inner communion with God. This

---

[18] 'Methods in Eschatology' in his *The Future of Creation* (London: SCM, 1979) 39–49.

[19] In a thoughtful way, Hendrikus Berkhof is an example of this, see his *Christian Faith*, 507–525; and his earlier, *Christ and the Meaning of History* (London: SCM, 1966) 169–78.

[20] *The Parables of the Kingdom* (London: Nisbet, 1935), *The Apostolic Preaching and its Developments* (London: Hodder & Stoughton, 1944 rev. ed.; original 1936) and *History of the Gospel* (London: Nisbet, 1938).

view is characteristically a-historical as regards the manifestation of the kingdom of God. The parousia tends on this view to be a symbol of a spiritual, even abstract, principle. However, although there are grounds for seeing some elements of this realized eschatology in the New Testament, especially in the gospel of John, the New Testament as a whole places these within a wider framework which it has taken up from the Old Testament. There is an overarching depiction of the coming of the kingdom of God as a massive intervention by God at a future time in human history to usher in what is arguably the historical age of the new heavens and the new earth. This future intervention is the consummation of Christ's bringing in of the kingdom in his own person and work.

In historical eschatology what is stressed is the coming of the kingdom of God into history as we experience it. A prominent place is given to the present-day realization of the promises of Christ on earth. Postmillennialism and certain forms of premillennialism fit here. But more especially in contemporary eschatological writings, the theologies of hope and liberation are important. The emphasis is this-worldly rather than other-worldly. For Wolfhardt Pannenberg, the coming kingdom is not a supernatural intervention into history but the destiny of present society. Jürgen Moltmann speaks of the fulfilment of history rather than a kingdom 'beyond history'. Moltmann does *not* claim that man creates his own future, but that he acts 'in the light of the promised future that is to come'. Christ's coming is not eternity breaking into history but 'the opening up of history'. The eschatological hope is seen as 'the future of man', and the 'socializing of humanity'.[21] Parousia, on this view, tends to be significative of a more concrete, earthly reality. In this way, the parousia has the status of *promise*. Thus, Moltmann has brought to the fore features of the New Testament presentation which have been neglected elsewhere. However, the New Testament also has two other stresses to which Moltmann does not appear to have given due weight: the fact that all the promises of God have already received their 'yes' and 'amen' in Jesus Christ (2 Cor. 1:20), and that between us and the new historical future which the kingdom of God brings in lies 'the day of the Lord', with its separation into 'sheep' and 'goats' (Mt. 25:32).

The writings of George Eldon Ladd represent a futurist eschatology. The kingdom involves two great moments: a fulfilment in

---

[21]   J. Moltmann, *Theology of Hope*, 222–3, 329.

history, in the coming of Jesus Christ, and a consummation at the end of history. There is a sharp distinction between the new order inaugurated by Christ and the age to come. In its present aspect, the Kingdom exists in humility beside the present order which is not disrupted. It is a present spiritual realm where such blessings of the Kingdom to come as forgiveness are experienced. Israel is temporally rejected and the Kingdom creates the church through which the powers and the keys of the kingdom work. The age to come, the future realm, is one of consummation, the destruction of satan, forgiveness, life and righteousness.[22]

In what Moltmann characterizes as a 'transcendent eschatology', Karl Barth describes three forms of Jesus' return. First, the resurrection, which has already occurred and which is the basis of the other two returns. Second, the outpouring of the Holy Spirit at Pentecost, which is our present reality in the church. Third, the parousia, by which Christ reveals and confirms to the whole of creation what has already been accomplished for the salvation of the world through his death and resurrection. For Barth, the first coming of Christ is inaugurated eschatology, whereas the second coming is consummated eschatology. The great events of the end of the world have already taken place in the resurrection and ascension of Christ, but they have still to take place in the history of the community of faith. The third coming is the revelation of the reality of the first two.

Here parousia is a real manifestation of God, a further and decisive in-breaking from God's side into present reality in which God unalterably changes our concrete existence. Barth's presentation has much to commend it, but questions have been asked as to the degree to which he will allow this manifestation of God to be thought of as an actual historical event.[23]

In understanding the character of that final event, it is helpful to see that the descriptions of the 'coming', 'arrival' and 'presence' of Christ which are expressed in the vocabulary associated with *pareimi* are used by the gospels not just to speak of the final coming of Jesus Christ, but also to highlight the key events of his earthly life and ministry. Thus, it is possible to see in the gospels, and

[22] Ladd, *Theology*, 64–9.

[23] See Moltmann, *Theology of Hope*, 45–58; A.A. Hoekema, *The Bible and the Future* (Grand Rapids: Eerdmans, 1978) 306–8; and B. Hebblethwaite, *The Christian Hope* (Basingstoke: Marshall, Morgan & Scott, 1984) 134–9.

especially in Matthew 24 and 25, five different 'parousias' of Christ:[24]

1. Jesus' birth at Bethlehem and his entry into the world. The concept of 'coming' is applied extensively to Jesus with regard to his earthly ministry (Jn. 12:46; Jn. 1; Jn. 7:28; 12:47; Mt. 5:7; 10:35; 20:28). At this first advent Jesus receives his eternal kingship (Lk. 1:30–3).

2. The presence or parousia (*hē parousia*) of the Son of Man which brings the destructive judgment of Jerusalem in 70 AD (Mt. 24:27; see also Mt. 25:31; Jn. 5:27; Lk. 19:44).

3. The coming (*erchomai*) on the clouds of heaven within the lifetime of Jesus' hearers (Mt. 26:64; 24:30, 34). This is an advent or parousia to the Father to receive the everlasting kingdom after his mediatorial death. 'Coming on the clouds' is equivalent to 'sitting at the right hand of God', since they are both metaphors for receiving universal and eternal authority from God (see Daniel 7). As the Daniel 7 passage refers to a coming on the clouds *to* the Ancient of Days, Matthew 26:64 could refer to the ascension.

   On the basis of the Son of Man receiving the kingdom from the Father, Jesus commissions his apostles for world mission (Mt. 28:16–20). The greatest practical outworking of this is seen in Matthew 24 to be after the fall of Jerusalem (Mt. 24:29–31): the world mission of the gospel would undermine and change established human institutions. Matthew 24:29–31; Isaiah 13:10; Ezekiel 32:7; Joel 2:28–32; and Acts 2:16–21 all use cosmic tribulation imagery to describe the overturning of human institutions by the hand of God.

4. The fourth advent or parousia of the Son of Man is the coming of the Holy Spirit at Pentecost (Jn. 14:18). 'I will not leave you orphans, I will come to you', says Jesus as he speaks of the gift of the Spirit.

   The coming of the Holy Spirit into the heart of the believer is the coming of Jesus for fellowship (Rev. 3:20; Jn. 14:3, 23). On this basis Jesus' title as *ho erchomenos*, 'the coming one', is transferred to the faithful believers. In Revelation 7:14 faithful believers are called *hoi erchomenoi*, the ones destined to come into the presence of the Father and receive the kingdom.

---

[24] See D.B. Knox, 'The Five Comings of Jesus: Matthew 24 and 25', *Reformed Theological Review* 34 (1975) 44–54.

5. The fifth and final parousia (*erchomai*) or advent is the coming of the Son of Man with the angels for the final judgment (Mt. 25:31).

Whether we identify two, three or five advents or parousias of Jesus, the notion of *advent* or parousia structurally dominated the life and work of Christ and the existence of the church. The last advent is but the last in a series of 'presences' of Jesus, whose presence has a further four distinctive theological characteristics which fill out for us the meaning of Christ's parousia. First, all of Jesus' appearances have to do with his mediatorial kingship. All of them are *pro nobis*, for us. Secondly, all of Jesus' advents are couched in terms of upset or judgment – upon sin, upon people, upon himself, for us. Thirdly, all of Jesus' parousias reconcile, prospectively or actually, positively or negatively, the creation upset by sin (Mt. 1:21; Col. 1:20; 2:15; Phil. 2:5–11). Finally, all these comings and their consequents form the content of the gospel, are executed by gospel proclamation, and fulfil the promise of the gospel (e.g. Rom. 2:16; 1:15–18; 1 Pet. 4:6, 17; Mt. 24:14; Rev. 14:7).

From this review we may conclude two things about the biblical presentation of the final advent of Christ. First, the final advent is irreducibly historical. It signals both the chronological end (*finis*) and the goal (*telos*) of present history. On the other side stands not a time-less-ness but a new quality of time, the history of the new heavens and the new earth. Secondly, the parousia is above all the sign of the gospel. Wherever the gospel is preached the day of judgment is imminent. The gospel is the prolongation of the new age already inaugurated in the life, death, and resurrection of Jesus Christ. This new age now confronts all humanity, calling for decision, for repentance. Thus the parousia is the antidote to all manifestations of our self-centredness, whether in materialism, self-actualization or the struggle for a utopian community on earth:

> Besides this you know what hour it is, how it is full time now for you to wake from sleep. For salvation is nearer to us now than when we first believed; the night is far gone, the day is at hand. Let us cast off the works of darkness and put on the armour of light; let us conduct ourselves becomingly as in the day . . . put on the Lord Jesus Christ, and make no provision for the flesh, to gratify its desires (Rom. 13:11–14).

The Angel of Revelation 14:7 was given an eternal gospel to proclaim to all peoples: 'Fear God and give him the glory, for the hour of his judgment has come.' Because the new age overlaps the old age, the last day, the absolute future which lies on the other side of Christ's final advent can even now be anticipated in faith and repentance.

Death and the Intermediate State

There is a certain artificiality in considering our last two topics, death and resurrection, separately, since the primary theological theme underlying their presentation in the New Testament is the correlative death and resurrection of Jesus Christ. However, beside the pedagogic value of treating them separately, there are also theological reasons for doing so. Although they are correlative in the one Man, Jesus Christ, they stand as polar opposites.

To put it another way, when death is focused through Jesus Christ, the proper Man, it is also at the same time focused through Adam, the first Man. So the major theological motif underlying the Bible's presentation of death is 'dying in Christ and dying in Adam' (Rom. 5:9; cf. Phil. 2:8; Rom. 6:5–8). But there is no such parallel in the biblical presentation of resurrection.

What then is the Christian attitude to death? In brief, it is seen as a present, thoroughly unpleasant experience, resulting from sin, which hedges around our whole existence. Death is a process as well as an event. This can be seen from the five distinct senses in which the New Testament speaks of death – physical death, spiritual death, the second death, death as a realm and death to sin.

Spiritual death refers to man's alienation from God, and the hostility towards God and from God that is evident in sin and in God's judgment on sin (Gen. 2:17; Rom. 5:15–16; Rom. 7:9, 24; Eph. 2:1–3; Col. 1:21). Both physical and spiritual death, and their present and future consequences, are 'in Adam', as a result of the fall. That the two are locked together is no surprise, for humanity is not thought of in Greek terms as a body and a soul, but as a psychosomatic entity. The 'second death' denotes the permanent separation from God that befalls physically dead unbelievers, that is, those whose state of spiritual deadness was not reversed during their lifetime through regeneration, with the result that their names are 'not found in the book of life' (Rev. 20:14–15; cf. 2:11; 20:6; 21:8). Occasionally death is regarded as a concrete thing, either as a realm (Rev. 1:18; 20:3) or as a person (1 Cor. 15:26; 20:14). In Romans 6, sin, death, law, and unrighteousness are regarded as the great enemies, the components of the old age, the sphere of the false lord which is opposed to the rule, age and sphere of the good Lord, Jesus Christ, who brings righteousness and life. For this reason, even as we live in the overlap of the two ages and are torn between two contrary and distinctive sets of experiences (Gal. 5, esp. vv. 16–17), we are to regard ourselves as 'dead to sin' in Christ (Rom. 6:11). That is, we are to see ourselves as unresponsive to the appeal and power of sin, but alert and responsive to the voice of God.

In the light of this presentation in the New Testament, may we see actual physical death in a positive light, as Hendrikus Berkhof does, as a 'fermentation' included in the renewal process?[25] No, for physical death is part of the judgment of God, and moreover, Jesus, the 'Resurrection and the Life', shows a boiling rage as he confronts death at the tomb of Lazarus his friend (Jn. 11:1–44). Death is the great enemy of God as well as man. In the resurrection of Christ, it is *conquered*. It is the sting of death which is removed (1 Cor. 15:50–57), not its status or its reality as a totally foreign intrusion into God's good purposes for his creation. The contrast between life and death that we see in the Adam–Christ comparison (Rom. 5:12–21; 1 Cor. 15:12–57) places 'hope', positive expectation, in the resurrection of Christ, and thus in our resurrection. To transfer this positive outlook to physical death is to miss the plain drift of the metaphors of 1 Corinthians 15:35–57, for the body in the ground is characterized as 'earthly', 'perishable', 'in dishonour', 'sown in weakness', 'of the dust', 'mortal'.

Traditionally, the term 'intermediate state' refers to the period that elapses between the death of the individual believer and the parousia of Christ or the consummation of all things. It is 'interme-diate' for one of three reasons: it lies between two definite temporal points; or, it is the period an incorporeal soul awaits embodiment at the parousia; or, it refers to the period in which, while individuals may have received spiritual bodies at death, the corporate Body of Christ awaits the parousia when it will achieve its full perfection.

Nowhere does the New Testament use the term 'intermediate state', nor does it say much about the idea. From the few references we can conclude that the focus is on the 'intermediate state' of the church, and not so much that of the individual believer. It is thus the interval between the first fruits of Christ's resurrection and the full manifestation of it as the completed Body of Christ. It is the interval between inauguration and consummation.

---

[25] *Christian Faith*, 484.

However, the history of theology throws us five pastoral and theological questions concerning the fate of the individual believer in this in-between time. Is it a time of consciousness or sleep? Is it a time of purification, as in the concepts of 'purgatory' or further sanctification in the presence of Christ? What does 'being with Christ' mean? Is it a state of disembodiment? Where are the Christian dead?

The New Testament gives us a number of clear statements in which we must seek our answers. We have to affirm that those who have fallen asleep are unconscious with respect to our world, but, not to their world of spirit, for they are 'alive to God' (Lk. 20:38b), or 'with (*meta*) me' (Lk. 23:43). They 'live spiritually as God does' (1 Pet. 4:6), 'they are with (*pros*) the Lord' (2 Cor. 5:8), 'with (*syn*) Christ' (Phil. 1:23). The 2 Maccabees 12:39–45 passage which refers to Judas Maccabeus making 'propitiation for them that died, that they may be released from sin' is non-canonical. The appeal to Matthew 12:31–2 to support the notion of purgatory fails because the passage speaks of forgiveness, God's gracious declaration over us, not a personal expiation. In the same way, the appeal to 1 Corinthians 3:11–15 depends on assuming your conclusion before appealing to the verses as a proof. Finally, the nature of resurrection makes a doctrine of purification after death an obfuscating disbelief, for Jesus Christ is not only our justification but also our sanctification (Rom. 4:24–5; 1 Cor. 1:30).

Luke 23:43, 2 Corinthians 5:8 and Philippians 1:23 speak of being 'with Christ'. In context, they point to an experience that follows death yet precedes the parousia. The idea of some sort of suspended animation is not plausible, for all these references witness to conscious fellowship with Christ, a better fellowship than now, not less.

As to the question of whether this is a state of disembodiment awaiting the general resurrection, there is little direct New Testament evidence. The accounts of the transfiguration (Lk. 9:30–33) and Dives and Lazarus (Lk. 16:23–4) are not in themselves interested in our question. In Revelation 6:9–11, the description of the souls of the martyrs supports a body-after-death view as they wear white robes. Paul's twofold use of *gymnos*, naked, might offer insight. But 1 Corinthians 15:37 views not the interim state is not in view but the dead physical body which is the seed for the spiritual body; bare seed becomes full plant when the physical gives way to the spiritual. Nothing is said of disembodiment, only of the change from one to the other. In 2 Corinthians 5:3 'nakedness' has traditionally been seen as a temporary bodilessness for all or for unbelievers only. But the 'nakedness' statement is rhetorical, for Paul is expressing his assurance of spiritual embodiment and rejecting any notion of a possible permanent disembodiment.

We may draw three conclusions from Paul's arguments. First, the final state of the Christian is one of embodiment. Secondly, irrespective of the anthropological question of the interim state, it is absolutely clear that 'Whether we live or whether we die, we belong to the Lord' (Rom. 14:8), secure in his possession of us and assured of sharing his destiny (Rom. 8:17). Finally, as 1 Corinthians 15 shows, it is a matter of finding suitable metaphors to describe a continuity and yet a radical discontinuity between present experience and future hope, between time as we have it now and as we will have it then. The weight of the metaphors which seek to express these tensions points to assurance of consummation. Hence we may conclude that 'then' we have all that has been promised, and thus are embodied.

As to the question of where the Christian dead are, there are two emphases in the New Testament. From our earthly point of view, they are resting in the grave (Jn. 5:28–9; 1 Thess. 4:16–17; cf. Acts 13:36), or are resident in Hades (Acts 2:27, 31), the invisible realm in the heart of the earth (Mt. 12:40) in which all the dead are temporarily resident. Secondly, from the viewpoint of Christian faith which is directed towards the invisible and coming kingdom of God, the Christian dead are in proximity to God in heaven: in table fellowship with Abraham (Lk. 16:23), in the resting-places in the Father's house (Jn. 14:2; Lk. 16:9), in fellowship with Christ in paradise or heaven (Lk. 23:43; Jn. 12:26; 2 Cor. 5:8; Phil. 1:23), or as martyrs, waiting under the heavenly altar (Rev. 6:9).

We may now draw a number of conclusions concerning the intermediate state. First, the New Testament is more concerned with the nature of the eternal state (e.g. Rev. 21:1–22:5) and with the determinative character of a person's life (Lk. 16:27–20; 2 Cor. 5:10) than with the transitory interval between death and consummation. The main interest is focused on the assured nature of the ultimate stage of God's purposes. Secondly, the Christian dead are asleep to the world, but alive to God in the presence of Christ (Lk. 20:38b; Phil. 1:23). Thirdly, the post-mortem state of the Christian is not marked by 'soul sleep' but by conscious, enriched fellowship with Christ. Finally, the ultimate destiny of the Christian is not emancipation from a body but acquisition of a perfected, spiritual body which is fit for one who is destined by God to be his fellowshipping vice-regent in creation.

Ground of Eschatology: Resurrection[26]

There is no doubt that the resurrection of Jesus Christ, and the consequent hope of our resurrection to eternal life, structurally dominates New Testament thought. The Old Testament contains statements which clearly show the writers' confidence that God has power over death, and that God will not be found faithless in the face of personal and national catastrophe (Ps. 16:10; 49:15; 73:24; Deut. 32; 1 Sam. 2:6; Hos. 6:1–3; 13:14; Isa. 26:19; Ezek. 37). Such is the strength of these statements that it is not surprising that both Jesus and Paul cite them in order to speak of the distinctive New Testament hope that springs from the raising of Jesus Christ from the dead (Mk. 12:26 f. = Exod. 3:6; 1 Cor. 15:55 = Hos. 13:14b). The one clear passage in the Old Testament that clearly expresses confidence in God's power over death in terms of the resurrection of the dead is Daniel 12:2. Several intertestamental writings evince a belief in the resurrection of the dead, but, as with Daniel 12:2, it is limited to Israel. The resurrection of Jesus the Messiah and the sending of the Spirit dramatically changes that.

At key points in his ministry, Jesus predicted his resurrection (Mk. 8:31; Lk. 9:22; Mk. 9:9, 31; 10:34). Mary Magdalene, and 'the other Mary' and 'the women who had come with him from Galilee', and the disciples bear testimony to his resurrection by referring to the empty tomb and meeting him (Mt. 28:1–10; Lk. 24:10–12, 13–53; Jn. 20:1–29; 21:4–23; Acts 1:22; 2:31 f.; 4:33). By a mighty act of God, the dead and buried Lord was raised to life again with a body which was new and material. It was new in that it was not identical with the old, and it was not merely visionary, for he met with his disciples in a form that could be seen and felt (Jn. 20:21, 27; Lk. 24:16, 31, 39; Acts 1:2, 9). This 'body and bones' resurrection becomes the irreducible foundation of apostolic preaching (1 Jn. 1:1–4; 1 Cor. 15:1–11 ff.; Rom. 4:16–25; Acts 2:22–36; 17:22–34). Now the disciples are certain that in Jesus Christ they have to do with the Lord, the Son (Rom. 1:4).

The resurrection clearly signals God's triumph over the power of sin and death in the person and work of Jesus. Because the crucified and resurrected One has entered the glory of God as the first-born

---

[26] I much indebted in what follows to the thorough review article on 'Resurrection' by Colin Brown and Lothar Coenen in C. Brown (ed.), *The New International Dictionary of New Testament Theology* Vol 3. (Exeter: Paternoster, 1978) 259–309.

among many brethren, the fall of Adam and all human slavery to sin which resulted from it has been cancelled. More than that, there is now a new start to the human race, a second Adam, whose life, death and resurrection has healed, at the very depths of our being, the alienation, corruption and dissolution characteristic of rebellious humankind and the creation which unwillingly bears that race (Rom. 5:12–21; cf. 4:25; Rom. 6:1–14; Col. 1:15–21; Rom. 6:15–19; 8:18–25; 1 Cor. 15:20–3). This message is the foundation of all Christian hope and preaching (1 Pet. 1:3; 1 Cor. 15). Resurrection is why baptism is a suitable sign of salvation (1 Pet. 3:21; Rom. 6:5).

But it is Jesus himself, in his very own person, who is 'the resurrection and the life' (Jn. 11:25). Resurrection then, for all its eschatological reality, has begun now, and is coextensive with the gospel ministry of the apostles and the Spirit and the belief it produces (1 Pet. 1:12, 23–5; cf. 1 Thess. 1:5–10; 2:13). The resurrected one has sent his Spirit, and those who are united to this Christ by faith are possessed of his power and already experience the beginning of the transition from this age to the age to come. They have moved from the kingdom of darkness to the kingdom of light, from sin and death to liberation and life (Eph. 1:15–2:10; Col. 1:13; 1 Pet. 2:9; Phil. 3:7–10). Right participation in the table fellowship of the Lord's Supper signifies the move from death to life through the death and resurrection of Christ (1 Cor. 10:14–22; 11:27 ff.; Jn. 6:54). Faith, then, is characterized as a dying and rising again with Jesus (Rom. 6:11; Jn. 5:24).

In the power of the resurrection of Jesus Christ, the believer now in his or her living has already entered the ethical realm and reality of the eschaton. On the basis of the indicative of Jesus' death and resurrection, the believer is to heed the imperative to put off the old life of self-centredness and sin and to put on the new life of faith in God and love of neighbour (Col. 3:1–17 ff.; 1 Cor. 6:12–20). On this side of the final parousia, the only way to enter into the power of Jesus' resurrection is by a willingness to share his sufferings, and so become like him in his death (Phil. 3:10–11). The bringing of the life of the age to come through a faith union with the resurrected Lord does not mean perfection has been gained now, but rather the power to persist in the new life under adversity, for the good of the neighbour and the glory of God (Phil. 3:1–4:1).

Given the universal scope of the person and work of Christ (Col. 1:15–20; Jn. 3:16–17), it is not surprising that Christ's resurrection means that, in contrast to the more limited outlook of Daniel 12:2, a general resurrection of all humankind from the dead is taught in the New Testament (1 Cor. 15:20–4; Rev. 20:11–15; Mt. 25:31–46). This is linked with the return of Christ and with judgment (Jn. 5:29; cf. 11:24). Faith in the Son of God is decisive here (Jn. 6:28–9). So different does this allegiance to Jesus Christ make the outcome that in several places the New Testament talks of a preceding 'first' resurrection of the righteous, the dead in Christ who will reign with him (Lk. 14:14; 1 Thess. 4:16; Rev. 20:4 ff.).

On the pattern of Christ's resurrection, the resurrection of those in Christ is not depicted as a reanimation of their corpses but as a transformation of their whole persons into the image of Christ (1 Cor. 15:20–4, 35–49). It is the resurrection not of a body, but a person. Although there is a radical discontinuity between 'what is sown' and 'what is raised', there is also a clear continuity of person-hood, of the transformed person (1 Cor. 15:49). Only those in Christ will be like Christ and possess 'spiritual bodies', since the 'spiritual body' is imperishable (1 Cor. 15:42, 50). Similarly controlled by the nature of Christ's person and work, immortality in the New Testa-ment is not a present possession of all humanity, but a future acquisition of Christians, for immortality is participation in the eternal life of God, that is, enjoying fellowship with Christ (2 Pet. 1:4; Lk. 23:43; 2 Cor. 4:8; Phil. 1:23). 'Life' and 'eternal life' are equivalent to 'immortality' (cf. 2 Cor. 5:4 and 1 Cor. 15:53 f.). 'Immortality' is a way of speaking about the reversal of the decay and deterioration which is characteristic of Adam's fallen race. Immor-tality is founded on and accompanies only Christ's resurrection and our participation in it by faith, for in the end it is only God who is immortal, and it is only Christ who leads us to the Father. In this way, immortality and resurrection are complementary notions.[27]

As for the unbelieving dead, they too will be raised, but to judgment and not to life, which amounts to a reanimation which leads to the 'second death' (Jn. 5:21a; Acts 24:15; Rev. 20:4 ff., 11–15). Thus there is a clear distinction between these two experiences of the one general resurrection, both of which are

---

[27] In recent scholarship it is Murray J. Harris who has done very careful exegetical work on the notions of resurrection and immortality. See his 'Resurrection and Immortality: Eight Theses', *Themelios* 1 (1976) 50–5, and more extensively in his *Raised Immortal: Resurrection and Immor-tality in the New Testament* (London: Marshall, Morgan & Scott, 1983). The former is summarized in Brown, *Dictionary of New Testament Theology*, 302–5.

determined in and by Christ and his resurrection (Jn. 5:25–9; 1 Cor. 15:20–4).

Scholarly debate about the theological meaning of 'resurrection' has quite appropriately centred on the significance of Christ's resurrection. Further, this has centred on the two pivotal issues of the historical status of Jesus' resurrection, and its eschatological meaning. With respect to the latter, Karl Barth speaks of the resurrection of Jesus as the breaking in of 'fulfilled time', the time of 'the pure presence of God'. In this way it is a presence of God without a future, an eternal present, for it fulfils the hopes of the Old Testament and those raised by the life and death of Jesus Christ. Thus, the Easter story 'does not speak eschatologically'. The eschatological, or the component of future expectation, lies in the confession of our own future resurrection. 'If we confess that Christ is risen and risen bodily, we must also confess our own future resurrection.' So the New Testament account of the Easter story is no mere Ebionite recollection, for 'the real New Testament says clearly that He who came is also He that comes'. This manifestation of the eschaton and the expectation it produced constitutes the very element by which Christ's church lives. In this short presentation in the early part of his *Dogmatics* Barth manages to focus for us most of the eschatological issues.[28]

The question of the actual historical character of the resurrection of Christ has been the focus of a long tradition of criticism since the eighteenth-century Enlightenment. Barth, and in a different way Bultmann, have pointed to the non-provability of the event, as it is without analogy to any event before or since; it is utterly unique in that it is entirely a work of God and not a work of man. Barth quite rightly insists that it must have been an event in history or it loses the very meaning the New Testament attaches to it, but will not go beyond 'the recollection, proclamation and reception of it'.

Within the tradition of biblical studies that takes as axiomatic Enlightenment views on history, a tradition that includes G.E. Lessing and Emmanuel Kant, the Easter events are not only denied historical existence, but tend to be reduced to religious experience. Such an approach tends to dismiss any claim to the historical facticity of the resurrection as a naive reading of the texts which ignores even 'the discrepancies that are only too apparent in a surface reading', let alone the allegedly more reliable evidence

---

[28] *Church Dogmatics* (Edinburgh: T. & T. Clarke, 1956) I. 2. 114–17.

which comes from redaction criticism that exposes the motives and the subsequent, inventive re-shaping of traditions by the editors of the gospels.[29] But that dismissiveness not only imaginatively overstates the discrepancies and underplays the similarities, it also fails to heed the warning of C.S. Lewis regarding the assumed certainty of a literary criticism which purports to see beyond the text and reconstructs its genesis.[30]

However, within both biblical and theological studies there has been a return by some to affirming the historicity of the events, in large part if not in full: so Alan Richardson, Hans von Campenhausen, C.F.D. Moule, G.E. Ladd, R.E. Brown, and Wolfhardt Pannenberg. Pannenberg has quite rightly insisted that analogy can only enable us to discern events of a similar kind, it cannot prejudge the historicity of events which are dissimilar.[31] Further, rigorously applied, such use of analogy destroys all historical work, for history yields its meaning very much from the dissimilarity of events. The biblical accounts purport to be historical, and there are quite clear historical markers around the actual resurrection itself which are open to modern historical investigation, and thus some assessment of the unique central claim that Jesus Christ arose from the dead. Further, given the historical facticity of this resurrection, its own peerless character and associated meaning demand that *it* becomes the decisive context for understanding and interpreting all of subsequent history, not the other way around.[32] Adapting Pannenberg's argument, the resurrection offers this possibility because questions regarding the meaning and unity of history by their very nature must rest on a transhistorical 'something' which can account for individuality and continuity at the same time. Unitary explanations, limited to human existence, consciousness and social experience, fail because 'the human spirit always exists only as an individual

---

[29] For example, Peter Carnley, *The Structure of Resurrection Belief* (Oxford: Clarendon, 1993) 12–19 ff.; his own understanding is that the resurrection faith of the early church is due to remembrance of Jesus' unique self-giving and the presence of the heavenly Jesus in the community's experience of forgiveness (see pp. 187–9, 221–2, 264–7, 296, 324–6, 367–8).

[30] C.S. Lewis, *Fern-seed and Elephants, and other essays on Christianity* (Glasgow: Fontana, 1975) 104–25.

[31] See Wolfhardt Pannenberg, *Basic Questions in Theology* (London: SCM, 1970) volume 1, 44–50; and his *Systematic Theology* vol. 2 (Grand Rapids: Eerdmans, 1994) 359–63.

[32] Brown, *Dictionary of New Testament Theology*, 302.

and for the individual.'[33] Finally, the historian in his or her quest for meaning must always look backward, look for the links to what has happened in the past, to something which offers itself as a genuine revelation of the transcendent explanation of all history.[34]

Theologically, the historicity of the bodily resurrection of Jesus Christ is completely undetachable from the hope of the gospel: that God will bring in a real, concrete new heaven and a new earth, where eternal life means not only a creation healed of its alienation but also a heaven where the inhabitants enjoy fellowship with each other and their God in a context of corporeality. The resurrection of Jesus Christ means that God has really and finally intervened in human history and existence to transform its 'form and matter', not abolish it by removing present human reality to a spiritual plane of non-concreteness, where disembodied spirits may enjoy heightened religious experience. The New Testament will not allow the hope of the resurrection to be detached from the hope of a renewed earth (Rom. 8:18–25). If God has not done what the apostle claims, then we are indeed 'of all people most to be pitied' (1 Cor. 15:19). The Enlightenment dismissal of the possibility of the resurrection of Jesus Christ being historical depends on the assumption of a closed instead of an open universe. But even David Hume from time to time needed to appeal to an open system;[35] and modern cosmological thought, especially that which takes its rise in physics, is pushed to acknowledge that the universe cannot be adequately explained on the assumption of it being a closed physical system. One must

---

[33] Pannenberg, *Basic Questions*, 74.

[34] See Pannenberg, *Basic Questions*, 66–80.

[35] Hume must assume a closed and rational system for his dismissal of miracles, and an open one in order to uphold Newtonian science and human moral experience. At a deeper level though, Hume is acutely aware that if, as he does, we deny that causation is rational or true, then far from having a closed system, we have no 'system'. To give Newtonian science a place he must invoke 'a trivial property of the fancy', a 'trivial property' which although unsupported by reason, is necessary. That is, he strongly argues on *pragmatic* grounds that we cannot live in the world his philosophy has constructed, acknowledging that 'Nature is always too strong for principle'. Questions of the moral nature of human existence, of ultimate meaning and the reliability of empirical science, i.e. common sense, force Hume to acknowledge the limits of his radical empiricism. See his *A Treatise of Human Nature*, vol. 1 (London: J.M. Dent & Sons, 1911) 178–9, 252–5; and *Enquiries Concerning the Human Understanding and Concerning the Principles of Morals* (Oxford: Clarendon, [2]1902) 160.

posit a transcendent intelligence.[36] It comes down to this, do we believe with Israel that the God who made the heavens and the earth and all that lives in them, in fact, has power over death?

OVER COFFEE

- Discuss what further judgment there may be beyond the cross.
- How is the kingdom of God relevant to the contemporary world?
- Does Christ's final return have to literally be 'bodily and visible'? What is at stake in your answer?
- 'For God's sake, we hope that hell will be a form of purification' (H. Berkhof). Discuss critically.
- Is the notion of 'resurrection to hell' theologically justifiable?

---

[36] For example, Paul Davies argues that the rules of physics 'look *as if* they are the product of intelligent design. I do not see how that can be denied.' However, he is wary of attempts to rationally construct a unitary theory of physics and metaphysics which would account for everything in 'a complete and self-consistent explanation'. See his *The Mind of God: Science and the Search for Ultimate Meaning* (London: Penguin, 1992) 214, 226, 231. From within a Christian tradition of physicists, John Polkinghorne points out that quantum theory and the existence and operation of complex dynamical systems quash the notion of a closed mechanistic universe in favour of an open process where the physical and metaphysical are related (*Science and Providence: God's Interaction within the World* [London: SPCK, 1989] 1–3).

3

Searching for the Fundamentals: Patristic Eschatology to Chalcedon

Actual eschatologies are often hammered out in the context of Christians seeking to understand and remain faithful to biblical revelation against prevailing social and religious pressures. Coming to an understanding of the various schemes will do two things for us. First, it will remind us that we too have histories, no matter how much we are unconscious of that fact, and our histories affect the way we think about biblical revelation. Second, it will expose some of the problems that have arisen as Christians have sought to understand the eschatological teaching of Scripture, and the solutions they have posited for those problems.

We may think of the difficulties the early Christian writers faced in this way. Obviously, any eschatology which wants to be seen as Christian must take seriously the particulars given in the New Testament: life after death, resurrection, judgment, heaven, hell, and the like. But how does one conceive of these elements in a *Christian* way, that is, in a way that reflects the major concerns of the New Testament? It is partly a matter of framework. As we will see, it is possible, with the Gnostics, to reflect on the resurrection with great earnestness. But reflect on the notion of resurrection within a frame of reference which in its essentials is not only non-Christian but anti-Christian, and the resulting eschatology ends up in direct opposition to that of the New Testament. In their eschatological reflection, what the orthodox Christian writers did by way of response was to find and affirm alternative frameworks which more palpably owed their shape to the great controlling themes of the Bible.

In this way then, the early Christian period is a search for fundamentals, not just with respect to details, but to overall interpretative frameworks. It is in a real sense a vigorous search for the big picture, the theological backdrop against which such pressing questions as 'What happens to us after death?' are to be answered. For that reason, it is an adventure.

Context

The period designated 'Patristic', from about AD 100 to the Council of Chalcedon in AD 451, is one of great excitement and richness as the Christian message, essentially a Jewish phenomenon, impacted on the diverse cultures of not only the world created by the civilizations of Rome and Greece, but also the more 'exotic' cultures on the fringe of the Roman empire. In communicating and defend-ing its message the growing church faced challenges posed by cultural differences and an almost constant buffeting by the vicis-situdes of political and social change. It is not surprising that we face several difficulties in coming to grips with the development of Christian eschatology over this period of about 350 years.

Difficulties of diverse experience, coherence, and orthodoxy

The first difficulty is the very diversity of the church's historical experience, each experience affecting in a unique way the eschato-logical content of Christian writings. The most distinctive feature of this history is growth, but growth under diverse conditions, which can be periodized like this:

1. DE-JUDAIZATION OF THE CHURCH: With Gentile believers far outnumbering Jewish Christians, the fall of Jerusalem in 70 and the crushing of the Jewish revolt in 115, the church was cut off from its Jewish roots with deleterious consequences for under-standing the Old Testament, and therefore the New. The church labelled as heretical the radical solution of Marcion (d. 160) who rejected the Old Testament outright, but could come to grips with the Old Testament themselves only by spiritualizing its message in a direction compatible with Hellenic thought. Old and New Testament apocalyptic was particularly troublesome. Paradoxically, after this de-Judaization of biblical studies came a later re-Judaization of the church's ministry, where the Old Testament models of priesthood and worship were re-embraced.[1]

---

[1] See Jaroslav Pelikan, *The Christian Tradition: A History of the Devel-opment of Doctrine* vol. 1 (University of Chicago Press, 1971) 12–27.

2. THE APOLOGISTS: A small group of Greek Christian authors of the second century defended Christianity in the face of persecution, slander and intellectual attack. They sought to make Christianity understandable and acceptable to both Graeco-Roman and Jewish audiences. Justin Martyr was the most important of the Apologists. In their work we see the beginnings of a systematic Christian construction from the theological content of Scripture.

3. PERSECUTIONS: Prior to 250, although sometimes savage and without the usual restraints embedded in Roman law, persecution of Christians was only sporadic and its extent was determined more by local feeling than by official government policy. This changed with Emperor Decius. In 250 he ordered that all his subjects should sacrifice to the state gods under pain of death. There was sporadic toleration under some of the later emperors. From 303 to 312 persecution reached ferocious heights. When Constantine became emperor in 312 he issued orders for toleration and showed imperial favour to Christians.

4. ARIAN CONTROVERSY: Arianism rent the church with controversy from 313 until its final expulsion from mainstream Christian thought, and the borders of the Empire, after the Council of Constantinople in 381. Arianism claimed that the Son of God was not eternal, 'there was a time when he was not', and that he was created by the Father from nothing as an instrument for creating the world. It reached its political and ecclesiastical height with its acceptance by the councils of eastern and western bishops, at Seleucia and Ariminum respectively, in 359. St Jerome wrote: 'The whole world groaned and marvelled to find itself Arian.'

5. RESURGENCE OF PAGANISM: After Constantine's accession, paganism continued as the major religious belief well into the fourth century. Its replacement by a folk-Christianity, or Christo-paganism, was slow. There was some official suppression of pagan sacrificial practices. This gradual change from paganism was sharply arrested by the coming to power of Julian (361–363). Julian was an apostate from Christianity, an intellectually able and moral promoter of an ambitious programme for the wholesale overhaul and reintroduction of a polytheism undergirded by the religious outlook of Neoplatonism. Christianity was not proscribed, but was vigorously combated by the retraction of legal and financial privileges accorded to Christians by his predecessors, by official discrimination

against Christians in public office, and by some administrative meddling in internal church affairs. Although less than success-ful where Christianized citizens were numerous, Julian's programme struck a responsive note among many.

6. POLITICAL AND SOCIAL TRIUMPH OF THE CHURCH: The policy of Valentinian I, the next emperor in the West (364–75) and a Christian, was one of official neutrality and enforced toleration in religious matters, extending to both heretics and pagans. However, direct intervention in affairs of religion was needed when public order was threatened by riots between sizeable Christian factions. At the same time, leaders like Pope Damasus (366–84) successfully fused old Roman civic pride with Chris-tianity so that the men of the Roman nobility more frequently became Christians. Secular and Christian understandings of religion and state were starting to flow together. From Bishop Ambrose of Milan (374–97) onward, the notion of an orthodox empire free from religious error gained currency in the West. Emperors from Gratian (d. 383) to Theodosius II (d. 450) obliged, the process reaching its climax with the Theodosian Code of 435. It covered both parts of the empire by 439. Book XVI dealt with religious affairs and contained bans on pagan-ism and penalties for heresy, as well as laws regulating the position of the clergy and determining the relation between church and state. However, pagan thought and literature generally remained free of control.

7. COUNCIL OF CHALCEDON, 451: This council, whose dogmatic decisions were accepted by both the eastern and western churches, marks a high-point of doctrinal consensus and stabil-ity. Christological controversy had not ceased with Arianism, and the affirmation by Chalcedon that the incarnate Jesus Christ is one person in two natures, which are united 'uncon-fusedly, unchangeably, indivisibly, inseparably', defined the limits of legitimate speculation, and brought some peace to the theological life of the church.

A second problem in understanding the thinking of this period is rooted in the content of the eschatological writings themselves. With few exceptions, they are not particularly coherent, even within the works of one author. This is partly due to the fact that most eschatological discourse occurred in the context of wider concerns. That is, these Christians were not seeking to be systematic, as such, though they were striving to be coherent, for they sought to bring together and make sense of the diverse strands of biblical thought in order to answer the questions which came to them out of their particular pastoral contexts. And as they did so, some themes emerged which acted as foundations for later theology to build on. It is the concern of this chapter to identify the more important of those themes, and to indicate some of their strengths and weaknesses as expositions of New Testament hope.

A third problem flows from defining just who and what was orthodox, and associated with this, just where was the unity in it all. Some were 'orthodox' in some respects, 'unorthodox' in others, bringing controversy as well as enlightenment for the church. Tertullian (*c.* 160–*c.* 225) and Origen (*c.* 185–*c.* 254) are prominent examples. The struggle to assert and understand New Testament themes is one indicator of orthodoxy, and it shapes a unity of content. The following beliefs are fairly plain in the writings of this period: a linear view of history with history having an origin and an end determined by the power and plan of God; bodily resurrection from the dead; God's universal judgment both on the world as a whole and on each individual; retribution and reward in that judgment; and the continued involvement in the life of the church by those who had died.[2] But the writers often disagreed amongst themselves and with the New Testament on the details of these beliefs. This should not be seen as entirely negative, for these differences often flowed from a sincere struggle to understand and apply the text of Scripture. Keeping empathy with them has the benefit of drawing our attention to truths in the text which a settled orthodoxy of later centuries may have overlooked.

For all these problems, there is no doubt that Christian writers did make effective use of eschatological themes. Ambrose of Milan, for example, although lacking a consistent eschatological theory, as a preacher held out to the faithful believers powerful images of Christian hope.[3] Eschatology acted, somewhat following the pattern in the New Testament (Mk. 13, 2 Pet. 3), as a theodicy both to believers who faced dreadful suffering and to non-believers who challenged the authenticity of the biblical claim of a decisive intervention by God in the affairs of humanity with its concomitant promise of victory over 'sin, the world and the devil'. Often, eschatological discourse with its promise of rewards and punishments served to exhort church

---

[2] Brian E. Daley, *The Hope of the Early Church* (Cambridge University Press, 1991) 219–23.
[3] Daley, 101.

members to greater faithfulness and perseverance. Turned towards pagan and sophisticated worlds on the outside, impending eschato-logical judgment, already evident in everyday affairs if viewed aright, provided a strong motive for repentance. Cyprian, bishop of Carthage during the turbulent years 248–58, echoing a Stoic theme of the *senectus mundi* (worn-out world), often states that human history has reached its evening; the world was dying from a depletion of its natural forces, and so showing the cumulative effects of sin.[4] With much vigour, Cyprian urges on his pagan reader the view that all the dissolutions of contemporary life are signs of the outpouring of God's wrath and constitute a call to repentance:

> Moreover, that wars continue frequently to prevail, that death and famine accumulate anxiety, that health is shattered by raging diseases, that the human race is wasted by the desolation of pestilence, know that this was foretold; that evils should be multiplied in the last times, and that misfortunes should be varied; and that as the day of judgment is now drawing nigh, the censure of an indignant God should be more and more aroused for the scourging of the human race. For these things happen not, as your false complaining and ignorant inexperience of the truth asserts and repeats, because your gods are not worshipped by us, but because God is not worshipped by you.[5]

Three departures from New Testament themes

The orthodox fathers developed their characteristic eschatological beliefs during the course of resisting three major departures from dominant New Testament concerns about the last things, namely Gnosticism, moralism and adventism.

Gnosticism

Gnosticism,[6] a movement of thought which established itself in the major centres of Christianity in the second century, taught as a basic

---

[4] Daley, 41. See Cyprian, *Epistle* 62.16 and especially *Address to Demetrianus* 3–8; ANF 5.363 and 458–60.

[5] *To Demetrianus*; ANF 5.459.

[6] Formerly, much of our information about Christian Gnosticism came from the anti-Gnostic writings of Hippolytus, Epiphanius, and most especially Irenaeus (*c.* 130–200) in his chief work, *Against Heresies*. The publication of the collection of Coptic Gnostic documents found at Nag Hammadi in Egypt in 1947 supplements the Christian sources. See James M. Robinson (ed.), *The Nag Hammadi Library in English* (San Francisco: Harper & Row, [3]1988).

tenet that through special and often secret revelations of knowledge about God and humankind, the spiritual element in human nature could receive redemption. The Gnostics treated both Jewish and Christian apocalyptic as symbolic, cryptic codes, not for the future but for present, spiritual, inner, knowledge.[7] In Gnostic systems the Christian expectation of the parousia and of the consummation and fulfilment of God's mighty redemptive acts which have caused his kingdom to be already operative is replaced by the theme of the soul's ascent to heaven.

The delay of the parousia and the fading of the early church's sense of eschatological crisis are partly the cause for this shift. However, there were also more immediate causes for the acceptance of Gnostic schemata: Hellenistic religious philosophy with its sharp dichotomy between body and soul; a general philosophical affirma-tion of a reality consisting of the real, heavenly Ideas radically separated by the *ho chōrismos* (the chasm) from their illusory earthly images or forms; and an emphasis on a vertical relationship between time and eternity. Gnostic schemes worked within these assumptions, which are common to Graeco-Roman culture but essentially foreign and antithetical to the New Testament.

Salvation is conceived as the restoration of the luminous elements in this world that belong to the highest, least material realm. These luminous elements are the souls of the followers of Gnosticism. The highest realm is the *plerōma*, or original 'full complement' of hierarchically ordered divine beings.[8] God is *pneuma* (spirit) and *dynamis* (power). Only the soul, imprisoned according to Basilides and Marcion in the body, is saved. Consequently, the key words in the Gnostic doctrine of redemption are those which emphasize the souls return to *plerōma* or fullness: 'ascend', 'escape from', 'when it had received power from that besprinkling of light which it possessed, it sprang back again, and was borne aloft.'[9]

The fate of human individuals is not clearly distinguished from the fate of the 'light' or 'dark' elements in the cosmos as a whole. The Gnostic *Gospel of Philip* describes the goal of salvation as the consummation of a mystical marriage between the soul and truth or light, foreshadowed in the church's liturgy.[10] Here then, we are

---

[7] Brian Hebblethwaite, *The Christian Hope* (Basingstoke: Marshall Morgan & Scott, 1984) 44–5.

[8] Daley, 26.

[9] Irenaeus, *Against Heresies* 1.30.3. See also *Against Heresies* ANF 1.24.5; 2.12.4.

[10] Daley, 27.

not far from the idea of 'deification' or 'divinization', which has its rise in the orthodox writing, 'To *Autolycus*' by Theophilus of Antioch (*c.* 180). In its fully developed form in the Eastern Orthodox churches, divinization is the finely nuanced belief that, in some ultimately mysterious way, the likeness of God in human-kind lost at the Fall is restored as we partake of the energies of God communicated to us by the Holy Spirit. Because the energies of God radiate from his essence and share its nature, to partake of God's energies is to partake of his very own nature and thus to come into such an intimate and holy communion with him that we may be said to be 'divinized' or 'deified'. However, in this we are not absorbed into the essence of God, but maintain our creaturely status. It is a process of sanctification in which our corruption and mortality are replaced by the incorruptibility and immortality of the divine Son of God, a transformation only brought to completion in the final consummation.[11] The concept of divinization was to become a commonplace amongst eastern theologians like Gregory of Nyssa, and is most noteworthy in the mystical writings of Denys (or Dionysius) the Areopagite (*c.* 500). Denys stands as the early medieval heir of many gnostic ideas and a most formative influence in the mystical theology of both eastern and western Christendom.

It is no surprise then that the promise of bodily resurrection becomes spiritualized. *The Treatise on the Resurrection* (*Epistle to Rheginus*) interprets the hope of resurrection as being a call to disregard fleshly existence and 'enter into the wisdom of those who have known the Truth'.[12] Resurrection, an event in history, has become simply the phenomenon of enlightenment. The writer urges his reader: 'Therefore do not think in part, O Rheginos, nor live in conformity with this flesh for the sake of unanimity, but flee from the divisions and the fetters, and already you have the resurrection.'[13]

As far as there is a single eschatological hope in a diverse Gnosticism, Brian E. Daley sees it in the promised continuity

---

[11] See H. Cunliffe-Jones (ed.), *A History of Christian Doctrine* (Edinburgh: T. & T. Clark, 1978) 149ff.; and S.B. Ferguson and D.F. Wright (eds.), *New Dictionary of Theology* (Leicester: Inter-Varsity Press, 1988) 189f.

[12] Cited from Daley, 28.

[13] Op. cit. Daley's citations are from James M. Robinson (ed.), *The Nag Hammadi Library in English* (New York: Harper & Row, 1977).

between the present enlightenment claimed by the sect and an eternal sharing in a saving, but largely hidden, truth. That is, in the vertical, a-historical relationship between time and eternity. Such a hope and relationship is evident in the following quotation from the *Gospel of Philip*: 'The mysteries of truth are revealed, though in type and image. The bridal chamber, however, remains hidden. It is the holy in the holy . . . If anyone becomes a son of the bridal chamber, he will receive the light. If anyone does not receive it while he is in these places, he will not be able to receive it in the other place.'[14]

Thus the New Testament hope of the parousia, resurrection of the body, the judgment, and the renewal of creation fade into the background where this line of thought dominates the thinking of Christians.

Moralism

The second departure from New Testament themes involves a moralism akin to that of the New Testament Judaizers which reduced the hope of the kingdom of God to simply a hope of 'heaven'. Heaven was thought of as the place or state of life in which those who have done good will be rewarded, and which is to be won as a prize for endurance. In the West, Tertullian's teaching on Christ proclaiming a new law and a new promise of the kingdom in heaven echoes this second departure. Christian writers continued to use popular expectations of future reward and punishment as an instrument for reinforcing their own social and moral message.[15] In so doing, eschatology became severed from its New Testament integration into the sweep of salvation-history from creation to new creation, and the biblical images were treated in isolation to answer particular questions on the nature of life after death, and the like, which come from the pastoral context. Tertullian can be credited with laying the foundation for Latin Christianity's doctrine of the last things,[16] and especially its understanding of repentance as 'doing penance'. Later, in the East, John Chrysostom (*c.* 344–407) shows the same moral concern and use of reward or punishment to further it, but he does place it within a wider context. Since the good so often

---

[14] Op. cit.
[15] Daley, 33–4.
[16] Daley, 37.

suffer and the wicked prosper in this world, if goodness and evil
are not punished in the afterlife, then our sense of justice is
rendered absurd and faith in God's provident care for the world
contradicted.[17]

Adventism
The third departure from New Testament concerns was an 'adventism', which stands as a polar opposite to the spiritualizing
tendencies of Gnosticism and which, in the light of some special
revelation of the true meaning of Jewish and Christian apocalyptic, particularly Daniel and Revelation, expected a literal, imminent parousia. Early hopes of a thousand-year earthly reign of
Christ which would heap rich bounty on faithful believers, 'millennialism' as it has become known, is credited to Cerinthus (*c.*
100) and Papias (*c.* 60–130) bishop of Hierapolis in Phrygia who,
according to Irenaeus, possessed teachings he attributed to Jesus
which described in vivid detail a coming millennial kingdom.[18]
Common to this chiliasm or millennialism is the 'belief in a
temporary, earthly, Messianic kingdom to be realized sometime
in the future'.[19] The leading second-century example of this tendency is Montanism. Montanus was a Christian convert in Asia
Minor who prophesied that the heavenly Jerusalem would soon
descend to a plain in Phrygia. Many left their homes and followed
Montanus to await its coming. Elsewhere Montanism became a
sect practicing extreme moral rigour and claiming special revelation from the Spirit. Tertullian was its most notable convert,
becoming a member in the third century.[20] Elsewhere, despite
Origen's (d. 254) powerful critique of literalistic millennial hopes,
and perhaps because of his spiritualizing tendencies, millennial
hope remained strong even in those parts of Christendom most
influenced by Origen and the other Alexandrian theologians of the
third and fourth centuries.[21]

---

[17] Daley, 105–6.
[18] Daley, 18.
[19] Charles E. Hill, *Regnum Caelorum: Patterns of Future Hope In Early
Christianity* (Oxford: Clarendon, 1992) 5.
[20] Hebblethwaite, *Christian Hope*, 60. Hill traces millennial belief until
Nicaea: in Irenaeus, Papias, Justin Martyr, Tertullian, Commodianus,
Methodius, Victorinus, and Lactantius; *Regnum Caelorum*, 4–40.
[21] Daley, 60.

Response

As already stated, how the fathers resisted these departures from orthodoxy to affirm a more New Testament-based eschatology is not really amenable to a simple formula as their writings in this area were neither always consistent nor always logically argued. But they did strive to affirm the biblical fundamentals of the birth, life, death, resurrection, ascension and promised return of Jesus Christ and the sufficiency of the biblical witness against Gnostic, moralistic, and adventist pressures.

In general, four features stand out in patristic eschatology.

1. History is fulfilled in Christ

The fathers stressed the linear aspect of history and were apprecia-tive of all redemptive history, including the Old Testament. They saw the past redemptive activity of the Old Testament and the associated hopes gathered up into and realized in Christ, and in turn becoming the ground of Christian eschatological expectation. Against Gnosticism, they affirmed the *future* realities of parousia, resurrection, judgment and final consummation.[22]

Although it is *Irenaeus* (c. 130–c. 200) who is rightly credited with weaving a coherent theme along these lines, *Justin Martyr* (c. 100–c. 165) states that it is the righteous judgment of a provident and all-knowing God, not the necessity of fate, that provides the final intelligibility of history as both morally and beneficently purposive.[23] Earlier still, in his epistles, Ignatius of Antioch (c. 35–c. 107) remarks that at the birth of Jesus all the dark powers of the 'old abolished kingdom' came to an end, as a logical consequence of 'a beginning which had been prepared by God'.[24]

In his *Demonstration of the Apostolic Preaching*, Irenaeus pre-sents Christ and Christianity as the fulfilment of Old Testament prophecy. Salvation history is structured according to the various covenants of God with man, and can be diagrammed as:

OT redemptive acts & hopes	➤	Jesus Christ	➤	future hope

---

[22] Hebblethwaite, *Christian Hope*, 45.
[23] Daley, 21. See to Justin's *First Apology* 43–44; ANF 1.177–8.
[24] Daley, 12; refer *Epistle to the Ephesians* 19; ANF 1.57.

Writing against Gnostic teachings in *Against Heresies*, Irenaeus proposed an interpretation of Scripture based on a summary of the apostolic preaching, the biblical doctrines of creation, redemption, and resurrection, and a millennial timetable painting the end of human history in traditional and vivid apocalyptic colours.

However, his unique contribution was to give linear eschatology a thorough christological basis with his doctrine of *recapitulation* (*anakephalaiosis*).[25] The fully divine Christ became fully man in order to sum up all humanity in himself. What was lost through the disobedience of the first Adam was restored through the obedience of the second Adam. Christ went through all the stages of human life, resisted all temptation, died, and arose a victor over death and the devil. The benefits of Christ's victory are available through participation in him. Even the literalism in his conception of the millennial kingdom seems to be to 'defend the inclusion of the material side of creation in the unified plan of God's salvation'.[26]

In estimating Irenaeus' contribution we need to understand that his theology was directed against Gnosticism, and is essentially a plea for the validity of ordinary Christian experience in an ordinary world. This he does by stressing unities. Daley helpfully lists these unities:

1. the unity of God as creator and saviour;
2. the personal unity of Christ, as both the eternal Word, the agent of creation, and a full participant in our fleshly human life;
3. the unity of every person, as a single composite of spirit and flesh, who is called as such to salvation through Christ;
4. the unity and continuity of all human history from creation through redemption, by the incarnation of the Word, to the goal of the lasting union of the human race with God.

But, for all his reliance on the Bible in stressing these unities, Irenaeus still conceives of salvation as not so much God's unexpected intervention in history to rescue believers, but rather as the end-stage of a process of organic growth, the outworking of creation's law implanted since the beginning. Irenaeus emphasizes the 'necessity' of events:

> It was necessary that the human person should in the first instance be created; and having been created, should receive growth; and having

---

[25] See the discussion of this in chapter 2, pp. 24–5.
[26] Daley, 31.

received growth, should be strengthened; and having been strengthened, should abound; and having abounded, should recover from [the disease of sin]; and having recovered, should be glorified; and being glorified, should see his Lord. For God is the one who is yet to be seen, and the beholding of God is productive of immortality, but immortality renders one near unto God.[27]

Immortality and incorruptibility in union with God is the goal of the divine plan, and is a gift. But, it is the gift of the beginning. Thus, Irenaeus' conception of gift, his 'necessitarianism', and lack of an appreciation of the interventional nature of God's dealings in history tend to drive grace, and consequently the gracious nature of God as Judge and Father, away from eschatology. For different reasons, in the thirteenth century Thomas Aquinas' great synthesis will also couple grace to nature, so that eschatology will have more to do with divine causality working from inside nature than with the in-breaking of the kingdom of grace from outside of creation.

Irenaeus has raised one further problem in his grand sweep, namely the goal of these cosmic salvific events as participation with God. The fathers took the promise of 1 Corinthians 15:28 that 'God may be all in all' with great seriousness. This final union with God is expressed in the New Testament as communion or fellowship with Christ and the Father (1 Cor. 1:9; 2 Cor. 13:14; Phil. 2:1; 3:10; 1 Jn. 1:3), and as incorporation into or membership of the body of Christ (Rom. 5 and 6; 1 Cor. 11:12–12:14; Eph. 1:3–14). However, Irenaeus merely expresses it as 'partaking of the divine nature' by believers, their 'communion with God', 'receiving God' as life and light and being made anew in God's image, with some possibility of growth and advancement toward closer union with God even after the final judgment.[28] Later writers, taking their lead from Origen's more far-reaching consideration, will first of all include the whole cosmos in this union, even unbelievers, and think of it as a divinization which almost excludes the creature–Creator distinction. In a way, this marks the extension of Irenaeus' interest in the centrality and processes of biblical and world history beyond the logic of Scripture, in keeping with the monism of Neoplatonic thought, and even to contradict his stress on history.

Origen (*c*. 185–*c*. 254) was the most controversial figure in the development of early Christian eschatology. Such was his influence

---

[27] *Against Heresies* 4.38.3; ANF 1.522; cited from Daley, 28–9.
[28] Daley, 31–2.

that after him virtually all writers at some stage in their thinking take pro- or anti-Origenist lines. Standing in the tradition of Alexandrian learning, Origen was attuned to the cosmology and ethical outlook of enlightened Greeks, notably the emerging Neo-platonism, but was no mere cipher for it. His theological approach was subtle, complex, very learned in Christian Scripture and Greek philosophy, and respectful of what he saw as the Christian basics confessed in the church. He 'was both a bearer and an imaginative interpreter of Christian tradition: a man of critical intelligence, unafraid of bold speculation, but also a man of the Church'.[29] As much as, and perhaps even more than Irenaeus, because of his pastoral concern he stressed the processes and goal of history. All of creation, both cosmic and individual, is in a process of growth towards union with God.

The heart of kingdom joy, according to Origen, is the contemplation of God as ultimate truth and beauty. Because of the limits of human intelligence and the incomprehensibility of God, such knowing of God will never be complete. Therefore, we can never speak of our knowledge of God as coming to rest, as 'reaching home'.[30] Further, this beatitude is not just individual but corporate, the fulfilment of the whole church's growth as the Body of Christ. The whole eschatological church will know God as the Son knows him. This is the key to understanding the promise of 1 Corinthians 15:28, that 'God may be all in all'. This knowledge is a mingling and union with God in love. God will ultimately be the totally satisfying object of every mind's activity.[31]

Origen's view of the scope of this salvation was all-embracive. He is insistent that all human souls will ultimately be saved, and will be united to God forever in loving contemplation. Hence, all punishment after death is ultimately medicinal and educational. He goes further though, and outlines a period of instruction for human souls between death and resurrection, a 'school for souls'. The extended treatment of this in *De Principiis* exposes as much of Origen's underlying philosophical assumptions about the nature of reality as it does his eschatological outlook:

> I think, therefore, that all the saints who depart from this life will remain in some place situated on the earth, which holy Scripture calls

---

[29] Daley, 47.
[30] *Homily 17 on Numbers*; cited from Daley, 50.
[31] Daley, 50–1.

paradise, as in some place of instruction, and, so to speak, classroom or school of souls, in which they are to be instructed regarding all the things which they had seen on earth, and are to receive also some information respecting things that are to follow in the future, as even when in this life they had obtained in some degree indications of future events, although 'through a glass darkly,' all of which are revealed more clearly and distinctly to the saints in their proper time and place. If any one indeed be pure in heart, and holy in mind, and more practiced in perception, he will, by making more rapid progress, quickly ascend to a place in the air, and reach the kingdom of heaven, through those mansions, so to speak, in the various places which the Greeks have termed spheres, i.e. globes, but which holy Scripture has called heavens; in each of which he will first see clearly what is done there, and in the second place, will discover the reason why things are so done: and thus he will in order pass through all gradations, following Him who hath passed into the heavens, Jesus the Son of God, who said, 'I will that where I am, these may be also.'[32]

The connectedness of all reality as it goes out and then returns to divinity, which is fundamental to Neoplatonic philosophy, is evident here, and will continue to exert an important influence on Augustine of Hippo and on into the medieval period. We will have to return to this point.

Origen's arguments about the remedial nature of punishment may be driven by his fundamental conviction about universal salvation, but they are also exegetically based. He is careful to point out that Scripture designates 'eternal fire' expressly for 'the devil and his angels', as if implying that it is not meant for human souls. [33]

'Joshua burnt Ai and made it a land which was uninhabitable for eternity' . . . Not quite like that uninhabitable place of the earth which is in eternity the uninhabitable place which will then be for the demons, when the devil and his angels will be delivered into the eternal fire, when our Lord Jesus Christ is seated as the king and judge and says to those who have conquered, the earlier and the later: 'Come, blessed of my father, receive the kingdom which has been prepared for you by my father.' But to the others he says: 'Depart into the eternal fire which God prepared for the devil and all his angels', until he acts on each soul

---

[32] Origen, *De Principiis*, 2.11.6–7; ANF 4.299–300.
[33] Origen, *Homilies sur Josue* 14.2, 8.5 Sources Chretiénnes. (Paris: Cerf, 1960) 71.328–9, 230–1.

(they which he himself knows) with the means of deliverance and 'all Israel is saved.'[34]

And *aiōnios* (eternal), as Origen uses it, seems to refer to long but limited periods of time or *aiōnes* (ages), rather than to eternity in the later Augustinian sense of timeless existence.[35] For Origen, universal salvation is an indispensable part of the end promised in 1 Corinthians 15:24–8. Christ will destroy all his enemies, even death, and hand over all things in subjection to his Father, who will be 'all in all'.

Sometimes Origen referred to the final state using the term *apokatastasis*, 'restoration' (see Mt. 17:11, Acts 3:21). Although in most second-century Christian works the word seems simply to have meant 'attainment' of a goal, Origen uses it to denote a retrospective as well as a prospective dimension; to go beyond mere human fulfilment to mean the re-establishment of an original harmony and unity in creation.[36] The concern for order and return to unity, and for it to be determined both theocentrically and christocentrically, are worth noting in the following extract:

Seeing then that such is the end, when all enemies will be subdued to Christ, when death – the last enemy – shall be destroyed, and when the kingdom shall be delivered up by Christ (to whom all things are subject) to God the Father; let us, I say, from such an end as this, contemplate the beginning of things. For the end is always like the beginning: and, therefore, as there is one end to all things, so ought we to understand that there was one beginning; and as there is one end to many things, so there spring from one beginning many differences and varieties, which again, through the goodness of God, and by subjection to Christ, and through the unity of the Holy Spirit, are recalled to one end, which is like unto the beginning: all those, viz., who, bending the knee at the name of Jesus, make known by so doing their subjection to Him: and these are they who are in heaven, on earth, and under the earth: by which three classes the whole universe of things is pointed out, those, viz., who from that one beginning were arranged, each according to the diversity of his conduct, among the different orders, in accordance with their desert; for there was no goodness in them by essential being, as in God and His Christ, and in the Holy Spirit. For in the Trinity

---

[34] *Homilies sur Josue* 8.5; SC 71.230.
[35] Daley, 57.
[36] Daley, 58.

alone, which is the author of all things, does goodness exist in virtue of essential being; while others possess it as an accidental and perishable quality, and only then enjoy blessedness, when they participate in holiness and wisdom, and in divinity itself . . . But those who have been removed from their primal state of blessedness [by sin] and have not been removed irrecoverably, but have been placed under the rule of those holy and blessed orders which we have described [angels, principalities, powers, thrones, etc]; and by availing themselves of the aid of these, and being remoulded by salutary principles and discipline, they may recover themselves, and be restored to their condition of happiness. From all which I am of the opinion, so far as I can see, that this order of the human race has been appointed in order that in the future world, or in ages to come, when there shall be the new heavens and new earth, spoken of by Isaiah, it may be restored to that unity promised by the Lord Jesus in His prayer to God the Father on behalf of His disciples: 'I do not pray for these alone, but for all who shall believe on Me through their word: that they all may be one, as Thou, Father, art in Me, and I in Thee, that they also may be one in Us.'[37]

In several places Origen made the suggestion which so scandalized many ancient authors, that even satan and the other evil spirits could be saved.[38] In the controversial passage in which he comments on the betrayal of Jesus at the hand of Judas Iscariot, the agent of the devil, Origen nine times uses the language of John to qualify Jesus as the One to whom 'the Father had given all things into his hands' (Jn. 13:3). He exegetes this encomium in terms of Paul's description of the eschatological goal of Jesus' mission in 1 Corinthians 15:20–28. All the principalities and powers are given to Christ. Further, Christ is the one in whom all will be made alive (*pantes zōopoiēsontai*), emphasizes Origen. And he will hand all things back to the Father. In the consummation of God's purposes, Jesus conquers death with life. 'For even the enemies of Jesus were some part of everything which Jesus knew, because of foreknowledge, to be given him from the Father'[39] In *De Principiis*, quoted above, he continues his theme and considers the possibilities for the devil and his angels:

---

[37] *De Principiis*, 1.6.2; ANF 4.260–1.
[38] *Com on Jn.* 32.3; A.E. Brooke, *The Commentary of Origen on S. John's Gospel* (Cambridge University Press, 1896) 2.152–5; *De Principiis*, 1.6.2–3; ANF 4.260–1.
[39] *Com on Jn.* 32.3 op. cit; *De Principiis*, 1.6.2 op. cit.

It is to be borne in mind, however, that certain beings who fell away from that one beginning of which we have spoken, have sunk to such a depth of unworthiness and wickedness as to be deemed altogether undeserving of that training and instruction by which the human race, while in the flesh, are trained and instructed with the assistance of the heavenly powers; and continue, on the contrary, in a state of enmity and opposition to those who are receiving this instruction and teaching. And hence it is that the whole of this mortal life is full of struggles and trials, caused by the opposition and enmity of those who fell from a better condition without at all looking back, and who are called the devil and his angels, and the other orders of evil, which the apostle classed among the opposing powers. But whether any of these orders who act under the government of the devil, and obey his wicked commands, will in a future world be converted to righteousness because of their possessing the faculty of freedom of will, or whether persistent and inveterate wickedness may be changed by the power of habit into nature, is a result which you yourself, reader, may approve of, if neither in these present worlds which are seen and temporal, nor in those which are unseen and are eternal, that portion is to differ wholly from the final unity and fitness of things . . . [in the meantime, individual progress is made towards restoration] . . . From which, I think, this will appear to follow as an inference, that every rational nature may, in passing from one order to another, go through each to all, and advance from all to each, while made the subject of various degrees of proficiency and failure according to its own actions and endeavours, put forth in the enjoyment of its power of freedom of will . . . For this renewal of heaven and earth, and this transmutation of the form of the present world, and this changing of the heavens, will undoubtedly be prepared for those who are walking along that way which we have pointed out above, and are tending to that goal of happiness to which, it is said, even enemies themselves are to be subjected, and in which God is said to be 'all in all.'[40]

But in other passages he speaks of the destruction of the devil in eternal fire.[41] In the end, he leaves the question open.[42]

In his eschatological thinking Origen stands out for his consis-tency. His aim was to give an explanation of Scripture and tradition that was true to its sources and intellectually responsible in the

---

[40] *De Principiis*, 1.6.3–4; ANF 4.261–2; see also 3.6.5; ANF 4.346.

[41] *Homilies sur Josue* 8.5; 14.2; SC 71.328–9, 230–1.

[42] Daley, 59.

world of his day. 'Origen was, perhaps, the first fully professional Christian thinker.'[43] In his writings, eschatology was part of the larger picture: the purposive, grace-filled growth towards God that is at the heart of Christian faith and practice.

Although often taking exception to some aspects of Origen's synthesis, other theologians continued to think through the histori-cal approach and extend Christian understanding of it. *Gregory of Nazianzus* (329–390) was a cautious Origenist, affirming our participation as human creatures in the Godhead, the purgative nature of punishment and the hope of universal salvation. What is remarkable is that he brings trinitarian language and understanding of the New Testament to bear on the problematic and paradox that lies at the heart of such affirmations. The divine Logos 'assumes the poverty of my flesh, that I may assume the riches of His Godhead. He that is full empties Himself, for He empties himself of His glory for a short while, that I may have a share in His Fullness.'[44] Gregory's description is magisterial, and was to prove enormously influential:

As these [terrible and mounting ravages of sin] required a greater aid, so also they obtained a greater. And that was the Word of God Himself – Who is before all worlds, and the Invisible, the Incomprehensible, the Bodiless, Beginning of Beginning, the Light of Light, the Source of Life and Immortality, the Image of the Archetypal Beauty, the immovable Seal, the unchangeable Image, the Father's Definition and Word, came to His own Image, and took on Him flesh for the sake of our flesh, and mingled himself with an intelligent soul for my soul's sake, purifying like by like; and in all points except sin was made man. Conceived by the Virgin, who first in body and soul was purified by the Holy Spirit . . . He came forth then as God with that which He had assumed, One Person in two Natures, Flesh and Spirit, of which the latter deified the former. O new commingling; O strange conjunction; the Self-Existent comes into being, the Uncreated is created, That which cannot be contained is contained, by the intervention of an intellectual soul, mediating between the Deity and the corporeity of the flesh. And he Who gives riches becomes poor, for He assumes the poverty of my flesh, that I may assume the richness of His Godhead. He that is full empties Himself, for He empties Himself of His glory for a short time, that I may have a share in His Fulness. What is the riches of His Goodness?

---

[43] Daley, op. cit.
[44] *Oration* 38.13; NPNF (2) 7.348–9; cf. *Oration* 7.23; NPNF (2) 7.237.

What is this mystery that is around me? I had a share in the image; I did not keep it; He partakes of my flesh that He may both save the image and make the flesh immortal. He communicates a second Communion far more marvellous than the first, inasmuch as then He imparted the better Nature, whereas now Himself partakes of the worse. This is more godlike than the former action, this is loftier in the eyes of all men of understanding.[45]

What is man, that Thou art mindful of him? What is this new mystery which concerns me? I am small and great, lowly and exalted, mortal and immortal, earthly and heavenly. I share one condition with the lower world, the other with God; one with the flesh, the other with the spirit. I must be buried with Christ, arise with Christ, be joint heir with Christ, become the son of God, yea, God Himself. See whither our argument has carried us in its progress. I almost own myself indebted to the disaster which has inspired me with such thoughts, and made me more enamoured of my departure hence. This is the purpose of the great mystery for us. This is the purpose for us of God, Who for us was made man and became poor, to raise our flesh, and recover His image, and remodel man, that we might all be made one in Christ, who was perfectly made in all of us all that He Himself is, that we might no longer be male and female, barbarian, Scythian, bond or free (which are badges of the flesh), but might bear in ourselves only the stamp of God, by Whom and for Whom we were made, and have so far received our form and model from Him, that we are recognized by it alone.[46]

The Holy Spirit can be proven equal to the Father and the Son by the fact that he 'makes me God, joins me to the Godhead' in baptism.[47]

God will be all in all in the time of the restoration (*apokatastasis*). I do not mean the Father, as if the Son were to be dissolved in him, like a torch that has been separated for a time from a great fire and is then rejoined to it . . . I mean God as a whole, at the time when we are no longer many, as we now are in our movements and passivities, bearing in ourselves nothing at all of God, or only a little; we shall then be

---

[45] *Oration* 38.13; NPNF (2) 7.348–9.
[46] *Oration* 7.23; NPNF (2) 7.237.
[47] *The Fifth Theological Oration: On the Holy Spirit* 4.28; NPNF (2) 7.318–9, 326–7; cf. *Oration* 7.23; NPNF (2) 7.237; 34.12; NPNF (2) 7.337.

wholly like God, receptive of God as a whole and of God alone. This, after all, is the perfection (*teleiosis*) 'towards which we strive.'[48]

Gregory of Nyssa (*c.* 335–94) further grounds universal salvation in the thought of the New Testament by insisting, much more so than Origen, on the importance of the bodily resurrection for union with God. The resurrection of the body, an event that he often presents as the first stage of the *apokatastasis*, or restoration of humanity to its original and ideal form, is a key to his conception of final human fulfilment. He conceives of this in terms of the restoration of the image of God. What is restored or recaptured in the resurrection is first of all the fullness of the rational creature's potential that is eternally present to the mind of God. This goal pre-exists the human race's historical journey of gradual growth towards God. In biblical terms, this goal is 'being transformed into the image of God'. Secondly, restoration is the realization, in the full number (*plērōma*) of human individuals, of the bodily and spiritual characteristics their ancestor Adam possessed before his fall.[49] As convincing as this may or may not be as an exposition of the image of God, it did firmly give a theological rationale for bodily resurrection as an integral part of restoration to union with God.

In the western church, although not as interested in the processes of biblical and world history as Irenaeus and Origen, *Hilary of Poitiers* (*c.* 315–67) is credited with the first use in Latin writings of the emerging Greek soteriology and eschatology of 'divinization' to describe the goal of the last things.[50] Two things in his description of this goal bear remark. First, the insistence that as in knowledge and prayer we can only approach the Father through the Son, so also we approach him in the eschatological order. Secondly, and concomitantly, the humanity of Jesus Christ, and therefore our humanity, needs be heavily qualified in this divinization. In the eschatological order we only become 'subject'

---

[48] *Oration* 30.6; cited from Daley, 84–5. There is another recent English translation by L. Wickham and F. Williams in F.W. Norris, *Faith Gives Fullness to Reasoning: The Five Theological Orations of Gregory of Nazianzen* (Leiden: E.J. Brill, 1991) p. 266; Greek text in A.J. Mason, *The Five Theological Orations of Gregory of Nazianzus*; (Cambridge University Press, 1899) pp. 117–18.

[49] Daley, 86–7.

[50] Daley, 96.

to the Father, experience his rule of us, by becoming 'subjected to the glory of the rule of [Christ's] body',[51] a subjection that appears to be realized or brought to fulfilment by our undergoing the same transformation in our bodies that the risen Christ has undergone in his:

> In His body, the same body though now made glorious, He reigns until the authorities are abolished, death conquered, and His enemies subdued . . . Then, when they are subjected, He, that is the Lord, shall be subjected to Him that subjecteth all things to Himself, that God may be all in all [1 Cor. 15:24–8], the nature of the Father's divinity imposing itself upon the nature of our body which was assumed. It is thus that God shall be all in all: according to the Dispensation He becomes by His Godhead and His manhood the Mediator between men and God, and so by the Dispensation He acquires the nature of flesh, and by the subjection shall obtain the nature of God in all things, so as to be God not in part, but wholly and entirely. The end of the subjection is then simply that God may be all in all, that no trace of the nature of His earthly body may remain in Him. Although before this time the two were combined within Him, He must now become God only; not, however, by casting off the body, but by translating it through subjection; not by losing it through dissolution, but by transforming it in glory: adding humanity to His divinity, not divesting Himself of divinity by His humanity. And He is subjected, not that He may cease to be, but that God may be all in all, having, in the mystery of the subjection, to continue to be that which He no longer is,[52] not having by dissolution to be robbed of Himself, that is, to be deprived of his being.[53]

This transformation of Christ, to become 'again entirely God',[54] will result in the transformation of 'us, the assumed humanity', into 'the perfect image of God'.[55]

Ambrose of Milan (*c.* 334–97), with Augustine of Hippo and Jerome one of the three most influential leaders in the Latin church in the late fourth century, continued to develop this line of thinking. He shared with Irenaeus and Origen the notion of a

---

[51] *On the Trinity* 11.36; NPNF (2) 9.213.
[52] The translator's footnote in the NPNF edition is apposite: 'The humanity is eternal, although He is no longer man'; NPNF (2) 9.215.
[53] *On the Trinity* 11.40; NPNF (2) 9.214–15.
[54] *On the Trinity* 11.43; NPNF (2) 9.215.
[55] *On the Trinity* 11.49; NPNF (2) 9.217.

ceaselessly growing eschatological fulfilment, but so carried on the process of spiritualization of the resurrection body that his conception of individual restoration 'is more centred on the fate of the soul after death than on resurrection and judgment in an apocalyptic, universal context'.[56]

What has happened here? 2 Peter 1:4 describes salvation, and in context, the hope and promise of salvation, as becoming 'sharers in the divine nature' (*theias koinōnoi physeōs*). This 'divinization', which describes our union with God conceived of eschatologically as God being 'all in all', even when only applied to believers, has so been conceived that our bodily resurrection, and indeed the real humanity of Jesus Christ after his ascension, has had to be spiritualized. This development in understanding divinization has in the end acted as a denial of creation, and therefore, a contradiction of one of the theological gains the christologically determined historical approach to eschatology has given the church. The reasons for it are ready at hand. Ambrose 'made both Neoplatonic philosophy and Origenist exegesis respectable in western Christian thought'.[57] The determinative effect of Neoplatonism on Christian eschatological thought will emerge clearly when we examine Augustine and his medieval successors.

2. The future is already at work in the church

A second theme which emerges in the course of countering Gnosticism and adventism is the notion that the eternal kingdom won by Christ, the age of fulfilment, although firmly tied to the future, is just as emphatically present here and now, inaugurated through the redemptive work of Christ. Here, countering adventism, alleged special revelations are disallowed, and the Lucan concept of a salvation history including an age of the church between Christ's resurrection and the parousia is developed.[58]

Origen, as part of his pastoral concern, emphasized the continuity between the present Christian life and its eschatological *telos* or goal. Eschatological statements must have a present as well as a future relevance, a relevance which is brought out by Origen's pushing the text of Scripture for its 'deeper' meaning by moving from historical to spiritual exegesis, often by allegory.

---

[56] Daley, 100.

[57] Daley, 97.

[58] Hebblethwaite, *Christian Hope*, 45.

The presence here and now of the age of fulfilment, and the special place of the church in eschatological understanding is seen in the patristic understanding of the sacraments of baptism and the Eucharist. These sacraments represent what has already happened and at the same time point forward to what is to come. The church is bound by the sacraments to Christ who is himself the kingdom. For Origen, the resurrection is not just a promise for the future, but is already anticipated 'in part' in the life of the baptized Christian.[59] Origen's concern for christologically defined progress, and the underlying assumption of the connectedness of all reality, is evident in the following citation where he links baptism and moral Christian living as the effective steps in realizing a resurrection already enjoyed:

> (181) Now just as he is 'light of men' and 'true light' and 'light of the world' because he enlightens and illuminates the intellects of men or, in general, of spiritual beings, so he is called 'the resurrection' from the fact that he effects the putting away of all that is dead and implants the life which is properly called life, since those who have genuinely received him are risen from the dead.
>
> (182) Now he effects this not only for those who can say at the present, 'We have been buried together with Christ by baptism' and we have risen with him, but much more when someone has completely put away all that is dead, even that related to the Son himself, and walks in newness of life; that is, when we have been aided in so remarkable a manner, 'we always carry about here the dying of Jesus in our body that the life of Jesus may be made manifest in our bodies.'[60]

This experience of the power of the resurrection in grace is the 'first resurrection' mentioned in Revelation 20, the 'baptism in water and the Holy Spirit' that will deliver the faithful from a 'baptism of fire' at the 'second' resurrection.[61] In the third and fourth centuries, *Cyprian* and *Cyril of Jerusalem* state that in the Eucharist the eschatological bread of heaven, the spiritual food of

---

[59] *Com Jn.* I.27 [25] 181–2, in R.E. Heine, *Origen: Commentary on the Gospel According to Saint John, books 1–10* (Washington: Catholic University of America, 1989) p. 70; *Com Rom.*, Greek text, in A. Ramsbotham, 'Documents: The Commentary of Origen on the Epistle to the Romans', *Journal of Theological Studies* 13 (1912) 363.
[60] *Com Jn.* I.27 [25] 181–2; R.E. Heine op. cit.
[61] *Homily in Jeremiah* 1.3; cited from Daley, 55.

Christ, is made available within the present order.[62] In the very different context of the late fourth century, the African Donatist *Tyconius* also links his very apocalyptic eschatological and eccle-siological outlook to the sacraments. The first resurrection of Revelation 20:3–6, which inaugurates the church's thousand years of rule with the triumphant Christ, is the rebirth of baptism, which brings release from the death of sin through a rigorous penance. Consequently, the saints are already enthroned with the trium-phant Christ, judging the world, for Christ has begun to judge the world by judging the church, bringing penance to its members through their mutual ministry.[63] Thus, over a broad spectrum of eschatological thought, there is a constant affirmation that in the sacraments the Christian has presented to him the entire mystery of salvation.

Besides the more generalized use of sacramental practices and theology to express a belief in the present working of future realities in the church there were attempts, in the more settled political conditions of the fourth century, to directly marry the contempo-rary church to a very realized eschatology. Tyconius, a Donatist experiencing persecution by an orthodoxy he considered spiritually lax because of its association with political power, is one example of this. In the very oppression his Donatist friends suffer, Tyconius not only sees the Antichrist at work but also, in their perseverance under suffering, the beginnings of the unmasking and defeat of this minion of hell.[64]

Eusebius of Caesarea (*d.* 339) goes further and, in an optimistic direction, realizes eschatology in the events of the contemporary church. Termed, 'the first political theologian in the Christian Church', Eusebius found in Constantine's rule a foretaste of the eternal kingdom. Contemptuous of millennialism and avoiding the book of Revelation, Eusebius asserts that God's judgments, both positive and negative, take place within history as well as after it. In his writings, the earthly kingdom takes on more and more the characteristics of the kingdom of promise. Future hope becomes just a backdrop for the theatre of human history, where humans either build Christ's ideal society or hinder its coming.[65]

---

[62] Cyril of Jerusalem, *Catechetical Lectures* 22:1–6,9; 23:4–9,15; NPNF (2) 7.151–2; 7.153–5. Cyprian, *Treatises* 4.18; ANF 5.452.
[63] See Daley, 130.
[64] Daley, 129.
[65] Daley, 78.

3. Decisive rescue is close

Thirdly, and somewhat paradoxically in the light of adventism being a problem, there was a strong strand of realistic eschatology evinced especially by the simple, lower-class majority of Christians, and to a certain extent by some theologians such as *Irenaeus*, *Tertullian* and *Lactantius*. Two differences may be detected between this set of beliefs and a less acceptable 'adventism'. Adventism promises a this-worldly hope for beleaguered believers, and it is intrinsically sectarian. The dividing line between this realistic eschatology and adventism can be thin. The African Donatist *Tyconius* is a case in point. By interpreting the future threats and promises of apocalyptic spiritually, he can apply all of them to the present state of the church. But his aim is not an earthly prosperity, but purification of the church before the end.[66] What distinguishes the realistic strand is its extreme urgency and the focus on individual Christians in dire circumstances as well as on the church.

Daley points out that in the first half of the third century Christian writings tended to take on sectarian and anti-intellectual tendencies. The devil was close, a closeness exacerbated by sporadic persecution, and thus classical paganism, Jewish teachings and the occult speculations of the Gnostics were attacked bitterly.[67] This realistic eschatology was based on notions of millennialism, bodily resurrection, and the reign of the saints with Christ. Charles Hill has shown that there is a correlation between these beliefs and belief in an intermediate state between death and the coming of the earthly kingdom (before ultimate entry into the kingdom of heaven). This is often depicted as residence in Hades, below the earth, where Christ went to visit the spirits in prison.[68] When decisive rescue is depicted as close, the belief in an intermediate state seems to be stressed less.

The social alienation experienced by Christians produced popular expectations of an immediate end which reached a fever pitch in many parts of the western Empire between 200 and 250.[69] P.D. Hanson's conclusions about the nature and function of apocalypticism in the biblical period are applicable. 'Genuine apocalypticism arose within a setting of alienation, and was never a theological programme self-consciously constructed in security and repose. Apocalyptic movements generated their alternative symbolic

---

[66] Daley, 127–31.
[67] Daley, 33.
[68] Hill, *Regnum Caelorum*, 9–40.
[69] Daley, ibid.

universes in periods within which the community of faith could be maintained only by retreat from the system of an oppressive soci-ety.'[70] Hill locates the sources of Christian millennialism before Nicaea in the Jewish apocalypses which were contemporary to the fall of Jerusalem, 2 Baruch and 4 Ezra.[71]

Scriptural promises of a kingdom and priesthood for believers were taken with the utmost seriousness and realism. Under perse-cution the suffering believer would rather hear that the present situation was the real thing, the climax of the war, the last great apocalyptic battle, than be content with an eschatology realized in the church's sacramental life. Christian apocalypses were not un-common in this period. Believers looked for and found quasi-physical tokens of their election, an assurance of their participation in the rule of Christ, when they received the baptismal sign of the cross. In the context of impending apocalypse, great emphasis is laid on martyrdom as the way to heaven, the assured way to participation in the reign of the saints with Christ.

Under conditions of social instability caused by barbarian inva-sions, the apocalyptic genre revived amongst both eastern and west-ern Christian writers in the late fourth and into the fifth century. As the century proceeded, the institutions of Roman civilization seemed, especially to the Latin West, to verge on collapse. Two features stand out in the apocalyptic speculation written on the edge of this abyss. First, in for example the *Apocalypse of Paul* by an anonymous eastern author, unfaithfulness in the church, notably the sinful clergy, will be punished. Secondly, various forms of periodization become com-monplace, often in the form of the six days of creation being interpreted as six ages of a thousand years. On any scheme, a correct reading of 'signs of the times' shows that the clock is very close to midnight of the last day before fiery intervention. But, as *Maximus of Turin* (c. 380–c. 468) puts it by way of succinct summary, the very perils which signal the coming of the end are cause for comfort:

> The reason for this is that the nearer we are to the end of the world, so much the nearer are we to the reign of our Savior. So the prospect of war proves that Christ is ever closer to us.[72]

---

[70] 'Apocalypticism', in *The Interpreters Dictionary of the Bible*, supp. vol. (Nashville: Abingdon, 1976) 33. Cf. his *The Dawn of Apocalyptic* (Philadelphia: Fortress, 1979) 442–4.

[71] Hill, *Regnum Caelorum*, 41–63.

[72] Cited from Daley, 125; see also 120–3, 124–31.

4. *The future is already at work in the individual*

If the future is already at work in the church, and apocalyptic rescue
is on its way from heaven for the believer in peril, it is also at work
in the believer. This is most evident in the eschatological writings
associated with the ascetic movement which took on its institution-
alized form in the Greek- and Latin-speaking churches after the end
of the persecutions. The ascetic movement arose not only as a way
of meeting 'new demands for discipline and sacrifice in a Church
that seemed to be losing its spiritual vigour',[73] but also to express a
deeply held belief about the way of salvation, that the way of the
cross could be interiorized by a radical denial of the external world.

Throughout the patristic period there was a fairly well defined
and understood concept of Christian spirituality, which the majority of Christians came to acknowledge to be the highest, if not
readily obtainable, goal of true religion. The second and third
centuries had believed martyrdom (from the New Testament word,
martureō 'I bear witness') to be the high road to heaven. But with
the conversion of the Roman Emperor Constantine in 312, this
option was no longer open, and so emerged a new path called the
via spiritualis, 'the spiritual way'. At root, this involved a radical
renouncing of the world and embracing a hermit-like existence in
the desert in order to pursue true knowledge of self and God. Thus
asceticism grew. By 451 this had developed into various forms of
monasticism, characterized by an existence separate from the secular world and vows of 'poverty, chastity, and obedience'. Through
self-denial and contemplation the spiritual Christian moved away
from the world and its sinful temptations towards a truer knowledge of God, with an ultimate, if fleeting, hope in this life of union
of the soul with God. This union would surpass knowledge as an
experience of pure love.

Given the interiorization characteristic of asceticism, it is no
surprise that its eschatology had a dramatic and realistic bent which
in its handling of traditional expectations about judgment, reward
and punishment after this life, as well as the drama of death itself,
focused on the present life of the individual. This is evident in the
very influential *Life of Antony* by Athanasius (*c.* 296–373), which
commended the Egyptian monastic ideal. In letters attributed to
Antony, the passage of recently departed Christian souls is depicted
as surrounded by warfare between demons and angels. One's own

---

[73] Daley, 69.

struggles and prayer life are similarly caught up in the constant warfare between God and the satan. The rewards and punishments of heaven and hell are conceived of in terms springing from ascetic aspirations. Hell is lonely, separation from the faces of the other damned, a place of painful silence and shame. Heaven is deliverance from the fear and loneliness inherent in human life.[74] In the west, *Jerome* (331–420) repeatedly takes apocalyptic predictions of the end of history as referring primarily to the individual's confrontation with death, or to his freely chosen anticipation of death in the ascetic life.[75] The notion that God's kingdom had already begun in the life of the monk was to become common to all forms of monasticism.[76]

Might we suspect here that we are starting to come full circle, that is, back to a second-century Gnostic emphasis on inner, spiritual knowledge? The answer is of course patently 'no', for Athanasius, Antony and Jerome are at pains to affirm bodily resurrection, the coming consummation and fulfilment of God's mighty redemptive acts for his creation. However, we are on better ground if we look to the seedbed of Gnostic appeal. Gnostic schemes worked within the assumptions common to Graeco-Roman culture, and made religious sense of them. These included the depreciation of the body and its separation from the soul, the latter being the only truly spiritual part of humanity; the connectedness of all reality as a coming forth and going back to divinity; and as part of this movement, an all-pervasive and underlying metaphysical hierarchy. That is, there is more to how Christian asceticism conceived of the last things, and asceticism itself, than notions of eschatological judgment impinging at the present time on the believer. But the present applicability of the last judgment is also a New Testament concern. The 'more' for the ascetics was mostly bound up with their dominant stress on 'interiority', and demonstrably had deep roots in their culture. However, at the centre of Paul's discourse on Christian living in the light of the last day, that day which is near (Rom. 13:11–15:33), is not interiority but exteriority, faith in the great promise of God expressed in love of neighbour: 'We do not live to ourselves, and we do not die to ourselves' (14:7).

This 'more' had always been a battle to the fathers, as much as it is a battle to us. Their achievement was to have engaged in theological

---

[74] Daley, 70–1.
[75] Daley, 101.
[76] Daley, 72.

construction which affirmed the concerns of New Testament escha-tology in the face of the 'more'. They asserted biblical outlooks against misunderstanding and attack. They evolved structures of thought which gave a coherence to the data of Scripture, and hence facilitated its use in pastoral and apologetic situations. In this, they were creating a distinctively Christian thought-world which allowed productive investigation of theological problems producing formu-lations which their inheritors were able to comfortably stand on. However, distinctively Graeco-Roman notions about cosmology and the metaphysical structure of reality bubble away in the background of patristic writings, and often impinge, both because of and in spite of their best efforts. But, somewhat paradoxically, it will be the medieval period after Chalcedon which will make these notions systematic to Christian thought, with far-reaching consequences. The hinge is Augustine of Hippo, as he looks out on a Neoplatonic world.

Primary Reading

Gnosticism	'The Gospel of Thomas (II, 2)'; James M. Robinson (ed.), *The Nag Hammadi Library in English* (San Francisco: Harper and Row, [3]1988) pp. 124–38.
Irenaeus	*Against Heresies*; The Ante-Nicene Fathers vol. 1 (Grand Rapids: Eerdmans, 1987):
	'Adam and Christ', bk. 3 chpt. 23, pp. 455–8
	'Christ in both covenants', bk. 4 chpt. 5, pp. 466–7
	'Abraham looked forward to Christ', bk. 4 chpt. 7, pp. 469–70
	'Christ came for all ages', bk. 4 chpt. 22, pp. 493–4
	'Christ predicted by the Old Testament Prophets', bk. 4 chpt. 34, pp. 511–13
	'Christ is Head of all things', bk. 5 chpt.s 20–2, pp. 547–51
	'End of world, fall of Roman empire, Antichrist, res-urrection, earthly kingdom of God', bk. 5 chpts. 26–36, pp. 554–67.
Origen	'On the End or Consummation of the World', *De Principiis* chpt. 6; The Ante-Nicene Fathers vol. 4 (Grand Rapids: Eerdmans, 1979) pp. 260–2.
Cyprian	*Address to Demetrianus*; The Ante-Nicene Fathers vol. 5 (Grand Rapids: Eerdmans, 1979) pp. 457–65

Athanasius   *Life of Antony* 20, 63–6; The Nicene and Post- Nicene Fathers, second series, vol. 4 (Grand Rapids: Eerdmans, 1978) pp. 201, 213–14.

Chrysostom   *Homilies on the Gospel of Matthew* 13; The Nicene and Post-Nicene Fathers, first series, vol. 10 (Grand Rapids: Eerdmans, 1978) pp. 80–6.

OVER COFFEE

- 'Hope, for the Christian disciple, is the indispensable link between faith and love: the affirmation of real possibilities for the world and oneself, the awareness of a promise for the future, which gives to the person of faith the freedom to give himself or herself away, to God and to his or her neighbour, with liberated imagination and with a generosity unhampered by the anxious need to secure the future on his or her own.' (Brian E. Daley, *Hope of the Early Church*, 217)
- How true today is Jesus' statement that 'the kingdom of heaven is like treasure hidden in a field'?

4

Time and Eternity: Augustine

Augustine (354–430), bishop of Hippo, stands as the heir of the patristic period. In the originality and profundity of his thought he is also the founding father of all the Latin theology which was to follow in the medieval period and beyond. His major contribution to theology lies in his formulation of the doctrine of grace, and hence of sin, for, before Augustine, 'free will' was an assumption in nearly all the writings of the major fathers. Three of his other contributions also determine the parameters of western theology to this day: his approach to and understanding of the nature and work of the Trinity, his development of sacramental theology, and the creation of a new human consciousness in which the objective character of the external world disappears before the new objectivity found in a deeply subjective experience of God or Truth within.[1] Moreover, Augustine's writings and personal journey are characterized by a concerted attempt to recover, and rediscover, unique teachings of Holy Scripture; some, like sin and grace, not clearly understood in the church, and all of them seemingly at risk of loss by an onslaught of ignorance both within and without the body of the faithful. This recovery of biblical doctrine was in the midst of an intellectually and culturally vigorous Neoplatonism which Augustine both opposed and used to structure his theology.

Eschatology

Augustine is also 'without a doubt the theologian who has most influenced the development of Latin eschatology'.[2] As to details,

[1] For a comprehensive and incisive introduction to Augustine see, O.J.-B. Du Roy, 'Augustine, St', *New Catholic Encyclopedia* (Washington: Catholic University of America, 1967) 1.1041–58.
[2] Brian E. Daley, *The Hope of the Early Church* (Cambridge University Press, 1991) 131.

Augustine's eschatology is traditional, drawing on the resources of the eastern church since Origen and of the western church since Tertullian and Hippolytus; what is new, and foundational for eschatology after him, is its systematic cohesion and integration into his broader theological outlook.[3] Augustine took, for example, prayers for the dead and made a theological sense of them in which God was left to be God, and humanity in the image of God left to be humankind on a journey to this God, by grace. The key to understanding all of Augustine's theology, and in particular, his eschatological hope, is 'the sharp, metaphysically grounded distinction he draws between time and eternity'.[4] We can diagram Augustine's understanding of eschatology as follows:

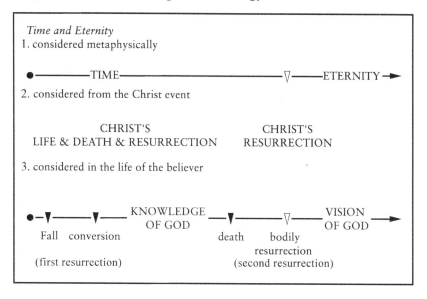

Time and Eternity
1. considered metaphysically

●————TIME————————————▽———ETERNITY➤

2. considered from the Christ event

CHRIST'S   CHRIST'S
LIFE & DEATH & RESURRECTION   RESURRECTION

3. considered in the life of the believer

●–▼————▼— KNOWLEDGE —▼————▽— VISION ➤
                OF GOD   OF GOD
Fall conversion   death   bodily
                                  resurrection
(first resurrection)   (second resurrection)

Augustine argues that the relationship between time and eternity can be seen from three different perspectives. He first views time in relation to God and eternity (1 above). Time is a created entity; created at the the creation of the world, it will finish on the last day. Further, time is radically different from eternity. Time is the 'place' in which we dwell, the place of change and corruption. Eternity is where God dwells, the place of changelessness and incorruption. The last day will usher us into God's eternity. Secondly, he views the relationship between time and eternity from the viewpoint of the One who brings in the end time, Jesus Christ (2 above). As the divine Son of God and the human Son of

---

[3] Ibid.
[4] Ibid.

Man, Jesus Christ stands as the mediator between time and eternity. It is the events of his birth, life, death and resurrection which bring about God's eternal purposes in the world, and lead us from this place of corruption to that place of incorruption, that is, from time to eternity. The really great eschatological event in Jesus' life, the event which ushered his human nature into eternity, was Jesus' own resurrection from the dead. Augustine's third perspective on time and eternity is therefore unsurprising (3 above). He views it from the viewpoint of the life of the believer. The 'fall' is Adam's disobedience in the Garden of Eden, resulting in the sinful nature we inherit as descendants of Adam. Because of Jesus Christ, 'resurrection' is the key to understanding the Christian life. The point at which we start to leave behind our time-bound corruption is when we are converted, which Augustine calls the 'first resurrection', the resurrection of our souls which before this point were dead in trespasses and sins. The 'second resurrection' a Christian undergoes is his or her bodily resurrection on the last day. This then places both soul and body in God's eternity, where we enjoy the eternal vision of God, which is the culmination of God's eschatological purposes and actions in the world in Christ. Note that for Augustine physical death lies on this side of eternity. The following text will expand on the reasons for this, and its implications.

Time is the place of human existence now, the place of history where we live as changeable spirits embodied in a finite, material universe. Eternity is the final existence we long for, released from the limits of space and time and united in unchanging knowledge and love of God, who is both the source of our creation and our goal. Eternity 'is the utterly simple, unchanging present of God's being'.[5] Eternity is God's way of existing; time is ours, on this side of the total transformation which comes with the resurrection from the dead. In his Confessions (397–401)[6] Augustine prays doxologically:

> In the eminence of thy ever-present eternity, thou precedest all times past, and extendest beyond all future times, for they are still to come – and when they have come, they will be past. But 'Thou art always the Selfsame and thy years shall have no end' [Ps. 102:27]. Thy years neither go nor come; but ours both go and come in order that all

---

[5] Daley, 132.
[6] In dating the writings I am following Du Roy, 'Augustine', 1049–51.

separate moments may come to pass. All thy years stand together as one, since they are abiding. Nor do thy years past exclude the years to come because thy years do not pass away. All these years of ours shall be with thee, when all of them shall have ceased to be. Thy years are but a day, and thy day is not recurrent, but always today. Thy 'today' yields not to tomorrow and does not follow yesterday. Thy 'today' is eternity.[7]

If the unchanging and transcendent nature of God, and the change-able and dependent nature of humanity mark the difference be-tween time and eternity, how is it possible for us, and the creation of which we are part, to cross this boundary? Only through the incarnation, life, death and resurrection of Christ.

When do we cross this boundary? For Augustine, the ultimate eschatological event, the final crossing of the dividing line between time and eternity, is the general or second resurrection of our bodies. But before this we experience the first resurrection of our souls, when forgiveness of sins issues in perseverance in love, an entrance on earth into the kingdom of Heaven. Behind both of these resurrections stands the action of God through the person and work of the Son. In a fine passage dating from 419–24, Augustine highlights the resurrection of our bodies as the proper work of the incarnate Son by contrasting it with the resurrection of our souls which is properly the work of the whole divine substance, Father, Son and Holy Spirit:[8]

'For as the Father raiseth the dead, and quickeneth them, so also the Son quickeneth whom He will;' but this according to the Spirit. The Father quickeneth, the Son quickeneth; the Father whom He will, the Son whom He will; but the Father quickeneth the same as the Son, because all things were made by him. 'For as the Father raiseth up the dead, and quickeneth them, so also the Son quickeneth whom He will.' This is said of the resurrection of souls; but what of the resurrection of bodies? He [Jesus] returns, and says: 'For the Father judgeth not any

---

[7] *Confessions*, book 11, chapter 13; in A.C. Outler (ed.), *Augustine: Confessions and Enchiridion*, Library of Christian Classics (Philadelphia: Westminster, 1955) 253–4. See also *Confessions* 11.10–28. Translations taken from any of the three volumes (6, 7, 8) devoted to Augustine's writings in the Library of Christian Classics series will be simply designated by LCC, and the page number.

[8] See Daley, 137.

man, but all judgment hath He given to the Son.' The resurrection of
souls is effected by the eternal and unchangeable substance of the Father
and Son. But the resurrection of bodies is effected by the dispensation
of the Son's humanity . . .[9]

Again commenting on John 5 in *The City of God* (413–427),
together with *On the Trinity* (399–422) regarded as his most
mature work, Augustine continues to tie the believer's expectations
to the work of the incarnate One, the Son of Man:

> For all the dead there died the one only person who lived, that is, who
> had no sin whatever, in order that they who live by the remission of
> their sins should live, not to themselves, but to Him who died for all,
> for our sins, and rose again for our justification, that we, believing in
> Him who justifies the ungodly, and being justified from ungodliness or
> quickened from death may be able to attain to the first resurrection
> which now is . . . And of this judgment He went on to say, 'And hath
> given Him authority to execute judgment also, because He is the Son
> of man.' Here He shows that He will come to judge in that flesh in
> which He had come to be judged . . . For 'the hour is coming and now
> is, when the dead shall hear the voice of the Son of God; and they that
> hear shall live,' i.e. shall not come into damnation, which is called the
> second death; into which death, after the second or bodily resurrection,
> they shall be hurled who do not rise in the first or spiritual resurrection
> . . . So are there also two resurrections – the one the first and spiritual
> resurrection, which has place in this life, and preserves us from coming
> into the second death; the other the second, which does not occur now,
> but in the end of the world, and which is of the body, not of the soul,
> and which by the last judgment shall dismiss some into the second
> death, others into that life which has no death.[10]

Augustine portrays the nature of Christian existence on this side
of physical death in thoroughly eschatological terms. Time now,
the time of the church between Christ's ascension and return, is
the time of the millennium of Revelation 20:1–6 ff. In his early
writings Augustine conceived of the millennial kingdom in terms
of the Sabbath rest to come, but soon abandoned this exegesis in

---

[9] *Homilies on the Gospel of John* 23.13; NPNF (1) 7.156.
[10] *City of God* 20.6; in Marcus Dods (trans.), *The City of God by St Augustine*, 2 vols. (New York: Hafner Publishing Company, 1948) 716–18.

favour of a realized, ecclesiological interpretation.[11] In keeping with the Alexandrian tradition which he embraced, Augustine's exegesis is spiritual, avoiding a literal duration of 1000 years and notions of earthly delights beloved by other writers. In *The City of God* 20.7–9 he explains this ecclesiological interpretation. The kingdom is explicitly identified with the earthly church, and the thousand years are seen as symbolic of all the years of the Christian era.

> But while the devil is bound, the saints reign with Christ during the same thousand years, understood in the same way, that is, of the time of His first coming. For, leaving out of account that kingdom concern-ing which He shall say in the end, 'Come, ye blessed of my Father, take possession of the kingdom prepared for you', the Church could not now be called His kingdom or the kingdom of heaven unless His saints were even now reigning with Him, though in another and far different way; for to his saints He says, 'Lo, I am with you always, even to the end of the world' . . . We must understand in one sense the kingdom of heaven in which exist together both he who breaks what He teaches and he who does it [Mt. 5:19], the one being the least, the other great, and in another sense the kingdom of heaven into which only he who does what He teaches shall enter. Consequently, where both classes exist, it is the Church as it now is, but where only the one shall exist, it is the Church as it is destined to be when no wicked person shall be in her. Therefore the Church even now is the kingdom of Christ, and the kingdom of Heaven.[12]

The thrones, and their endowment of authority to judge (Rev. 20:4), are those of the rulers by whom the church is now governed. Their activity is a veritable binding in heaven by dint of having bound on earth (Mt. 18:18). But, as expected from his description of this manifestation of the kingdom of heaven on earth, the millennium is not a time of peace, but of daily struggle by the church militant and its faithful members. In the details of Augustine's exegesis of that other 'binding and loosing' of the devil (Rev. 20:2,7) we do not see the triumphalism of some segments of the institutional church of, say, the Middle Ages, which appropriated his identification of the age of the church with the millennium and accepted the con-ferred thrones with too much enthusiasm. Instead we see a pastoral

---

[11] Daley, 133.
[12] *City of God* 20.9; Dods, 364–5.

and theological concern that the gates of hell will not prevail against Christ's flock.[13]

> It is then of this kingdom militant, in which conflict with the enemy is still maintained, and war carried on with warring lusts, or government laid upon them as they yield, until we come to that most peaceful kingdom in which we shall reign without an enemy, and it is of this first resurrection in the present life, that the Apocalypse speaks . . .[14] But the binding of the devil [Rev. 20:2] is his being prevented from the exercise of his whole power to seduce men, either by violently forcing or fraudulently deceiving them into taking part with him. If he were during so long a period permitted to assail the weakness of men, very many persons, such as God would not wish to expose to such tempta-tion, would have their faith overthrown, or would be prevented from believing; and that this might not happen, he is bound.
>
> But when the short time comes he shall be loosed. For he shall rage with the whole force of himself and his angels for three years and six months; and those with whom he wages war shall have power to withstand all his violence and stratagems. And if he were never loosed, his malicious power would be less patent, and less proof would be given of the steadfast fortitude of the holy city: it would, in short, be less manifest what good use the Almighty makes of his great evil.[15]

Augustine is concerned to point out that even in those terrible days before the end, children will continue be born to Christian parents, and others will be able to struggle to the font of baptismal grace:

> On the contrary, we are rather to believe that in these days there shall be no lack either of those who fall away from, or those who attach themselves to the Church; but there shall be such resoluteness, both in parents to seek baptism for their little ones, and in those who shall then first believe, that they shall conquer that strong one, even though unbound . . .[16]

Besides battling temptation, with both success and failure, what might a Christian hope for? Unequivocally, the resurrection of the

---

[13] Daley, 134, however, understands Augustine's ecclesiological emphasis more in terms of a subordination to the sharp disjunction he maintains between time and eternity.

[14] *City of God* 20.9; Dods, 365.

[15] *City of God* 20.8; Dods, 360–1.

[16] Ibid.

dead, 'the one genuinely eschatological event'.[17] The hope that marks off the followers of Christ from the wise among the pagans, Plato, Plotinus and Porphyry whom in many respects Augustine greatly admired, is the resurrection from the dead.

> Our hope is the resurrection of the dead, our faith is the resurrection of the dead. It is also our love, which the preaching of 'things not yet seen' [Heb. 11:1] inflames and arouses by longing . . . If faith in the resurrection of the dead is taken away, all Christian doctrine perishes . . . If the dead do not rise, we have no hope of a future life; but if the dead do rise, there *will* be a future life.[18]

'What happiness did he promise you?' If the happiness of this age, the age of endless change and disappointment, then we have every ground for grumbling against Christ. 'What but in the resurrection from the dead?'[19]

With the resurrection definitively marking the boundary between time and eternity, and the only proper object of our hope, it is no surprise that the time between death and the last trumpet does not really belong to the eschaton. This side of bodily resurrection, the souls of believers continue to belong to the earthly church and are fitting subjects of its continued ministrations:

> 'And the souls,' says John, 'of those who where slain for the testimony of Jesus and for the word of God,' understanding what he afterwards says, 'reigned with Christ a thousand years,' – that is, the souls of the martyrs not yet restored to their bodies. For the souls of the pious dead are not separated from the Church, which even now is the kingdom of Christ; otherwise there would be no remembrance made of them at the altar of God in the partaking of the body of Christ, nor would it do any good in danger to run to His baptism, that we might not pass from this life without it; nor to reconciliation, if by penitence or a bad conscience any one may be severed from His body. For why are these things practiced, if not because the faithful, even though dead, are His members? Therefore while these thousand years run on, their souls reign with Him, though not as yet in conjunction with their bodies. And therefore in another part of the same book we read, 'Blessed are the dead who die in the Lord from henceforth: and now, saith the Spirit, that they may rest

---

[17] Daley, 141.
[18] *Serm* 361.2; cited from Daley, 139–40.
[19] *Enarrations in Psalms* 36.I.9; cited from Daley, 141–2; NPNF (2) 8.73.

from their labours; for their works do follow them' [Rev. 15:13]. The Church, then, begins its reign with Christ now in the living and the dead.[20]

The fate of believers is thus deferred until the End. However, Augustine is at pains to point out in his later writings that the souls of the dead are immediately judged at the end of their lives, and that they enter the place of reward or punishment without their bodies, although they may receive a sort of likeness, a phantasm of their resurrection bodies. Further, the ability of the dead to profit from prayers for them and good works offered on their behalf depends on the desert they obtained in their lifetime. But such rewards and punishments experienced in the time after death are only foretastes of the final state to come. However, the prayers of the church for the forgiveness of sins, and even a purgative effect of temporal punishment if it turns the heart of the sinner away from himself to God, may release the souls of some from condemnation to salvation before the general resurrection.[21]

> But temporal punishments are suffered by some in this life only, by others after death, by others both now and then; but all of them before that last and strictest judgment. But of those who suffer temporal punishments after death, all are not doomed to everlasting pains which are to follow that judgment; for to some, as we have already said, what is not remitted in this world is remitted in the next, that is, they are not punished with the eternal punishment of the world to come.[22]

We may well see here the theological justification for the later development of the doctrine of purgatory, but, as Daley points out, Augustine never presents this temporal punishment as being carried out in a distinctive 'place', nor, of itself, having a cleansing effect on the sinner. Augustine is contemptuous of the attempts of soft-hearted Christians to see all punishment as purgative and therefore temporary, and devotes a considerable part of chapter 21 (sections 17–27) in *The City of God* to repudiating the idea. He sees all such punishment as retributive in itself, but with the possibility of it occasionally having a purgative side-effect.[23]

---

[20] *City of God* 20.9; Dods, 366.
[21] See Daley, 137–40.
[22] *City of God* 21.13; Dods, 440–1; slightly altered following the translation and suggestion of Daley, 139 and endnote 21.
[23] Daley, 140.

The resurrection of the dead, then, brings the end of time and the beginning of eternity for the creation. The boundaries of heaven and hell are thus fixed. What, for the believer who has persevered, is the nature of this radical transformation? Augustine, in keeping with the philosophical culture of Neoplatonism, maintained throughout his writings that the soul was immortal, and in keeping with Christian tradition, that it was immortal by the creative act of God. In *Concerning the Immortality of the Soul* (387) he argues for its immortality along accepted philosophical lines. Later Augustine takes a more explicitly Christian approach, arguing for immortality on the basis of the soul's being made in the image of its Creator[24] or the natural desire for beatitude that the Creator has implanted in it, a yearning which requires unending existence if it is not to be frustrated.[25] Further, in *The City of God* 13.2 he points out that natural immortality is of itself of limited value since the soul experiences a kind of death if abandoned to hell by its Creator due to sin.[26]

In keeping with this trend towards a distinctively Christian description of eternity, Augustine emphasizes that it is in the resurrection of the body that humans will be in the fullest sense, 'conformed to the image of the Son' of God.[27] Thus he opposes any understanding of Christian hope that would allegorize bodily res-urrection. Against both the Manichees and Platonists, Augustine insists that 'the saints will in the resurrection inhabit those very bodies in which they have here toiled.'[28] As God is the creator of both our souls and bodies, he will be the restorer of both.[29]

There is a progression in Augustine's understanding of the exact nature of the resurrection body. In his earlier writings, the spiritual nature of this body (see 1 Cor. 15:35–50) is stated in such a way that the 'flesh and blood' which Paul says 'will not inherit the kingdom of God' (v. 50) is at the moment of its spiritual transfor-mation no longer flesh and blood, 'but simply a body'.[30] Later, 'flesh

---

[24] *The Magnitude of the Soul* 2.3 (AD 388), in *Writings of Saint Augustine*, The Fathers of the Church, a new translation (New York: CIMA, 1947) vol. 4 pp. 61–2; Daley, 142.

[25] *On The Trinity* NPNF (1) 3:14.8.11.

[26] Daley, 142.

[27] *The Trinity* 14.18.24.

[28] *City of God* 13.19; Dods, 544.

[29] *Serm* 277.3; cited from Daley, 143.

[30] *Faith and the Creed*; LCC, 368.

and blood' are interpreted to mean either an immoderate love of the works of the flesh, or the flesh's present corruptibility. Thus, the 'spiritual body' of 1 Corinthians 15:44 refers first to the incorruptibility of the risen body,[31] and secondly to its perfect subjection to the human spirit.[32] In passages which will later find exact echoes in Thomas Aquinas, Augustine develops the idea that the resurrection overcomes the warfare between 'spirit' and 'flesh', between the inner and outer person, by giving us bodies which no longer suffer corruptibility but are in full, integrated support of the godly desires of our souls.[33]

> But if any one says that the flesh is the cause of all vice and ill conduct, inasmuch as the soul lives wickedly only because it is moved by the flesh, it is certain he has not carefully considered the whole nature of man . . . We are . . . burdened with this corruptible body; but knowing that the cause of this burdensomeness is not the nature and substance of the body, but its corruption, we do not desire to be deprived of the body, but to be clothed with its immortality. For then, also, there will be a body, but it shall no longer be a burden, being no longer corruptible . . . the corruption of the body, which weighs down the soul, is not the cause but the punishment of the first sin; and it was not the corruptible flesh that made the soul sinful, but the sinful soul that made the flesh corruptible.[34]
>
> But, say they, Porphyry tells us that the soul, in order to be blessed, must escape connection with every kind of body . . . For what we say is, that the God who, even according to Plato, does impossible things, will do this. It is not, then, necessary to the blessedness of the soul that it be detached from a body of any kind whatever, but that it receive an incorruptible body. And in what incorruptible body will they more suitably rejoice than in that in which they groaned when it was corruptible? . . . they shall have those bodies to which a return was desired, and shall, indeed, be in such thorough possession of them, that they shall never lose them even for the briefest moment, nor ever lay them down in death.[35]

Answering objections raised by opponents who attacked resurrection by pointing to the absurd implications of the doctrine – what happens

---

[31] *Enchiridion* 23.91; LCC, 392; *City of God* 22.21.
[32] *City of God* 22.21.
[33] Daley, 143–4.
[34] *City of God* 14.3; Dods, 4–5.
[35] *City of God* 22.26; Dods, 531–2.

to the body of a dead man cannibalized by an emaciated neighbour during a famine? – and to assuage pastoral anxiety, Augustine gives considerable space to sketching a concrete picture of the resurrected body. It is a fully healed, mature body of ideal proportions, intact even down to its sexual organs, although they will not be used. It is a body free from any connection with shame or passion. It is nothing less than a complete transformation, the entry into a completely new phase of created existence, bodies which serve and are in themselves without time or corruption, that is, changeless, like God.

> But their way is to feign a scrupulous anxiety in investigating this question, and to cast ridicule on our faith in the resurrection of the body, by asking, Whether abortions shall rise? . . . What, then, are we to say of infants, if not that they will not rise in that diminutive body in which they died, but shall receive by the marvellous and rapid operation of God that body which time by a slower process would have given them? . . . from the words, 'Conformed to the image of the Son of God,' some conclude that women shall not rise women, but that all shall be men . . . For my part, they seem to be wiser who make no doubt that both sexes shall rise. For there shall be no lust, which is now the cause of confusion. For before they sinned, the man and the woman were naked, and were not ashamed. From those bodies, then, vice shall be withdrawn, while nature shall be preserved. And the sex of woman is not a vice, but nature. It shall then indeed be superior to carnal intercourse and child-bearing; nevertheless the female members shall remain adapted not to the old uses, but to a new beauty, which, so far from provoking lust, now extinct, shall excite praise to the wisdom and clemency of God, who both made what was not and delivered from corruption what He made.[36]

The great purpose which these bodies serve, and which is Augustine's apical description of the believer's existence in eternity, is the vision of God. Throughout his works Augustine stresses the direct contemplative vision of God as being at the heart of eternal rest for believers. The more precise nature of this vision emerges in his discussion of whether Christians might see the essence of God with the bodily eyes of their transformed bodies or, as is now occasionally vouchsafed to us in our earthly pilgrimage, see him only in the internal, metaphorical sense of 'seeing with the heart'. In earlier writings, Augustine is scornful of the notion of bodily eyes being involved, but later is more conciliatory to the possibility, while still preferring a kind of spiritual

---

[36] *City of God* 22.12–17 ff.; Dods, 504–17; cf. *Enchiridion* 23.84–93.

vision. In the final book of *The City of God*, while still having philosophical reservations about a corporeal vision of God, he encourages the reader to take a more daring view: [37]

> ... the bodily eyes also shall have their office and their place, and shall be used by the spirit through the spiritual body ... Wherefore it may very well be, and it is thoroughly credible, that we shall in the future world see the material forms of the new heavens and the new earth in such a way that we shall most distinctly recognize God everywhere present and governing all things, material as well as spiritual, and shall see Him ... by means of the bodies we shall wear and which we shall see wherever we turn our eyes ... Either, therefore, the eyes shall possess some quality similar to that of the mind, by which they may be able to discern spiritual things, and among these God – a supposition for which it is difficult or even impossible to find any support in Scripture, – or, which is more easy to comprehend, God will be so known by us, and shall be so much before us, that we shall see Him by the spirit in ourselves, in one another, in Himself, in the new heavens and the new earth, in every created thing which shall then exist. [38]

The pressure of Neoplatonic philosophical culture, plainly evident in the developing mysticism and monasticism of the period, might lead us to expect Augustine to conceive of the beatific vision as a passive, solitary activity. On the contrary, to be in that heaven after the end is to be in the society of angels (*societas angelorum*), a member of the single heavenly community, in the perfect harmony and peace of the 'common life (*societas*) of those who enjoy God and one another in God', [39] and, engaged in the active praise and hymning of God. The activity of praise is the one activity perfectly appropriate to eternal rest. [40]

> How great shall be that happiness, which shall be tainted with no evil, which shall lack no good, and which shall afford leisure for the praises of God, who shall be all in all! ... All the members and organs of the incorruptible body, which now we see to be suited to various necessary uses, shall contribute to the praises of God ... 'That God may be all in all'. He shall be the end of our desires who shall be seen without end, loved without cloy, praised without weariness. This outgoing of affec-tion, this employment, shall certainly be, like eternal life itself, common

---

[37] Daley, 145.
[38] *City of God* 22.29; Dods, 537–540.
[39] *City of God* 19.13; cited from Daley, 147.
[40] Daley, 146–7.

to all ... There we shall rest and see, see and love, love and praise. This is what shall be in the end without end. For what other end do we propose to ourselves than to attain to the kingdom of which there is no end?[41]

Who does not long for that city, where no friend leaves and no enemy enters, where no one tries or disturbs us, no one divides the people of God, no one wearies God's Church in the service of the devil? ... We will have God as our common sight (*spectaculum*), we will have God as our common possession, we will have God as our common peace.[42]

Athens and Rome: Neoplatonism and Law

Religious Neoplatonism

Augustine inhabited a world which was intellectually dominated by Platonism or, more accurately, the religious Neoplatonism of the pagan philosophers Plotinus (*c.* 204–*c.* 270) and his disciple Porphyry (*c.* 232–*c.* 305). Augustine's self-acknowledged dependence on Neoplatonism for understanding the metaphysical structures of the universe is evident right from his first enthusiastic use of their ideas in his earliest Christian writing, *Answer to Skeptics* (386),[43] to a direct acknowledgment later in the *Confessions* (397–401). In *Confessions* 7.10.16 ff. he acknowledges his personal indebtedness to 'certain Platonic books' which, during his conversion experience, led him to search for truth within the soul, the immaterial, spiritual world, instead of in the crass material world of the Manichees who, to that point, had held him in thrall. Even towards the end of his life, in *The City of God* (413–427) where in book 10 he most sharply attacks Porphyry's rejection of Christ's mediatorship for a *via universalis* (universal way) to the heavenlies by the practice of beneficial magic, and in his *Retractions* (426–7) where he regrets that he had overpraised the Platonists,[44] Augustine can still esteem

---

[41] *City of God* 22.30; Dods, 540–45.
[42] *Enarrations in Psalms* 84.10; cited from Daley, 147.
[43] 'I am confident that I shall find among the Platonists what is not in opposition to our Sacred Scriptures' (III.20.43), in Writings of Saint Augustine, volume 1, FOCn, 5.220.
[44] 'I have been rightly displeased, too, with the praise with which I extolled Plato or the Platonists or the Academic philosophers beyond what was proper for such irreligious men, especially those against whose great errors Christian teaching must be defended'; FOCn, 60.10.

the Platonists as 'the noblest of philosophers' because they under-stood that the true happiness of the soul is in its union with God, and that this end cannot be reached without persons cleaving to this unchangeable God with a pure and holy love.[45] Augustine's combi-nation of dependence on Neoplatonism and Aristotle mediated through Neoplatonism, and independence as he strove to assert biblical teachings on the person and work of Christ and the createdness of the world from nothing (*ex nihilo*) by a divine act of pure grace, is well documented. It marks him as an eclectic user of both the speculative philosophy of Athens and the practical phi-losophy of Rome.[46] This close relationship, surprising perhaps to modern thought, is congruous in an age where all philosophy was in the end theology, 'inasmuch as it sought an understanding of that first principle of thought and being which might be referred to variously as the Good, or the One, or *ho theos*'.[47]

What then were the basic metaphysical structures that Augustine accepted from Greek philosophy, either uncritically or in a qualified way? What, if any, effect did they have on his eschatology? Three main interconnected areas of influence from Neoplatonism stand out: cosmology, epistemology, and the doc-trine of God. All these are integrated in what was arguably Augustine's greatest theological achievement, his understanding

---

[45] *City of God* 10.1.

[46] John J. O'Meara, 'The Neoplatonism of Saint Augustine' in Dominic J. O'Meara (ed.), *Neoplatonism and Christian Thought* (Norfolk, Vir-ginia: International Society for Neoplatonic Studies, 1982) 34–41 gives a useful summary of the debate to 1981. See also Robert Russell, 'The Role of Neoplatonism in St Augustine's De Civitate Dei' in H.J. Blumenthal and R.A. Markus (eds.) *Neoplatonism and Early Christian Thought: Essays in Honor of A.H. Armstrong* (London: Variorum Publications, 1981) 160–70; E.G.T. Booth, 'St Augustine's *De Trinitate* and Aristotelian and Neo-Platonist Noetic', in E. Livingstone (ed.) *Studia Patristica* 16/2 (1985) 487–90; G.J.P. O'Daly, '*Sensus interior* in St Augustine, *De Libero Arbitrio* 2.3.25–6.51' in E. Livingstone (ed.) *Studia Patristica* 16/2 (1985) 528–32; Mary T. Clark, 'Augustine's Theology of the Trinity: Its Rele-vance', *Dionysius* 13 (1989) 69–84; Christos Evangeliou, 'Porphyry's Criticism of Christianity and the Problem of Augustine's Platonism', *Dionysius* 13 (1989) 51–70. For useful commonsense on what the issues are see R.D. Crouse, 'St Augustine's *De Trinitate*: Philosophical Method' in E. Livingstone (ed.) *Studia Patristica* 16/2 (1985) 501–10.

[47] Crouse, 503.

of grace expressed in his doctrine of the Christian life. If we can appreciate the operation of Greek, Roman and scriptural components in Augustine's major area of theological reconstruction, we will be better able to see their relative contributions to his eschatology.

1. *Metaphysical cosmology*

The prevailing cosmology in which the stationary earth was over-arched by the heavens was given its most influential theoretical expression by Ptolemy in the second century AD. This physical cosmology was but the expression of a metaphysical view of existence in which earth was transitory and designed to reflect ultimate heavenly reality. Everything that happened on earth corresponded in some way to an eternal pattern in the heavens. Thus the whole purpose of life could be described in terms of *imitatio* (imitation) or conformity to this heavenly reality. Neoplatonism related the overarching heavenly reality of Ptolemaic cosmology to its earthly counterpart by means of a series of emanations from the One or the Good, to the *Nous* or Mind, to the *Psyche* or World-Soul, to matter, and back again by way of a returning or conversion. In Plotinus, the One, Mind and Soul are three Hypostases, or a triad in linear and subordinate descent. The final cause of all is the One, termed Father, to which all things return by their conversion in knowledge and desire back through the *Psyche* and the *Nous*, as shown in the diagram on p. 100.

The earliest importance of this Neoplatonic schema for Augustine was that, in his personal journey back to the catholic faith of his upbringing, it allowed him to understand how in the doctrine of the Trinity, which he took as axiomatic, generation or relationships take place between fundamental spiritual entities.[48] The key to this doctrine of returning to the One is a programme of contemplation, by which the higher part of man, his mind, is able to come to a knowledge of the eternal verities, and even into union with the One itself in 'the home country'.

---

[48] See Clark, 69–75 ff.; O'Meara, *passim*.

NEOPLATONISM (3rd to 6th centuries AD)

- a religious philosophy,
- basic tenet: 'only the intelligible really is'
- fiercely monistic, all multiplicity being less than perfection
- metaphysically hierarchical, with reality being a constant *exitus et reditus*, a coming forth from the One, the First Principle, into increasing complexity and return to the One by way of conversion through desire and knowledge as in the following diagram:

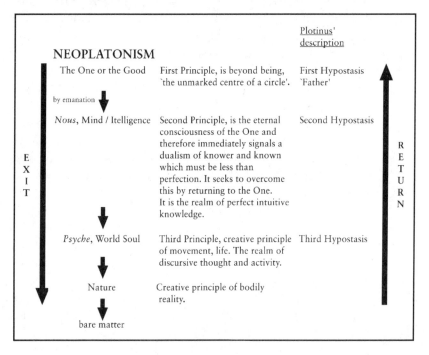

- humanity is microcosm containing matter, nature, soul and mind in itself, longing to return to the One by contemplation and have all dualities overcome.

2. Doctrine of God

Augustine's escape from Manicheaism was facilitated by his acceptance of the Neoplatonic doctrine of an incorporeal creator, the immutability of the One, and also the existence of Providence and mediatory salvation.[49] Although translated into orthodox trinitarianism and into the unique Christian confession that creation was *ex nihilo*, out of nothing by the free act of God, Augustine used Plotinus' doctrine of the *Logos* (Word) to articulate his own

---

[49] O'Meara, 37.

philosophical understanding of creation in Genesis, and Porphyry's idea of *spiritus* in his fundamental and philosophical
understanding of the afterlife.[50] But most especially, Augustine
depends heavily on Plotinus' and Porphyry's doctrine that the
Father, the One, is beyond being and beyond not only all sensory
but also all rational or even intellectual perception. Rejecting the
Neoplatonic notion that the Father is without being, because in
trinitarianism his being is asserted and defined in his relationship
to the Son and the Spirit, Augustine nevertheless appropriated
their notion of the fundamental unknowability of God. 'God',
Augustine says, 'is known better in not being known.'[51] It is in the
area of epistemology then, that we most see Augustine's use of
Neoplatonic conceptions. Further, because he viewed salvation
primarily in terms of 'knowing God', we see Neoplatonic conceptions operating powerfully in Augustine's teachings on the Christian life as it is expressed in the doctrine of justification, that
doctrine, mostly shorn of his epistemology, which so much determined later Latin redemptive theology.

3. Epistemology

As we have already seen, for Augustine the eschatologically determined goal of the Christian life is the beatific vision of God promised
to us in heaven. The following diagram illustrates how Augustine's
understanding of the Christian life fits into his Neoplatonic thought
structures:[52]

AUGUSTINE'S NEOPLATONIC EPISTEMOLOGY	
temporal world	changeless world
temporal truth	eternal truth
knowledge (*scientia*)	wisdom (*sapientia*)
reason (*ratio*)	intellect (*intellectus*)
faith (*fides*)	sight (*visio*)

---

[50] O'Meara, 39; cf. Clark, 76.

[51] *De ordine* II.16.44; cited from O'Meara, 40, which see for a fuller
discussion of Augustine's dependence here.

[52] These structures in Augustine's thoughts can be seen from reference to
the following, *On the Trinity* 2.17.28–29; 4.18.24; 14.2.4 ff.; *Spirit and
the Letter* 15(ix); 49–52; 34.

Platonic thought makes a qualitative distinction between the temporal world of images and the changeless world of the forms. From the temporal world of change and corruption we have knowledge (*scientia*) of sensible and perishable things, by the operation of reason (*ratio*) processing the information which comes to us through the senses. In the sphere of the Christian religion, the Bible calls this knowledge 'faith', in contrast to 'sight' which is reserved for the eternal world to come (2 Cor. 5:7; cf. 1 Cor. 13:12; Heb. 11:1–2). By contrast *sapientia* (wisdom) is the knowledge of eternal and immutable realities, whose primary object is God. Here intellect (*intellectus*) operates to perceive supersensible realities, the eternal truths which are pointed to by and in turn underlie temporal truths. In the area of religion, such knowledge is known as 'sight'. In terms of the analogy between temporal and eternal truth as image and form, this sight is an *intellectus fidei*, a grasping of the real meaning, the object of our faith, to which the articles of the creeds and the record of God's activities in the Scriptures point. Further, following on the mysticism innate to Neoplatonism, Augustine insists that the pursuit of *sapientia* is an interior journey, into the soul, where one is most like God, by a process of illumination. In this journey God is progressively known in three ways. First, *scientia*, the inevitable starting point, is left behind as it is realized that God is the cause of all creatureliness, and thus not one of the creatures. Second, there is an apprehension of the relation between time and eternity. God and self are contrasted in their respective and distinctive immutability: the soul as a contingent self-knowing identity having immortality, and God as the unchanging Creator of this identity and immortality. Finally, God is grasped or known in the moment of self-knowledge when the soul, through Christ, knows itself to be the image of God. This last phase is truly a reaching of the soul's own centre, where it is united with God. There it grasps the trinitarian Principle by an inward vision which is as much a matter of giving God his worth (as Father, Son and Holy Spirit) as of self-integration (as body, mind and soul).[53]

---

[53] See Crouse, 503–9; James Doull, 'What is Augustinian "Sapientia"?', *Dionysius* 12 (1988) 61–7. Ramon Williams, 'Sapientia and the Trinity: Reflections on the *De Trinitate*', in *Collectanea Augustiniana: Melages T.J. Van Bavel*, 2 vols. (Leuven University Press, 1990) 317–22. In a splendid analysis of *de Trinitate* XIV and XV Williams shows how for Augustine *sapientia* is properly a way of describing in trinitarian terms

But the person who engages in this contemplative pursuit of knowledge is very much a sinner. Technique or formal knowledge of metaphysics is not enough. How can a sinner 'know God'?

Doctrine of the Christian Life: Justification

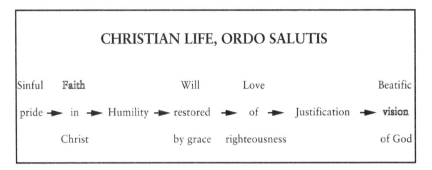

Sinful	Faith		Will	Love			Beatific
pride ➤	in ➤	Humility ➤	restored ➤	of ➤	Justification ➤		vision
	Christ		by grace	righteousness			of God

CHRISTIAN LIFE, ORDO SALUTIS

Augustine's epistemology places the will at the foundation of knowledge. Unless we desire (*cupiditas*) knowledge, or rather the object of our knowledge, we will not gain it. With respect to knowledge of higher things, and above all of God, we would rather desire or love darkness than light. Our root problem is hubris, or pride, which stops us turning to God even if we manage to turn and desire other higher things.

Faith in Christ cures this pride.[54] But note the place of faith. Augustine regards 'faith' as an activity characteristic only of this life, which on the basis of his understanding of 1 Corinthians 13:12 and 2 Corinthians 5:6 f. must give way to 'vision' as the characteristic of the next life. Faith, like reason and knowledge, only operates on earthly realities, and so is the way we apprehend Jesus Christ, the incarnate Son of God in his earthly ministry. Vision, which is direct apprehension of God, operates with respect to the heavenly realities. Because Jesus Christ is essentially

---

[53] *(continued)* what it means for God to be God. *Sapientia* is neither a static or self-centred entity, as in much thought even nowadays, but an active and relational one, for it exists by being love in search of an object. When understood in terms of God, this *sapientia* is another way of describing the Spirit and thus the Spirit's role in that relational entity which is the Trinity. Hence, granted his Neoplatonic epistemology, Augustine's understanding of *sapientia* allows a profoundly Christian integration, even fusion, of theology and anthropology.

[54] Cf. Clark, 80, 83.

revealed in the earthly sphere where faith operates, he *drops out of view* as we pass to the heavenly, direct vision of God. In heaven, in heavenly matters it is the eternal Word, not the incarnate Word revealed in history, who teaches us. Thus, Augustine's christology is truncated:[55]

> But all these things which the Word made flesh did and suffered for us in time and place belong, according to the distinction which we have undertaken to point out, to science [knowledge] and not to wisdom. But because the Word is without time and without place, He is co-eternal with the Father and is wholly present everywhere . . . therefore, the Word made flesh, which is Christ Jesus, possesses the treasures of wisdom and knowledge. If these two so differ between themselves that wisdom has been attributed to divine things and science to human things, I recognize both in Christ, and everyone who believes in Him agrees with me. And when I read: 'The Word was made flesh and dwelt among us', I recognize the true Son of God in the Word, and the true Son of man in the flesh, and both are united together into the one person of God and man by ineffable liberality of grace . . . Christ, therefore, is our science, and the same Christ is also our wisdom. He Himself plants the faith concerning temporal things within us; He Himself manifests the truth concerning eternal things. Through Him we travel to Him; through science we proceed to wisdom; but we do not depart from the one and the same Christ, 'in whom are hidden all the treasures of wisdom and knowledge'.[56]
>
> And this is thy Word, which is also 'the Beginning', because it also speaks to us. Thus, in the gospel, he spoke through the flesh; and this sounded in the outward ears of men so that it might be believed and sought for within, and so that it might be found in the eternal Truth, in which the good and only Master teacheth all his disciples. There, O Lord, I hear thy voice, the voice of one speaking to me, since he who

---

[55] Lamenting Augustine's depreciation of the material character of the exterior aspect and use of the sacrament, R. Prenter asks rhetorically: 'Is the human nature of the incarnate Lord in the same manner a transitory value, which must be left behind when man, by following Christ in his humility, succeeds in attaining the divine Logos as the true food of the rational soul? Is the "imitatio Christi" then any more than a necessary preparation for the contemplation of the heavenly logos?'; 'Metaphysics and Eschatology in St Augustine', *Studia Theologica* 1 (1947) 21.

[56] *The Trinity* 13.19.24; FOCn, 404–6; cf. *The Trinity* 4.18.24; 1.2.4; 14.2.4f.

teacheth us speaketh to us. But he that doth not teach us doth not really speak to us even when he speaketh. Yet who is it that teacheth us unless it be the Truth immutable? For even when we are instructed by means of the mutable creation, we are thereby led to the Truth immutable.[57]

This pursuit of immutable Truth during the course of the interior journey has consequences now, this side of heaven, for if the soul is understood as intellectual activity, it is there, by introspective reflection, that one is most likely to find experiences, structures and analogies which help us understand and theologize about the Trinity. However, we need to carefully note that this is not the rampant natural theology of later periods, for Augustine's order of thinking is deliberately 'faith in search of understanding'. That is, he starts from faith in the biblically grounded statements of the creed about the trinitarian nature of God, and then seeks by introspective analysis to find structures and activities of the soul which will help him better understand and explain the Trinity. But because there is a great deal of this sort of theologizing in Augustine, not just in *On the Trinity*, the 'left-Jesus-behind' way of describing the Christian life gets a lot of emphasis. This implies that one can adequately describe the Christian life without Jesus, the incarnate Christ, remaining at its centre at every stage.

Turning to Augustine's doctrine of justification, it should be noted that he was working within an Aristotelian–Ciceronian view of justice or righteousness, expressed in Roman law and later medieval theology, which affirmed that:[58]

(i)   'righteousness is a virtue which renders to each man according to his due' (*iustitia est virtus reddens unicuique quod suum est*);

(ii) 'without respect to persons' (*sine acceptione personarium*);

and that therefore

---

[57] *Confessions* 11.8.10; LCC, 250.
[58] See, G. Kittel (ed.), *Theological Dictionary of the New Testament* (Grand Rapids: Eerdmans, 1964) 2.193; Alister E. McGrath, 'Divine Justice and Divine Equity in the Controversy between Augustine and Julian of Eclanum', *Downside Review* 345 (1983) 312–319; *Iustitia Dei: A History of the Christian Doctrine of Justification*, 2 vols. (Cambridge University Press, 1986) 1.9–35 passim.

(iii) 'equity distinguishes merit, justice gives reward' (*et equitas merita distinguit, iustitia premia reddit*)

(This understanding is also known as 'distributive righteousness').

The Christian theologian's problem was to show how salvation preserved equity and justice, and yet was a matter of grace. The Pelagian bishop, Julian of Eclanum, abandoned grace and completely embraced the distributive view of righteousness to show why grace was *not* an appropriate way to think of man's salvation. Man had to save himself by an exercise of his free will towards moral improvement, spurred on by the example of Christ, otherwise God would be liable to a charge of injustice. Against this, Augustine insisted that the whole of justification was by God's grace, both prevenient and continuous.

In explaining how grace operated, Augustine drew on his novel, but unhappy, interpretation of *iustificare* in the Latin Bible as meaning *iustum facere*, 'to make righteous', a totally unacceptable interpretation of a verb considered the Latin equivalent of *dikaiō* as used in the Septuagint.[59] For Augustine 'justification' means *being made just*, and it is a *process*. In order to enjoy eternal felicity with the righteous God, man under grace must more and more love and do the righteousness of God as it is reflected in the law. Our loving of and obedience to God's law, which is the expression of his righteousness is thus an integral part of our justification. In this way, we are saved by the works of the law performed under grace; as he argues in *Spirit and Letter*, 'grace may restore the will and the restored will may fulfil the law'.[60] Thus, 'merit' is integrated into justification, even if Augustine insists that in rewarding human merit God only rewards his own gifts.

---

[59] McGrath, *Iustitia Dei*, 1.14.

[60] See *Spirit and the Letter* 15 (ix)–16 (x); 5 (iii); 49. Note the flow of the argument: law does not save, only faith does because it is faith which heals the will, not law; the will then goes on to fulfil the law because hatred and fear of the law have been replaced by love of the righteousness it embodies. God 'by his Holy Spirit make[s] . . . the delight of his precepts greater than the attraction which obstructs the keeping of them. The law of faith which is the love of him written and shed abroad in our hearts, is perfected unto them that hope in him; so the healed soul may work that which is good, not in fear of punishment, but through love of righteousness' (51; LCC, 235–6).

On the basis of Neoplatonic outlook and his own Christian understanding of the importance of love, Augustine stressed that the faith which justifies is 'faith working through love' (cf. Gal. 5:6; 1 Cor. 13:1–3). That is, love is the desire (*cupiditas*) for the good, the Word of God, the law and righteousness of God. Thus it is inaccurate, as Luther tended to do, to summarize Augustine's doctrine as 'we are justified by faith alone'. It is love rather than faith which has the power to convert man from his self-centred pride. Thus Augustine's position can be summarized as 'we are justified by love alone'.[61]

Augustine's doctrine of justification is central to his theology because justification encompasses all of the Christian life – taking up his major work on the nature of grace and knowledge of God – from the first moment of faith, through increase of righteousness before God and man, to the final perfection of righteousness in the heavenly city. It reflects the influences of both the philosophy of Athens and the legal interests of Rome on his theological reconstruction of the data of the Bible. But Augustine's inability to show how the incarnate Christ himself carries us into heaven and remains our Saviour there, and not just at the beginning of our pilgrimage, and his concurrent emphasis on vision within a Neoplatonic framework, opened the way for a thoroughly anti-Christian understanding of our identification with God in Christ. In my opinion, Augustine opened a way for Hellenic mysticism to appear Christian. But our present interest lies in his eschatology. Does it too suffer from a christological truncation?

Neoplatonism, Immutability and Eschatology

When viewed in its details, and in the polemical context of Por-phyry's denial of Christ as God's appointed Mediator and of the reality of the resurrection of the body, Augustine's eschatological schema stands as a magnificent affirmation and interpretation of New Testament motifs. Yet one one may point to instances of Neoplatonism supplying more than just the language to describe and defend the Christian doctrine of the last things, and to a constant struggle between this Neoplatonism and contrary data from Scripture. For example, take the concept of the purification of our minds throughout this present life, the period between death and the final resurrection of the dead. This purification involves a

---

[61] McGrath, *Iustitia Dei*, 1.30.

movement from *scientia* to *sapientia*, that is, a process of learning to love God and God's justice on his terms and not ours. Behind this process of 'purgation' lies the axiom of all pagan, Hellenic mystical theology, that *only like can know like*. We cannot reach the beatific vision of God until we love God with the same love with which he loves us. Augustine's reading of Romans 5:5 – 'the love of God [i.e. as an objective genitive, where God is the object of our love] has been poured into our hearts through the Holy Spirit which has been given to us' – made the presence and activity of the Spirit in the Christian soul the presence and activity of love, in which God's love becomes our love for God. 'God is love', writes St John, and we are saved, brought into God's presence, only by matching, ourselves becoming, in our souls, that love. Given our sinful en-slavement to the lower appetites, salvation can only be eschatologi-cally understood as a process of illumination until the culmination of the final vision.

The difficulty Augustine has with the possibility of corporeal eyes having a direct vision of God in heaven is another case in point. Yes, the Neoplatonic view which centres on assimilation of the mind with God is an option, a solution, however tentative, to this problem.[62] But why is corporeality such a problem for Augustine? It is due to his conception of God being beyond creation because God, in Neoplatonic terms, is immutable, unchangeable, incorrupt-ible, even unreachable, whereas creation is the place of change and corruptibility. The problem of God is central to all of Augustine's theology. How can he assert a Christian doctrine of creation in relation to a God who is, above all, immutable? God inhabits the changeless mode of eternity, not time. Corporeality, for Augustine, always remains in some sense in the arena of time, not eternity.

Thus the very distinction between time and eternity which is so fundamental to his eschatology is also heavily influenced by Neopla-tonism. It preserves the immutability of God. In terms of the witness of the New Testament, 'immutability' is God's unchanging goodwill towards his creation in Jesus Christ, his faithfulness to his promise to Abraham (Gen. 12:3; cf. 2 Cor. 1:19–20; 2 Tim. 2:8–13; Jas. 1:17–18). But Augustine also felt the pressure of a philosophical definition of immutability which isolates the One, the supreme transcendent Principle, not only from everything material, but also from all description and being itself. It is a severe monism where the One's self-knowledge must be placed at a level below it in the *Nous*

---

[62] *City of God* 22.29.

or Mind because self-knowledge implies knowledge and a knower, and is therefore dualistic. A severe monism not only needs the dualism and descending multiplicity that comes from the One's creative overflow, in the order Mind, World-Soul, and material reality, to express itself, but must also overcome all such multiplicity and dualism by a return of all being back to its source in the One. Although Augustine eschewed this Neoplatonic doctrine of God in his work on the Trinity,[63] he readily used it to describe God's relationship to his creation.[64] He protects God's being from change in the act of creation by interpreting Genesis 1:1–2 in terms of Neoplatonic cosmology, placing around God in his creative act concentric circles of first 'the heaven of the heavens', then 'formless-ness', then the material creation.[65] The Christian doctrine of creation confessed not only that God himself was the creator but also that the physical universe was not eternal (as in Greek thought) but existed within the limitations of time, and thus came into existence from the midst of the eternity where God exists and where once the creation did not exist; therefore implying change in this God, in the eternity in which he inhabited. To overcome this implication, and thus further protect God's immutability, Augustine posited that creation was a timeless idea in the mind of God.

That the creation is a timeless idea in the mind of God fits perfectly into Ptolemaic cosmology and its metaphysical precursor, Platonism. This philosophical view of God and nature espoused in the Neoplatonism which Augustine was both contending and using was carried over into the relationship between heaven and earth, and into the theological relationship between the kingdom of God, which is a central eschatological entity, and the earthly church. Nature, and especially the mind of man, was regarded as containing the mirror images of the heavenly forms, so that the eternal pattern embedded in nature could be read off by philosophical reflection. Likewise the earthly church was regarded as in a mimetic relation-ship to the heavenly kingdom of God. Thus the end-time purposes of God became 'domesticated' or tamed within the institutional church, instead of standing over it, ever threatening judgment and destruction. This is most clearly seen in Augustine's interpretation of the millennium of Revelation 20:1–8 as being the present age of

---

[63] Williams, passim.

[64] See for example the doxological conclusion to *Confessions*, books 11 to 13.

[65] *Confessions* 12.1–12 ff.

Christian existence, and the church in this age being in truth the kingdom of Heaven on earth. Because of the mimetic conformity of the earthly institution to the heavenly kingdom of God, the church was in principle static, and unreformable. Its job, as the church militant here on earth, was simply to be that church, that kingdom of God by word and sacrament in a timeless fashion, until Christ should return.

In Platonism, the eternal or divine works in the world through material things which act as signs, or sacraments, that draw us upward to the higher values. In Augustine, with Christ now in heaven, God works in the world through the sacraments, accompanied by his Word. But, for all the Christian echoes in that formula, his conception of the operation of the sacraments once again betrays the Neoplatonic underpinnings of his thought in general and eschatology in particular. He writes, 'the whole import of the sacraments of salvation has to do more with the hope of future goods than with the retaining or attaining of present goods.'[66] The efficacy of these ministerial activities must be sought in the future, after the resurrection, when eternity embraces us, not now in the arena of time. But, according to the New Testament, the efficacy of God's activity in the world in word and sacrament is now, in time. The disciples eat the Last Supper as an appropriate sign because of something that is happening in their very midst, Christ is defeating sin on the cross, the last great Exodus is happening. For Augustine, eschatological salvation is the transfer from the change and corruption of time to the changelessness and incorruptibility of eternity. For the disciples, eschatological salvation consists of being transferred, now, from the vicious, evil kingdom of satan to the kindly, good kingdom of God. In the New Testament, what underlies eschatology is not the qualitative difference between time and eternity, but the difference between the now and not-yet of God's direct and decisive acts for our salvation.

Augustine had a significative view of the universe in which the sacraments of the church were tightly bound to their heavenly counterparts so that they really did have a heavenly effect, and, conversely, because they spoke of heavenly realities, their earthly effects were immutable. Thus, for example, because marriage was a sacrament of the heavenly marriage between the Christian soul

---

[66] *Enchiridion* 17.66; LCC, 378. See Prenter for a full and sympathetic discussion of Augustine's understanding of the sacraments and their relation to eschatology.

(and the church) with Christ, even divorce could not break it, and therefore re-marriage was infidelity, or better put, idolatry.[67] In this way the Neoplatonic elements in his eschatology more than assisted in determining the shape and implications of his doctrine of the church, sacraments and the nature of the Christian life.

But if, despite the firmness of his stand against Porphyry's depreciation of Christ's role as mediator and of the Christian hope of bodily resurrection, we still feel impelled to assign a fundamental influence to Neoplatonism in Augustine's eschatology, a puzzle remains. Augustine makes the resurrection of Christ not only the key to our first resurrection of forgiveness of sins, but also to the consummation of history when Christ comes in final judgment. The general resurrection is *the* eschatological event, and behind this stands Christ, God incarnate, who even more properly than the Father, determines the 'second resurrection'. Augustine wrote: 'The resurrection of souls is effected by the eternal and unchangeable substance of the Father and Son. But the resurrection of bodies is effected by the dispensation of the Son's humanity . . .'[68] We need to hear the grand, all-encompassing swell of that theme, (for it is Augustine, the Christian, at his best), before we listen further and recognize that it was not, after all, the ultimate note, but somehow acts as a penultimate tension which must then be resolved by a small collection of notes in a minor key in counterpoint. 'The resurrection of bodies is effected by the dispensation of the Son's humanity, *which is temporal, not co-eternal with the Father (resurrectio vero corporum fit per dispensationem humanitatis Filii temporalem, non Patri coaeternam.)*'[69]

It is true that 'The Lord Christ is the principle by whose incarnation we are purified',[70] and, against Porphyry, all parts of us – intellect, spirit and body.[71] But, 'this way purifies the whole man and *prepares* the mortal in all his parts for immortality',[72] we note. The humanity of Christ, and the works of that humanity, are limited

---

[67] See, *Homilies on the Gospel of John* 9.2; NPNF (1) 7.63; *On the Profit of Believing*; NPNF (1) 3.349; *On the Good of Marriage*; NPNF (1) 3.400–13, passim.

[68] *Homilies on the Gospel of John* 23.13; NPNF (1) 7.156.

[69] Ibid., emphasis mine; and *Corpus Christianorum Series Latina* (Turnholti, 1954) 36.242.

[70] *City of God* 10.32; cited from Evangeliou, 65.

[71] See Evangeliou, 64 ff.

[72] *City of God* 10.32; Dods, 434.

in Augustine's eschatology, as in his doctrines of the Christian life, to time, as a preparation; they do not carry us through and beyond into eternity. For there, only the eternal Word, not the temporal Word who is the incarnate Jesus Christ, can operate. As far as our progress to beatific vision is concerned, Augustine's Neoplatonic understanding of eternity and God's immutability forces him to leave the humanity of Christ at the threshold.

Evaluation

Great care is needed in evaluating the influence of Neoplatonism on the whole of Augustine's theology,[73] not just his eschatology. O'Meara's conclusion is judicious: 'There is no simple statement adequate to describe Augustine's use of the Neoplatonists.'[74] That doyen of Augustine studies, Etienne Gilson, judges that Augustine inhibited Neoplatonic influence in the west rather than transmitted it.[75] At one level, Augustine reformed philosophy so that it might truly bring us to knowledge of God by exposing the false paths of Plotinus and Porphyry, showing that the mediation of the incarnate Christ is the only proper way, and that true self-knowledge occurs only, and is thus only unitive with the divine, when it is a discovery of self in the image of the Triune God.[76] However, the play and consequences of Neoplatonism in his eschatology need to be ac-knowledged. In the significative universe which Augustine be-queathed to the Latin west, the earthly church is regarded as being in a mimetic relationship to the heavenly kingdom of God. The end-time purposes of God become 'domesticated' or tamed within the institutional church, instead of standing over it, threatening judgment and destruction.

Augustine needs to be divorced from his Platonism by a fuller christology which acknowledges the continuing relevance in heaven of the person and earthly work of Jesus Christ, who in his humanity as our high priest and king continues to intercede for us and rule over us at the right hand of the Father. That is a work

---

[73] E.g., the reputed triumph of philosophy in Augustine's trinitarian theology. See both Williams and Crouse, passim.

[74] O'Meara, 41.

[75] Ibid.

[76] Crouse and Williams in different ways show good grounds for that conclusion in Augustine's 'The Trinity.'

which is in its eschatological import the complete fulfilment of the promise of God to Abraham, and thus begets faith as the all-embracing response; faith which by grace unites the unlike, the ungodly, to the Unlike, God (Romans 3:21–4:5 ff.). Thus divorced, we can better appreciate the contribution of Augustine: a coherent schema which is determined by the life, death and resurrection of Jesus Christ and which is well integrated into all of (his) theology; the sharp distinction between time and eternity, a dramatic acknowledgment of the 'quantum leap' between the now and not-yet which will be resolved at the last appearance of Christ; the making sense of the reality of corporeal resurrection and hell, against the scornful attacks of unbelief; recognition that Christian existence at the End will image trinitarian existence in its sociality, as opposed to a solitary individualism, and as activity not passivity, the activity of praise.[77]

Primary Reading

Augustine   *City of God*, books 20 to 22

Augustine   *Enchiridion*, chapters 23 to 33, in *Augustine: Confessions and Enchiridion*, Library of Christian Classics (Philadelphia: Westminster, 1955) pp. 390–412.
(The *Enchiridion* was written for a layman, aiming to sum up the Christian faith in the briefest possible manner. It represents Augustine's fully matured theological perspective and is worth reading in full.)

OVER COFFEE

- Critically evaluate the place of prayers for the dead.
- In heaven, will we see God with our bodily eyes?
- In heaven, what will happen to faith?
- What place does the New Testament give to the resurrection of Jesus Christ in determining Christian eschatology?

---

[77] See Williams, 331–2.

5

Heaven and History: Medieval Eschatology

The medieval period covers the thousand years from the fall of the western Roman Empire in AD 476 to the Renaissance and Reformation dated from about AD 1500. Although regarded by the Renaissance writers, who invented the notion of a 'middle age' between theirs and Graeco-Roman antiquity, as one of cultural decadence, it was one of the most creative and fruitful periods in world history. During this time, western or Latin Christendom realized its ideal of a Christian unity encompassing every activity and thought, all religion and culture, the sacred and the secular, both church and state. Central to this ideal was eschatology.

In this period eschatology suffused all Christian and western thinking. It was a time when the details of eschatology were worked out in detailed and picturesque ways which both captured the mind and inflamed the heart. Perhaps the best example of this total, eschatologically driven world-view, is Dante's epic poem, *The Divine Comedy* (*c.* 1314). As the accompanying diagrams indicate, astronomy and geography, time and spiritual realities could all be integrated into a metaphysical whole. A great chain of being, which binds all existence to God as its source and end, underlies this grand vision. Note first Dante's understanding of the created sphere in which both the physical and spiritual are embodied (see p. 116), and then the relationship of this sphere to the multi-layered heavens (see p. 117). In his vision, Dante travels during Easter week, 1300, from a dark forest on the northern or known side of the world down through hell to satan at the centre of the earth and up the seven terraces of the Mount of Purgatory, an island in the Antipodes opposite Jerusalem, to its summit, the earthly paradise, where Adam and Eve were created. Up to this point, the great poet of classical Rome, Virgil, has been his guide. But now he meets his beloved, and deceased, Beatrice who conducts him through the nine planetary and stellar spheres to the

THE EARTHLY SPHERE OF DANTE'S *DIVINE COMEDY*[2]

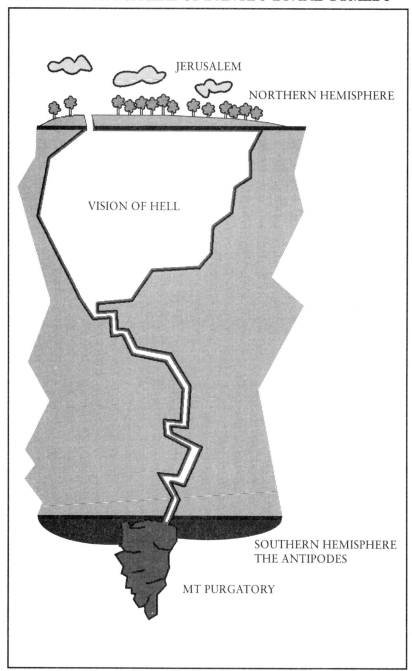

[2] Design work by Sarah Doyle, with computer assistance from Elizabeth Doyle.

THE MULTI-LAYERED HEAVENS

10. EMPYREAN
Eternal and infinite home of God and his saints
THE SNOW-WHITE ROSE OF PARADISE

9. CRYSTALINE HEAVEN
of the *Primum Mobile*, which gives motion to below

8. STARRY ★ HEAVEN
of fixed stars GEMINI

7. HEAVEN OF SATURN

6. HEAVEN OF JUPITER

5. HEAVEN OF MARS

4. HEAVEN OF THE SUN

3. HEAVEN OF VENUS

2. HEAVEN OF MERCURY

1. HEAVEN OF THE MOON

Empyrean, where St Bernard of Clairvaux, prince of Latin mystics (later to be much esteemed by John Calvin), takes over from her. Bernard presents Dante to the Blessed Virgin Mary, at whose intercession the poet is granted a glimpse of the 'beatific vision', the final vision of God.

The poem is more than just a religious epic working within the licenses granted by Dante's imagination and contemporary literary convention; it is also a statement of scholastic thought. As such, certain assumptions about the nature and content of the physical sciences, cosmology, philosophy and theology operate to make possible this sweeping vista, which is driven by an all-encompassing eschatology. The result is a thorough integration of all human knowledge and endeavour, whether secular or spiritual, time-bound or eternal.[1]

Now, the long duration of the Middle Ages and the multiplicity of elements its best thinkers sought to successively embrace, change or reconcile, make medieval thought complex in itself, and also in its theological development. Therefore, for the purpose of under-standing the period's contribution to eschatological thought, I will concentrate on two outstanding and representative trends; trends whose formative influence stretch beyond their own age and well on into our time. These two, opposing, trends emerge in the work of Thomas Aquinas (*c.* 1225–74) and Joachim of Fiore (*c.* 1132–1202). As it was Aquinas' work which was the most influential and characteristic of the period, we will examine it first and at length, paying special attention to the foundational factors which made his conception of eschatological reality possible.

'Hope' or 'Desire'?

Thomas Aquinas, a Dominican philosopher and monk, is regarded as the most important and influential scholastic theologian and philosopher in the Roman Catholic Church. In the Middle Ages he was honoured and referred to by titles such as 'Doctor Communis' (in the thirteenth century) and 'Doctor Angelicus' (in the fifteenth century), and in 1923 declared by Pope Pius XI to be one whom the

---

[1] The geographical, astronomical and religious details of the Universal 24-Hour Clock demonstrate this integration. There is a useful description and depiction of this in Mark Musa (trans. & comm.), *Dante, The Divine Comedy*, vol. 2: *Purgatory* (New York: Penguin Books, 1985), 369.

church has made 'her very own'.[3] But in approaching his eschatological understanding, two severe criticisms cut across this general
approbation. These criticisms come from Thomas F. Torrance and
Jürgen Moltmann, both of whom stand within the Reformation
heritage. Moltmann writes:

> By contrast [to Joachim of Fiore], Thomas replaces the biblical history
> of promise with a finalistic metaphysics. He replaces the hope which
> seeks the fulfilment of the promise with the natural striving for happi-
> ness which according to Augustine can come to fulfilment only in God
> himself. The 'coming God', *ho erchomenos, Deus adventurus*, is re-
> placed by the 'unmoved Mover' who draws all creatures to him by
> virtue of *eros*. The eschatological promise of the 'new heaven and new
> earth' – 'Behold, I make all things new' (Rev. 21.5) – is replaced by the
> *visio Dei beatifica in patria*, i.e., in heaven, the bliss of the pure spirits
> in the world beyond. 'In this way the whole of eschatology and the
> whole eschatological tension of the Christian promise is set off against
> the idea of a goal understood in transcendentalist terms.' Thomas did
> not translate biblical language into any other language or mode of
> thought, but basically liquidated it. His 'theology of hope' is in truth
> not the theology of a biblical 'hope' but the anthropology of the natural
> desire (*appetitus naturalis*) of the inner self-transcendence of human
> beings which finds its answer in the metaphysical theology of the
> supreme good (*summum bonum*).[4]

That is, Moltmann says, Aquinas has reduced the biblical hope of
God coming to recreate the whole universe to one of mere human
'desire'. Torrance's earlier criticisms are no less sweeping, as he
places Thomas in the wider context of a certain understanding of
God and his relationship to the world:

> In the medieval Roman Church the Greek view of God and nature was
> carried over into the relation of heaven and earth, the Kingdom of God
> and the Church. Nature was regarded as impregnated with final causes,

---

[3] See W.A. Wallace and J.A. Weisheipl, 'Thomas Aquinas, St', *New
Catholic Encyclopedia* (New York: McGraw-Hill, 1967) 1.102–15.
[4] 'Christian Hope: Messianic or Transcendent? A Theological Conversation with Joachim of Fiore and Thomas Aquinas', in *History and the
Triune God: Contributions to Trinitarian Theology* (New York: Crossroad, 1992) 95. 'Messianic or Transcendent?' first appeared in *Münchner
Theologische Zeitschrift* 33 (1982) 241–60.

so that the eternal pattern embedded in nature could be read off by natural theology or deductive science. Likewise the Church was regarded as impregnated with the Kingdom of God, so that the pattern of the Kingdom embedded in the earthly structure of the Church could be read off the historical consciousness of the Church by the teaching office. Here the *Eschaton* is so domesticated and housed within the Church that far from standing under final judgment the Church dispenses it by binding and loosing; far from being repentant and reformable, the Church can only develop according to her own immanent norms which correspond to the fixed pattern of the Kingdom . . . When St Thomas, for example, considered the questions raised by Joachim, he removed the eschatological end to a realm beyond history, and concluded that the Church, which has the pattern of that end embedded within it, is as static as history.[5]

That is, on the basis of his doctrines of God and creation, Aquinas as the heir of Augustine, has developed an eschatology which fits a Ptolemaic world-view in which earth is transitory and designed to reflect an ultimate heavenly reality.

These criticisms, and notably the more recent one of Moltmann, have not gone unchallenged.[6] Therefore, in an endeavour to understand the power of St Thomas' teaching on the last things, I will first outline its details and then analyse them in terms of his overall theological schema and purpose.

Aquinas' Eschatology of Hope

Development in topics of eschatology

Concerning the usual topics of eschatology – death, the intermediate state, resurrection, the last judgment and the beatific vision,

---

[5] 'The Eschatology of the Reformation', in W. Manson (ed.) *Eschatology: Four Papers Read to the Society for the Study of Theology*, Scottish Journal of Theology Occasional Paper No. 2 (Edinburgh: Oliver & Boyd, 1952) 37–8.

[6] See Joseph T. Merkt, 'The Discovery of the Genetic Development of Thomas Aquinas' Theology of Hope and its Relevance for a Theology of the Future', in Robert J. Daly (ed.) *Rising from History: U.S. Catholic Theology Looks to the Future*, The Annual Publication of the College Theology Society, 1984 (New York: University Press of America, 1987) 104–23.

Thomas Aquinas by and large embraces the traditional details and places them into the flow of his own particular apologetic and philosophical theology. Some development, however, is discernible on the precise nature of the intermediate state, the immortality of the soul and the final vision of God.

Immortality of the soul and resurrection

Aquinas followed Aristotle in asserting that reality was to be understood in terms of form and matter that must go together, rather than being separated as posited by Plato. A form, or a universal, only exists as expressed in a particular object, or matter. Moreover, form determines matter. Thus the 'appleness' of an apple does not exist in its own right; it is the union of the form 'apple' with the matter (the distinctive shape, colour, texture, and smell of apple that the senses perceive) which identifies an individual apple as the real thing. When this sort of analysis is applied to the immortality of the soul and a defence of bodily resurrection, Aquinas is able to bring the soul's immortality and bodily resurrection neatly together in a way that a more Platonic line of argument cannot. Since the soul is the form which determines human existence, which is expressed in the matter of the body, therefore after death the soul in the intermediate state carries a natural orientation towards forming a body. It cannot fulfil all its potentialities and thus in a sense longs for the resurrection.[7] Of course, in using Aristotle as an ally of Christian truth, he had to interpret Aristotle as believing in the soul's survival of bodily death.[8]

The intermediate state

The precise nature of what happens between the moment of death and the final resurrection is clarified throughout medieval theology. For his part, Thomas maintains that 'souls immediately after their

---

[7] *On the Truth of the Catholic Faith: Summa Contra Gentiles* translated by A.C. Pegis et al., (New York: University of Notre Dame Press, 1955–6) book 4 chapter 79 sections 10–11, pp. 299–300 (abbreviated SCG 4.79.10–11; Pegis et al., 299–300).

[8] See *SCG* 2.78–9; Pegis et al., 249–58; cf. *Summa Theologiae: Latin Text and English Translation, Introductions, Notes, Appendices and Glossaries*, 61 volumes (Blackfriars, Cambridge in conjunction with McGraw-Hill, New York et al., 1964–80) *Prima pars, quaestio* 90 *articulis* 4; Blackfriars volume 13 p. 15 (abbreviated ST 1a.90,4; Blackfriars, 13.15).

separation from the body become unchangeable in will, with the result that the will of man cannot further be changed, neither from good to evil, nor from evil to good.'[9] Consequently, immediately 'after death the souls of men receive either punishment or reward according to their merits.'[10] There is no need for souls to wait for the resumption of their bodies before experiencing this, for the soul, in its operation of the will, has directed the body in acts of sin or love and not the body the soul. Thus, 'since the souls had priority in the fault or the merit, they have priority also in being punished or rewarded.'[11] Even before the resurrection of their bodies, the souls of the pious can enjoy God on a par with the spiritual angels who enjoy the vision of him in heaven.[12] If it be asked how souls awaiting their bodies can suffer punishment when such punishment is described in the Bible in terms of bodily torment by fire, Aquinas argues that such descriptions contain metaphorical elements point-ing to torture by remorse of conscience. He also comes up with an ingenious explanation whereby non-bodily substances suffer by being placed in a certain bondage to bodily fire. As demons in the New Testament could be confined to bodies such as those of the swine, so bodily fire confines, which is not only punishment in itself but also brings a greater humiliation: 'they know they are in bondage to the lowliest things as punishment.'[13]

Purgatory

For Christians who die in venial, as opposed to mortal, sin, purga-tory awaits as a staging post to heaven. Thomas' theological rationale and description of purgatory is a sophisticated synthesis of the Anselmic notion of sin as a debt needing payment, the Augustinian notion that in the process of justification the soul's love or positive inclination toward God saves, the medieval emphasis on merit and reward in justification, the distinction between temporal and eternal punishment in the sacrament of penance, and Augustine's insistence that all punishment is retributive:

> But by sin the soul is unclean in its disordered union to inferior things. To be sure, the soul is purified from this uncleanness in this life by

---

[9] *SCG* 4.92.1; Pegis et al., 338–9.
[10] *SCG* 4.91.1–2; Pegis et al., 334; *ST* 3a.59,5; cf. *ST* 1a.64,4.
[11] *SCG* 4.91.4; Pegis et al., 335.
[12] *SCG* 4.91.8–9 f.
[13] *SCG* 4.90; Pegis et al., 332–4.

penance and the other sacraments, as was said above, but it does at times happen that such purification is not entirely perfected in this life; one remains a debtor for the punishment, whether by reason of some negligence, or business, or even because a man is overtaken by death. Nevertheless, he is not entirely cut off from his reward, because such things can happen without mortal sin, which alone takes away the charity [love] to which the reward of eternal life is due. And this is clear from what was said in Book III. They must, then, be purged after this life before they achieve the final reward. This purgation, of course, is made by punishments, just as in this life their purgation would have been completed by punishments which satisfy the debt; otherwise, the negligent would be better off than the solicitous, if the punishment which they do not complete for their sins here need not be undergone in the future. Therefore, if the souls of the good have something capable of purgation in this world, they are held back from the achievement of their reward while they undergo cleansing punishments. And this is the reason we hold that there is a purgatory.[14]

As well as hell for the damned and purgatory for those dying in venial sin, Thomas makes two other clarifications in regard to the nature of the *infernum* (lower world). The lower world has two regions (called 'limbo' by Albert the Great (1200–80), which border hell; one inhabited by the patriarchs, the other by infants dying without baptism. At the advent and death of Christ, the holy patriarchs of the Old Testament era were 'in *inferno* only on account of original sin', awaiting its removal by the Redeemer's passion. In the descent of his soul into hell, Christ released them to eternal glory.[15] But that descent had no effect then, or since, on the souls of infants who died without baptism, for they neither were capable of faith in the death of Christ nor had the sacrament of that faith. They are preserved from the hell of the damned by the fact that although dying in original sin, they are innocent of personal guilt. Hence, in this *limbus infantium* (as it was to be called), although never to enjoy the beatific vision of God, they enjoy full natural happiness.[16]

---

[14] *SCG* 4.91.6; Pegis et al., 336.

[15] *ST* 3a.52,2; Blackfriars, 159.

[16] *ST* 3a.52,2,7–8; *Scripta super libros Sententiarum* II d.33 q.2 a.2. See, George J. Dyer, *Limbo: Unsettled Question* (New York: Sheed & Ward, 1964) 44–52.

The last judgment and general resurrection

The last judgment, effected by Christ clothed in his humanity, brings the general resurrection to either an eternity in heaven or an 'eternity' of pain in hell, experienced as the passing of time without end.[17] The new bodies are suited to their ends: 'some will receive bodies which are incapable of suffering and glorious; but others, bodies capable of suffering and ignoble.'[18] Both the wicked and the good will see Christ in the form of his humanity, but only the good his divinity, as 'the sight of His divinity . . . makes men blessed.'[19] 'When, therefore, the last judgment is completed, saved human nature will be entirely established in its goal.'[20] That goal is the beatific vision; to be 'entirely established' refers to the two support - ing structures of this vision: the resurrection body and the rest of material creation. 'Since everything bodily is somehow for the sake of man . . . at that time, also, the entire bodily creation will be changed – and suitably – to be in harmony with the state of the men who then will be. And because men will then be incorruptible, the state of generation and corruption will then be taken away from the entire bodily creation.'[21] The details of these changes reveal a good deal of Thomas' thinking about the nature of resurrection, life after death, and the beatific vision of God.

As the death of Christ brings about the remission of our sins in the sacraments, so the resurrection of Christ effects our liberation from death which we will receive at the end of the world, 'when we shall all rise by the power of Christ'.[22] Against those who might raise philosophical and pastoral objections to the propriety of embodiment for the beatific life, and addressing concerns about the possibility of reconstruction of a body after it is has 'resolved even into the primary elements', Thomas is at pains to point out that this resurrection body is not just some spiritual entity, but a real, material body, and wholly new, without defect or corruption of any kind.[23] In answering these objections Thomas engages in an elabo - rate exposition of the relation between the form (soul) and the matter (the body), as we saw above, and appeals to the power of

---

[17] *ST* 1a.10,4.
[18] *SCG* 4.96.1.
[19] *SCG* 4.96.2; Pegis et al., 346.
[20] *SCG* 4.97.1; Pegis et al., 346.
[21] Ibid.
[22] *SCG* 4.79.3–5; Pegis et al., 297.
[23] *SCG* 4.79–81,84–85; Pegis et al., 297–308, 320–325.

God: 'Resurrection is natural if one considers its purpose, for it is natural that the soul be united to the body. But the principle of resurrection is not natural. It is caused by the divine power alone.'[24] The resurrection body will perfectly serve the goal of the soul, the vision of God. 'The life of the risen, moreover, is ordered to the preservation of perfect beatitude.'[25] This vision, in which the soul is united to God, also works with the soul to perfect the body in its support of the end of humanity:

> But the glory and power of the soul elevated to the divine vision will add something more ample to the body united to itself. For this body will be entirely subject to the soul – the divine power will achieve this – not only in regard to its being, but also in regard to action, passion, movements, and bodily qualities. Therefore, just as the soul which enjoys the divine vision will be filled with a kind of spiritual lightsomeness, so by a certain overflow from the soul to the body, the body will in its own way put on the lightsomeness of glory . . . the consequence will be the soul's utter obedience to the spirit's wish. Hence, the bodies of the blessed when they arise are going to have agility.
>
> Furthermore, the soul which is enjoying God will cleave to Him most perfectly, and will in its own fashion share in His goodness to the highest degree; and thus will the body be perfectly within the soul's dominion, and will share in what is the soul's very own characteristics so far as possible, in the perspicuity of the sense knowledge, in the ordering of bodily appetite, and in the all-round perfection of nature; for a thing is the more perfect in nature, the more its matter is dominated by its form.[26]

This is Thomas at his best; a fine, theocentric portrait of extraordinary beauty and power, where the conjunction of grace and nature gives us a view of the perfection of heaven that stirs longing and calls for praise. It also helps explain his rejection of sexual activity and eating in heaven. They belong to the corruptible life, for their end is to produce new life and to assist bodily growth. Biblical descriptions of eating in the paradisal, the post-resurrection, state are to be understood spiritually. Christ 'ate after the resurrection not out of necessity, but to establish the truth of His resurrection. Hence, that food of His was not changed into flesh, but returned to the prior

---

[24]   *SCG* 4.81.14; Pegis et al., 307–8.

[25]   *SCG* 4.83.11; Pegis et al., 315.

[26]   *SCG* 4.86; Pegis et al., 325–6.

material state.' Not even for pleasure will one engage in sex or food, for God alone and above all will be our pleasure, and indeed, in both activities pleasure is not the proper end, only the accompaniment. Sexual differentiation and organs will be retained, although there will be no use for the latter, except 'to re-establish the integrity of the natural body', and as a sign or witness to the divine wisdom which disposes all things in a certain order.[27]

The beatific vision

Aquinas has a radical solution to the role of the rest of creation in supporting the beatific vision. On the basis of his Aristotelian metaphysic in which the stars in themselves have an intermediary role in creation and by their motion a causal role in the change and generation of humankind, the stars will have perpetuity but will stop dead in their movements in the heavens. 'But the other animals, the plants, and the mixed bodies, those entirely corruptible both wholly and in part', that is, without any eternal nature, will entirely disappear. It is here the biblical picture of the fiery judgment of creation applies; it consumes the corruptible, it is 'the consumption of the things which ought not to remain in the future state'. What is left is believers clothed with bodies not only 'freed of corruption but also clothed with glory'. In this way 'even the bodily creation will achieve a kind of resplendence in its own way'. This, Thomas says as he closes his *Summa Contra Gentiles*, is the new heaven and the new earth promised in Revelation 21:1 and Isaiah 65:17–18.[28]

As much as this description of the new person in the new heavens and new earth may elicit our admiration, the all-attracting centre is the beatific vision of God.[29] In a long section of *Summa Contra Gentiles* (book 3, chapters 37 to 63), Aquinas places and develops his understanding of this vision firmly within the framework of his Aristotelianism. The Neoplatonists, the Christian Platonists and Christian theology in general owe to Aristotle the articulation of a notion which was to prove very fruitful: God is 'self-thinking thought'. In philosophy and Christian theology this understanding of God produced a foundation on which two key theological ideas could be understood and explained. First, that the interior life of

---

[27] *SCG* 4.83,88; Pegis et al., 311–20, 328–9; cf. *ST* 1a.97,3.

[28] *SCG* 4.97; Pegis et al., 346–9.

[29] For the human intellect to reach ultimate felicity, it must know not just that the First Cause *is*, but *what* it is; *ST* 1a2ae.3,8.

divinity (however that might be conceived) is self-sufficient and real (as opposed to the notion of the ultimate One as above all being, understanding and description). Secondly, the vexed question of how ultimate spiritual entities might be related to each other, and to the world. The latter problem exists because *the* ultimate spiritual entity to which all things are to relate is *God*, who is unique. To solve this, Aquinas posited that the nature of those relationships was intellectual or rational, through *logos*, in keeping with the definition of God as 'self-thinking thought'. To the theology of the Middle Ages which most associated itself with Thomas, this description of the being of God, the perfect coincidence of his essence and existence, gave the priority to reason or intellect over will in its doctrine of God and revelation. Further, the real nature and goal of existence created in the image of God, as exemplified in the crown of creation, humankind, is intellectual. The importance of this framework to Thomas can be seen in his argument for the vision of God making the pilgrim a partaker of eternal life:

> Furthermore, the intellective soul is created 'on the border line between eternity and time,' as is stated in the *Book on Causes*,[30] and as can be shown from our earlier statements. In fact, it is the lowest in the order of intellects, yet its substance is raised above corporeal matter, not depending on it. But its action, as joined to lower things which exist in time, is temporal. Therefore, its action, as joined to higher things which exist above time, participates in eternity. Especially so is the vision by which it sees the divine substance. And so, by this kind of vision it comes into the participation of eternity; and for the same reason, so does any other created intellect that sees God.[31]

Thomas starts his exposition by asserting, against other legitimate but penultimate sources of happiness, that 'the ultimate felicity of

---

[30] An anonymous treatise consisting mostly of extracts from Proclus' (Neoplatonic philosopher, 410–85) *Elements of Theology* and translated into Latin *c.* 1167. Aquinas wrote an extensive and appreciative commentary on it in the last years of his life. For Proclus' role in the wider absorption of Neoplatonism by Thomas Aquinas see Cornelio Fabro, 'The Overcoming of the Neoplatonic Triad of Being, Life, and Intellect by Saint Thomas Aquinas', in Dominic J. O'Meara (ed.) *Neoplatonism and Christian Thought* (Norfolk, Virginia: International Society for Neoplatonic Studies, 1982) 97–108.

[31] *SCG* 3.61.5; Pegis et al., 201; cf. *ST* 2a2ae.175,4.

man lies in the contemplation of truth', that truth which is the very being of God, which Thomas often calls the 'first truth', and occasionally when borrowing from Augustine, the 'eternal Word'.[32] He then examines what this does not consist of, what it does consist of, and how we attain it. This contemplation does not consist in the knowledge of God which is generally possessed by most men, nor in the knowledge of God gained through demonstration in that science which is theology, nor indeed in the knowledge of God which is through faith. Why does faith fail us here? Felicity is a perfect operation of the intellect. 'But in the knowledge of faith, there is found a most imperfect operation of the intellect.' Not because of the object of faith, but on the side of the intellect. 'For the intellect does not grasp the object to which it gives assent in the act of believing.' Furthermore, 'through felicity, because it is the ultimate end, natural desire comes to rest. Now, the knowledge of faith does not bring rest to desire but rather sets it aflame, since every man desires to see what he believes. So, man's ultimate felicity does not lie in the knowledge of faith.'[33] That is, the point at which felicity does lie is static.

What does it mean to see God?

Thomas has another obstacle to clear away, one raised in the course of Augustine's pilgrimage to the heavenly city: in this life, can God be known as he really is? The answer is noteworthy because it also concisely expounds Aquinas' theory of knowledge:

> Although this mirror, which is the human mind, reflects the likeness of God in a closer way than lower creatures do, the knowledge of God which can be taken in by the human mind does not go beyond the type of knowledge that is derived from sensible things, since even the soul itself knows what it is itself as a result of understanding the natures of sensible things, as we have said. Hence, throughout this life God can be known in no higher way than that whereby a cause is known through its effects.[34]

---

[32] *ST* 1a.10,3; Blackfriars, 2.143 and f.n. b. The editor notes: 'The joy of the saints in heaven is the vision of God face to face. Since the Word, the second person of the Trinity, is the self-revelation of God, the vision is often referred to, especially by St Augustine, as the vision of the Word.'
[33] *SCG* 3.40; Pegis et al., 130–2; cf. *ST* 2a2ae.1,3.
[34] *SCG* 3.47.9; Pegis et al., 161.

Thus, man's ultimate felicity does not come in this life, but in the life to come. What does it mean 'to see God'?

> It is already sufficiently apparent from what we have said what should be the mode of this vision. For we showed above that the divine substance cannot be seen intellectually by means of any created species. Conse-quently, if the divine essence is seen, it must be done as His intellect sees the divine essence itself through itself, and in such a vision the divine essence must be both what is seen and that whereby it is seen.[35]

> In this vision, of course, we become most like unto God, and we are partakers in His happiness. For God Himself understands His own substance through His own essence: and this is His felicity.[36]

The point of stasis and beatitude is God's own self-knowledge, the self-knowledge of the Unmoved Mover thinking thought, about himself. The Aristotelian language to one side, this is a remarkable passage. What bliss is, what heaven is, is to participate in the very life of God himself, and it is only because of that life, both within itself and outside itself in effecting our salvation, that we participate in God's own life. As Thomas has cast it, there are several moves in his thought here:

(i)   God fundamentally is his self-knowledge, and in that self-knowledge there is the perfect conjunction of God's essence (*what* God is) and existence (*how* he is; the actualizing of his essence).
(ii)   All being is related to God by creation.
(iii) There is a chain of causality between God and the creation which images him as cause to effect.
(iv)   God's fundamental nature as intellect is the clue as to what our real being means: knowledge, and above all that knowl-edge which is direct knowledge of the Knower who is our origin.
(v)   And it is along the chain of causality, under the impact of the Self-knower in his self-knowledge that he alone is God – fit to be worshipped and adored – that the human soul in its intellective capacity moves back to the source, to the Self-Knower.

---

[35] *SCG* 3.51.2; Pegis et al., 175.
[36] *SCG* 3.51.6; Pegis et al., 177.

That is, we only know anything, and above all God, because God knows himself, and our knowledge is in and through his self-knowledge. And again remarkably, the beatific vision of God in the life to come is not in any way second-hand, but of the divine essence itself; at the heart of the universe.

What is it like to experience seeing God?

Because the power of insight in our minds is not as strong as God's – after all he made us as 'a little lower than the angels', not as gods co-equal with him – 'though the created intellect may see the divine substance, it does not know all that can be known through the divine substance.'[37] But it does know a lot!

> Since the vision of the divine substance is the ultimate end of every intellectual substance, as is evident from what we have said, and since the natural appetite of everything comes to rest when the thing reaches its ultimate end, the natural appetite of an intellectual substance must come to rest completely when it sees the divine substance. Now, the natural appetite of the intellect is to know the genera and species and powers of all things, and the whole order of the universe; human investigation of each of the aforementioned items indicates this. There-fore, each one who sees the divine substance knows all the things mentioned above . . . Therefore, God shows the intellect that is seeing Him all things which He has produced for the perfection of the universe.[38]

The beatific vision is a wonderful experience. In it every human desire is fulfilled, says Thomas, as he takes us by the hand and shows how all the right and proper desires of human nature are satisfied in God: the desire for knowledge of the truth, to live in accord with virtue, for honour, glory, wealth, the enjoyment of pleasures, for preservation. 'And so, it is evident that through the divine vision intellectual substances obtain true felicity, in which their desires are completely brought to rest and in which is the full sufficiency of all the goods which, according to Aristotle, are required for happi-ness.'[39] The wonder of it answers the question as to the possibility of boredom in an eternal vision:

---

[37] *SCG* 3.56.1; Pegis et al., 188; cf. *ST* 1a2ae.3.8.
[38] *SCG* 3.59.1,3; Pegis et al., 195–6.
[39] *SCG* 3.63.9; Pegis et al., 208–9.

Furthermore, nothing that is contemplated with wonder can be tire-some, since as long as the thing remains in wonder it continues to stimulate desire. But the divine substance is always viewed with wonder by any created intellect, since no created intellect comprehends it. So, it is impossible for an intellectual substance to become tired of this vision.[40]

With some justification, Hebblethwaite regards the doctrine of the beatific vision as the high point of the medieval understanding of the last things.[41]

The puzzle

But, for all the wonderment of it, to be at the heart of the universe, to see all things which God has produced for its perfection, in gazing on God's substance, his essence, does one actually see *God, Deum in se*, God in himself? Does one (even) see God as Father, Son and Holy Spirit? There is a curious silence about this in *Summa Contra Gentiles*, and in *Summa Theologiae*. But in one place of the *Summa Theologiae* there appears to be a more hopeful statement. However, it is ambiguous in that God is spoken of here as the 'first truth': 'In the home country there will be the vision of the first truth in accordance with what it is in itself, according to: "When he appears we shall be like him, for we shall see him as he is [1 John 3:2]" (*visio patriae erit veritatis primae secundum quod in se est, secundum illud*)'.[42] Certainly, there are things regarding God that one *cannot* see. We go back to Aquinas' statement: 'if the term *all* means all the things that God knows in seeing His own essence, then no created intellect sees all things in God's substance, as we have showed above.' He goes on: 'But this can be considered under several points. First, in regard to those things which God can make but has not made, nor will ever make. Indeed, all things of this kind cannot be known unless His power is comprehended, and this is not possible for any intellectual creature, as we showed above.' And

---

[40] *SCG* 3.62.9; Pegis et al., 205.
[41] Brian Hebblethwaite, *The Christian Hope* (Basingstoke: Marshall, Morgan & Scott, 1984) 65.
[42] *ST* 2a2ae.1,2. The Blackfriars translation (31.15) is a little misleading: 'the first truth as he is in himself'. The older, more literal Dominican translation (*The 'Summa Theologica' of St Thomas Aquinas*, London: Burns, Oates & Washbourne, 1916; vol. 9 p. 6) agrees with mine: 'the object of the heavenly vision will be the First Truth seen in itself'.

not only do we not comprehend, that is, see intellectually, God's power, but also neither the divine goodness nor wisdom nor will.[43] An analysis of the beatific knowledge of God in the soul of Jesus yields similar results.[44] Again, in thinking about the vision which angels have, Thomas denies that any actual vision of God can be identified precisely with the object of that vision, that is, God. It is a matter of degree:

> There must then be some definite objective towards which each such creature is moved as to his final end.
>
> This objective is the vision of God. Yet we cannot identify it precisely with the *object* seen in that vision; for the supreme truth is seen by all the blessed in varying degrees. What we have to say then is that the objective intended by him who guides the blessed to their end has been decided in advance in respect of the *manner* of seeing that truth; and in various ways according to various degrees. For while intellectual creatures are indeed led towards the sight of the supreme essence, they cannot be led to the absolutely supreme mode of manner of seeing it, which would be the perfect comprehension of it; for this mode, as we have seen, belongs to God alone. But since such perfect comprehension of God implies an infinite intellect, and since intellect in the creature is finite, and since between the finite and the infinite there are infinite degrees, we can see that created intellects may be brought to see God in countless ways and with greater or less perspicuity; and consequently, that while bliss itself consists in the vision itself, there are degrees in bliss corresponding, each of them, to a special mode of vision.[45]

This is a puzzle we will return to later.

Hope

For all the cohesiveness and power of Thomas Aquinas' exposition of the last things, his major contribution is on the nature of Christian *hope*. To this he devoted a section in the *Summa Theologiae*,[46] and to this Moltmann has taken great exception. Before turning to an overview of Thomas' theology as a whole, against

---

[43] *SCG* 3.59.7–10; Pegis et al., 197–8.
[44] *ST* 3a.9.2 and 3a.10–14.
[45] *ST* 1a.62,9; Blackfriars, 9.243, 245.
[46] *ST* 2a2ae.17–22; Blackfriars, 33.1–123.

which I will seek to evaluate his eschatology, the following is a summary, based largely on the work of S.M. Ramirez, of the main thrust in Thomas' understanding of hope.[47]

Hope as 'operative habit'

Hope, faith and love are the three theological virtues. Hope, as a virtue, is an operative habit. Following Aristotle, Aquinas defines a habit as a quality that disposes a subject well or badly in itself or in relation to action.[48] It is thus an internal disposition or orientation by which a person is ready or prepared for something. Operative habits are acquired dispositions that prepare the powers of an organism for stable patterns of action.

A supernatural habit, in distinction to natural habit, is 'a super-natural, internal, permanent quality modifying the soul or its faculties in relation to the supernatural ultimate good'.[49] Supernatural habits provide the power to act supernaturally, that is, they allow the soul to know and be orientated towards God.

Hope, then, as a theological and operative habit, is defined by its relation to what it is directed to, its *proper object*, and to what it does, its *proper act*. The *proper object* of hope is twofold, material and formal. The material or terminative object that hope seeks to obtain is the 'future goods' promised by God, namely eternal life, the complete and secure enjoyment of God himself, and the means to that ultimate end.[50] The means include the gifts of nature and of grace. That is, they include 'daily bread', all the means of grace the church offers and the merits of the Christian as he or she pilgrimages towards heaven. Hope then, as defined by its material object of eternal life and the means to it, has a very large scope in Thomas' theology, encompassing both physical and metaphysical reality.

The formal or motive object of hope is the real and objective foundation of hope. It is God, God alone who is our hope. In the end, it is God alone who can and will move us to himself as the divine Agent:

---

[47] S.M. Ramirez, 'Hope', *New Catholic Encyclopedia* 7.133–41. Ramirez follows Thomas' reconstruction.
[48] *ST* 1a.83,2; 1a2ae.54,1; 1a2ae.82,1.
[49] R.J. Tapia, 'Habit (In Theology)', *New Catholic Encyclopedia* 6.884–885. M. Stock has an analysis on the wider notion of 'habit' in the same volume, pp. 880–5. Both Tapia and Stock follow Thomas' reconstruction.
[50] *ST* 2a2ae.17,1,4; 1a2ae.40,1; 2a2ae.18,2.

Now an effect should match its cause, and so the good we should rightly and chiefly hope for from God is an unlimited one, matching the power of God who helps us. For it belongs to his limitless power to bring us to limitless good. Such a good is life eternal, consisting in the joyful possession of God himself. This is simply to say that we should hope for nothing less from God than his very self; his goodness, by which he confers good upon creaturely things, is nothing less than his own being.[51]

The second major parameter defining hope is its *proper act*, which consists of the principle act and secondary acts, or effects, such as joy and patience. The principle act of 'the very habit of hope itself', is 'the expectation of beatitude', which 'is in no way caused from merits but is a pure gift of grace'.[52] With respect to its end, hope is the fixation of the intention upon God alone as one's ultimate goal. Here Thomas examines the love or desire that characterizes and drives hope. It is not the perfect love of charity – the love of another for their own sake, as in friendship, and pre-eminently in loving God for himself – but the imperfect love of desire (*amor concupiscentiae*), since the one who hopes is intending something for himself. In the trilogy of faith, hope and charity, charity enjoys a natural primacy in excellence. Faith and hope put us in contact with God as a means of raising us up to him, but it is charity that unites us to him. Thus charity renders hope more perfect.[53]

The other property of the act of hope in relation to its end is the lifting up of the will to the level of God himself. The will marshals its forces and dares to aspire to the achievement of the divine good despite the difficulties that lie in the way.[54] The formal motive, or driving power, gives the act of hope firmness and certainty that is unshakeable and absolute, for nothing can be firmer or more certain than that which drives it. God has promised the needed help, his omnipotence can overcome any obstacle. However, this is not the certainty of faith or knowledge, but has with it the element of a holy fear that one may not arrive at the heavenly vision. This fear is not that God may fail to give help, but that the pilgrim may not use it.

---

[51] *ST* 2a2ae.17,2; Blackfriars, 33.9; cf. 1a2ae.1,8 and 3,1.

[52] *ST* 2a2ae.17,1; Blackfriars, 33.7; 2a2ae.17,6.2.

[53] *ST* 2a2ae.17,8; Blackfriars, 33.27; 1a2ae.66,6; Blackfriars 23.219; Ramirez, 138–40.

[54] *ST* 2a2ae.17,6; Blackfriars, 33.21; 1a.59,4.2–3; 2a2ae.18,1 and 2; Ramirez, 138.

Both hope and fear are necessary. Hope without fear leads to presumption; fear without hope brings despair.[55]

Moltmann's criticism
At first glance, Moltmann's criticism seems all too true:

> Thomas replaces the biblical history of promise with a finalistic meta-physics. He replaces the hope which seeks the fulfilment of the promise with the natural striving for happiness which ... can come to fulfilment only in God himself ... Thomas did not translate biblical language into any other language or mode of thought, but basically liquidated it. His 'theology of hope' is in truth not the theology of a biblical 'hope' but the anthropology of the natural desire (*appetitus naturalis*) of the inner self-transcendence of human beings which finds its answer in the metaphysical theology of the supreme good (*summum bonum*).[56]

To properly assess the strong criticisms of Moltmann and Torrance, we will need to examine Aquinas' eschatology more closely against his overall theological schema.

At the Heart of the Universe

Frederick Copleston points out that for all his incisive reflection on questions of epistemology, Augustine of Hippo did not set out to give a systematic and carefully defined philosophical account of his concerns.[57] The same cannot be said for Thomas Aquinas, for in his two *Summae* – *Summa Contra Gentiles* and *Summa Theologicae* – he is concerned to show how God is the foundation of all reality, and how everything relates back to him as its First Cause.

Method

Aquinas' method in this is not, as it is sometimes portrayed, to move self-consciously from philosophy to theology, as if building a great

---

[55] *ST* 2a2ae.18,4; 1a2ae.64,4; 2a2ae.17,6.2. 'The inducements to fear are enough to rule out presumption, in the same way that the inducements to hope suffice to exclude despair', 2a2ae.22,2; Blackfriars, 33.121; Ramirez, 138.
[56] 'Christian Hope – Messianic or Transcendent?', 95.
[57] *A History of Philosophy*, vol. 2 (Westminster, Maryland: Newman, 1950) 67.

theological system in an architectonic way on certain rational presuppositions. Thomas' explicit starting point is the 'holy teaching' of the Bible and the creeds, and his aim is 'to convey the things which belong to the Christian religion in a style serviceable for the training of beginners'. He goes on: 'In order to keep our efforts within definite bounds we must first investigate this holy teaching and find out what it is like and how far it goes.'[58] A distinction is made between examining the God-question 'in the light of natural reason', philosophical theology in our terms, and 'in the light of divine revelation', which Aquinas identifies with his own projected 'theology of holy teaching'.[59] Further, although his own focus will be on the data of the Bible and the creeds, the other sciences can and will be useful in the enterprise:

> Holy teaching can borrow from the other sciences, not from any need to beg from them, but for the greater clarification of the things it conveys. For it takes its principles directly from God through revelation, not from the other sciences. On that account it does not rely on them as though they were in control, for their role is subsidiary and ancillary; so an architect makes use of tradespeople as a statesman employs soldiers. That it turns to them so is not from any lack or insufficiency within itself, but because our understanding is wanting, which is the more readily guided into the world above reason, set forth in holy teaching, through the world of natural reason from which the other sciences take their course.[60]

Well, in point of fact, more than *merely* useful, for his order of theological investigation is the same as Anselm's in *Proslogion* – *Fides Quaerens Intellectum* (faith in search of understanding). Thomas is very confident about the power of philosophy to clarify, and most importantly, about the complementary relationship between the different sciences:

> All the same holy teaching [i.e. Scripture] also uses human reasoning, not indeed to prove the faith, for that would take away from the merit of believing, but to make manifest some implications of its message. Since grace does not scrap nature but brings it to perfection, so also natural reason should assist faith as the natural loving bent of the will

---

[58] *ST* 1a. Prol. and 1,1; Blackfriars, 1.3,5.
[59] *ST* 1a.1,1.2; Blackfriars, 1.9.
[60] *ST* 1a.1,5.2; Blackfriars, 1.19; cf. 1a.1,8.2.

bends to charity. St Paul speaks of *bringing into captivity every under-standing unto the service of Christ*. Hence holy teaching uses the authority of philosophers who have been able to perceive the truth by natural reasoning.[61]

It is to the language and conceptions of philosophy that Thomas turns to explain the foundation, scope and method of his task of explicating holy teaching. For Thomas, theology is the theology of the First Principle upon which everything else in creation depends. These determinative parameters are evident in his early career as he lectured on the *Sentences* of Peter Lombard (1100–60):

> Since sacred doctrine intends to deal with divine things, since also a thing is understood to be divine inasmuch as it is related to God as its principle or its end [*ut principium vel ut finem*] . . . this doctrine will consider things as coming forth from God as from their principle, and as being brought back to God as to their end. Hence, in the first part, he [Peter Lombard] determines about divine things in their proceeding [*exitum*] from their principle, in the second in their returning [*reditum*] to their end . . . The theologian . . . looks at creatures as they come forth from their first principle [*a primo principio*], and as they return to their end, which is God. Hence, the knowledge of the theologian is rightly called divine wisdom, because it considers the highest of all, which is God.[62]

This is no small order or hesitant faith on Thomas' part: every being, every event, every object of nature becomes an object of theology because everything is and can be understood with reference to God. How do all these things relate to God *ut ad principium et finem*? Thomas has already given us his first metaphysical paradigm which, like Augustine, he has taken from Neoplatonism and will use to give intelligibility to theology: they all relate to God (maintaining of course the ontological separation between God and the universe by the characteristic Christian doctrine of creation 'out of nothing') as *exitus et reditus* (progression from God and conversion back to God).

At the beginning of the later *Summa Theologicae*, Thomas makes clear that what follows is the unrolling of that grand plan: 'The

---

[61] *ST* 1a.1,8.2; Blackfriars, 1.31.
[62] I *Sent.*, d.2, div. textus, cited from M.-D. Chenu, *Toward Understanding St Thomas* (Chicago: Henry Regnery, 1964) 306.

fundamental aim of holy teaching is to make God known, not only as he is himself, but as the beginning and end of all things and of reasoning creatures especially.'[63] The structure of the *Summa* precisely follows the Neoplatonic conception of movement to and from divinity:

First Part (I)	Emanation from God, the principle
Second Part 1st half (I–II)	God as the end of humankind
Second Part 2nd half (II–II)	Humankind's return to God
Third Part (III)	Christ as the way of humankind's return to God

At the beginning of the second part, another Neoplatonic tenet occurs to organize and explain his material: 'Now that we have treated of the *exemplar*, i.e. God, and of those things which came forth from the power of God in accordance with His will; it remains for us to treat of His *image*, i.e. man.'[64] But more than Neoplatonism informs Thomas' method.[65] If we ask how the relation between things which have God as their origin and end and God himself is to be explained and understood, the answer comes from Aristotle:

> Though we cannot know what God is, nevertheless this teaching employs an effect of his, of nature or of grace, in place of a definition, and by this means discusses truths about him. Some of the philosophical sciences adopt a similar method, of grounding the argument on the effect, not on the definition, of the cause when demonstrating something about a cause through its effect.[66]

---

[63] *ST* 1a.2 prol; Blackfriars, 2.3.

[64] *ST* 1a2ae.1 prol; Dominican, 6.1, emphasis mine.

[65] The literature on Thomas' appropriation of Neoplatonism is growing apace. The older work of Chenu has much to recommend it, pp. 301–18. Cornelio Fabro's, 'The Overcoming of the Neoplatonic Triad' is a detailed study of Thomas' exposition of the anonymous Neoplatonic work, *De causis*, which is considered to be the final step in the process of his absorption of Neoplatonism. More recently, W.J. Hankey, *God in Himself: Aquinas' Doctrine of God as Expounded in the Summa Theologiae* (Oxford University Press, 1987) is a magisterial study. Two critical but appreciative reviews of Hankey's book offer some balance in the debate: B. Carlos Bazan, *Speculum* 65 (1990) 166–70, and Brian Davies, *Journal of Theological Studies* 40 (1989) 290–4.

[66] *ST* 1a.1,7.2; Blackfriars, 1.27.

Aristotle's contribution

As we noted earlier, Thomas followed Aristotle in asserting that
form determined matter. This view required a theory of causation
to account for the determinative conjunction of form and matter,
the 'effect'. Aristotle pointed to four senses in which the word
'cause' may be used. A cause may be 'formal' – the form which in
conjunction with matter makes the new object a distinct entity;
'material' – the matter upon which the form is imposed; 'final' –
the end which in the process of growth and change determines the
course of the development; and 'efficient' – the motive power which
produces the event. Ultimately there was a First Cause, who, and
this is Thomas' advance over Aristotle, brings into being and
sustains all that is. This new existence of things, their being by
creation, is what links them to God and, in that link, acts as a sign
of their relation to that source.[67] What is characteristic of being,
therefore, is the ability to *act*. The fact that things have been acted
upon, and share in God's action by acting upon other things, defines
being, and is therefore analogous to God's being. Only existing
things can act. To be is to act, to move towards an end. In God, of
necessity, as the First Cause, existence and essence are identical.
This God was the *Unmoved* Mover because, Thomas pointed out,
in him every possible perfection was wholly realized; he, unlike
created substances which were in a state of constant change or
movement towards their ends, has no unrealized potentialities; he
alone is *actus purus*.

Akin to the hierarchy of being in Neoplatonism, a chain of cause
and effect, a chain of being, stretched from earth to heaven, to the
Unmoved Mover who alone as the efficient, formal and final cause
accounted for the existence of the world as a whole. But this chain
of causality is not conceived of as a relay or linkage between two
states of affairs – a parent state and a descendant state – but rather
as a second complementary analysis of any single state of affairs.
Any state of affairs can be analysed as the doing of an agent
pursuing its goal in that matter.[68] The Agent is God, and this gives

---

[67] *ST* 1a.45,5; see David B. Burrell, 'Aquinas and Scotus: Contrary
Patterns for Philosophical Theology', in Bruce D. Marshall (ed.), *Theology
in Dialogue: Essays in Conversation with George Lindbeck* (Indiana:
Notre Dame University Press, 1990) 109–11.
[68] Timothy McDermott, *Summa Theologiae: A Concise Translation*
(Westminster, Maryland: Christian Classics, 1989) xxvi.

Thomas' (and Aristotle's) work its great unity, a unity which can be expressed in terms of *exitus et reditus*. A created being acts upon others by sharing 'in the action proper to another, not by its own power, but instrumentally, as acting in the power of the other'.[69] In the chain of causality, in their very existence, all lower beings are sharing in the one great act of the One Great Agent who, in the eschatological language of 1 Corinthians 15:27–8, will on the last day 'be all in all'.

This then is not a universe where God operates through impersonally operating causes and effects as in, say, the later Newtonian view of things, and in some Protestant understandings of Aquinas. It is *God* who is the first, final, exemplary and efficient cause of every act. The entire created universe and everything in it – its substance (true being), its accidents (qualities), and the mode of relationship which connects one thing to another – are seen as co-inhering in one simultaneous whole. What to us is an immeasurable and puzzling succession of multiple events is in the final vision revealed to us as God sees it. Thus Thomas created a powerful picture of the theocentric unity of all things which was to galvanize generations to follow and inspire the greatest of Italian medieval poets, Dante Alighieri (1265–1321).[70]

The big picture

Using Neoplatonic and Aristotelian philosophical structures, working on the data of the Bible and the creeds, Thomas set out to make God *known* in his relation to everything, whether in the heavens above or on the earth below (cf. Philippians 2:9–11).[71] It is, as Peter Kreeft underlines, truly a powerful picture of cosmic unity. 'God is the ontological heart that pumps the blood through the arteries of creation into the body of the universe, which wears a human face, and receives it back through the veins of man's life of love and will. The structure of the *Summa*, and of the universe, is dynamic. It is not like information in a library, but like blood in a body.'[72] Kreeft's diagram is helpful:

---

[69] *ST* 1a.45,5; Blackfriars, 8.45.
[70] Dorothy L. Sayers and Barbara Reynolds, *The Divine Comedy*, vol. 3, *Paradise*, 18.
[71] *ST* 1a.1,8; 1a.2 prol.
[72] Peter Kreeft, *A Summa of the Summa* (San Francisco: Ignatius Press, 1990) 15.

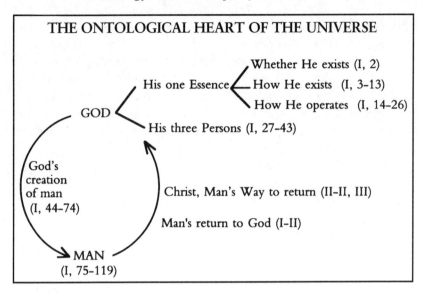

Aquinas Evaluated

Moltmann criticizes Thomas as not having a true theology of hope at all, but an ontology of desire, because his theology of hope is built on the concept of God as the final end. Joseph Merkt has acknowledged that the seminal idea is a definition of hope as a virtue which concentrates on the emotion-of-being-hopeful (*spes passio*) and the goal of a future good which is the beatific vision of God. However, Merkt argues that the emotion-of-being-hopeful is no mere internal feeling in Thomas. In his early commentary on the *Sentences* that deals with hope, Thomas stresses the arduousness of Christian hope due to the great distance between us and God, itself a product of our frailty and God's transcendence. Further, as we see in the 'big picture', *spes passio* must be seen in terms of the motion of the whole cosmos from God and back to him as a dynamic and outwardly directed movement, and not an intense inner desire in the modern romantic sense. Merkt's real defence lies in the observation that Thomas' fully developed doctrine of hope incorporates God's promise of future assistance towards the end goal, as well as the certainty of the presence of divine help now through secondary and created agents. In this way, Merkt argues, Thomas' notion of hope reaches out and embraces 'all of God's governance or providence over the world and His action within salvation history beginning with creation itself'.[73]

---

[73] Merkt, 108; 106–10.

Viewed against his understanding of God as the ontological heart of the universe, it is certainly true that Aquinas' notion of hope is dynamic and big enough to embrace all of creation. But two aspects of Moltmann's criticisms remain. In the New Testament

- the God who brings in the last things is *Deus adventurus* not *finis ultimus*, the God who comes to us, not the unmoved Mover;
- the last things are not the *visio Dei beatifica in patria*, the bliss of pure spirits in the world beyond, but the eschatological promise of the 'new heaven and new earth' – 'Behold, I make all things new' (Rev. 21.5).

Merkt's defence of Thomas on the question of *Deus adventurus*, and that of Louis Week on which he draws, are untenable. They do not meet the points that Moltmann has raised. Further, in their main defence that hope is not something that comes from within the nature of the human person but is the gift of God, they fail to give weight to the fact that such a grace is inexorably connatural.[74] The notion of 'connatural grace' is very important to Aquinas. 'Con-natural' means that a grace arises not only from God but also, in some way at least, from being natural to the human person. 'Hope', like love, must be a truly human habit. However, to say that hope is 'a truly human habit' does not exclude God, for God works also in and through nature. Aquinas' God is not the impersonal, unin-volved God of a later Deism. But, even in God's work in nature, God is working from 'out-there', working along the chain of being, so to speak. In the resurrection hope offered by the New Testament, it is not the working of a God in our world through secondary causes which is promised, but the *direct* work of God himself, *in person*. As Torrance saw earlier, Aquinas' conception of church and world do not quite place church and world under that imminent and fiery judgment which God *himself* brings in 'his coming to us'. In the light of this, it is no surprise that Aquinas' 'new heavens and the new earth' come about by a too-easy transfiguration. Even more tellingly, 'the new heavens and the new earth' become mere meta-phors for the static ontological structures which surround our enjoyment of the beatific vision.

Although philosophically much more sophisticated and coherent than the world-view of Augustine, Aquinas' theological under-standing of the last things is still essentially Ptolemaic, with the

---

[74] Merkt, 110–13.

earth merely transitory and designed to reflect an ultimate heavenly reality. Indeed, Thomas' philosophical theology strengthened the notion that everything which happens on earth corresponds in some way to an eternal pattern in the heavens. This relationship of correspondence is strengthened by Thomas' belief in both the presence of the universals in the particulars, which in turn means that the starting point and controlling factor for knowledge is always 'what is', and the detailed articulation of an *exitus-reditus* scheme, which sought to account for the progression from God, and the conversion into God of absolutely everything in the universe.

Torrance's critique is apposite. Aquinas regarded nature as impregnated with final causes, so that the eternal pattern embedded in nature could be read off by natural theology or deductive science. Likewise the church was regarded as impregnated with the kingdom of God, so that the pattern of the kingdom embedded in the earthly structure of the church could be read off the historical consciousness of the church by those with a teaching office.

In this way the eschaton *is* domesticated and housed within the church. The church does not so much stand under the final judgment as it dispenses it by binding and loosing in the sacrament of penance. Such was the perceived correspondence of the earthly church to the heavenly reality that even though medieval theology formally declared that the jurisdiction of the church on earth did not extend beyond death, the developing doctrine of indulgences promised remission of the temporal penalty of sin, even for the dead already in purgatory. Strictly speaking, such an indulgence for the dead was only a form of prayer and therefore not a heavenly exercise of earthly ecclesiastical jurisdiction, but the Ptolemaic logic of the situation supported the common belief (held, too, by popes and clergy!) that an indulgence was more than a mere petition. Thomas is not directly responsible for the excesses of the doctrine of indulgences, but he so clarified the notions of the intermediate state in terms of an ontological framework of cause and effect that this popular domestication was all but inevitable.

The theological understanding of the last things which Thomas bequeathed to the medieval church reduced the importance of history as the theatre of God's activity, the place where he always manifests his judgment, the place of our present experience of the last judgment (1 Peter 4:17). The major consequence of this was that far from being repentant and reformable, the church could only develop according to her own immanent (i.e. divinely implanted) norms which correspond to the fixed patterns of the kingdom. This eschatology, to say the least, is *a*historical.

However, although Ptolemaic eschatology has the twin disad-vantages of turning eschatology into an ecclesiocentric concept and into a mere transmutation of nature, Aquinas' synthesis has the advantage of making nature serve the ultimate heavenly purposes of God. The now perfected, incorruptible bodies of the blessed are completely under the control of their souls. The soul, now perfectly and properly embodied, is able to exercise all its potentialities in the enjoyment of God in the beatific vision of God. This marks the high point of the medieval understanding of the last things.[75]

But even here we must see that Thomas' Aristotelian approach has limited his Christian appreciation of the last things. God is indeed wonderful, but the 'final vision' of him is not static (an intellectual relationship between 'substances'); it is relational (between persons) and mutual, as the Bible makes plain, for 'the Lord's delight is his people'.[76] And this relational mutuality of knowledge and love and service between the gracious God and his redeemed people is surely a better clue as to why heaven will not be boring. An eschatology rooted in the philosophy of Aristotle and the cosmology of Ptolemy must in the end fail to appreciate the dynamics of relationship as ultimates, because in their view personal relationships seem uniquely characteristic of the inferior nature and thus opposed to a conception of divinity as 'eternal essence' or 'limitless substance'. God as 'limit-less substance' cannot, by definition, find ultimate joy in the love, service and knowledge of man. The bliss that God enjoys in heaven is eternal, but self-centred. Being 'eternal essence' he cannot find true joy in something inferior. On Aquinas' view, eschatological bliss can therefore only be static, and one-way.

And again, even here, in the enraptured contemplation of the Creator by the creature, there is another problem evident. Thomas denies that any actual vision of God can be identified precisely with the object of that vision, that is, God. It is a matter of degree, the degree to which one sees Truth, or Principle. In detailing the vision in terms of understanding species and genus, that is, seeing how everything relates to the great ontological heart, Thomas does not, and cannot, identify the God we gaze on as: 'Father, Son and Holy Spirit'. Nowhere does Thomas say that the vision of God is a vision of the Trinity.

---

[75] Hebblethwaite, 65.
[76] Deut. 32:9,10; Eph. 1:14.

In my estimation this is no incidental omission on Thomas' part, but is consistent with his approach to knowledge of God. Thomas means to start with the creeds, but in building his system he does not start where they do, that is, with the triune God. Thomas does not start with God who is, and is only known, in the relations of Father, Son and Holy Spirit, but, to serve his apologetic purpose, begins with the generalized God of Aristotle and the Neoplatonists who is *principium*, a simple unity. Further, Thomas' use of Aristotelian epistemology swallows up the reliance he really does want to place on biblical revelation. As things can be known only by their effects, and God is known by his effects in creation, the knowledge we have cannot be of God's essence, but only of his existence. Otherwise, we affirm the unchristian doctrine of pantheism. Hidden in the founda-tions of Thomas' *Summa* is an essential split in our knowledge of God: his essence is split from his existence, his person from his activity in the world. The best we can say is what God *is not*; God, in his coming to us in the knowledge we have of him, cannot be personal. Further, and here is the unarticulated embarrassment hidden in Aquinas' approach, because our knowledge of God as a Trinity is also the result of an effect of his in the world – the formation and giving of Holy Scripture – philosophically we cannot equate the triune Person of God with his essence. His essence must remain, essentially, hidden. Therefore, given that God *in se* is Father, Son and Holy Spirit, not only can we not have knowledge of God *in se* in this life, but also not even in the beatific vision of the next. Thomas as a philosophical theologian cannot affirm what he really does want to affirm as a biblical and credal theologian.

But, for all that, for all the essential hiddenness of God in the eschaton, for all the fact that our participation in that God is only by degree, Thomas does affirm the truth that at the heart of this *principium* is Love. In the next generation, Dante (1265–1321) captured in poetry for his and successive ages the grandeur of this ontological vision of Christian reality at the End. His last song in *Paradise* is a fitting, if unintended, tribute to Thomas, and in its trinitarian description, to Thomas the Christian theologian:

> Oh abundant grace, whereby thus daring grown
>   I fixed my vision through the eternal light
>   so far, that sight I wholly spent thereon!   84
> Within its depths I marked how by the might
>   of love the leaves, through all creation strowed,
>   bound in a single volume, there unite;

substance and accidents with each its mode,
   fused as it were together, in such wise
   that as one undivided flame they showed.
Methinks I saw the essential form that ties
   this knot, because I feel, while saying this,
   a more abundant joy within me rise . . .

In that exalted lustre's deep, clear ground
   methought that I beheld three circles flow,
   of threefold hue, in one dimension bound;   117
and one by the other seemed as bow by bow
   reflected, and the third was like a flame
   which equally from either seemed to flow.
How scant is language, all too weak to frame
   my thoughts! And these are such, that, set beside
   my vision, 'faint' is word too weak for them.
O light that aye sole in thyself dost bide,
   sole knowest thyself and, being self-understood
   and knowing dost love thyself, self-satisfied! . . .

Flight too sublime for my own wings to essay,
   had not a flash of insight countervailed,
   and turned my blindness into sudden day.   141
The lofty phantasy here vigour failed;
   but, rolling like a wheel that never jars,
   my will and wish were now by love impelled,
the love that moves the sun and all the stars.[77]

The Apocalyptic Tradition

Alongside of the mainstream of thought typified by Thomas Aquinas was an apocalyptic tradition which reiterated the *temporal* relevance of the last things, and directly tied eschatology to world history. Bernard McGinn has collected representative readings of over sixty writers and movements covering the period 400 to 1500, indicating their roots in the contemporary ups and downs of church and political affairs and their relation to each

---

[77] Geoffrey L. Bickersteth (trans.), *The Paradiso of Dante Alighieri* (Cambridge University Press, 1932) 295–9.

other.[78] They provide 'visions of the End – visions of terror and dread, visions of peace and of glory'.[79] Two will be mentioned here, both from the period of the reformed papacy and the ferment in religious life which accompanied it: Otto of Freising (1114–58), and Joachim of Fiore (1132–1202) who was very influential in the high and late Middle Ages, and on into the Reformation century and beyond.

In her essay on the originality and influence of Joachim of Fiore, Marjorie Reeves points out that both Jews and Christians saw history as moving in one direction to a definite 'end'. The reason for this was the fact that it was in the context of history that God had revealed himself to humankind. The Old and New Testaments disclosed in a 'salvation history' God's providential ordering of world events so that a fallen creation, and especially humankind, might move along the road back to paradise. Living on the other side of the close of the canon of Scripture, Christians had to think through the meaning of contemporary secular history. While they were being persecuted, secular history needed no other meaning than as a manifestation of satan. 'But the recognition of the Church by Constantine necessitated a new effort of the imagination.' The historical imagination of Christians had to be expanded beyond the confines of salvation history to include universal history, and the key to understanding the contemporary operation of God's unfolding providence lay in discovering a way to include Rome within the divine plan.[80]

In the early church, two writers created the framework within which medieval thinkers viewed the meaning of history. Eusebius (*c.* 260–340) in his *History of the Church* gathers the life of the people of God from Abraham to Constantine into one great movement in which the Roman Empire becomes the latest instrument of God. Orosius (early fifth century) expanded the concept of Rome as the chosen nation progressing towards a full Christianity. Orosius' main legacy was in showing the possibility of making a synthesis between national history and biblical exegesis. We have already noted some of the apocalyptic and millennial ways the early church conceived of the end towards which events were marching.

---

[78] Bernard McGinn, *Visions of the End: Apocalyptic Traditions in the Middle Ages* (New York: Columbia University Press, 1979).

[79] Ibid., 1.

[80] Marjorie Reeves, 'The Originality and Influence of Joachim of Fiore', *Traditio* 36 (1980) 270.

In the fifth century Augustine set his face against the optimism of Eusebius and disapproved of Orosius, his one-time disciple. The millennial dream of progress within history, or of a climactic foretaste of the kingdom of Heaven at its end, was effectively relegated to the sidelines. There are 'no verbs of historical movement in the *City of God*, no sense of progress towards ends that may be achieved in history'.[81] However, the affirmation of divine purpose in the secular historiography of Eusebius and Orosius continued to influence a strand of eschatological thinking which came to a high point in the writings and influence of Joachim of Fiore.[82]

Otto of Freising

The investiture struggle and the rise of papal monarchism in the eleventh century, with all its political and ecclesial conflicts, made it possible to wonder what role the popes would play in the last times. The 'Great Reform', as it has been termed, had its most profound repercussions in Germany, the home of the Holy Roman Empire.[83] *Otto of Freising*, monk and bishop, reformer and imperial propagandist, wrote a history of the two cities described by Augustine. Augustine had insisted on the transcendent nature of the city of God. Otto, however, equated this city with the Roman Church, and thus wrote a history of the Church and Empire as cities of God and Man, both now centred on Rome:

Otto made much use of Daniel and Revelation to support and systematize two theories about the course of history:

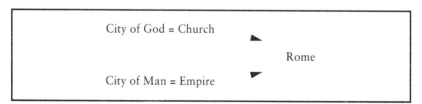

1. The translation (movement) of power and faith from East to West.
   - *translatio imperii* (the translation of imperial power) had by the birth of Christ settled the temporal power in Rome, where it would last until the end of time.

---

[81] Peter Brown, cited in Reeves 'Originality and Influence', 273.

[82] Reeves, 'Originality and Influence', 271–4.

[83] McGinn, *Visons*, 94 ff.

- *translatio religionis* (the translation of religious faith) from the Jews to Christians had finally succeeded after the many difficulties depicted by Revelation and recorded by Eusebius, establishing the Church of Rome.

The Emperor Constantine is depicted as the one who united both streams of prophecy and set the stage for an *indeterminate* millennium of the saints' rule with Christ until his second coming.

2. The Revelation of John depicted the history of the church through three stages:
   (i)   the time from Christ to Constantine
   (ii)   the indeterminate millennium of satan's bondage
   (iii) the final forty-two months of the world's history, during which history would be dominated by plagues and trials preparing the church for Christ's second coming for the purpose of the final judgment.

We need to note, however, that although Otto saw the structures of the prophesies of John as historical, the relevance for the twelfth century and for an indefinite future remained spiritual in nature. During the second stage, the function of the prophecies was to warn Christians of the trials to come and to promise them the final translation of the church to a heavenly state following the judgment.

Although Otto's apocalyptic understanding seeks to add an historical dimension to medieval eschatology, it really does little to challenge the basic philosophical, ahistorical, and church-centred eschatology which approached a peak in Thomas Aquinas. Indeed, as regards the latter parameter, Otto strengthens ecclesiocentricity by centring God's eternal purposes on the earthly Rome.

Joachim of Fiore

Joachim of Fiore's eschatological schema was more innovative, although he too believed that history reflected a divine and prede-termined pattern.[84] Fiore's thought revolves around three central issues: the interpretation of Scripture, the mystery of the Trinity,

---

[84] The literature on Fiore is vast. By way of introduction, see Steven Ozment, *Age of Reform 1250–1550: An Introduction and Religious History of Late Medieval and Reformation Europe* (New Haven: Yale University Press, 1980) 103–8 ff. An excellent critical survey of the issues involved in Joachite studies is Morton W. Bloomfield's, 'Joachim of Fiore: A Critical

and the meaning of history. Joachim, abbot and monastic visionary in Calabria, maintained a consistently literal expectation of the fulfilment of prophecy throughout the history of the church. To him, the seven seals of the Apocalypse symbolize a succession of periods in the church's history from Christ through Constantine and beyond to the end of time.

Joachim was not, for the most part, a systematic thinker: 'often his style is murky and his method rhetorical rather than logical.'[85] He was a lyrical thinker, and systemization of his views runs the risk of doing violence to the reality of his vivid thought. Joachim's unique contribution was to bring together and develop two ideas in a most powerful way: the trinitarian structure of history, in which the Lord of all history is successively revealed as Father, Son and Holy Spirit, and the imminent arrival of a second turning-point (i.e. second to the Christ event) ushering in a blessed time yet to be expected within history.[86]

The whole of universal history fell into three stages, each dominated by a member of the Trinity:

1. The *Age of the Father* was the time until the end of the Old Testament dispensation, from Adam to the birth of Christ, in which humankind lived under the law. This age is characterized by the *ordo conjugatorum* (the order of that which is fleshly). The culture of this age is patriarchal. Here the father-dominated family, in which hierarchical authority reigns supreme, is the model.

2. The *Age of the Son* was the New Testament dispensation, the age of the church to 'these times', which is lived under grace. Joachim thought that this would last for 42 generations of about 30 years each, i.e. 1260 years. This age is characterized by the *ordo clericorum* (the order of the clergy). The culture of

---

[84] *(continued)* Survey of his Canon, Teachings, Sources, Biography and Influence', *Traditio: Studies in Ancient and Medieval History, Thought and Religion* (New York: Fordham Press, 1957) 249–311. More recently, Reeve's 'Originality and Influence' is magisterial. See also Delno C. West and Sandra Zimdars-Swartz, *Joachim of Fiore: A Study in Spiritual Perception and History* (Bloomington: Indiana University Press, 1983), and Bernard McGinn, *The Calabrian Abbot: Joachim of Fiore in the History of Western Thought* (New York: Macmillan, 1985).

[85] Bloomfield, 260.

[86] See Reeves, 'Originality and Influence', 269–97.

this age is priestly-clerical, with many independent units of authority, reflective of the autonomous monasteries and fiefdoms of the Middle Ages.

3. The *Age of the Spirit* will be lived in the liberty of the *spiritualis intellectus* (the spiritual mind) proceeding from the Old Testament and the New Testament, and would be inaugurated around AD 1260. The culture of the dawning age of the Spirit is to be communitarian as monastic values penetrate society at large. Joachim characterized it as an *ordo monachorum* (the order of the monk, or 'solitary dwellers'), an *ordo contemplantium* (order of contemplation). 'Here authority and status are democratized within communities of men and women who consider themselves equals.'[87] In this way, as the Saracens and the Jews were converted, a monastic church would embrace all humankind. This age would see the rise of new religious orders destined to convert the whole world and to usher in the *Ecclesia Spiritualis* (the spiritual or true church). By counting the generations one could calculate the position of the present in the scheme, and the new age was close!

Joachim did maintain that the future remained unknowable in any detail; but he also maintained that Christians did have scriptural assurance of an approaching time of peace and perfection of the Spirit here on earth before the cataclysm of the final judgment.

It needs to be stressed that this is not a simple pattern of progress in which one person of the Trinity succeeds another so as to leave the other behind in a Sabellian fashion. The interpenetration of the persons of the Trinity, their coinherence, is important to Joachim's conception. Often in his thoughts are the 'Wheels of Ezekiel' – wheels within wheels, ultimately drawing history to its focus around the central caption of 'charity' – the symbol of the third stage. The 'verb with which he expresses the relationship of the stages is *inesse*'. There appears in his writings a multilayered structure of significances in which the persons interchange parts, that is, interpenetrate each other. But, none of these complex and shifting patterns detracts from the horizontal thrust of the Abbot's insistence on the age of the Spirit soon to appear.[88]

---

[87] Ozment, 105.
[88] Reeves, 'Originality and Influence', 289–93.

Joachim himself never advanced his doctrine of the third age to a point of danger to ecclesiastical authority. The church would continue to exist, but the sacraments would be spiritualized. The role of the papacy seemed somewhat dubious, but probably the church would continue to be presided over by a purified bishop of Rome. This historical optimism and its implied dethronement of religious power centred on Rome was very influential. Joachism was by its very nature bound to have a political significance that could be used by both optimists and pessimists.[89]

What Joachim meant by spiritualization of the sacraments is not exactly clear. It did at least mean a purification of the earthly church and its ministers. But, however much it is modified, Joachim's position does imply that the New Testament is not the final revelation of God.[90] Certainly, it was on that ground that Thomas Aquinas challenged the Calabrian's philosophy of history. Thomas asks, 'Is the New Law [i.e. the New Testament] to last till the end of the world?' He reviews the possibility of a third age of the Spirit succeeding those of the Father and the Son, and of the first place accorded to clerics concerned with wisdom being given to *spirituales viri* (spiritual men), and concludes, 'No state of our present life can be more perfect than the state of the New Law; for nothing can be closer to the last end than something which immediately leads into it.' The variation that occurs within this perfect state of the New Law is the greater or lesser degree to which the pilgrim receives the grace of the Holy Spirit.[91]

The contribution of Joachim's approach to theology is three-fold. First, it brought contingency, or dependence on the sovereign will of God, much more to centre stage in eschatological under-standing. His most basic tenet was God's active involvement in the three stages of history. Steven Ozment points out that Joachim's prophecy, more than Ockhamist philosophy, stressed to medieval man the contingency of the world as presently experienced.[92] God was in control of the historical future, and it was very different from the church-dominated culture of the present. It was no longer possible to regard the present earthly church as merely the static image of the eternal and the place where God's purposes could not dramatically change their expression.

[89] Bloomfield, 266–70 ff.; cf. Ozment, 106–8. ff.
[90] Bloomfield, 267.
[91] *ST* 1a2ae.106,4; Blackfriars, 13–19.
[92] Ozment, 107.

Second, and related to the first, Joachim's approach involved a decisive rejection of Augustine's conception of the church as the fulfilment of the prophecies of Revelation 20, that is, of the millennium as the age of the church. Against Augustine's view, Joachim stressed that the real millennium, after the overthrow of the Antichrist which would usher in the new age of the Spirit, would entail the purification of the church and the conversion of the heathen. That is, the church as an historical entity was, and would be, reformable in principle. It is difficult to estimate the influence of Joachim's views.[93] Bloomfield's estimation is not injudicious: 'it is at least true that his works and the works associated with his name helped to create the ferment that was eventually, in a few centuries, to make men feel that they were in a new era of rebirth and that a period of darkness lay behind them.'[94] The use of Joachite themes by the radical followers of Francis of Assisi, Petrus Olivi and Ubertino da Casale in the late thirteenth and early fourteenth centuries placed them in direct conflict with the papacy. In the late Medieval, Renaissance and Reformation eras, names such as Dante, Wycliffe, Huss, Christo- pher Columbus, Bullinger, Bale, Knox and Munster are suspected of having been influenced by Joachite writings. Studies are under way on his influence on such nineteenth- and twentieth-century scholars as Schelling, Hegel, Nietzsche, and Jung.[95]

Thirdly, Joachim's approach raised to a new level the question of the relationship between eschatology and historiography. What is the relationship between salvation history and the secular and church history which follows it? Augustine's answer was clear and unequivocal, and remains dominant to this day. The progression of the divine revelation in time reached its consummation in the first advent of Christ. Even though Augustine's schema had symbolic patterns of threes and sevens, and even an eight, it placed the alluring ideas of millennialism and a sabbath age outside history and thus beyond historical speculation.[96] But the old questions remained. Was there to be a final, climactic struggle and period of peace within history before the last judgment? Was the ultimate

---

[93] See especially Reeves, 'Originality and Influence', 297–316; cf. Bloomfield, 294–307; McGinn, 'Calabrian Abbot', 205.

[94] p. 250; cf. McGinn, 'Visions', 129.

[95] West and Zimdars-Swartz, 103–10; but cf. Reeves, 'Originality and Influence', 297–316, esp. 315 ff.

[96] Reeves, 'Originality and Influence', 273.

victorious battle near, or do we have to continue in suffering comforted only by the ministry of the church and the bleak hope of death as personal release? How should change and progress in history be viewed in a Christian way? How do change and diversity relate to unchanging realities? Joachim's historicization of eschatology tied these concerns firmly back into the heart of the knowledge of God as Trinity, and offered concrete, earthly hope, soon. His trinity of the ages corresponded to the divine Trinity, and it satisfied a desire for order and rationality in history. 'Concordance is the key-word for Joachim's method.'[97]

Primary Reading

Thomas Aquinas   'Bodily Resurrection' through to 'The State of the World after the Judgment', in *On the Truth of the Catholic Faith: Summa Contra Gentiles*, book 4 chapters 79 to 97 (New York: University of Notre Dame Press, 1956) pp. 297–349.

Thomas Aquinas   'The Vision of God', in *On the Truth of the Catholic Faith: Summa Contra Gentiles*, book 3 chapters 37 to 63 (New York: University of Notre Dame Press, 1956) pp. 123–208.

Thomas Aquinas   'Hope', *Summa Theologiae* 2a2ae q17–22; Latin text and English translation, Introductions, Notes, Appendices and Glossaries (Blackfriars, with McGraw-Hill: New York) vol. 33 pp. 1–121.

Alighieri Dante   *Paradise*, canto xxxiii, in Dorothy L. Sayers and Barbara Reynolds trans., *Dante, The Divine Comedy 3, Paradise* (London: Penguin Books, 1962) pp. 343–7.

Joachim of Fiore   'Joachim's Vision of the Meaning of Revelation', 'Commentary on an Unknown Prophecy', 'The Three *Status*', 'The Papacy and the Spiritual Men', in Bernard McGinn, *Visions of the End: Apocalyptic Traditions in the Middle Ages* (New York: Columbia University Press, 1979) 130–7.

---

[97] Bloomfield, 264.

OVER COFFEE

- 'Celibacy, for the medieval church, was a means of escaping the body and the world with its shameful desires and lusts.' How may eschatology help account for this view?
- How successfully does millennialism challenge determinism in eschatological thought?
- What did Jesus hope for?
- Does hope remain in heaven?
- How, if at all, can we give the place to eschatology that the Middle Ages did?

6

Faith at the End: Martin Luther

In the last chapter we saw that the prevailing Ptolemaic eschatology, following the logic of its doctrine of God and his relationship to the world, tended to see earthly history, and the earthly church in history, as static. Properly understood, Christian activity was in a mimetic relationship to the heavenly kingdom of God. Earthly history was static because it was determined by fixed heavenly realities. It was not seen as progressive, or developmental, as we now tend to understand history. Further, the church was in essence unreformable.

Not even the radical apocalypticism of Fiore could sufficiently challenge this static view of the church and history. For he too continued to conduct his ordinary Christian activities within a Ptolemaic framework, and thus at almost every point reinforced its dominance. With the rest, Fiore said mass and was a monk. In keeping with life in a sacramental universe, in the mass the offering of the body of Christ (whom the church insisted had died once and for all time on Golgotha) was seen as a definite re-immolation, a re-sacrificing. The logic of the situation demanded it be seen as a re-offering, for within the medieval church's understanding of the relationship between heaven and earth, it is by mimesis that heavenly benefits are bestowed.[1] It was true that it was during his earthly ministry that Jesus Christ had won his

---

[1] Cyprian (248–258) is an early exponent of this view of ministry and mimesis which conforms to those Greek thought forms which saw the relationship between earth and heaven in metaphysical terms of image and reality. The priest 'fulfils the role of Christ when he imitates what he did, and only then does he offer a true, complete sacrifice in the Church to the Father when he begins to offer it after the pattern of Christ's offering.' (*Epistle* 63, cited by J.N.D. Kelly, *Early Christian Doctrines* (London: A. & C. Black, 1965); text in ANF 5.358–64.

merits so as to be able to forgive sins, but now he was the *heavenly* Christ and those merits were in a heavenly treasury. Further, essential to Fiore's view of history was the rise of a purer monasticism, an ideal which he not only prophesied but also actively pursued.[2] The idea of the *vita spiritualis* (spiritual way) underlying such monasticism, with its extreme asceticism to release the soul from the downward pull of the flesh so that it might contemplate God, represents a thorough concession to Platonic religious philosophy and practice in its anthropology and notion of the Christian life as one of the soul's journey from earthly to heavenly realities. The logic of Augustine's synthesis of Neoplatonism and Christianity is again triumphant.

As we continue to trace the development of eschatology, what is of particular interest is that the sixteenth-century Reformers broke the back of Ptolemaic eschatology while at the same time seeing the physical universe and epistemology in Ptolemaic terms. The reason for that success lies in the fact that they struggled to understand the Bible on its own terms, and refused to let the logic of their general Ptolemaic world-view override the implications of the plain teaching of Scripture. The living God of the Bible was rediscovered, the God who actively intervenes in the affairs of humanity and is Lord and Judge of history. Consequently, in a powerful way they realized the historical relevance of eschatology.[3]

Reformation Breakthrough

T.F. Torrance points out that, like earlier Christians the Reformers continued to believe in a heavenly reality overarching the earth and its history. But they asserted their belief in the temporal or earthly relevance of the heavenly realm in a way that denied the metaphysical implications of Ptolemaic cosmology and its consequences for theology. Torrance's most fruitful observation is that they achieved this by thinking election, the beginning, and eschatology, the end, into each other.[4]

---

[2] See Bernard McGinn, *The Calabrian Abbot: Joachim of Fiore in the History of Western Thought* (New York: Macmillan, 1985) 17–30.

[3] T. F. Torrance, 'The Eschatology of the Reformation', in W. Manson (ed.) *Eschatology* (Occasional Paper No. 2, *Scottish Journal of Theology*, 1952) 38.

[4] Ibid. 39.

Martin Luther and John Calvin rejected the medieval doctrine of predestination which had prevailed at least since Peter Lombard. In this understanding, predestination was conceived of as *pars providentiae* (a subset of God's providential care of the world), and election was discussed under the doctrines of God and creation. However, Luther and Calvin placed election where the Bible does, under the doctrines of Christ and salvation. This is most clear in John Calvin who in his Institutes deals with predestination towards the end of his work in book 3, that is, after his treatment of the doctrines of Christ, the cross, sanctification and justification, and prayer, in order to answer the puzzling question of why anyone at all responds to preaching. For Calvin, predestination must always be contemplated 'in Christ', who is both the author and mirror of election.[5] Although Luther does not deal with predestination in the course of a systematic exploration of all of Christian doctrine, from his earliest writings onward he addresses it in the context of grace and salvation.[6] Thus both agreed that predestination should be understood in the light of grace and salvation, that it was uncaused, and that it lay in the absolute will of God. However, there is a difference between Luther and Calvin which centres on how they conceived of the 'absolute will', a difference whose importance we will explore at the end of the chapter.

In three powerful ways, their approach to predestination changes the way we think about how election determines world events, that is, how God operates in the world:

1. The Reformers' strong (Augustinian) doctrine of predestination leaves no room for humanity to influence God in the shape and content he gives to the new creation, or the events which lead

---

[5] *Ins* 3.22.7; *Concerning the Eternal Predestination of God* 8.6, J.K.S. Reid (ed.) (Edinburgh: James Clarke, 1961) 126–30.

[6] E.g. *Lectures on Romans* (1515–16), Luther's Works, American Edition (St Louis: Concordia, 1955–86) vol. 25 pp. 80–3, 162–4, 372–77; *Disputation Against Scholastic Theology* (1517), LW 31.10–11; *A Sermon on Preparing to Die* (1519), LW 42.106–10; *Sermons on the Catholic Epistles* (1523), LW 30.158–9; *Bondage of the Will* (1525), LW 33.138–40; *Lectures on Genesis* (1539), LW 4.142–5; *Appeal for Prayer against the Turks* (1541), LW 43.234–7. For Luther's early understanding and use of the doctrine of predestination see, Heiko A. Oberman, '*Facientibus Quod in Se Est Deus Non Denegrat Gratiam*: Robert Holcot, O.P. and the Beginnings of Luther's Theology', *Harvard Theological Review* 55 (1962) 317–42.

up to it. Many theologians of the medieval period were semi-Augustinian or semi-Pelagian in their treatment of predestina-tion, and thus gave the free or semi-free will of the human person a role in determining whom God would elect to eternal life, and thus a role in giving shape to the End. However, it needs to be strongly emphasized that the particulars of Luther's and Calvin's doctrine of predestination had been commonplace in medieval theology from Augustine onward, and were embraced by influential theologians of both the *via Antiqua* (old) and *via Moderna* (new) strands of scholastic theology.

2. But predestination can no longer be equated with the operation of the secondary causes and effects by which God cares for creation. Election is to personal faith in the gospel promises of the personal God who is our 'Father'. That is, and most especially in Calvin, election to life is the gracious, personal and free choice of God, whose heart beats with fatherly love for his lost creation. Although Thomas Aquinas insisted that it was God who was the first, final, exemplary and efficient cause of every good act, his teachings on secondary causes tended to leave this God somewhat remote from events as the unmoved Mover. This, in spite of his defending the notion that the traces of God in creation can be anchored in the relations of the Persons of the Trinity and are not just marks of the unity of God's nature.[7] In the circumstances Calvin found himself in, a chain of secondary cause and effect looked too much like the atheism and disorder of the 'Epicureans', who deemed God remote and uninvolved with the world.[8]

3. The God who determines events, driving them toward their end in Christ by his electing activity, is not just the God who, in a doctrine of creation considered apart from the doctrine of salvation, is purely heavenly. For this God has entered our history in the person and work of Jesus Christ. God himself has crossed the gap between heaven and earth and continues to

---

[7] *Summa Theologiae*, 1a.45,7; Blackfriars edition, vol. 8 pp. 55–9: 'the likeness of trace concerns those essential attributes of divinity especially accented when we think of one of the Persons;' 'without denying the essential causality proper to the divine nature, the comings forth of the divine Persons are modulating causes and reasons in the doctrine of creation.'

[8] See William J. Bouwsma, *John Calvin: A Sixteenth Century Portrait* (Oxford University Press, 1988) 167–9.

work across that gap, not by the church acting mimetically but personally by his word, the word of the gospel, the Word who is Christ Jesus.

Once removed from the doctrine of creation, predestination cannot mean that there is a predetermined, ontological pattern which can be read-off from the structure of the church on earth, but rather that the whole history of the church, the individual and the world is *contingent* on the *will of God* who is directly carrying out his own personal purposes in the world to gather all things into Christ in his own good time. Further, although the pattern of predestination is discernible in principle, so to speak, *in Christ*, in the Word of the gospel, it remains essentially a mystery and cannot be known in advance, but only from the final end, by apocalyptic manifestation at the advent of Christ. The Bible makes it plain, especially in the vivid and transcendent pictures of the Apocalypse of John, that reality at the end time, although at one level showing some continuity with present Christian experience, is a quantum leap of unfathomable proportions. To look at the earthly church and say, 'There is the mirror image of the New Jerusalem' is to confuse a seed with the plant which grows from it, and that only after the seed has died.[9]

This makes the history of the church essentially ambiguous. The perfect face of the new creation, while partially disclosed in the life of the church and Christians, does not yet fully appear. When the biblical doctrines of election and the last things are thought into each other, Torrance points out, history has a double aspect:[10]

1. There is an earthly future and an earthly consummation by dint of new creation. It is true that eschatology gives meaning to history, but not in the old Ptolemaic way.

    Earthly history is not independent or autonomous as in later secular thinking, but *neither* is its dependence that of a reflection of heavenly reality. The heavenly end in election, which controls earthly history, has moved into time and travels through time – the Christ event and the subsequent promise of new creation show us that. Thus history, because it is dependent only on God's will and nothing else, is not dependent on the church or a heavenly Idea. Because creation is *ex nihilo*, separate

---

[9] Torrance, 'Eschatology of the Reformation', 39–40.
[10] Ibid.

but dependent on God, the history of creation can be understood on its own grounds. Therefore history is significant in
itself, even in a secular interpretation which may not match
ecclesiastical trends!

2. It is only by faith that we may discern the other aspect of history,
   its Christian or eschatological aspect. It is by faith that we
   understand the signs of the times, the faith which has discerned
   the perfect pattern of the kingdom in Jesus Christ, 'the mirror
   of election' (Calvin).[11] Thus Christians can penetrate behind the
   outward facade of history to discern the face of the new creation
   that is about to be revealed. One of the questions we have to
   continually address is what the Bible leads us to expect when
   we penetrate this facade. We have already noted the easy
   conjunction between the secular and churchly history of
   Rome espoused by Eusebius and Freising, and present-day
   ethnocentric millennialism, as answers.

We now turn to look at the eschatological schemata thrown up by
the writings of Martin Luther and John Calvin.

Martin Luther's Eschatology

With good reason, Luther's eschatology has been said to be mainly
an eschatology of judgment, while Calvin's eschatology has been
said to be mainly an eschatology of resurrection. But the distinction
should not be overdrawn.[12] In a homely analogy, Luther insists that
because Christ the Head is already risen, we must think of the
resurrection of the church, which is his Body, as already more than
half behind us. 'As in the birth of man and of all animals, the head
naturally appears first, and after this is born, the whole body
follows easily.'[13]

Nevertheless, the idea that dominates Luther's thought – and
thus makes it thoroughly eschatological – is the dialectic between
heaven and earth, grace and nature, gospel and law. He reacted
strongly against the easy relation of grace and nature and the easy
transfiguration of nature which he found in medieval theology. The
Bible, and experience, convinced him that grace and nature were in
the sharpest tension because nature is radically affected by sin. He

---

[11] Calvin, *Concerning Predestination*, 8.6.
[12] Torrance, 'Eschatology of the Reformation', 40.
[13] *Commentary on 1 Corinthians*, LW 28.110.

saw that the same tension ran clean through the official church from top to bottom. The church lay under judgment.

How did Luther think election and eschatology into each other? We may discern three 'stages', or rather, strands in his eschatological thinking, for mirroring the complexity of 1500 years of Christian reflection on the Bible, church and society, Luther's thought developed on several fronts at once. Three major ideas define Luther's outlook: his apocalyptic view of history, the doctrine of justification by faith alone, and the way he conceived of the relationship between the two ages or two kingdoms.

Apocalypticism

Luther's apocalyptic view of history appears early in his writings, and with some force in his lecture on Psalm 69. He was shocked by the spiritual laxity he saw in his fellow Christians, and later by the opposition of the papal church to his understanding of justification as being by faith, a Christian being *simul justus et peccator* (at the same justified and a sinner), which he saw as the heart of the gospel. This shock led him to see his own period as a fore-shadowing the final judgment of Christ when the children of light would be divided from the children of darkness. He believed that he was living in the last times, and adapted a form of medieval historical apocalypticism influenced by Augustine, Bernard of Clairvaux, Otto of Freising and Joachim of Fiore.[14] Luther's threefold schema looked like this:

THE THREE AGES OF PERSECUTION

	against the	by	defended by
1.	FATHER	TYRANTS (up to Constantine?)	BLOOD of the MARTYRS
2.	SON	HERETICS (up to Chalcedon?)	WRITINGS of CHURCH FATHERS
3.	HOLY SPIRIT	EASE, GOOD WORKS false followers, Antichrist = papacy/Turk	JESUS CHRIST by restoring the light of the gospel

[14] See Heiko Oberman, *Luther: Man between God and the Devil* (New Haven: Yale University Press, 1989) 50–81, for an historical treatment. Some feel for the force and direction of Luther's apocalyptic can be gained from his Prefaces to his translations of Revelations, Daniel and Ezekiel, LW 35; and his commentary on Psalm 69, LW 10.351–402.

Unlike in her two previous temptations or persecutions, the church could expect no relief or salvation from any emperor or temporal ruler in this final temptation of the Antichrist. Only the Lord's return would destroy the *Endechrists Regiment* (kingdom of the Antichrist). The very fact that the Antichrist had been revealed in the papacy (and in the Turk and the Anabaptists) attested to the imminence of Christ's reappearance.

> So I think that now that the Roman Empire is almost gone, Christ's coming is at the door, and the Turk is the empire's token of the end, a parting gift to the Roman Empire.[15]

> It is my belief that the angels are getting ready, putting on their armour and girding their swords about them, for the last day is already breaking, and the angels are preparing for the battle, when they will overthrow the Turks and hurl them along with the pope, to the bottom of hell. The world will perish shortly. Among us there is the greatest ingratitude and contempt for the Word . . . I believe that the last day is not far off, for this reason: the gospel is now making its last effort . . .[16]

> If the last day were not close at hand, it would be no wonder if heaven and earth were to crumble because of such blasphemy [by the papacy in its persecution of Christians who put their faith in God's word, etc.]. However, since God is able to endure this, this day cannot be far off.[17]

> But the last hour has come, as we Christians know, and in it the papacy and its members, as Daniel [11:36] and Paul [II Thess. 2:3–4] say, will be the most terrible example of God's wrath, and the true and final abomination. No power on earth, not even the holy Church itself will destroy it, but only the Lord Christ himself, for by the spirit of his mouth he will slay it, and by his coming he will destroy it [II Thess. 2:8].[18]

---

[15] *On War Against the Turk* (1529), LW 46.199–200. Cf. Luther's view of history in his Psalms lectures of 1513–15, e.g. *First Psalm Lectures: Ps. 69*, LW 10.352–3, 360–3.

[16] Cited from H.T. Kerr, *A Compend of Luther's Theology* (Philadelphia: Westminster, 1943) 244–5.

[17] *On the Councils and the Church* (1539) LW 41.13, see also 150–72 on the marks of the true church on earth and how the devil constantly harries it, especially now.

[18] *Against Hanswurst* (1541), LW 41.244–5.

Until that moment the church must remain as a poor, little band, strengthened by prayer, doctrine, and admonition.

That is where Martin Luther fitted. He identified himself with Noah – one man standing against a licentious, ungrateful world; and through faith enduring terrible temptations and haunting doubts. Jesus Christ was the true Reformer. The church would only be reformed, become fitting as the bride without blemish or spot, when Christ returned. That return would be in Luther's lifetime.[19] Until then, Luther saw his role as urging into the ark as many sinners as possible:

> The number of holy and godly preachers is on the decline. All men yield to their desires. But what will happen is that the last day will come upon the world like a thief (I Thess. 5:2) and will overtake men who in their smugness give free reign to their ambitious desire, tyranny, lusts, greed, and all sorts of vices. Furthermore, Christ has foretold these develop-ments, and so it is impossible for us to believe that He has lied. But if the first world, which had so large a number of most excellent patri-archs, became so pitiably depraved, how much more should we fear when the feebleness of our nature is so great? Therefore may the Lord grant that in faith and in the confession of His Son Jesus Christ we may as quickly as possible be gathered to those fathers and die within twenty years, so that we may not see those terrible woes and afflictions, both spiritual and physical, of the last time. Amen.
>
> Thus it is clear that the smugness of the first world was exceedingly great. Although it had a hundred and twenty years, it stubbornly persisted in its lusts and even laughed at its pontiff, the herald of righteousness, Noah (2 Peter 2:5). Today, when the day of the Lord is drawing near, the situation is almost the same. We urge the papists to repent. We urge and warn our nobleman, burghers, and peasants not to continue to despise the Word; for God will not leave this unavenged. But we are spending our strength in vain, as Scripture says. Few faithful are edified; these are gradually taken away before the calamity, and 'no one understands', as is stated in Is. 57:1. But after the Lord has thus beaten out the wheat and has gathered the grain in its place, what do

---

[19] Luther thought that 1530 was likely to be the year of Jesus' return, and shortly before his death in 1545 he believed it less than 100 years off. Note though that in 1533 Luther dealt severely with Michel Stifel for calculating that the world would end at 8 a.m. on 19th October 1533! See T.F. Torrance, *Kingdom and Church: A Study in the Theology of the Reformation* (Edinburgh: Oliver & Boyd, 1956) 18–21, 20 f.n. 3.

you think will happen to the chaff? It will inevitably be burned with unquenchable fire (Mt. 3:12). This will be the lot of the world.[20]

What is the significance of Luther's apocalypticism? First, it over-throws the easy relation between nature and grace, heaven and earth characteristic of much of scholastic theology. It overthrows it by arguing from the apocalyptic strand of Scripture that the gap is much greater than we have hitherto been willing to admit. In the development of Luther's own thought, it poses more acutely the great question of the medieval church, 'What must I do to be saved?' How is the gap to be bridged so that I can withstand the impending judgment as 'saved' instead of 'sinner'? Secondly, as Heiko Ober-man has highlighted, Luther's formulation of history cuts him off radically from both the world of the Middle Ages and our world.[21] We have here a totally alien Luther, neither modern nor medieval. What characterized Joachim of Fiore's apocalyptic in particular and medieval theories of history in general was the expectation of a messianic reign of peace. The belief in a reign of peace, secularized since the Enlightenment of the eighteenth century, is a major driving force behind the important social and political ideas of contempo-rary western civilization, whether in the former Soviet Union or in the United States. The cataclysms of war and famine in the twentieth century, which have done so much to temper our belief in the possibility of an earthly utopia, have left us still with a firm belief in progress towards some kind of perfection. Against all this, Luther says that only God himself can and will bridge the stark gap between the hopeless mire of human wretchedness and heavenly perfection, and he will do so with fiery judgment.

Justification by faith

The answer to the question about how God saves us in the light of the wrath to come lies in St Paul's teaching on justification. In the doctrine of justification by faith Luther asserted that the believer, although sinner or *peccator*, knew himself to be *justus* or justified by an eschatological act of pure grace which anticipated Christ's ultimate vindication of the sinner at the final judgment. God himself has crossed the gap in the person of Jesus Christ to restore order,

---

[20] *Lectures on Genesis* (1535–6) 5:1, 6:3, LW 1.336; 2.24; see also 2.16–17, 20–5, 49–57, 101–3.
[21] *Man between God and the Devil*, 61–4.

and the nature of this justification, or setting-right, calls for eschato-logical fulfilment. In a structured way in the later Lutheran theology of the *Apologia* for the Augsburg confession (1530), and with less precision in Luther's own writings,[22] the term *imputatio* (imputation) is used to describe the relationship between us as sinners and God's act of justification for us, outside of us. It is used in two ways:

1. *Imputatio* indicates that justification is forensic; it is grounded on the judgment of Christ on the cross which has already occurred.
2. It also indicates that what happened on the cross for us is yet to be fully disclosed at the advent of Christ.

Imputatio is the concept which holds together these two great events in history, the forensic event and the eschatological one:

CROSS ———————————————————— PAROUSIA

forensic   eschaton

imputation

(the Christian is at the same time *justus*, justified, and *peccator*, sinner)

The believer possesses a righteousness which is *real*, though not yet fully *realized*. It is a relationship between having and not-having, and it is at the heart of Martin Luther's eschatology. In the sixteenth-century debate on justification, the Reformers argued that because righteousness is to be primarily thought of as *imputed*, it begs for a later, eschatological realization, or 'impartation'. With St Paul, Luther moved the focal point for the fuller realization of imputed righteousness from the life of the Christian now to the appearance of Jesus at his second coming with its apocalyptic ushering in of the new age.

Therefore Martin Luther's eschatology is neither a realized escha-tology nor a futurist eschatology. It is a dialectical eschatology of *simul justus et peccator*, the Christian is at the same time justified and a sinner. Because of the completed nature of the Christ event, the ultimate has already happened. The end, re-creation and salvation,

---

[22] See Alister McGrath, *Iustitia Dei: A History of the Doctrine of Justification*, 2 vol. (Cambridge University Press, 1986) 2.25, 31–2.

has already come on the cross. It is grasped personally by the Christian in the eschatological moment when he accepts what God has done for him in Christ. The resolution of the dialectic of *simul justus et peccator* comes only at the apocalyptic end of the world.[23]

The two kingdoms

The characteristic way in which Luther stated his whole position was his doctrine of the two kingdoms, the *geistliches Regiment* (spiritual kingdom) and the *weltliches Regiment* (worldly kingdom); which was his way of expressing the biblical doctrine of the two ages:

ou monon en aiōni toutō alla kai en tō mellonti[24]

'not only in this age but also in the age to come'

The Christian who is *simul justus et peccator* lives in two times or two ages.[25] The Christian exists on the boundary of time and

---

[23] Torrance, 'Eschatology of the Reformation', 41–2. For a fuller discussion of Luther's doctrine of justification in its historical context see Alister McGrath, *Iustitia Dei*, both volumes and especially 2.1–32.

[24] Ephesians 1:21. In the New Testament the present and future aeons are mentioned in the Synoptic Gospels, in the Pauline writings, and in Hebrews. In the gospels prominent examples are in Mk. 10:30 (Lk. 18:30); Lk. 16:8; 20:34 f.; Matt. 12:32. In Paul the phrase ὁ τὶ· Α«Ρ«μ occurs seven times – Rom. 12:2; 1 Cor. 1:20; 2:6 twice; 2:8; 3:18; 2 Cor. 4:4; and ὁ τὶ· Α ὁ ΄ΑΒ· μ π«ΑΔ«μ once – Gal. 1:4. This π«ΑΔ«μ is characteristic of the way in which Paul speaks of the present aeon as that of sin. For ὁ τὶ· Α «Ρ«μ there can be substituted ὁ ΅τ ΑΚμ«Ρ«μ (Mk. 10:30; Lk. 18:30), ὁ ΑΡΑ ΅τ ΑΚμ (Rom. 3:26; 8:18; 11:5; 2 Cor. 8:14), ὁ ΅«Β ««μ«Ρ«μ (1 Cor. 3:19; 5:10; 7:31; Eph. 2:2). In the Johannine writings this expression is normally used instead of ὁ τὶ· Α«Ρ«μ, which does not occur – Jn. 8:23; 9:39; 11:9; 12:25, 31; 13:1; 16:11; 18:36; 1 Jn. 4:17. In Heb. 6:5 there is reference to the ¤ΡΑ - ΄Αμ - ΄ΟΟ«Α«μτ ὶ· Αμ, i.e. the pneumatic or angelic powers of the future world whose ministry believers have already experienced, see 1:14.

  In the eschatological framework of the New Testament ὁ τὶ· Α-΄ΟΟ Α is not merely in the future. Believers are already redeemed from this present evil τὶ· Α(Gal. 1:4) and have tasted the powers of the future τὶ· Α(Heb. 6:5). Though as yet concealed from the eyes of men, the new aeon has already begun in and with the resurrection of Christ, inasmuch as this is the beginning of the general resurrection (1 Cor. 15:20, 23).

[25] *Commentary Galatians* 3:23 (1535), LW 26.335–45, esp. 340–3.

eternity. The Christian and the church already live in the end time.[26]

Thus Luther's doctrine of the two kingdoms, the two ages, is primarily dialectical. This poses for us the problem of how we should value history. Apocalyptic pointed not so much to the ongoing kingdom of God in history, as to the abrupt termination of history. Is the only meaning of history, contemporary history, that it is the moment just before the end, the world on the edge of the abyss? Does our earthly history have any meaning beyond this? Is it legitimate to think of history in any real, linear fashion, with all the implications of development and progress that come with it? Has the new creation in any concrete sense started already? We will return to these questions.

The range of expressions Luther used to describe this dialectic demonstrate how foundational the concept is in his thinking: spiritual kingdom / corporeal kingdom; reign of grace / reign of reason; reign of faith / reign of works; reign of Christ / reign of Caesar; eternal kingdom / secular kingdom; empire of believers / empire of sinners; and the like. But, the two regimes are *not* two principalities, excluding each other or competing with each other for rule; they are two overlapping aspects of one *regnum dei invisible* (invisible kingdom of God).

Hence the kingdom of God assumes a *dual* aspect within the world – each inseparable, each distinct from the other. Both are involved in our relation to God the Creator and Redeemer. In the spiritual realm the relationship to the kingdom of God is direct, in the secular, indirect – God's right hand and his left; Word and law:

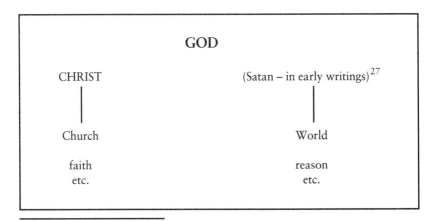

$$GOD$$

CHRIST   (Satan – in early writings)[27]

Church   World

faith   reason
etc.   etc.

[26] See Torrance, *Kingdom and Church*, 16–60 for a detailed exposition.

[27] 'This wretched life is a kingdom of all sin and wickedness, under one lord, the evil spirit, the source and head of all wickedness and sin; but Thy

Luther stressed that to confuse the two kingdoms or to mingle them, as the papacy had with its political pretensions, is the great mark of the Antichrist. Christians as Christians must keep themselves separate from the world, and 'wait'.

Is there any positive connection now between the two kingdoms in history which faith may discern, or have we to wait for the parousia? That is, can we see the grace of God in Jesus Christ working in the world as 'world'? Luther's answer is a tentative and qualified 'yes'. The connection is not concrete, but is the Word of God, which in turn is the divine *ordinatio* (ordinance) which created and recreated. But the Word of God is masked behind the *larva Dei* (mask of God).

The *larva Dei* is a key concept of Luther's which flows from his doctrine of God and expresses his understanding of how God reveals himself in the world. The *larva* is a mask, an actor's mask through which he expresses his character. In the paradox of drama, the mask both reveals and conceals, and suggests a ghostly presence. Luther works with a distinction basic to all scholastic theology but especially prominent in the *Via moderna*, the modern strand. God is understood in two ways. First, 'in himself', in his essence (*quid sit*) where in his majesty he dwells in light inaccessible. Here God, who in the second Person of the Godhead is the Eternal Word, is hidden, *Deus absconditus*, and with his completely sovereign will wields absolute power, *potentia absoluta*, free to decide and do whatever he likes, so long as it is not in contradiction to his nature. This transcendent God, the hidden God, is by definition completely inaccessible to human knowing, unless he chooses to reveal himself, chooses to speak. That is, God is masked by the dazzling glory of

---

[27] *(continued)* kingdom . . .' A Brief Explanation of the Ten Command-ments, the Creed, and the Lord's Prayer (1520), LW 2.377. This work is Luther's, and is indeed the world's first evangelical catechism. His major catechisms appeared 1529 f. Luther has the same thought in a sermon on the Lord's Prayer in 1517: 'To understand this is to know that there are two kingdoms. The first kingdom is a kingdom of the devil . . .', LW 42.38. Later, outside the more immediate context of the Christian life, as political concerns became more pressing, Luther thought more closely about the role of God and worldly princes in this second kingdom. At this stage in his thinking, satan, although active, is not the true head, God is; secular government is understood as 'God's left hand', and the governing author-ity and its sword as a divine servant. The matter is expounded at length in *Temporal Authority: To What Extent it Should be Obeyed* (1523), LW 45.77–129.

his being. Secondly, when he stoops and accommodates himself to our understanding in divine self-disclosure, and supremely in the incarnation, life and death of Jesus Christ, he is the revealed God, *Deus revelatus* in the incarnate Word. In this revelation we see that God in the freedom of his *potentia absoluta* binds himself to work in specified or ordained ways to save his fallen creation, *potentia ordinata*. This revealed God is thus God 'as he is towards us', *qualis sit*, the Word who is Jesus Christ. Here again, Luther saw from his wrestling with his own misery of conscience and the New Testa-ment's presentation of the gospel that God is masked even in his spoken Word. In his revelation in Jesus Christ, in the suffering and humiliation of the cross, he has two masks. To the world, the cross appears as judgment, wrath, humiliation and defeat. To the Chris-tian, that suffering reveals the mercy, triumph and power of God to save. That is, in the world, the Word of God is ghostly, wrathful and masked due to our estrangement. In the church, by the gospel, by preaching and sacrament, we behold a positive *larva dei, unveil-ing* God's mercy and grace in Jesus Christ and establishing the kingdom of God.[28]

It is *faith* which engages us with Christ and his kingdom. Hence Luther's eschatology is titled by T. F. Torrance 'the eschatology of faith'. There is no corporeal or concrete embodiment of the Word, no concrete connection in history between the two kingdoms, like the institutional church as the papal Christians believed. The new creation really remains buried. The world opposes both faith and the Word, and thus the new creation, and therefore the Word, generally bring violence on the world, which is a foretaste of the final judgment of God. For these reasons, in the dialectic between now and not-yet, in a general sort of way apocalyptic functions as the best language for describing a Christian's experience of the kingdom of God. In graphic language which is as foreign as it is repugnant to our modern sensibilities, Luther describes both the assured hope of Christ's kingdom and the failing struggle with satan's:

Now since [the resurrected] Christ has passed over and reigns above in heaven over sin, death, devil and everything, and since He did this for our sake to draw us after Him, we need no longer worry about our

---

[28] For fuller discussions refer to Torrance, *Kingdom and Church*, 34–45; and David C. Steinmetz, 'Luther and the Hidden God' in idem. *Luther in Context* (Bloomington: Indiana University Press, 1986) 23–31.

resurrection and life . . . And in that way we have the two best parts, much more than half, of the resurrection behind us. And because Christ animates and renews the heart by faith, He will also surely drag the decomposed rascal after Him and clothe him again, so that we can behold Him and live with Him . . . No matter when or how God ordains that we die, whether in bed or in the fire, in the water, by rope or by sword, the devil, death's master and butcher, will surely seek to be killing us and carrying out his trade, so that we will not be able to choose or select a mode of death. But no matter how he executes us, it shall not harm us . . . He may now take life and limb while we are lodging here in his inn, where he does nothing but kill and slaughter daily, similar to a hangman or a butcher in a barn filled with sheep. And since we eat and drink in such an inn, we must naturally also pay him for our keep. He dispenses no other food than pestilence and every sickness and pours no other wine or drink than pure poison. Therefore we can expect nothing else than that he will fill us with this and then butcher and flay us.

But with all that done, he has still stripped us of nothing. For the goods and the treasure which we Christians have are not those which the world seeks and possesses in this life on earth. No, we have already secured our possession against the devil, so that he cannot take it from us. It is in the safe custody in this Firstfruits of the dead, who is seated on high, who has ascended from the den of murderers and has taken our life and all with him.[29]

The Christian in the world

What does Luther's eschatology, expressed in his doctrine of the two kingdoms, imply about the role of the Christian in the world? In the face of the fact that apocalyptic points not so much to the ongoing of the kingdom of God in history but to its abrupt termination, we might expect a kind of frightened, or at best scornful, withdrawal from secular matters. But at root, Christian understanding of apocalyptic flows from God's act of justification and the faith it demands. Because justification by faith unites us to Christ, we like Christ are servants of all, and slaves of none. The Christian life, then, is built on God's great act of justification. In the seminal treatise of 1520, *Freedom of a Christian*, Luther sums it up:

---

[29] *Commentary on 1 Corinthians* (1534), LW 28.110–12.

We conclude, therefore, that a Christian lives not in himself, but in Christ and in his neighbour. Otherwise he is not a Christian. He lives in Christ through faith, in his neighbour through love. By faith he is caught up beyond himself into God. By love he descends beneath himself into his neighbour. Yet he always remains in God and in his love.[30]

This thesis marks the beginning of the modern era and the end of the old. No longer are the secular good works of a cobbler inferior to the sacred good works of a monk. 'There is no true, basic difference between laymen and priests, princes and bishops, between religious and secular, except for the sake of office and work, but not for the sake of status . . . A cobbler, a smith, a peasant – each has the work and office of his trade, and yet they are all alike consecrated priests and bishops', writes Luther in 1520.[31] 'All the estates and works of God are to be praised as highly as they can be, and none despised in favor of another . . . God is a great lord and has many kinds of servants.'[32] Nor are good works, secular or sacred, done for the sake of religious self-fulfilment or merit before God. For, because of Christ and faith, one is complete in God and completely in God. The Christian is now free to serve his neighbour for his neighbour's sake, as Christ did. And he must, and does, so serve for that is what a Christian is. Reformation of a Christian, Luther insists, does not entail domination but service of the world.[33]

An extension of justification is that all believers are members of the priesthood. The cobbler and the prince are as much priests in Christ's kingdom as the monk and the pope; and with the same responsibilities to minister the Word and forgive sins. This is the point Luther is making in his statement about the parity between layman and priest. The difference between them is not one of kind, but of time and recognition. The priest has the ministry of the Word full-time, and receives public recognition for this role by ordination. The layman is necessarily engaged in the same ministry, but infor-mally as opportunity presents itself. Thus both advance the spiritual kingdom, the new kingdom of Christ.

Further, both are also members of the old kingdom, the secular one, and thus serve God here too as they serve their neighbours in

---

[30] LW 31.371.
[31] *To the Christian Nobility* (1520), LW 44.129–30.
[32] *A Sermon on Keeping Children in School* (1530), LW 46.246.
[33] Oberman, *Man between God and the Devil*, 64.

good works. Daily work establishes and maintains human relationships. Behind such relationships is God. For this reason, mundane
activities are holy, for they maintain God's world. 'Where such
stations operate as they should, there things go well in the world,
and there is the very righteousness of God. But where such stations
are not maintained, it makes for unrighteousness. Now God declares concerning these stations that they must remain if the world
is to stand.'[34] In this way, 'even the godless may have much about
them that is holy without being saved thereby'.[35]

Although mundane activities maintain God's right order for his
world, they reveal nothing of God to us in themselves, for behind
them, as we have already noted, God is doubly masked – both by
his glory and our faithlessness. Against the medieval *theologia
gloriae* (theology of glory) Luther uncompromisingly asserted the
theologia crucis (theology of the cross). In reality, God is appre-
hended only in the cross, in the suffering and humiliation of Jesus,
and through the ministry of the Word. Further, although Luther
can evaluate daily work positively in terms of its contribution to
joy, its main worth is its holding back of unremitting evil.

Secular government is especially to be esteemed in the task of
restraining wickedness and maintaining order, and is a most fitting
arena for Christians to serve their neighbours in. On behalf of
himself, a Christian will suffer every evil and injustice without
redress, but 'on behalf of others he should and may seek vengeance,
justice, protection, and help, and do as much as he can to achieve
it'.[36] It is the realm of secular government which facilitates this high
calling. Priests serve here too. Faithful preaching of the gospel
creates appropriate attitudes towards civil government and justice.

> Peace, the greatest of earthly goods, in which all other temporal goods
> are included, is really a fruit of true preaching. For where the preaching
> is right, there war and discord and bloodshed do not come; but where
> the preaching is not right, it is no wonder that there is war, or at least
> constant unrest and the desire to fight and to shed blood.[37]

Thus, on the basis his understanding of justification by faith alone,
the priesthood of all believers, and the nature of God's twofold rule

---

[34] *Commentary on Psalm* 111 (1530), LW 13.358.
[35] *Confession Concerning Christ's Supper* (1528), LW 37.635.
[36] LW 34.161.
[37] LW 46.226.

in the world, Luther laicized the clergy, and sanctified the laity not only in their Christian activities but also in their secular occupations. Luther was often consulted by Christian princes seeking Christian guidance on social policy. He wrote letters, treatises and pamphlets on a wide range of issues from schooling to social welfare, trade and usury, marriage, warfare, and jurisprudence. What was the basis of his secular ethical discourse, and how was the Bible used?

The mutual duties of love and helpfulness encompassed life. Instruction in this came from reason and commonsense (*Vernünft*). For Luther, marriage, family, and natural and civil laws in the Roman law tradition were blessed by God and were the pillars of an orderly creation. 'In the preaching office Christ does the whole thing, by his Spirit, but in the worldly kingdom men must act on the basis of reason – wherein the laws also have their origin – for God has subjected temporal rule and all of physical life to reason (Gen. 2.15).'[38]

Luther's views on natural law were unexceptional. Moses' law, the decalogue, was but the clearest expression of it. Christian princes were not bound to embrace Old Testament law in order to rule properly in the secular realm. Reason and imperial (pre-Christian Roman) law would suffice. Against radicals who said that the imperial code was unjust and unchristian, Luther replied that he knew nothing in it which was contrary to God.[39] In his longest treatise on usury, he examines the problem from a number of theological, historical, legal and economic vantage points. His advice is not an inflexible reiteration of the Old Testament's ban on all usury, but control of it by limiting it to about 5%. To ease the unjust burden of a fixed amount of goods or cash having to be paid in perpetuity to the original seller of a property, Luther suggests the Jubilee year of the law of Moses, not as a binding precedent, but as a wise possible solution. After all, God is 'certainly as wise as human reason can be, and we need not be ashamed to keep the law of the Jews in this matter, since it is useful and good.'[40]

In the end, for all his interest in and approval of a wide number of secular pursuits, Luther's estimate of their worth is based on

---

[38] LW 46.242.
[39] 'Letter to Elector Frederick, June 1524', I. D. K. Siggins, *Luther* (Edinburgh: Oliver & Boyd, 1972) 143.
[40] *Trade and Usury* (1524), LW 45.310. See also *How Christians Should Regard Moses* (1525), LW 35.166–7.

spiritual considerations. 'Man's labor is to be his discipline in this life, by which he may keep his flesh in subjection.'[41] His main initial concern for secular government was that its Christian rulers should serve the spiritual realm, the church, by calling a reforming council. As fellow priests, in this matter kings have the same obligation as the pope. His later concern was in the same direction, keeping peace and restraining lawlessness so that the gospel may be heard. Why? Not because of a latent ecclesiastical or clerical-centredness, but because the old kingdom is passing away, and the new and ever-lasting kingdom of Christ, which is established only by his Word, is the all-determinative reality. Luther's Preface to his translation of Ezekiel gives a good summary of these tensions as he articulates his expectations for God's left-handed rule in the secular regimen:

> For so the old, worldly, temporal government remains in all the world, and does not at all prevent the establishment upon earth of the new, spiritual, everlasting rule and kingdom of Christ under it and within it, a kingdom that has its own peculiar nature, as we clearly see. Especially is this the case where there are righteous kings and princes, who in their old government tolerate this new everlasting kingdom of Christ, or who themselves accept it, promote it, and desire as Christians to be in it. Otherwise the greater part of the kings, princes, and lords of the old government hate the new covenant and kingdom of Christ as poi-sonously and bitterly as the Jews at Jerusalem. They persecute it and would wipe it out; and, like the Jews, they go to destruction because of it. That is what happened to Rome; it will happen to others also. Christ's new kingdom must abide for it is promised it shall be an everlasting kingdom, and the old kingdom must perish in the end. It is well to remember, too, that since God himself calls this kingdom a new kingdom, it must be a far more glorious kingdom than the old kingdom was or is. It was God's will to make it a far better kingdom than the old one. Even if this new kingdom had no other glory, this alone would be enough to make it glorious beyond measure: that it is to be an everlasting kingdom that will not come to an end like the old, worldly kingdom.[42]

Luther, then, had no expectation that the new kingdom of Christ would make any significant, let alone permanent, mark on the old,

---

[41] *Exposition of Psalm 127, for the Christians at Riga in Livonia* (1524), LW 45.326.
[42] LW 35.289.

temporary, worldly kingdom; it would just replace it at the last day. In this latter regime it was not the gospel, but commonsense that ruled. Because of what God had done on the cross by way of justification, Christian social involvement was not only necessary, it was motivated by a love of one's neighbour which was essentially devoid of self-interest because it flowed from union with Christ who was the perfect servant of all, yet subject to none. The value of Christian living lay more in it's keeping one focused on Christ in faith, and on one's neighbour by love, than in progress. It is not that Luther denied sanctification outright as basic to Christian experience, but that in the light of the impending last judgment the task at hand was to more clearly and tenaciously grasp Christ and get on with more determined service of one's neighbour. As the clergy were laicized and the laity sanctified, and Christ's return was not yet, Luther's views marked the beginning of a social revolution.

Gains and Problems in Luther

Luther's achievement is monumental. Unlike even Fiore, he broke the back of Ptolemaic eschatology by grasping the implications of the active intervention in human affairs by the living God who is Lord and Judge of history. Apocalyptic showed that the gap be-tween grace and nature, God and his fallen creation was radically greater than hitherto conceived. The doctrine of justification showed that God himself has crossed the gap in the person of his Son to restore order by an eschatological act of pure grace on the cross. The notion of two kingdoms was not new to Luther, and their existence together to form that unity known as Christendom, where citizens were also Christians, was a commonplace. By and large, the medieval church did not make the mistake of confusing the spiritual kingdom, one's churchly activities, with the everyday activities of the temporal kingdom. But the two, as expected of members of one body, were intimately related. God ruled both, and, it was the especial duty and privilege of kings to serve the church, to 'Kiss the Son, lest he be angry and you be destroyed in his way' (Ps. 2). Further, with the rise and dominance of the theory of papal monarchism, Christ's Vicar, his direct vice-regent on earth, was the Roman pontiff. Kings only ruled by the permission of the pope, and wielded the sword on behalf of the church only at his express command. The essential unity of Christendom was expressed in the institution of the papacy. Luther's achievement was to find the point of unity not in the pope but in the active, judging God of the Bible. Everything in all of creation was absolutely contingent on the will of God, under the eschatological judgment of the cross. The church was, and must be, reformable. Under the impact of the incarnate Word's activity, everything could change, and must change, except that Word itself, the word of the gospel.

Luther's achievement was to write a theology which did not have an eschatology, but was an eschatology. Under its impact the Christian life was radically changed, and made devastatingly simple: we live in God by faith and for our neighbour by love. The Christian life consists of hanging on by faith against the unrelent-ing onslaught of hell, and waiting, while serving one's neighbours. Luther's conception not only showed how profoundly eschatologi-cal all of Christian existence is, but also gave us a language in which to express it, that of apocalyptic. This parallels, and to some extent is influenced by, the language he used to describe the believer's experience of justification, as opposed to its content, which he drew from the mystical tradition, using terms such as *Anfechtung* (buffeting/temptation at the hand of God), 'the dark night of the soul', 'the abyss' and the like. In all of this, Luther formed an alternative way of thinking about God's promise for the future which stands beside the eschatology of the Middle Ages (which in both its contemplative and historicizing forms, still powerfully motivates large numbers of those who confess Christ before the world).

However, there are three problems left hanging from Luther's formulation: an elusive assurance about the nature of the final outcome; perplexing questions about the present progress of the kingdom of God on earth and of the individual believer; and a nagging doubt about the language he uses to describe our participation in the kingdom.

First, for all Luther's affirmation of the free grace of God in salvation, his understanding of predestination, which forms the foundation for his approach, has at its heart a nasty doubt intrinsic to his treatment of the 'absolute will' of the electing God. In his most mature work, *The Bondage of the Will*, 1525, fighting off the assault on the grace of God posed by Erasmus' insistence on a freedom being left to the will of humanity even after its fall, Luther insists that only God's will is and must be free, and therefore mankind's will is and must be in bondage. God must be left to be God. God is the cause of both sin and salvation. Humanity sins by compulsion, but not by necessity. God in his predestination in an uncaused way elects some to salvation and reprobates others to damnation. But, objects Erasmus in his appeal to numerous texts of Scripture, Ezekiel 33:11 says, 'I desire not the death of a sinner'. 'Does the good Lord deplore the death of his people which he himself works in them? If he does not will our death and if we nonetheless perish, it is to be imputed to our will.'[43] That is, God's predestination must in some sense be caused and our wills in some sense be free.

Luther's reply is explosive, and devastates Erasmus' denial of free grace. He appeals to the medieval commonplace about the difference between 'God as he is in himself' and 'God as he is towards us', between the unknowable God hidden in his majesty and the God known to faith, revealed in his Word of the cross, that is, between the absolute will within God and an ordained will he exercises in the world. *Deus absconditus* predestines to salvation and damnation. That will we do not know, with that God we have nothing to do. In that will he is completely free. We have to do with *Deus revelatus*, and only that God and his ordained will. It is *Deus revelatus* 'who desires not the death of a sinner'.[44] *Deus revelatus*, 'the good God does not weep over the death of his people which he works in them, but he weeps over the death which he finds in his people and desires to remove it from them'. On the other hand *Deus absconditus*, 'God hidden in his majesty neither weeps nor takes away death, but works life, death, and all in all. For there he has not bound himself by his word, but has kept himself free over all things.'[45] Then to drive the point inexorably home, Luther points to Jesus weeping over Jerusa-lem. 'Jerusalem, Jerusalem, you who kill the prophets and stone those sent to you! How often have I desired to gather your children together, as a hen gathers her chicks under her wings, but you were not willing!' (Mt. 23:37). But that activity cannot be credited to the hidden God of the absolute will. God in himself, *Deus absconditus*, does not weep over the death of sinners, only *Deus revelatus*, God as he is towards us, only the incarnate Word weeps.[46]

In locating the place where God is most God in his hiddenness and opposing it to his revealedness, Luther was at this point following the theological outlook of both scholasticism and mysticism. Although Luther rejected the main tenets of mysticism, from the

---

[43] LW 33.136.
[44] LW 33.138–41.
[45] LW 33.139–40, WA 18.685.18–24.
[46] Cf. *Lectures on Genesis* (1536), LW 2.49–50.

German mystic Tauler (*c.* 1300–61), and even the sixth-century 'founding father' of Latin and German mysticism, Dionysius the Areopagite, he not only appropriated the language of mystical experience to express the experience of being justified by faith but also stressed the ultimate hiddenness of God.[47] Further, the logic implicit and explicit in the scholastic doctrine of God and revelation from Aquinas to Occam, where God can only be known in his effects, whether in nature or Scripture or church, and not in his immutable essence, also prevails here in Luther. Consequently, for the best of reasons, to oppose Erasmus on free will, but with the worst of results, Luther makes a radical split between God in himself and God as he is towards us; and that at the most foundational of places, in his doctrine of predestination. Because of this, the end is not finally assured for the individual believer as regards either its nature or his or her participation in it. *Deus absconditus* is not bound to his word of revelation, to Jesus Christ, but has kept himself free over all things. There is always the possibility, then, that both our acceptance in Christ and the felicitous nature of the promised end may not avail.

Although it is never as starkly stated as in *The Bondage of the Will*, in all his writings on predestination Luther consistently main-tains the split between God hidden and revealed.[48] He did this to safeguard the freedom of God and his grace, and to keep his parishioners away from a speculative predestinarianism which seeks certainty by attempting to peer into the naked majesty of God and finds only 'the abyss of horror and hopelessness'.[49] Luther's

---

[47] See Steven Ozment, *The Age of Reform 1250–1550: An Intellectual and Religious History of Late Medieval and Reformation Europe* (New Haven: Yale University Press, 1980) 115–34, 239–44; Gerhard O. Forde, 'When the Old God's Fail: Martin Luther's Critique of Mysticism', in C. Lindberg (ed.) *Piety, Politics, and Ethics: Reformation Studies in Honor of George Wolfgang Forell* (Kirksville, Missouri: Sixteenth Century Jour-nal & Northeast Missouri State University, 1984) 16; Erwin Iserloh, 'Luther's Christ-Mysticism', in J. Wicks (ed.) *Catholic Scholars Dialogue with Luther* (Chicago: Loyola University Press, 1970) 41; David G. Schmiel, 'Martin Luther's Relationship to the Mystical Tradition', *Concordia Journal* March 1983, 46.

[48] E.g. *Lectures on Romans* (1515–16), LW 25.389; *Sermons on the Catholic Epistle* (1523), LW 30.159; *Lectures on Genesis* (1536), LW 2.48, 72; *Lectures on Genesis* (1539) LW 3.171; *Lectures on Genesis* (1541) LW 5.45; cf. *Appeal for Prayer against the Turks* (1541), LW 43.235–6.

[49] LW 25.389.

doctrine of predestination is so uncompromising that, in order to make some theological sense of the extent of the death of Christ and the predetermined fate of the reprobate, he even briefly enter-tains the thought of Gottschalk (*c.* 804–869), that in an absolute sense Christ did not die for all, but only for the elect.[50] Good reason indeed, then, to keep away from 'the mazes of the Divine Being' characteristic of the hidden God.[51] However, it is abundantly clear that Luther was not happy with the problems thrown up by his formulation of God hidden and revealed. Towards the end of his life, feeling death near,[52] in his long drawn-out series of lectures on Genesis, Luther reminds his listeners of what he had said in *The Bondage of the Will*. He reiterates his distinctions and warnings about the hidden God: 'With regard to God in so far as he has not been revealed, there is no faith, no knowledge, and no under-standing.' We are to flee speculation. In spite of the fact that God has given us the sacraments, absolution, and the rest of the divine ordinances, deep doubt still remains in the hearts of some:

> But you will say: 'I cannot believe'. Thus many are troubled by this trial, and I recall that at Torgau a little woman came to me and complained with tears in her eyes that she could not believe . . . God says to you: 'Behold, you have My Son. Listen to Him', and receive Him. If you do this, you are already sure about your faith and salvation. 'But I do not know', you will say, 'whether I am remaining in faith'. At all events, accept the present promise and the predestination, and do not inquire too curiously about the secret counsels of God. If you believe in the revealed God and accept His Word, He will gradually also reveal the hidden God; for 'he who sees Me also sees the Father', as John 14:9 says. He who rejects the Son also rejects the unrevealed God along with the revealed God. But if you cling to the revealed God with a firm faith, so that your heart is so minded that you will not lose Christ even if you are deprived of everything, then you are most assuredly predestined, and you will understand the hidden God.[53]

---

[50] *Lectures on Romans* (1515–16), LW 25.376.

[51] *Lecture on Genesis* (1536), LW 2.45: 'I follow this general rule: to avoid as much as possible any questions that carry us to the throne of the Supreme Majesty. It is better and safer to stay at the manger of Christ the Man. For there is very great danger in involving oneself in the mazes of the Divine Being.'

[52] LW 5.50.

[53] LW 5.46.

Luther reinforces this again and again by saying that Christ is our God who was made flesh for us, that the highest form of worship he requires is our conviction that he is truthful, that God is well disposed towards us on account of Christ, that we should cling to the Child and Son Jesus Christ because if you have him you also have the hidden God together with him who has been revealed.[54]

At that moment the holy angels over Wittenberg wept tears of joy, but the fact remains that Luther did not, and indeed could not, retract the position he stated in *The Bondage of the Will*, and consistently maintained, even in 1541. It is a contradiction in Luther; his deep piety and trust in God's work on the cross leads his pastoral heart to affirm what his theological mind denies, that the hidden God also weeps over Jerusalem because his Word weeps. David Steinmetz sums it up in these terms: 'The central theological problem for Luther remains the problem of God. The mercy and compassion of God are always set against the background of his hiddenness . . . The thought which terrifies Luther is not that the devil is his enemy but that God might be.'[55] The 'uncertainty principle' in Luther's doctrine of God casts a theological pall over the End, even if existentially its edges can be lifted by appeal to the promise and suffering of the Beloved Son.

The other two problems can be mentioned briefly. May we not expect some manifestation of the coming kingdom of God in terms of its present progress in the world, and in the individual believer as sanctification? From his reading of St Paul, Luther strongly affirmed that we can never progress past Christ and justification by faith, since the saving acts by God through his Son on Good Friday and Easter Sunday are the only grounds on which the believer is justified. In that sense, the most advanced Christian is always a

---

[54] LW 5.47–50 passim; see also LW 4.144–5; 2.49; 25.164. This perspective is not entirely lacking in earlier pastoral works, *A Sermon on Preparing to Die* (1519), LW 42.108–9: 'Thus when you look at Christ and all his saints and delight in the grace of God, who elected them, and continue steadfastly in this joy, then you too are already elected . . . This sign and promise of my salvation [the death of Christ and the Eucharist] will not lie to me or deceive me. It is God who has promised it, and he cannot lie either in words or in deeds. He who thus insists and relies on the sacraments will find that his election and predestination will turn out well without his worry and effort.'

[55] *Luther in Context*, 31.

beginner, and true progress is never to depart from the starting point.[56] In maintaining these Pauline emphases, in comparison to the later Protestant and evangelical tradition, Luther expresses little optimism about personal and corporate sanctification. But in the Acts of the Apostles, and elsewhere, there is an optimism about the movement of the kingdom, against all odds, through the boundaries of ignorance and culture. Therefore, is merely keeping them faithful by the skin of their teeth the Christians' only real expectation for the presence now of God's future? Finally, how adequate is apocalyptic as a language to describe eschatological experience? Are we bound always to be seeing the devil, that bloody butcher, lurking in the shadows?

Primary Reading

Two Kinds of Righteousness (1519), LW 31.293–306.
Preface to the Revelation of St John I (1522) and *II* (1530/1546), LW 35.398–411.
First Lectures on the Psalms, Ps. 69 (1514), LW 10.351–84.

This last is a fine example from the early Luther of his eschatological outlook on history, and the background problems he is wrestling with in the church and his own experience. He writes here as a medieval exegete and 'decodes' the psalm by recourse to historical, tropological, anagogical and allegorical meanings (the last three to unlock the spiritual secrets in the text). Refer to a dictionary of theology, or Heiko Oberman's *Luther: Man between God and the Devil*, 1989, pp. 250–4, for more details on this method. However, this psalm marks a turning point in his approach to Scripture, and is a pointer to how he was to apply his christological insights to the wider question of justification. Watch for his treatment of 'standing' (*substantia*) early in the psalm. Note how he eschews a philosophical treatment and treats it in a way we would recognize as appropriate to biblical theology.

---

[56] 'However, to stand still on God's way means to go backward, and to go forward means ever to begin anew.' *Lectures on Romans*, W. Pauck (trans. and ed.), Library of Christian Classics (Philadephia: Westminster Press, 1961) 370–1.

OVER COFFEE

- How are election and eschatology related? What is the importance of that relationship for Christian living?
- 'God's kingdom may be advanced by Christians and non-Christians alike.' Critically discuss this statement.
- How important is 'apocalyptic' to a Christian view of history?

7

Determined in Christ: John Calvin

The importance of John Calvin to the development of Christian eschatology needs to be appreciated. Without formal theological training, his prodigious intellectual abilities were turned to under-standing the message of Scripture on the basis of a literary approach to the original text. But by the pinnacle of his theological career, which is marked by the 1559 edition of his *Institutes of the Christian Religion*, Calvin had engaged in considerable critical interaction with the theology of the Reformation, the Middle Ages and the church fathers. Four things distinguish Calvin's contribution to the development of eschatology:

1. Throughout his writings, with the exception of his early book, *Psychopannychia* ('soul sleep', an eschatological topic), Calvin's thinking on eschatology forms a very well-integrated system which embraces the whole range of the subject – personal, corporate and universal.
2. His eschatology is not only well informed from the history of theology, but distinctively biblical in its source and expression. Calvin, like his contemporaries, is deeply indebted to the pre-vailing exegetical tradition.[1] However, in comparison, for ex-ample, to Luther's early writings on the Psalms and Romans, he is relatively free from the language and agendas of medieval philosophical theology. Calvin's clarity of expression and con-formity to the thought forms and language of the Bible is one of the reasons his *Institutes* remain in print and appreciated four hundred years later. If we are familiar with the main themes of the Bible, we can understand Calvin.

---

[1] See David C. Steinmetz, 'Calvin and Abraham: The Interpretation of Romans 4 in the Sixteenth Century', *Church History* 57 (1988) 443–55.

3. Most especially, he gave full systematic expression to the place the New Testament gives Jesus Christ and the Spirit in all of theology, including the last things. That is, he is self-consciously trinitarian in his approach.

4. In doing this he offers a resolution of many of the difficulties the church has faced in thinking about eschatology, a resolution which in my opinion is of lasting benefit.

Differences between Calvin and Luther

Although there are many substantial dissimilarities in character, social setting and ideational background between Martin Luther and John Calvin,[2] two important differences in approaching the task of theology in general and eschatology in particular help illuminate Calvin's distinctive contribution to eschatological thought: his use of the Bible and trinitarianism.

Use of the Bible

First, as already signalled, Calvin's approach is what we may term 'biblical theology'. He saw his commentaries and the *Institutes* as complementing one another, the *Institutes* embracing and expanding on the topics or *loci* that the scriptural text itself suggested as important. To put it another way, in the *Institutes* he sought to expound the simple data of the Apostle's Creed in terms of the flow of God's story unfolded in biblical revelation. The result, as we have it in the *Institutes*, is manifestly coherent, but it does not fall victim to its own logic. On the contrary, it is part of Calvin's strength that he reflected the tensions within the biblical material itself; more so than Luther, I would argue. He aimed to provide a work which 'can be a key to open a way for all children of God into a good and right understanding of Holy Scripture'.[3] But,

---

[2] Two biographies in particular throw the contrast into sharp, if unintentional, relief: compare William J. Bouwsma, *John Calvin: A Sixteenth Century Portrait* (Oxford University Press, 1988) and Heiko A. Oberman, *Luther: Man between God and the Devil* (New Haven: Yale University Press, 1989).

[3] *Institutes of the Christian Religion*, 'Subject Matter of the Present Work' (1560), p. 7 in Ford Lewis Battles' translation, Library of Christian Classics (Philadelphia: Westminster, 1960). All citations from Calvin's

'above all, I must urge [them] to have recourse to Scripture in order to weigh the testimonies that I adduce from it.'[4]

The most obvious difference with Luther is that the German did not attempt to write a handbook of systematic theology, let alone one following the major heads of the Creed. As a monk schooled in professional theology, in a sense, Luther inherited his systematic theology. Most of his works, including even his commentaries, are critical adjustments of that system. But the major difference between Calvin and Luther lies in their approaches to the text of the Bible, which helps account for their distinctive emphases in eschatology.

Luther had ushered in a revolution in biblical interpretation which Calvin both accepted and improved on. In brief, Luther had moved Bible reading away from the methods of *lectio divina* which sought to dig out the spiritual secrets below the surface of the text. Luther did this by moving from the fourfold (literal, allegorical, tropological, anagogical) exegetical method of the Middle Ages to a literal-prophetic method, which gave a christological focus to the historical or literal meaning of Scripture, emphasizing promise and faith and the placement of all Bible passages in their wider context of Jesus Christ being the 'Amen' to all of God's promises (2 Cor. 1:20).[5]

---

[3] *(continued)* works are taken from the most modern translations available. For his commentaries on the New Testament, this is the series of translations edited by David W. and Thomas F. Torrance, published by Saint Andrew Press in Edinburgh. For Calvin's commentaries on the Old Testament I have used the nineteenth-century translation of the Calvin Translation Society (CTS). Translations of tracts and treatises are more diverse, and I have tried to indicate their source when a work is first cited. With the exception of Ephesians and Job, translations of sermons date back to the sixteenth century (some have been reproduced by Banner of Truth). Occasionally I have supplied my own translation from the *Corpus Reformatorum* (Brunsvigae: Schwetschke et Filium, 1864–97) which contains the *Calvini Opera*. I have given the CR volume number. For the French and Latin originals of the *Institutes* I have used the *Opera Selecta* (Munich: Chr. Kaiser, 1926–36) edited by Peter Barth and William Niesel.

[4] *Institutes*, 8.

[5] For fuller discussion of this see S. Ozment, *Age of Reform* (New Haven: Yale University Press, 1981) 63–72, which has a detailed discussion and summary of the medieval background and the scholarly debate over Luther; cf. A.E. McGrath, *Luther's Theology of the Cross* (Oxford: Blackwell, 1985) 75–81, McGrath emphasizes Luther's debt to the late medieval hermeneutical tradition; Heiko A. Oberman, *Man between God and the Devil* 168–74, 224, 250–4.

Further to this, Luther redefined the medieval understanding of 'meditation' away from seeking, in an inward way, the application of the secrets of the Bible to one's own soul.[6] For Luther, meditation is 'reading and rereading' (*lectio et relectio*), reading and rereading of the letter, the litero-prophetic flow of the text, wherein lies the spirit of the divine author.[7] And the end result is not an inward directed gaze which says a spiritual journey has begun or the conditions for grace have been fulfilled, but a looking without which recognizes, by faith, that God has already done everything for you outside of you. The clue to successful Bible study is no longer the finding of secret allegories, but the openly demonstrable cohesiveness of the main ideas in the text, the book, and the whole Bible. And of course, how these show that the God whom you have deeply offended by your sin is 'for you'.[8]

Calvin accepted these two advances. In a sense, Luther's revolution had to do with an attitude to Bible reading, the overall approach. Calvin's difference with Luther on the use of the Bible lies more in the 'hands-on' exegetical methods used. This is mainly evident in the different way they wrote Bible commentaries. As T.H.L. Parker has pointed out in his study of the exegetical work of John Calvin, Calvin moved on from the method of interrogating literature pioneered by the humanists, and by Rudolph Agricola in particular. Agricola's method can be summed up in two words, *inventio* and *loci*. *Inventio* was the searching out in a document of its leading concepts, the *loci*. The 'leading concepts', were those which, when taken together, comprehended the meaning of the whole document.[9] This method was favoured by the Lutherans at

---

[6] G.R. Evans, *The Mind of St Bernard of Clairvaux* (Oxford: Clarendon Press, 1983) 44–49 has a more extensive discussion on 'Bernard of Clairvaux' use of the Bible in the Cistercian tradition.

[7] See Heiko A. Oberman, ' "*Iustitia Christi*" and "*Iustitia Dei*": Luther and the Scholastic Doctrines of Justification', *The Dawn of the Reformation* (Edinburgh: T. & T. Clark, 1986) 108–14.

[8] D.R. Reinke, 'From Allegory to Metaphor: More Notes on Luther's Hermeneutical Shift', *Harvard Theological Review* 65 (1973) 386–96, has a very helpful statement of the nature and significance of the change, and summarizes scholarly debate about it to 1973. For a careful analysis and comparison between Luther and medieval commentators on one particular passage of Scripture, see David C. Steinmetz, 'Luther and the Ascent of Jacob's Ladder', *Church History* 55 (1986) 179–92.

[9] T.H.L. Parker, *Calvin's New Testament Commentaries* (London: SCM Press, 1971) 31.

the University of Wittenberg, as well as elsewhere. Parker summarizes its use by Melanchthon, Luther's young and influential colleague: 'The critic's way is one of search and discovery, his purpose is to find and co-ordinate the major concepts, his office to reduce confusion to order.'[10] The Bible commentaries resulting from this approach are characterized by the dominance of concepts arranged under headings. A distinguishing mark of the method is that the explanation of the leading concepts in texts tends to be much more doctrinal in nature than exegetical. In fact, putting together all the concepts produces a systematic theology of the author.

But, for all the humanist flavour of this method, it is not modern, in our terms! The best modern commentaries on the Bible are characterized by continuous exegesis of the language of the text to unfold the field of meanings and associations implicitly contained in the text itself.[11] Humanism did not pioneer this; John Calvin did. In the preface to his commentary on Romans, Calvin gently rejects the method followed by Melanchthon and others. There will be no *loci*, no excursus; an understanding of the total meaning is reached by continuous exegesis and exposition of the language, *perspicuous brevita* (brief clarity) is the phrase he uses.[12] This preface and his commentary on 1 Corinthians 2:11 reveal Calvin's views on his own method: (1) The method is only a means to an end; no final claims should be made for it. The most important thing is that Scripture should be understood. (2) Calvin is completely convinced of the superiority of the method he uses, which is characterized by continuous exegesis and exposition of the language and lucid brevity. (3) In his commentary on 1 Corinthians 2:11, Calvin states once again that the paramount duty of the expositor is to reveal the mind of the writer as it is poured out on the page. Here, two assumptions are involved. (i) The writer is able to give expressions to his thoughts. (ii) The expositor is able to understand that expression. Why is this possible? Because, 'language is the *character mentis* (mark of the mind)'.[13] And in the end, whose mind is exposed? Who is the final author behind the human writer? The mind of God.[14]

---

[10] Parker, 33.
[11] David C. Steinmetz, 'Abraham and the Reformation', in *Luther in Context* (Bloomington: Indiana University Press, 1986) 43.
[12] 'John Calvin to Simon Grynaeus', *Commentary on Romans and Thessalonians*, pp. 1–3.
[13] Parker, 50–6.
[14] *Com 1 Cor.* 2:11.

Where does Luther fit?[15] Although his commentaries never quite show the same studied use of divisions and subdivisions, heads and subheads, as do those of other Reformers who used the *inventio* method, his commentaries on the epistles of St Paul do have a corresponding concentration on *loci*, leading concepts, and more precisely, theological concepts. So much so that, in the absence of a work by Luther devoted to systematically outlining and explain- ing his understanding of the whole counsel of God, these *loci* are most valuable in reconstructing Luther's theological mindset. How- ever, when Luther comments on narrative, another picture emerges. For example, in his commentary on the Noah stories in Genesis 6 to 9, although very verbose and with a predilection to sidetrack on pastoral matters,[16] Luther tends to stick to the storyline and explain all the verses. There are therefore two approaches in Luther, the humanist style of *inventio* and *loci* in commenting on the more doctrinally orientated epistles of the New Testament, and a continuous exegesis of narrative approaching that of Calvin.[17]

However this difference between Luther and Calvin is more than just one of refinement of a method. Calvin has only one method in scriptural exegesis, and he has clearly grasped and expressed its import for Christian thought: continuous exegesis is the best way to expose the mind of God in Holy Scripture, and systematics is the art of embracing and expanding on the topics that the scriptural text itself suggests as important. This indicates that if we are to under- stand Calvin we need first of all to treat him as a biblical theologian, and then as a systematist. In keeping with this, Calvin will be seen as actively seeking to cast his understanding of eschatology in the thought forms of the New Testament.

---

[15] B. Lohse *Martin Luther: An Introduction to His Life and Work* (Edinburgh: T. & T. Clark, 1986) 14–16, and McGrath, *Luther's Theol- ogy of the Cross*, 40–53, have useful discussions on the humanist background to Luther.

[16] See, for example, his exposition of Genesis 6:1–2, LW 2.10–12, and the problems raised by sexual intercourse with demons resulting in the birth of deformed children, a reality which neither Luther nor his audience doubted. As important and useful as this exposition is, Luther admits it is a sidetrack contributing 'nothing to the passage before us'.

[17] In an interesting article comparing Luther with the 'narrative exegesis' approach to Scripture espoused by Brevard Childs and Hans Frei, Mark Ellingsen demonstrates the continuing modernity of Luther's exegetical methods. See Mark Ellingsen, 'Luther as Narrative Exegete', *Journal of Religion* 63 (1983) 394–413.

Trinitarianism: the epistemological relevance of the Holy Spirit

His second major difference from Martin Luther is in Calvin's more thoroughgoing trinitarianism. Much more thoroughly and consistently than any other Reformer, and indeed any other theologian until Karl Barth, Calvin saw in what way Jesus Christ was the ground and grammar of theology, and therefore of eschatology. In the same way that he stabilized the Protestant doctrine of justification by anchoring the insights of Luther more firmly into their christological base (thus saving the doctrine from massive misunderstandings by some of his Swiss and Lutheran contemporaries),[18] Calvin treated Protestant eschatology. This thoroughness is echoed in his treatment of the Spirit. Jürgen Moltmann stands in this line of development.

It is not that Luther was *not* trinitarian, that would be an absurd claim, but that, read against his late medieval background, Luther is in a real sense much more a theologian of the 'Word' than a theologian of 'Christ'. Further, there is not a lot of systematic treatment of the role of the Holy Spirit,[19] as evidenced by Luther's comparatively underdeveloped, somewhat pessimistic view of progress in sanctification in contrast to that of the urban Reformers like Calvin.

Luther's emphasis on the Word springs from the nominalist stress on God in himself being inaccessible – hidden in his majesty and working according to his absolute and secret will, known only in his effects, that is, as he is towards us. Against the older form of scholasticism, nominalism stressed that *the* effect by which God reveals himself is his Word, and especially his contractual word or *pactum* by which he expressed his ordained and public will that defined and restricted how humanity might approach God in the sacraments and the religious life. In nominalist epistemology, because he is not an immediately present object susceptible to our senses, God *cannot* be known directly by intuition but only abstractly: through abstraction from his existence or through abstraction from some other thing. God is not known experientially and directly, but knowledge of him rests solely in statements put out by

---

[18] See Alister E. McGrath, *Iustitia Dei: A History of the Christian Doctrine of Justification*, 2 vols. (Cambridge University Press, 1986) 2.10–39.

[19] For a contrary view see Regin Prenter, *Spiritus Creator: Luther's Concept of the Holy Spirit* (Philadelphia: Fortress, 1953).

the church and in Scripture. These in turn cannot be analysed or rationally understood in terms of the reality they witness to (because God is not known directly), but can only be the target of an essentially blind 'fideism'. That is, not only does everything hang on the words of God in the Bible and the church, but the response must be a literalist faith, or a 'fundamentalism', to use a modern pejorative and risk overstating the case.

In Luther, this tendency can be seen in his unrelenting insistence to the Swiss Reformers at the Marburg Colloquy, and in various associated writings, that when Jesus said, 'this is my body, this is my blood' in the Last Supper, they must believe, contrary to all reason if necessary, that the flesh and blood of our Lord are literally present in the elements of Holy Communion. Of course, at Marburg, Luther did acknowledge the possibility of overthrowing his literal exegesis by showing how it contradicts the teaching of the creeds on the person and work of Jesus Christ, and offered a theological rationale for this in the form of the *communicatio idiomatum* (the communication of the properties): in the Supper, the divine nature of Jesus Christ lends the property of ubiquity (being everywhere) to his human nature. However, a reading of the proceedings at Marburg indicates that these offers are made in scorn as a concession to what he repeatedly labels as the wicked rationalism of the Swiss. What he insists on again and again is that the Swiss must believe the text literally, against all reason, by faith.

T.F. Torrance has argued extensively that Calvin broke the impasse posed by nominalist epistemology between the fideistic knowledge of absent objects which pertains to God and direct or rational knowledge of immediate objects in ordinary life by advancing a position of 'intuitive, audative knowledge of God.'[20] That is, God has made himself known to us personally and presents himself to us in Person as Father, Son and Holy Spirit by and in his Word. God gives himself personally to be known directly in his Word. Thus the words of institution, 'this is my body, this is my blood', must be understood by subordinating them to the thing they witness to: the full humanity of Jesus Christ, now ascended and seated at the right hand of the Father. Therefore they must be understood metaphorically: 'this bread and wine of the Passover feast symbolize

---

[20] 'Knowledge of God and Speech about Him according to John Calvin', *Theology in Reconstruction* (Grand Rapids: Eerdmans, 1975) 76–98; more recently and fully in *The Hermeneutics of John Calvin* (Edinburgh: Scottish Academic Press, 1988).

my body and blood soon to be broken and shed for you on the cross.' This advance by Calvin not only tends to make his theology much more rational (that is, understood against the objective reality of God's being) than Luther's, but also more self-consciously trinitarian. This latter stress is evidenced by the fact that the four books of Calvin's *Institutes* follow the four heads of the Creed: Father, Son, Holy Spirit and church. In this structuring, Calvin is falling back on the approach of Peter Lombard (c. 1095–1169) whose most influential *Four Books of Sentences* objectively summarized the opinions of the church fathers and near contemporaries on Christian doctrine under four heads: (1) the Trinity, (2) Creation and Sin (3) Incarnation and Virtues (4) the Sacraments and the Last Things.

STRUCTURE OF THE INSTITUTES

The structure of Calvin's *Institutes of the Christian Religion* reveals the systematic structure of his theology:

Book 1	Book 2	Book 3	Book 4
Father	**Son**	**Holy Spirit**	**Church**
Creator	Redeemer		
	incarnation and atonement	union with Christ │ faith │	church │ baptism │
	'all parts of our salvation complete in Christ'	repentance │ sanctification │ justification │ election	Lord's Supper │ civil government

To put it another way, the key to Calvin's breakthrough is the epistemological relevance he saw in the Holy Spirit. Why may listening to the gospel lead to a direct, rational apprehension of the God who is really and actually present? Because the Holy Spirit speaks the words of the gospel, and where the Spirit of the Father and the Spirit of the Son is, there is the triune God himself in Person. Calvin's emphasis on the Spirit in the foundations of his theology will be mirrored in his eschatology.

Having considered the differences between Calvin's and Luther's approaches to the use of the Bible and trinitarianism, we can now turn to Calvin's exposition of the great themes of biblical revelation through which he expresses and organizes his systematic under-standing of the last things. Throughout his commentaries and the *Institutes*, Calvin comments on and uses these themes as principles of interpretation.

Three Controlling Pictures

At the basis of John Calvin's eschatology is what we in contem-porary terms would call a 'biblical theology'. Calvin's overarching theological concerns as he thinks about the eschaton come from the patterns he sees in the biblical revelation itself. He sees three major biblical patterns or motifs to be the basis of how we are to reflect on God's final purposes for the world: the kingdom of God, the phenomena of promise and fulfilment, and the pouring out of the Holy Spirit at Pentecost. In contrast to an atomistic approach to eschatology, which is limited to a treatment of the particulars of the last things, Calvin's treatment of them is controlled by three big pictures.

Kingdom of Christ and God

Calvin insists that there are *not* two different kingdoms, but one kingdom of God and Christ; 'God's kingdom . . . is expressly said to be the kingdom of Christ; and why? Because it has been pur-chased for us by his blood.'[21] Although the administration by Christ of this kingdom will change at the last day when he hands it over to the Father (1 Cor. 15:28), Christ's reign remains eternal.[22] Specifically, Christ by his reign does two things: he *restores right-eousness* in God's people,[23] and he renews all things in the *restora-tion of order*.[24] These two effects of the reign of Christ are characteristic emphases in Calvin's writings.

Two observations are in order here. First, the kingdom of God is defined theocentrically and christocentrically as God taking his

---

[21] *Serm Eph.* 5:3–5 (London: Banner of Truth, 1973) 197; CR 79.677–8; *Com Acts* 28:31, etc.
[22] *Com Isa.* 9:7.
[23] *Com 1 Jn.* 3:8.
[24] *Com Mt.* 5:12.

people, the elect, the church, into his rule. This re-ordering or restoration of a fallen humanity is effected by the Word of the gospel. The kingdom of God is therefore not only the *rule* of God but also the *realm* over which he rules, and both find their apotheosis in Jesus Christ, who is not only the perfect Ruler but also the perfect subject, as seen in his perfect obedience to the Father. Secondly, the coming of the kingdom of God is *dynamic*, unlike the rather static conception of scholastic theology. This dynamism can be seen in the following exchange in Calvin's catechism of 1545:

> M: In what sense do you pray this kingdom come?
> C: That the Lord may daily increase the number of the faithful and load them repeatedly with new gifts of his Spirit.
> M: Are these things not done daily?
> C: They are so far done that one can say the kingdom of God is begun. Therefore we pray that he assiduously increase and advance it, until it reach the summit of its power, which we hope for only at the last day, when God, having reduced all creatures to order, will alone be exalted and pre-eminent, and thus be all in all. [25]

Thus the eschatological fellowship, the *coniunctio per Christum* (union with Christ) that is its purpose, is achieved:

> In fact, the kingdom of God is set up and flourishes only when Christ the Mediator unites men to the Father, both pardoned by the free remission of sins and born again to righteousness, so that, while they *begin* the heavenly life on earth, they may always desire to reach heaven, where they will have the complete and full enjoyment of glory. [26]

Promise and fulfilment

Calvin is interested in understanding the meaning of the historical order apparent in biblical revelation. He encapsulates this in his model of promise and fulfilment which, because of the way God has dealt with us in the advent and the ascension of Jesus Christ, is thoroughly eschatological in nature. Three movements are seen here in Calvin's thought:

---

[25] *Catechism of the Church of Geneva* (1545), in J.K.S. Reid, *Calvin: Theological Treatises* (Library of Christian Classics; Philadelphia: Westminster, 1954) 125.
[26] *Com Acts* 28:31; emphasis mine.

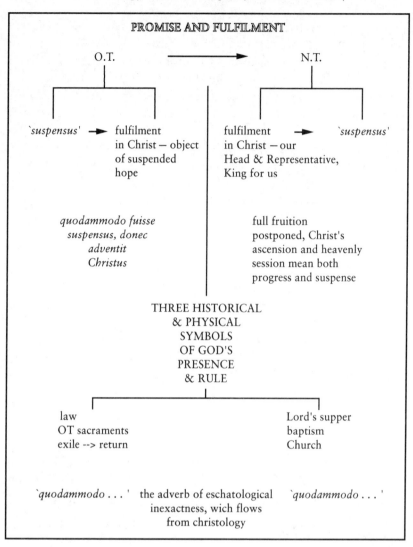

1. The christological description of the fulfilment of promises in the Old and New Testaments.

In the Old Testament all of God's promises to his people find their fulfilment in Christ. The efficacy of the Old Testament covenant lies in this. Until the advent of Christ, 'the promises under the Old Testament were fulfilled to the godly, as far as was good for them, but at the same time they were in a sense suspended till Christ came (*quodammodo fuisse suspensus, donec adventit Christus*)',[27] the

----

[27] *Com 2 Cor.* 1:20.

Object of their suspended hope. On the other hand, the New Testament stands in a back-to-back relationship to the Old Testament: 'The Kingdom of Christ is now a present fact for us . . . the full fruition of which is postponed to the resurrection and the age to come.'[28]

There are two reasons why this is so: First, Christ our Head and Representative, by his birth, life, death, resurrection, ascension, and heavenly session, has received the authority of the kingdom of God for *our* salvation. Secondly, our incarnate Head has ascended into heaven to intercede for us, and to rule his kingdom from there by the power of the Spirit, until his return and the full revelation of his kingship.[29] That is, Christ determines the nature of eschatology, all eschatology.

Hence, and this is most important in Calvin, the full manifestation of the fulfilment of God's promises to his people is in *suspensus* (suspension).

2. The changing symbols of God's presence and rule.

For the sake of our flesh, during our present experience of satanic warfare, God has ordained three symbols of his presence and present rule. These symbols differ in the Old Testament and the New Testament, but their purpose is the same, to nurture our hope. Under the Old, these symbols were the law, the Old Testament sacraments of circumcision and Passover, and the exile with its return. In the New, these symbols of God's dealings with us are the Lord's Supper, baptism, and against all odds, the continued existence of the church.

3. The tension between 'now' and 'not-yet'.

Our present union with Christ, under the condition of suspensus, and the christological reality governing the kingdom mean that the central problem of eschatology is the realization in time of the presence of Christ. Because we are united to Christ, we are in the direct presence of God. That is, because of Christ's union with us, and ours with him, he only reigns in us directly. But because our location is earthly, and he in his incarnate humanity is in heaven (but will one day return), Christ is 'in a manner (*quodammodo*)

---

[28] *Com Heb.* 10:1.
[29] *Com Acts* 1:11.

present with us', and 'in a manner (*quodammodo*) absent'. *Quo-dammodo* functions in Calvin as the adverb of eschatological inexactness!

Outpouring of the Holy Spirit

In book 3 of the *Institutes*, where he examines how we receive the grace of Christ, Calvin begins with a programmatic statement about union with Christ, belief, and the work of the Holy Spirit:

> We must now examine this question. How do we receive those benefits which the Father bestowed on his only-begotten Son – not for Christ's own private use, but that he might enrich poor and needy men? First, we must understand that as long as Christ remains outside of us, and we are separated from him, all that he has suffered and done for the salvation of the human race remains useless and of no value for us. Therefore, to share with us what he has received from the Father, he had to become ours and to dwell within us . . . Yet since we see that not all indiscriminately embrace that communion with Christ which is offered through the gospel, reason itself teaches us to climb higher and to examine into the secret energy of the Spirit, by which we come to enjoy Christ and all his benefits.[30]

Behind this fine trinitarian statement lies Calvin's appreciation of the work of the Spirit.

The outpouring of the Spirit at Pentecost, marks, as it were (*quasi*), the beginning of the reign of Christ and the renewal of the world.[31] It is *quasi*, because properly understood Christ's reign began when God first formed his church by calling it out of exile in Babylon, and again when Christ gathered some of the church by his preaching before his departure. However, the Christian church only began to exist in its proper form (*legitima forma*) when the Spirit was poured out after the ascension of its Lord.[32] The church, then, and the progress of the kingdom of God in the world, undergoes a paradigm shift with the coming of the Spirit promised by the Father, such that it is only by the Spirit that the church can be repaired and a doorway opened 'for us to enter into all the

---

[30] *Ins* 3.1.1.
[31] *Com Acts*, 'Theme'
[32] Ibid.

treasures of spiritual blessings, and even into the kingdom of Heaven'.[33]

But, unlike Augustine and Fiore who tended to leave the Son behind in their understanding of Pentecost and the subsequent history of the church, and for all the radicalism the Spirit's coming brings, Calvin ties his pneumatology very closely to christology. So close that Calvin's stress on the Spirit can be overlooked. For it is Christ, as well as the Father, who sends the Spirit. Why? So as 'to make the whole Church partakers of [Christ's] life'.[34] Calvin is at pains to reflect a trinitarianism he sees in the New Testament where our approach to God is through the Son, in the Spirit, to the Father. This is reflected in his carefully structured comment on baptism and the gifting of the Holy Spirit in Acts 2:38: 'the whole efficacy of baptism is contained in Christ; although Christ cannot be grasped by faith without the Father by whom He was given to us and the Spirit by whom He renews and sanctifies us.'[35]

The role of the Spirit in the progress of the kingdom of God thus follows from the latter's christological definition. Christ is reigning when he subdues the world to himself by the preaching of the gospel.[36] As already stated, it is characteristic of Calvin that God in Christ rules the world through his word of the gospel, not remotely as if by some distant edict, but in person. What distinguishes the Old dispensation from the New is that now, after Pentecost, the same word of God is accompanied by the Spirit of God. This accounts for its present efficacy in the lives of men and women and the extension of God's kingdom beyond Israel to the world.[37] Now, the efficacious work of the Holy Spirit is not just a matter of the anthropological change he brings in renewing our hearts and minds towards the gospel, but primarily lies in the fact that in the preaching of the gospel post-Pentecost, 'God speaks to us openly, as it were face to face, and not under a veil'.[38]

It is in this binding of Word and Spirit together in the preaching of the gospel that the importance of Calvin's pneumatology for his eschatological outlook emerges. Most often, Calvin expresses this in the *Institutes* and in his commentary on John 14–17 and

---

[33] *Com Acts* 2:17.
[34] *Com Acts* 2:32.
[35] *Com Acts* 2:38.
[36] *Com Acts* 1:8.
[37] *Com Jer.* 31:31–2; *Com Acts* 1:6.
[38] Ibid.

1 Corinthians 2 in terms of 'the inner and secret testimony of the Holy Spirit'. This 'inner testimony' has three closely linked meanings in Calvin. First, it is this secret witness, the Holy Spirit in his teaching office, that accounts for belief when the gospel is preached.[39] This aspect of the inner testimony is not, as some misunderstand it, a second revelation beside that of the Scriptures in which the Holy Spirit says extra to Scripture, 'these words are true, believe them'.[40] It is more fundamental. Through the Scriptures we have real, unambiguous knowledge of God, God himself, because in the Scriptures God speaks from the heart about himself, speech which is as persuasive as it is true:

> We ought to remember what I said a bit ago: credibility of doctrine is not established until we are persuaded beyond doubt that God is its author. Thus, the highest proof of Scripture derives in general from the fact that *God in person speaks in it . . . we ought to seek our conviction* in a higher place than human reasons, judgments, or conjectures, that is, *in the secret testimony of the Spirit . . . the testimony of the Spirit is more excellent than all reason.* For as *God alone is a fit witness of himself in his Word,* so also *the Word will not find acceptance in men's hearts before it is sealed by the inward testimony of the Spirit.* The same Spirit, therefore, who has spoken through the mouths of the prophets must penetrate into our hearts to persuade us that they faithfully proclaimed what had been divinely commanded.[41]

In the controversial context thrown up by papal religion and the Anabaptists, who in different ways claimed that the Spirit speaks words extra and other to those of Scripture, commenting on John 14 to 16 Calvin affirms again and again that the content of this inner testimony of the Spirit is the words of scriptural revelation and only those words.[42] These words are to be understood in a trinitarian way. All that Christ has he has from the Father, and that he communicates to us by his Spirit.

---

[39] *Com Acts* 2:38.

[40] For an older, and still apposite, treatment of 'the inner testimony', see Bernard Ramm, *The Witness of the Spirit* (Grand Rapids: Eerdmans, 1959) 11–19.

[41] *Ins* 1.7.4, emphasis mine.

[42] *Com Jn.* 14:26–7, 16:12; 'the Spirit bestows on us nothing apart from Christ; but He takes from Christ what He sheds on us', *Com Jn.* 16:14; 16:25.

Secondly, the Spirit, who is from the Father and the Son, comes from the very heart of the Trinity to bring us the word of that Trinity.[43] That is, it is 'the secret and inner testimony of the Holy Spirit' because the speech the Spirit brings to us is the conversation within God itself. Here Calvin approaches the understanding of Augustine that the Spirit is the mutual possession of Father and Son, their inner communion. It is thus appropriate that in the donation of the Spirit by the Father and the Son we have the gift of God himself, the communication of God's own personal being. This accounts for the vivifying work of the gospel. In the preaching of the gospel it is the Spirit of *God* at work, bringing life to the dead.

Thirdly, and this is treated in more detail in his commentary on 1 Corinthians 2:10–11, the Spirit, who is the Spirit of the Father and the Son, through the words of the gospel which he speaks, lifts us up to heaven itself, into the 'Holy of Holies, inaccessible to men', into the very presence of the Father and the Son. As we have already seen, another way Calvin has of expressing this is union with God, union with Christ. The Spirit unites us to Christ 'as members to the Head, that by hope they posses Heaven along with Him. Hence, the grace of the Spirit is a mirror in which Christ wishes to see Him.'[44] Being lifted up into the very presence of God himself and confronted with his majesty and his very own voice, it is no surprise then that 'He makes us surer of those things which are otherwise hidden from our perception.'[45]

In this way, the Spirit has two functions in Calvin's eschatology. First, Christ's rule by his gospel is direct because it is personal. All of God is present to us in the kingdom work done by the gospel. Then, this work of the Spirit bridges the gap between the now and not-yet. In the now of earthly existence we participate in the not-yet of heaven by the Spirit binding us to Christ, Christ clothed with his promises. Calvin applies the same pneumatological solution to the problem of the presence of Christ in the Lord's Supper. It is not that the humanity of Christ is dragged down from heaven to be localized

---

[43] 'Let us then willingly leave to God the knowledge of himself. For, as Hilary says, he is the one fit witness to himself, and is not known except through himself. But we shall be "leaving it to him" if we conceive him to be as he reveals himself to us, without inquiring about him elsewhere than from his Word.', *Ins* 1.13.21; cf. *Ins* 1.7.4, 1.6.1–2; *Com 1 Cor.* 2:10; *Com Jn.* 15:26–27.

[44] *Com Jn.* 16:16.

[45] *Com 1 Cor.* 2:11.

in the 'now' of the elements, but that, as we testify in that ancient liturgical formula, the *sursum corda* ('lift up your hearts, we lift them up to the Lord'), by faith in the gospel promise the Holy Spirit lifts us up into heaven where we commune with Christ, as 'bone of his bone, flesh of his flesh'.

After elucidating the logic of the eschatological patterns thrown up by the Bible, Calvin turns to more systematic considerations which deal with our present Christian experience. The Genevan applies his three big themes first to secular history and then to the life of the believer.

Applied to Secular History

Our view of the theological nature of history mirrors our view of the nature of eschatological living here and now.

As one might suppose from the promise and fulfilment model, John Calvin's eschatology is thoroughly, but not exclusively, his-torical. He regards history as necessary to faith, and sees God using some unwittingly as his instruments, and others, like John Calvin in aspiration, willingly. God's purpose in history, unveiled in Christ, is the restoration to order of all that is lying waste upon the face of the earth. He is concerned even with the conquest by the gospel of the Antipodes![46]

Secular history and apocalyptic history are inseparable because they witness to the same reality, which is the march of the kingdom of Christ through time, and yet they are distinct, and in that distinction allow comparison in the way they speak of the same truth. In the interpretation of apocalyptic symbolism, allegorization is firmly rejected in favour of a metaphorical explanation which must conform to both salvific and secular history, and natural reality. The ultimate principle for interpreting apocalyptic symbol-ism is the 'purpose' of history, that is, the dramatic unveiling of God's will towards us in the first advent of Jesus Christ.

An example of this approach can be seen in Calvin's comments on the progress of the kingdoms in Daniel from Gold, Silver, Bronze and Iron to Clay. Calvin finds parallels to this metaphor in secular poets who invented fables about the first four kingdoms. But the ultimate explanation comes from the history of salvation, and therefore the five ages in Daniel are witness to a retrogression

---

[46] *Com Mt.* 24:14.

into increasing disorder until the advent of the One who comes to set things right by the proclamation of the gospel and the manifestation of his kingdom. In accord with this sort of accommodation by God in Scripture to our limited understanding, apocalyptic time is symbolic, not literal; and is this way for our comfort and encouragement amidst distress.

More importantly, the kingdom of God's historical nature is seen in its advancement, its progression in time. The kingdom of God increases, stage upon stage, to the end of the world.[47] That is, Calvin is optimistic about history, a theological optimism.[48] However, he is always at pains to stress, on the analogy of the two conditions of Christ's humanity,[49] that this progress is hidden behind the veil of the Suffering Servant, and in the present hour the history of the kingdom of God is experienced as suffering. Calvin's view of Christian history, then, is a modified form of Luther's. If Luther's may be characterized as 'brinkmanship now', Calvin's is 'brinkmanship and progress now'.

In thinking theologically about how the eschaton impinges on history, Calvin emphasizes four things which he considers foundational for our Christian thinking about this theological problem.

Prius of election

Brian Hebblethwaite, finding Calvin's doctrine of predestination 'morally incredible', fails to understand the theological importance of election to the Genevan's eschatological thought.[50] For Calvin, election, the decree of God, is the *prius* (first principle or starting point) of eschatological history. 'Here the prophet understands how nothing happens accidentally, but all things are carried on in the world in their own time as God has decreed them in heaven'.[51] The only way to apprehend this *prius* and gain comforting certainty is through its author, the only and true mirror of election, Jesus Christ:

---

[47] *Com Mt.* 6:10.
[48] See Robert C. Doyle, 'The Search for Theological Models; The Christian in his Society in the Sixteenth, Seventeenth and Nineteenth Centuries', in B. Webb (ed.) *Explorations 3: Christians in Society* (Sydney: Lancer, 1988) 44–8.
[49] See ahead to 'Applied to the Believer'.
[50] *The Christian Hope* (Grand Rapids: Eerdmans, 1984) 79–80.
[51] *Com Dan.* 7:12 etc.

When we talk of this decree we are astonished [dismayed], as men worthy of death, but if Jesus Christ is our guide, we may boldly be merry.[52]

Election, then, is not an abstract and impersonal datum amenable to speculative thinking about 'the hidden recesses of God', but when interpreted in Christ is seen to be the personal and beneficial beginning of God's final purposes.

In the context of thinking about eschatology, two things must be affirmed about election:

1. Election is prescriptive, telling us the way by which God brings us into possession of his kingdom, into salvific union with his Son. That is, election is prescriptive to *faith* in Christ, the only gate into the kingdom of God.[53] This faith is the temporal bridge between the *prius* and *posterius* (end result) of election, 'a certain intermediate passage from eternal predestination to future glory'.[54]

DECREE / ELECTION	HEAVENLY POSSESSION
	OF KINGDOM OF GOD
faith	
PRIUS ►	POSTERIUS

2. The goal of God's decree is the re-ordering or restoration of the whole world in Christ,[55] the extension of the kingdom of God to the furthest limits of the earth and in the heavens, so that all, whether willingly or unwillingly, render obedience to his will.[56] That is, election and God's eschatological purposes are greater than the individual. Further, Calvin stresses, this goal is congruent with the perpetual and Abrahamic covenant that lasts until the renovation of the world.[57] Its fountain, the 'material

---

[52] *Serm 2 Tim.* 1:9–10.
[53] *Eternal Predestination*, 'Author's Introduction', trans. J.K.S. Reid (London: James Clarke, 1961) 50.
[54] *Ins* 3.13.4.
[55] *Com Eph.* 1:1–8.
[56] *Catechism* (1545); Reid, 125.
[57] *Com Gen.* 17:7.

cause', is the universal atonement wrought by Christ. The dramatic end and completion of this re-ordering will be the resurrection of both the elect and the reprobate.

Church history

Brian Hebblethwaite highlights the central place Calvin gives to the church in his eschatology. He concludes that Calvin is more confident than Luther about the historical mission of the visible church and its positive role in the ordering of human society in general.[58] But although right about the importance of ecclesiology in Calvin, it is not the visible church as such which is engaged in eschatological restoration, but rather that which forms and re-forms the church.

Calvin does firmly tie the restoration of the world to the course of the church. God's decree to reorder the whole world,

> is very openly manifest in all places and in all events, but he promises that he will do this especially in protecting and delivering his Church, and not without good reason, for the delivery of the Church from its commencement down to the coming of Christ might be called a renewal of the world.[59]

> Because the renewing of the Church would mean the beginning of a new age, Peter refers it to the last days.[60]

> This world is embraced by the eternal condition of the Church.[61]

But eschatological restoration is tied to the course of the church because of the nature of God's rule in his kingdom – he rules by his Word and Spirit. Thus, the renewal that the kingdom of Christ brings is tied to the progress of gospel preaching, its activity in the conversion of the world and the consequent spread of the church.[62] For that reason we can say that 'the Church is Christ's kingdom, [for] he reigns by his Word alone'.[63] Therefore 'the complete reign of God over all' becomes a metaphor for the church.[64]

---

[58] *Christian Hope*, 78–9.
[59] *Com Isa.* 40:5.
[60] *Com Acts* 2:17.
[61] *Com Isa.* 9:6.
[62] *Com Col.* 1:23; *Com Acts*, 'Theme'; *Com Ps.* 22:30, *Com Dan.* 7:27.
[63] *Ins* 4.2.4.
[64] *Com Dan.* 7:27.

The restoration of the church can even be considered as eternal,[65] so long as we realize that this permanence is heavenly, while the earthly church is like shifting tents.[66] Because of the close and necessary tie between the church and the world, eschatological history is metaphorically the history of the Christian church in its trials and tribulations amidst the cosmic and personal upheavals brought by the gospel of the kingdom.[67] Finally, because the sceptre of Christ is his gospel, and this gospel restores order, both individual and corporate, the church *must* be reformed and reformable. Thus the history of the church is a history of reformation, which is only ever an experience of the cross. The triumph of the church, like the permanency of its restoration, is heavenly.

Supra-history

Because our life is hidden in Christ,[68] eschatology is also supra-historical. The 'heavenly' aspect of the kingdom is not only prior, in that Christ possessed supreme power in heaven and earth before his advent; but also because 'he truly inaugurated his kingdom only at his ascension into heaven'.[69] This heavenly aspect means that the kingdom transcends earthly and celestial geography, man's political and personal experience, and history.

Apart from the ascension rendering eschatology essentially heavenly, it also confers three trans-historical benefits on earthbound believers:

1. It keeps their hopes in suspense, and therefore alive in the face of adversity.[70]
2. It means Christ's personal, spiritual presence with all believers to the end of the world.[71]
3. It means Christ's heavenly session on our behalf so that we a) already in our Head possess heaven, b) are given reconciliation with the Father and the possibility of prayer to him, c) having

---

[65] *Com Isa.* 66:22.
[66] *Com Isa.* 54:2.
[67] *Com Acts*, 'Theme'.
[68] *Com Col.* 3:3.
[69] *Ins* 2.16.14.
[70] *Com Mt.* 19:28.
[71] *Catechism* (1545); Reid, 101.

despoiled our enemies by the cross and resurrection he exercises his glorious might in the majesty of heaven over and for the church.

Because Calvin's evaluation of the biblical data sees that the con-tent, or product, of eschatological re-ordering is at its heart a new humankind in fellowship with God in Christ, these three benefits are true and most appropriate experiences of God's end purposes. They are not somehow just secondary, mere foretastes.

In this context Calvin points out that earthly eschatological disturbances and present kingdom benefits – which are the concrete content of our present history – are for the purpose of turning our eyes to contemplate Christ in heaven, where our true treasure and stability are.[72] It is therefore a fundamental error to seek or con-struct the kingdom of God on earth, because it is in reality, *heavenly*; it is only implemented on earth by God's hand through his Word.[73]

Nature

Calvin lets the Pauline perspective of 'the creation groaning in travail, longing for the revelation of the sons of God' impress onto his thinking, and so must tackle the question of how we are to view natural reality in light of the promised end. Several strands in the Genevan's answer should be noted. The disorder apparent in nature is anthropocentric, and accidental to God's purposes. Nature will undergo *transformation*, not transfiguration as in medieval thinking. This re-ordering will mean that there will be no deformity or impermanence in the natural order. Economic and social stability while ephemeral in themselves, hint of this prom-ised end. In general, nature as it sits under the curse now serves as a witness, an example (usually accusatory) of the patience and the hope of the resurrection which the eschatological promises of God call for amongst humanity.[74]

---

[72] *Com Heb.* 13:14.

[73] *Com Isa.* 11:11.

[74] See R.C. Doyle, *The Context of Moral Decision Making in the Writings of John Calvin: The Christological Ethics of Eschatological Order* (Ph.D. Thesis submitted to the University of Aberdeen, 1981) 206–8 for more details.

Applied to the Believer

Living in the last days: the two conditions of the kingdom

Living in the nasty, brutish age which was the sixteenth century, Calvin shows great concern for how believers should perceive their personal relationship to God's end purposes. What sort of 'knowledge of self'[75] should we have in the light of the eschaton? In brief, we are to see that our life is tied to the course of the life of Jesus Christ, and in that is our true self-understanding and comfort.

As far as our place in time is concerned, history is to be understood against the *prius* of election and the *posterius* of that eschatological entity, the kingdom of God. Thus, for the reasons we have already explored in Calvin's understanding of promise and fulfilment, our present situation is defined by two ages: the old world, and the world to come, and these two ages overlap. Further, we live in that overlap, which is defined in terms of the new creation that Christ brings, and is understood in terms subservient to christology.

To put it another way, sometimes Calvin speaks of the kingdom as wholly future, as the fulfilment of blessedness,[76] and occasionally as realized, as the present experience by some of God's judgment at the hands of men.[77] But his emphasis is on the presence of the future, the presence of a trans-historical heaven by a believer's union with Christ in our real historical present. We are thus in a situation of tension. In exploring the meaning of this tension Calvin goes to great lengths to point out that this presence of the future is tied to the humanity of Jesus Christ. And for this reason, this presence of eschatological renewal is to be thought of in terms of *hiddenness*:

> But because the mode in which he reigns is hidden by his flesh, its manifestation is properly delayed until the last day.[78]

> For we have this hope of our resurrection and of our ascension into heaven: that Christ rose again and ascended, and, as Tertullian says, bore the guarantee of our resurrection with him to heaven.[79]

---

[75] *Ins* 1.1.1.
[76] *Com Mt.* 5:6.
[77] *Com Mt.* 7:1.
[78] *Com Lk.* 10:22.
[79] *Ins* 4.17.29.

A wonderful consolation – that children of God who now lie sunk in foulness or are hidden and worthless or even are covered with reproaches will then shine truly and clearly as in a bright and cloudless sky.[80]

We are like dead men departed from this world . . . our life is hidden with God in Jesus Christ.[81]

The apprehension by the Christian believer of his present kingdomly status as christocentric hiddenness can be schematized in the following way:

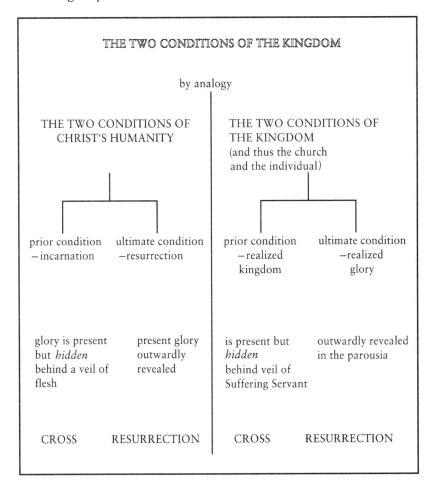

THE TWO CONDITIONS OF THE KINGDOM

by analogy

THE TWO CONDITIONS OF CHRIST'S HUMANITY		THE TWO CONDITIONS OF THE KINGDOM (and thus the church and the individual)	
prior condition – incarnation	ultimate condition – resurrection	prior condition – realized kingdom	ultimate condition – realized glory
glory is present but *hidden* behind a veil of flesh	present glory outwardly revealed	is present but *hidden* behind veil of Suffering Servant	outwardly revealed in the parousia
CROSS	RESURRECTION	CROSS	RESURRECTION

---

80   *Com Mt.* 13:43.
81   *Serm Eph.* 1:13–14.

The Christian then, by analogy to the two conditions of the humanity of Jesus Christ, labours under both the condition of the cross and the condition of the resurrection. Calvin emphasizes both of these in describing the believer's position in the world, but he is especially noted for his use of the resurrection analogy. The resurrection and heavenly ascension of Jesus Christ acts as a sign for us of three realities: (1) that our hope is assured, because this is a visible and historical harbinger of what is to come for us; (2) that we already by dint of union with this Christ participate in heavenly renewal, and is thus a spur to striving for Christ-likeness; and (3) that the history of the church is 'a continuous sequence of resurrections'.[82]

Now, if because of his christological understanding of eschatology Calvin emphasizes the essential ambiguity, humiliation or hiddenness of Christian experience in the church, what are his expectations for civil life?

Living in society

In his reflection on the relationship between society at large and society organized around the Word of God, and the relationship of both to God, John Calvin generally worked within the parameters of Luther's two kingdoms theory. But the Genevan reworked the material along lines which better appreciated the unitary nature of the two Testaments. Calvin saw that the Bible grounds both gospel and law in the person and work of Christ. Because of his more thoroughgoing christological treatment of the problem, Calvin saw more clearly the continuity between nature and grace, God's 'left hand' and 'right hand', while affirming with Luther their radical discontinuity and the limits this places on the theological understanding of Christian social involvement.

However, Calvin's position, with its greater interest in time and history, and the summing up of all things in Christ their Head, has been perceived by some to be not just a fine-tuning of Luther, but much more positive than Luther about the value of Christian civic involvement. So H. Richard Niebuhr will say that Calvin saw Christ and his gospel as the transformer of culture, whilst Luther places the two in paradox, such that Christians in their cultural activities are merely enduring while awaiting a transhistorical

---

[82] *Concerning Scandals*, trans. John W. Fraser (Grand Rapids: Eerdmans, 1978) 46.

salvation.[83] After elucidating Calvin's thinking, we will return to this question.

In the last chapter of the *Institutes* Calvin insists that the qualitative distinction he (in company with Luther) makes between the 'two governments', under the one reign of Christ and God, 'does not lead us to consider the whole nature of [secular] government a thing polluted, which has nothing to do with Christian men'.[84] But in spite of this protest, the sparseness, almost absence, of any direct references to Jesus Christ in his discussion of secular government after his long and thoroughly christological exposition of the Holy Catholic Church, does make their relationship appear somewhat antithetical. However, Calvin has two main ways of explaining the role and significance of secular government which show that it is in essence christocentric, if not in practice: his use of the 'image of God', and a few explicit references to Jesus Christ and the state.

Not only is the image of God in all humankind to impel us to such duties of love as equity, justice, courtesy, and the like,[85] but the same image, precisely because of the order and equity which is inherent in it, can be said to be the ground of our duty to the state and its duty to us:

> ... the image of God which ought to have shone in the magistrate.[86]

> ... no king nor prince in the world should reign with tyranny and pride, but God's image should shine forth in them.[87]

> ... while magistrates ought to bear the image of God, I reply that the order established by God ought to be so highly valued by us as to honor even tyrants when in power.[88]

This ethic-producing image of God to which Calvin appeals can be either the product of creation or redemption.[89] This is because,

---

[83] *Christ and Culture* (London: Faber, 1952) 56.

[84] *Ins* 4.20.2.

[85] *Ins* 3.7.6, *Com Mt.* 5:43, *Com Jn.* 13:34, *Serm Gal.* 6:9–11 where Calvin applies the 'image of God', and our consequent duties towards each other, at all levels of relationship – family, street, state, world, and church; *Ins* 2.8.55.

[86] *Ins* 4.20.24.

[87] *Serm Titus* 2:15–3.2, *Serm Deut.* 5:17.

[88] *Com 1 Pet.* 2:14.

[89] *Com Jas.* 3:9, *Serm Deut.* 5:17, *Com 1 Jn.* 4:17, *Serm Eph.* 1:15–18.

due to the horrible deformity done to the image by Adam's rebellion, we can only really know what it is like from its restoration in Jesus Christ.[90] Typically in his ethical exhortations Calvin brings together both the image of God by dint of creation and by dint of redemption:

> Love is, indeed, extended to those outside, for we are all of the same flesh and are all created in the image of God. But because the image of God shines more brightly in the regenerate, it is proper that the bond of love should be closer among the disciples of Christ. Love seeks its cause in God; from Him it has its root; to Him it is directed . . . Christ here speaks of the highest degree of love; but we ought to believe on the other hand, just as the goodness of God extends to and is shed upon the whole world, so we ought to love all, even those who hate us.[91]

> What is added about the creation may refer either to the first creation of man, or to the reformation effected by the grace of Christ. Both expositions will be true. Adam was at first created in the image of God, so that he might reflect, as in a mirror, the righteousness of God. But that image, having been wiped out by sin, must now be restored in Christ.[92]

In all this, of course, Calvin insists that the image of God is only actually restored by union with Christ by faith, that is, in believers. He is equally insistent that contemplating people in the image of God is contemplating them '*in God*, not in themselves'.[93] Hence the graciousness inherent in the restored image in Christ throws its mantle over all with respect to our perception of our duty towards them; as is witnessed by the fact that this image even 'cancels and effaces their transgression, and with its beauty and symmetry allures us to love and embrace them'.[94] So Calvin in his moral writings often refers to both the original and restored image in the same passage,[95]

---

[90] *Ins* 1.15.4; *Serm Job* 1:6–8; Psychopannychia, in Henry Beveridge and Jules Bonnet eds, *Selected Works of John Calvin: Tracts and Letters*, 7 vols. (Grand Rapids: Baker, 1983) 3.424–5.

[91] *Com Jn.* 13:34.

[92] *Com Eph.* 4:24.

[93] *Ins* 2.8.55.

[94] *Ins* 3.7.6, *Serm Gal.* 5:14–18, *Ins* 3.7.4, cf. *Serm Eph.* 4:1–5.

[95] *Ins* 3.7.6, *Serm 1 Tim.* 2:1–2, *Serm Gal.* 6:9–11, *Serm Eph.* 4:31–5.2, *Serm Job* 31:9–15.

sometimes not even bothering to distinguish between them.[96] Therefore we must say that the state in the image of God also sits under the shadow of Christ.

But Calvin is prepared to go even further than this and talk of the state's direct relationship to our Lord Jesus. The state must 'kiss the Son', who is the redeemer: 'For where David urges all kings and rulers to kiss the Son of God [Ps. 1:12] he does not bid them lay aside their authority and retire to private life, but submit to Christ the power with which they have been invested, that he alone may tower over all . . . He entrusts the condition of the Church to their protection and care'.[97] The magistrate kisses the Son, or acknowledges Christ's rule, by following the church in matters of discipline, 'for a good emperor is within the Church, not over it'.[98] Further, Christ has invested the officers of the state with divine titles, making them nothing less than God's vice-regents. Governments may even be called 'Christian'.[99] Very explicitly, civil government is said to fulfil a vital role in the advancement of the spiritual kingdom of Christ:

> This consideration makes a true king: to recognize himself a minister of God in governing his kingdom . . . He is deceived who looks for enduring prosperity in his kingdom when it is not ruled by God's sceptre, that is, his Holy Word.[100]

> Princes must be protectors of Christianity, and Queens must be nurse-mothers.[101]

Outside of personal example and persuasion, this nursing and protection of the kingdom of Christ consists of defending the Church's doctrine and discipline by the sword.[102] Since, 'unquestionably you see that it is a work of immense difficulty to establish

---

[96] *Ins* 2.8.39–40, *Serm Gal.* 6:9–11.
[97] *Ins* 4.20.5, *Serm 1 Tim.* 2:1–2, 'Letter to King of France, 28 Jan 1561' (refer to last 4 volumes of the 7-volume selection *Selected Works of John Calvin: Tracts and Letters*).
[98] *Ins* 4.11.4.
[99] *Ins* 4.20.3–4.
[100] 'Letter to John Cheke, 13 Feb 1553'.
[101] *Serm 1 Tim.* 2:1–2.
[102] 'Letter to King of Poland, 5 Dec 1554'; *Com Acts*, 'Dedicatory Epistle to second part'.

the heavenly reign of God upon earth',[103] this earthly battle is spoken of in the same terms as the eschatological warfare that the church is involved in.[104]

But there is inevitably a distinct reserve or hiddenness in the state's relationship to its true lord. Partly it is a matter of compre-hension. The state only really grasps its role when its leading officers are converted. Hence Calvin's enthusiastic exhortations, and often misplaced expectations, in his letters to Christian leaders – Edward VI of England, the King of Poland, the King of Navarre, the Count of Wurtemburg, James Stuart, the King-Elect of Denmark and Norway.[105] As he reminds the King of Navarre in a protracted correspondence, the greater the apprehension of Christ, the greater the responsibility to his kingdom and accountability to its King.[106] This indirectness in the relationship is also due to the fact that Christ's kingdom *is* spiritual and heavenly, and therefore only rightly ordered by the Word and the Spirit (as in the church) and not by the sword. In the end, although God has given the power of the sword to rulers, its use is incidental, ineffectual, and full of ambivalence.[107] 'The depravity of the world causes the kingdom of Christ to be established more by the blood of martyrs than by the aid of arms.'[108]

Therefore, because the state is all but blind to Jesus Christ, and because the nature of his kingdom is spiritual, and because of the tension placed on all things because of the double condition of the kingdom, the inherent christocentricity of the state must be muted, and is so in Calvin's exposition. This is congruent with the fact that the image of God, as a natural datum, is only perceived by the believer.[109] This means that the Christian perception of the one kingdom of Christ still requires a twofold government for

---

[103] 'Letter to Nicholas Radziwill, 13 Feb 1555'.

[104] Eg. in 'Letter to King of Navarre, 14 Dec 1557', 'Letter to King of Poland, 5 Dec 1554'.

[105] See variously letters of 4 July 1552, 5 Dec 1554, 14 Dec 1557, 12 July 1558, 11 July 1561; *Com Acts*, 'Dedicatory Epistle to second part'.

[106] 'Letter of 14 Dec 1557'.

[107] *Com Jn.* 18:36; *Com Isa.* 11:4; 'Letter to Joachim Wadian, 24 July 1545'; 'Letter to Bullinger, 24 July 1545'.

[108] *Com Jn.* 18.36.

[109] This was the case with the sailors and Jonah; the sailors, although perceiving that the shedding of blood was against nature, did not know the greater truth of the image of God, and therefore, 'here we must go far beyond them', *Com Jon.* 1:13–14.

humanity. 'One aspect is spiritual, whereby the conscience is instructed in piety and reverencing God; the second is political, whereby man is educated for the duties of humanity and citizen-ship that must be maintained among men'.[110] The civil aspect of Christ's kingdom may be, in a sense, anomalous, but is neverthe-less an act of God's loving power, and it is to beget in us gratitude, and willing obedience.[111]

What were Calvin's expectations for the believer in society, and the society which contained them? The seventeenth-century English Puritans, who rightly or wrongly saw themselves as Calvinists, developed an eschatology which in its optimism for life in the world we might consider 'postmillennial'. As the gospel spread, things would gradually improve until Christ should come, and top-things-off, so to speak. Richard Niebuhr sees Calvin in this optimistic tradition. 'More than Luther he looks for the present permeation of all life by the gospel.' Calvin's characteristic emphases 'lead to the thought that what the gospel promises and makes possible, as divine (not human) possibility, is the transformation of humankind in all its nature and culture into a kingdom of God in which the laws of the kingdom have been written upon the inward parts'.[112]

Undoubtedly the Genevan's careful working out of biblical themes and the consequent christological appreciation of eschatol-ogy make for a much closer identification of the two governments of the one kingdom of Christ and God, and thus open up the way for seeing, and perhaps even promoting, the notion of a rule of Christ in secular society. In review, the specific elements which support this drift start with the fact of the oneness of the kingdom of Christ and God, and with the fact that this kingship is especially understood as the headship of the incarnate One, a headship which, although overwhelmingly speaking of Christ's relationship to the church, is still an anakephalaiosis, a summing up of all things in Christ.[113] Calvin's treatment of the 'dissolving of the elements', and the 'new heavens and the new earth' (2 Peter 3) also tended to treat these as metaphors, emphasizing not discontinuity but continuity,

---

[110] *Ins* 3.19.15, *Com 1 Cor.* 8:6, *Ins* 4.20.1; to be sure Calvin initially confuses the issue a little when in *Ins* 3.19.15 he also, tentatively, calls the two governments, the two kingdoms; but it is an equation that he never repeats.

[111] *Ins* 4.20.1–2, *Serm Job* 36:4–14, *Com Mt.* 22:21.

[112] *Christ and Culture*, 217.

[113] See R.C. Doyle, *Context of Moral Decision Making*, 304–22.

and the present spiritual renovation of the believer. Finally, there is the clear statement by Calvin on Isaiah 35:1 that the promised restoration, the re-ordering of wilderness to habitable land, began with the return from Babylon, which theologically marks the beginning of the kingdom of Christ and its promise of universal restoration 'which will be completed at the Last Day, which on that account is called "the day of renovation and restoration" '.

But against the conclusion drawn by Niebuhr, and others, about Calvin's optimistic view of the operation of the kingdom of Christ in the present world, we need to remind ourselves of his dominant emphases. Christ's kingdom is a *spiritual* kingdom, for not only does its Lord rule by Word and Spirit, but also he in his humanity is ascended to the right hand of the Father, so that 'our life is hid with Christ'. Further, 'meditation on the future life', and *contemptus mundi* (contempt of the world) are the central hallmarks of Christian activity. Niebuhr acknowledges that the social optimism of Calvin is repressed, broken by an eschatology of physical death.[114] Eschatology, yes, but of the risen and reigning Christ who veils his present earthly rule in the church under the form of the Suffering Servant.

Further, this kingdom is shaped in its movement in history and its final form because of its *prius* in the electing activity of God; an election which in time and history is to faith in Christ. There can be no true, real and everlasting manifestation of this kingdom without faith in the Crucified One. Society is not renovated society unless it is a fellowship of believers. There is no real new humanity which is not repentant, believing humanity. What was essentially lost in Adam was faith, and fellowship with God and the rest of humanity. Finally, where a desert is restored, it is *God* who does it as a concomitant of a redeemed community, not man through better agriculture or social engineering. Niebuhr has this right, it is the conversion of man in his culture and his society, not divorced from it, which brings the change.[115] For humankind in fellowship with God is humankind in fellowship with man. On Isaiah 2:4 Calvin comments, 'when the gospel shall be published, it will be an excellent remedy for putting an end to quarrels; and not only so, but that, when resentments have been laid aside, men will be disposed to assist each other.' Yes, we note, there is an optimism

---

[114] *Christ and Culture*, 218.
[115] Op. cit. 56.

here, for this is Calvin's expectation where Christ reigns by Word and Spirit, an expectation which firmly sees Isaiah's promise about 'swords into ploughshares' applying to the present proclamation of the gospel. It will have its fulfilment at the last day, but it begins wherever Christ is honoured. 'The fulfilment of this prophecy in its full extent must not be looked for on earth. It is enough if we experience the beginning, and if, being reconciled to God through Christ, we cultivate mutual friendship, and abstain from doing harm to anyone.'[116]

Evaluation

Luther and Calvin's contributions to eschatological thought spring from their appreciation of the Christ event and the warp and woof of biblical theology. Calvin is characteristically more thorough than Luther. Calvin's genius lies in the fact that he has so much more thoroughly understood that the person and work of Jesus Christ is the ground and interpretative key to the biblical data on eschatology. Four developments follow, three in relation to Luther, and one in relation to their common upset of Ptolemaic eschatology:

1. In line with his healing of the split between Word and Spirit and word and sacrament, Calvin heals the radical split between the being and activity of God, between *Deus absconditis* and *Deus revelatus*, which so bedevilled medieval theology, and Luther. Calvin could never say that 'Jesus weeps, but God in his majesty does not weep' over sinners.[117] For Calvin, God is everywhere 'the Father'; and in dealing with the hidden, secret will of God he ties it to the will and word of God, rejecting the notional distinction between the absolute and the ordained power of God.[118] Further, Calvin explicitly, and implicitly, identifies the

---

[116] *Com Isa.* 2:4.

[117] 'And by His tears He bore witness, not only that He had a brotherly love for those for whose sake He became man but that also there was poured into His human nature by God the spirit of fatherly love.'; *Com Lk.* 19:41.

[118] *Ins* 3.23.2. David C. Steinmetz, 'Calvin and the Absolute Power of God', *Journal of Medieval and Renaissance Studies* 18 (1988) 65–79, reviews Calvin's use of this notion at various points in his writings.

God who makes secret and incomprehensible decisions in predestination and salvation as the Father.[119] Calvin eschews knowledge of God 'as he is in himself' (that is, *quid sit*) in favour of knowledge of 'God as he is towards us' (that is, *qualis sit*). He rejects the first because of its speculative abuses at the hand of the Scholastics.[120] From knowledge of God as he is towards us, Calvin moves to God as he is in himself. God may speak sparingly of his essence, but speak he does, and that trinitarian word is to be believed with joy.[121] The God revealed in Jesus Christ *is* God. Hence, in a way that is somewhat dissimilar to Luther, our assurance of the end, both as to its nature and our participation in it, is certain.

2. Calvin's understanding of the nature of the kingdom of Christ as the dynamic and personal rule of Christ in the world by the inner and secret energy of the Spirit through the preaching of the gospel makes it clear that we may expect some manifestation of the coming kingdom of God in terms of its present progress in the world and in the individual believer as sanctification. The existential experience of life-long regeneration, or sanctification, is repentance, which in turn has two parts: mortification and vivification. Calvin's stress on mortification in terms of self-denial and *contemptus mundi* (contempt for the world) certainly makes him appear pessimistic about individual progress,[122] but such denial is to deal with the fierceness of *philoutia*, self-love, so that we may by meditating on the glory of the future life be free to cast our faith upon God and love our

---

[119] 'It is the Father's good pleasure to both forgive sins by his own free decision anterior to the cross and to do so by the merits of Christ won on that cross', *Ins* 2.17.1–5 passim. The 'secret good pleasure' of God in election is that of the Father and the Son, *Ins* 3.22.7.

[120] *Ins* 1.2.2; 1.4.1; cf. 1.5.1, and especially 1.10.2.

[121] *Ins* 1.13.1, 1.13.21; 1.11.1.

[122] Not without reason, Karl Barth accuses Calvin of being too gloomy in his exposition of mortification and vivification: 'The doctrine of Calvin obviously suffers . . . from a curious over-emphasising of *mortificatio* at the expense of *vivificatio* . . . What we have called the divine call to advance is in Calvin so overshadowed by the divine summons to halt that it can hardly be heard at all. The result is that his presentation is not merely stern, as is inevitable, but sombre and forbidding. And this is quite out of keeping with the themes presented.' *Church Dogmatics* (Edinburgh: T. & T. Clarke, 1956) 4.2.575.

neighbours as much as we love ourselves.[123] Calvin expects progress in love of neighbour.[124]

3. With Luther, Calvin also finds the dialectic between the two ages pivotal to any proper understanding of eschatology. How‐ever, more than Luther he incorporates this in his christology and moves from 'two kingdoms' to 'one kingdom of Christ and God with two governments', and ties the Church's experience of this kingdom to the two conditions of Christ's humanity. Because of our union with the humanity of Christ, in the midst of eschatological turmoil we can be assured of remaining in the victory Christ has decisively and completely won on the cross. For example, in an age when the reality of demons and the demonic was never in doubt as it continued to hold the general population in fearful enslavement, and also fascinated many theologians, Calvin quite simply had no time for it. If Luther, while eschewing demonologies with their overtones of sympa‐thetic magic, nevertheless saw and dealt with satan and his minions as they oppressed him from the shadows in an obscene implementation of James 4:7b, Calvin left them chained and tamed at the foot of the cross. Because eschatology is deter‐mined in Christ, Calvin maintained that apocalyptic is not the best language to describe eschatological experience, christology is.

4. Against the 'heavenly' emphasis of both papal and anabaptist Christianity which remained very much in a Ptolemaic frame‐work and thus tended to deny earthly reality its proper place and encourage in different ways a progressive programme of religious works to move us to the heavenly ideal, Calvin showed that life is indeed heavenly now on earth because we are united with Christ and thus permanently at the right hand of the Father. Calvin comes very close to seeing that 'heaven' in the New Testament is a metaphor for the untrammelled rule of God and not a state of other-worldly-being to be achieved. There‐fore, when Calvin urges on us *contemptus mundi* and medita‐tion on the future life, the world he denies is not that of earthly existence but the world which is in ungrateful rebellion against its Creator.[125]

---

[123] *Ins* 3.3.8–15, 3.7.1–10.
[124] *Com Isa.* 2:4.
[125] See *Ins* 3.6–10.

But there is a criticism to make. Calvin was right in showing the essential christological basis of the secular state in his 'one kingdom of Christ and God, two governments', and thus overcoming any dualism that might be lurking in Luther's understanding of civil government as 'God's left hand'. But his formulation does tend to so explain the benefits of government by Christians that Calvin's theological descendants, and we, are left with some sort of belief that the kingdom of God may be advanced by the secular as well as by the spiritual.[126] On this question, in my opinion, Luther has better grasped the New Testament.

Returning to the three contemporary issues we highlighted in the first chapter, Calvin has the following to say:

1. Time, eternity and history
   As to the relationship between history and revelation, or the future promised by God and the present, Calvin has tied them closely together by showing that revelation, the future kingdom of God, has entered our present in Jesus Christ. The present is understood and defined by God's future, but not in a directly equivalent way as with the medieval idea that the earthly church is the Platonic reflection of the heavenly ideal. The way to understand this relationship is to think of it in terms of the One who has determined it, that is, christologically. Thus, since Christ has ascended in the clouds to rule us in his heavenly session, the future is 'in a manner' present now. Further, since Christ will return to usher in the new heavens and the new earth, that future has to do with a fellowship with God under the kingship of Christ in a creation which will better serve that purpose than it already does. It is like our present enjoyment of fellowship, only more real.

2. Hermeneutics and language
   Calvin has given us an appropriate language in which to speak about eschatology: the language of christology – union with Christ, restoration of order, the kingdom of Christ and God, the two conditions of the humanity of Jesus Christ, and the church as his body, the sphere where his rule by Word and Spirit is recognized. In seeking for the principles of hermeneutics suggested by Scripture itself appropriate to eschatological

---

[126] See Doyle, 'Search for Models', 27–72; also H. Berkhof, *Christian Faith: An Introduction to the Study of the Faith* (Grand Rapids: Eerdmans 1979) 499–520.

assertions in church theology, Karl Rahner unintentionally pays Calvin a great compliment: 'It can . . . also be said that *Christ* himself is the hermeneutic principle of all eschatological asser-tions. Anything that cannot be read and understood as a Christological assertion is not a genuine eschatological asser-tion. It is soothsaying and apocalyptic, or a form of speech which misses and misunderstands the Christological element, because [it is] couched in a style and an imagery borrowed from other sources.'[127]

3. God and creation

As to the relationship between transcendence and immanence, from the christological considerations we have already out-lined, Calvin offers us both a theological and a practical solu-tion, not a metaphysical one. The transcendent God is immanent to us because we are already seated in the heavens, united to the flesh of his Son. We express this concretely in the activity and attitude of the Lord's Supper as we in the words of the *sursum corda* 'lift up our hearts' to where our ascended Lord and Brother reigns and engages in his heavenly session on our behalf. 'Meditation on the future life' is a recurrent theme in Calvin, and most important to his practical eschatology, and as we would expect, grounded in christology.

Primary Reading

'The Final Resurrection', *Institutes of the Christian Religion* 3.25.
'The Life of the Christian Man', 'Denial of Ourselves', 'Meditation on the Future Life', 'Bearing the Cross', 'Use of the Present Life', *Institutes of the Christian Religion* 3.6–10.

---

[127] 'The Hermeneutics of Eschatological Assertions', *Theological Investigations* IV (Baltimore: Helicon, 1966) 342–3.

OVER COFFEE

- How, and with what consequences, did the sixteenth-century Reformers dismantle the Ptolemaic eschatology of the Middle Ages?
- How and why, if at all, should we be optimistic about the progress of the kingdom of God in the contemporary West?
- What is the relationship between the church and the kingdom of God?
- What place has Jesus Christ in eschatology?

8

'Millennialism' in the modern era

After Calvin, the next major development in eschatological thought belongs in a way to the nineteenth century, for 'millennialism', as we now often see it among conservative evangelicals in North America, gained its present shape more than 150 years ago.

In general, eighteenth-century eschatological thought[1] was a diminution of earlier developments which adds little to our under-standing of the subject. There was a move from the great eschato-logical schemas of previous periods to either a mere defence of biblical particulars, or the replacement of a vibrant hope in God's ultimate future with a philosophically grounded belief in the immortality of the soul.

In the nineteenth century, liberal protestantism was to play down the ultimate Christian hope and to equate the kingdom of God with the perfect ethical community towards which humanity, under God, was progressing.[2] The eschatology of conservative groups such as the Evangelical Revival, the Oxford Movement, and ultra-montane Roman Catholicism was largely traditional and other-worldly. The only development that is of contemporary importance was millennialism, to which we now turn.

Although the North American form of millennialism known as 'premillennialism' may be the one we are most acquainted with nowadays, it is only the more obvious survivor of a long and multi-faceted history of millennial thought in the modern era, that is, since the sixteenth century. If 'millennialism' appears today to be the preferred outlook of only a sizeable minority and no longer a majority of Christians in the evangelical theological tradition, then that is arguably the reverse of the situation from the sixteenth

---

[1] See B. Hebblethwaite, *The Christian Hope* (London: Marshall, Morgan and Scott, 1984) chapter 6.
[2] *Christian Hope*, 129.

till the beginning of the twentieth centuries, when millennial ideas were both normal and influential, not only in the church but also in society at large.[3]

What is millennialism? Millennialism is a way of thinking often structured around the 'thousand-year reign' of Revelation 20:1–10. It is concerned with the chronology of coming events just as secular history is concerned with the study of the record of the past.[4] Narrowly defined in terms of attitudes taken to the thousand years of Revelation 20, contemporary millennialism may be categorized as pre-, post- or amillennial. The premillennialist believes that Christ will return before the thousand-year reign, and that his return will be preceded by signs including wars, famine, earth-quakes, the preaching of the gospel to all nations, a great apostasy, the appearance of Antichrist, and the great tribulation. The thousand-year reign will be one of peace and righteousness. Postmillennialism interprets the millennium as symbolic of a period in which the world becomes largely christianized, after which Christ returns. Amillennialists view the millennium as not a literal period of history, but as symbolic of this whole present age in which the

---

[3] The literature on the nature and import of millennial thought from the Middle Ages to the twentieth century is vast. Several foundational studies are worth noting: Norman Cohn, *The Pursuit of the Millennium*, rev. ed. (New York: Oxford University Press, 1970); Marjorie Reeves, *The Influence of Prophecy in the Later Middle Ages: A Study in Joachimism* (Oxford: Clarendon, 1969); C.A. Patrides & Joseph Wittreich (eds.) *The Apocalypse in English Renaissance Thought and Literature* (Ithaca, New York: Cornell University Press, 1984); Katharine R. Firth, *The Apocalyptic Tradition in Reformation Britain, 1530–1645* (Oxford University Press, 1979); Richard Bauckham, *Tudor Apocalypse* (Appleford, Oxford: Sutton Courtenay Press, 1978); Robin Bruce Barnes, *Prophecy and Gnosis: Apocalypticism in the Wake of the Lutheran Reformation* (Stanford University Press, 1988); Bryan W. Ball, *A Great Expectation: Eschatological Thought in English Protestantism to 1660* (Leiden: E.J. Brill, 1975); James West Davidson, *The Logic of Millennial Thought: Eighteenth-century New England* (New Haven: Yale University Press, 1977); W.H. Oliver, *Prophets and Millennialists: The Uses of Biblical Prophecy in England from the 1790s to the 1840s* (Auckland University Press, 1978); Richard H. Popkin (ed.) *Millenarianism and Messianism in English Literature and Thought 1650–1800* (Leiden: E.J. Brill, 1988); Ernest R. Sandeen, *The Roots of Fundamentalism: British and American Millenarianism, 1800–1930* (Grand Rapids: Baker, 1970).
[4] R.G. Clouse, 'Millennium, views of the', in W.A. Elwell (ed.) *Evangelical Dictionary of Theology* (Grand Rapids: Baker, 1984) 715.

gospel is preached. On this view, Christ returns after the millennium. Both pre- and postmillennialism have in common an optimism about earthly history, that is a political optimism about the 'city of man' as distinct from the final 'city of God'. But in premillennialism it is an optimism about a period which only occurs after earthly history first experiences the great tribulation prior to Christ's coming to rule the earth. Postmillennialism believes that we are in that good age now, or just about to enter it. It is this historical optimism which categorizes the wider pool of ideas termed 'millennial'.

The Apocalypse of John portrays the millennial period as one of blessedness, when all our Christian yearnings for an ideal society characterized by peace, freedom, material prosperity, and the rule of righteousness will be realized.[5] Because of this focus on a well-defined and strongly anticipated ideal future in concrete terms, which in turn shapes perceptions and activities in the present, we may see 'millennialism' as a phenomenon not restricted to schemes which have definite, or any, views on Revelations 20:1–10. Defined as the expectation of an actual earthly paradise coming by supernatural means, anthropologist have found millennial beliefs in traditional religions, including those of the Pacific islands.[6] Further, drawing on the pioneering work in biblical studies by Paul Hanson,[7] we ought to see millennialism against the backdrop of a phenomenon called 'apocalypticism'.

Apocalypticism is more than merely the occurrence of apocalyptic literature in the Bible and elsewhere, or even its use, but is a way of thinking. In biblical and related literature, it is a system of thought produced by visionary movements which generates a symbolic universe opposed to that of the dominant society.[8] Imminent deliverance coming from the cosmic realm is awaited. In the history of Christian apocalyptic in and since the Middle Ages, apocalypticism is 'the expectation of an imminent, final crisis, which will bring

---

[5] Clouse, 'Millennium', 714.

[6] E.g., see G.W. Trompf, *Melanesian Religion* (Cambridge University Press, 1991) 47 f.

[7] Paul D. Hanson, *The Dawn of Apocalyptic: The Historical and Sociological Roots of Jewish Apocalyptic Eschatology* (Philadelphia: Fortress Press, 1979).

[8] Paul D. Hanson, 'Apocalypse, genre' and 'Apocalypticism', in *The Interpreter's Dictionary of the Bible*, Nashville: Abingdon, 1976; supplementary vol., 27–34.

to an end the present, corrupt era and inaugurate a new one, whether within history or outside it'.[9] The actualization of the new, paradisal age will be the work of God.

What all forms of millennialism (except amillennialism) have in common is an historical optimism in which God is the primary and dramatic agent who ushers in a new era of well-being which encompasses earthly political life.

What are the theological features which characterize this millennialism, and what issues do they raise for eschatological thought?

Millennialism addresses problems that are often overlooked in other eschatological schemes. Many Christian theologians limit themselves mainly to discussing the consequences of eschatology for the individual. By contrast, millennialism is especially concerned with the future of the human community on earth. In its focus on chronology it is concerned with the integration of a prophetic or apocalyptic timetable of divine interventions in human affairs with the timing of the main events of secular history. In this way, in its most highly developed schemes, it forms another 'big picture' eschatology, seeking through its particular outlook to unite all reality into one dynamic theological panorama.

These features raise a number of important questions. Given the present inbreaking of the kingdom of God in Christ (Mk. 1:15; Lk. 7:18–28), just what may we expect now? Is historical optimism justified, and if so, just what is the nature and content of that optimism? How ought we to read and apply the prophetic and apocalyptic parts of the Bible which have eschatological concerns? How ought we to think about earthly political life, both now and in the future?

In order to pursue these concerns I will briefly sketch the rise of apocalyptic thought amongst the heirs of the Protestant Reforma-tion, and then look in more detail at three representative examples in the English-speaking world: John Owen in the seventeenth century, Jonathan Edwards in the eighteenth century, and the dispensational millennialism of the nineteenth and twentieth centuries.

---

[9] E. Randolph Daniel, 'The Spread of Apocalypticism, 1100–1500: Why Calvin could not reject it', in J.H. Leith (ed.), *Calvin Studies V: Presented at a Colloquium on Calvin Studies at Davidson College, North Carolina*, (Calvin Studies Society, 1990) 61.

Apocalyptic Tradition of the Sixteenth Century

It is now widely conceded that in the late Middle Ages and at the beginning of the Reformation apocalyptic and millennial ideas which we have seen typified by Otto of Freising and Joachim of Fiore were not confined to a few radical visionaries, but were common currency amongst the intelligentsia, and may also have had wide circulation amongst the peasantry. Certainly, with respect to the latter, the leaders of various peasant revolts from the Middle Ages to the revolt of 1525 in Germany, which so appalled Luther, laced their manifestos with apocalyptic ideas and expectations.

In this context it is no surprise that Protestantism engendered its own unique version of apocalypticism.[10] At base was, and remains, a question of the relationship between biblical prophecy and history outside of the Bible. The focus falls especially on the prophecy in the more apocalyptic portions of Scripture, and the New Testament in particular – Matthew 24–25; Mark 13; Luke 21; Romans 9–11; 2 Thessalonians 2; 2 Peter; 1 John 2; Jude; and Revelation. The Protestant apocalyptic tradition on the European continent was formed from three sources: the book of Daniel which prophesied the fate of the Roman Empire, Revelation which traced the history of the church, and the Prophecy of Elias which encompassed and limited the duration of the world. Unlike the other two, the Prophecy of Elias is non-canonical, originated in a third-century Midrash, was rewritten several times, and came into the Protestant tradition through the translation of the Talmud made by the humanist John Reuchlin and published around 1523. This prophecy divided the history of the world into three great periods. In an early English translation it reads:

The Sayenge of Helias house.
Thee worlde shall stand syxe thousand yeres and after shall it falle.
Two thousande yeares wythout the lawe
Two thousande yeares in the lawe
Two thousande yeares the tyme of Christ.
And yf these yeares be not accomplyshed oure sinnes shall be the cause, whiuch are great and many.[11]

---

[10] In what follows I am much indebted to Katharine R. Firth, *Apocalyptic Tradition*, 1–31.

[11] Cited from Firth, *Apocalyptic Tradition*, 16–17.

Several Lutheran scholars were responsible for bringing together these and other sources into an interpretation of the history of the church in both its past and present manifestations. That Phillip Melanchthon, Luther's young associate and the emerging leader of the German Reformation, was amongst them demonstrates how central the apocalyptic tradition was to Lutheranism. Eventually, this emerging tradition would lay great emphasis on predicting the future of the church from canonical and extra-canonical sources.

Of prime importance in assembling the tradition was *Carions' Chronicle*, 1532. John Carion was a mathematician and student of astronomy and astrology who intended his work to be a guide to memorable dates in both biblical and world history and argued for the use of astronomy as the means to determine correct dates. His draft work was revised by Melanchthon, who was probably responsible for including in its published form interpretative material from Daniel and the Prophecy of Elias. Beside the importance of *Carion's Chronicle* in assembling and disseminating the apocalyptic tradition first in Germany and later in England, the book also demonstrates the interdisciplinary nature of the enterprise. The tendency of secular disciplines to become intimately involved in interpreting and applying prophesy both pre-dated the Reformation [12] and was to become a major component of it right up to at least the late seventeenth century. Perhaps inevitably, the movement was to produce quite distinctively heterodox configurations which by the early seventeenth century were perceived as direct threats to Protestant orthodoxy in Germany. Examples of these include Rosicrucianism and the pansophical or theosophical hopes for a 'new Reformation'. [13]

---

[12] A good example of this can be seen in the intellectual roots and contemporary conversation partners of Girolamo Savonarola in his prophetic reform activities in Florence, 1494–8. Donald Weinstein has identified among others the humanists, the Medici, and the Platonic Academy of Florence. See his 'Savonarola, Florence and the Millenarian Tradition', *Church History*, 27 (1958) 291–305.

[13] As Firth points out, in Britain the Protestant apocalyptic tradition was to enjoy a consensus and respectability denied it on the continent; *Apocalyptic Tradition*, 2. However, the picture on the continent was not even. Throughout the sixteenth century Lutheran churchmen were highly tolerant of astrological prophecy, unlike French (Calvinist) clergy who repeatedly sought to limit or control astrological prediction. The foundational Rosicrucian writings of 1604 and 1614, although anonymous, are now widely acknowledged to have been the work of a Lutheran pastor, J.V. Andreae (1586–1654). Meant to be satirical, these esoteric and mystical

How, in general, did the early apocalyptic tradition in Protestantism apply prophecy to history? We have already seen an
example of this in Luther's periodization of the past history of the
church, with the present viewed as the immediate precursor to the
imminent Last Judgment. Other schemes evolved, but common to
all was firstly seeing the history of Rome as the fulfilment of
scriptural prophecy and secondly identifying the prophesied Antichrist with the pope, and in Germany, with the threat posed by the
Turk. As the movement entered the seventeenth century, prophecy
was applied to predicting certain kinds of future events.

Before examining John Owen, it needs to be noted that there was,
at least in the first half of the sixteenth century, a powerful and not
ineffective alternative approach to the relation between prophecy and
history. Erasmus, as Wycliffe had done before him in England,
believed that the prophecies depicted an allegory acted out on an
eternal plane, illustrating a completed and changeless revelation of
truth. For Erasmus, scriptural events were types, the study of which
gave men insight when dealing with the less-than-perfect examples
thrown up by secular history.[14] In the early stages of the Reformation
in England, although fond of applying the term 'Antichrist' to the
pope and the Roman Church, William Tyndale was explicitly Erasmian in preferring a spiritual interpretation of relevant passages of
the Bible over historical interpretations. John Frith, another early
English Reformer, in his prefatory letter to his translation in 1529 of
Luther's *The Revelation of Antichrist* (which is a commentary on
Daniel 8) is, like Tyndale, Erasmian in his outlook. Luther himself,
in contrast to many who followed him, is best categorized as a
modified Erasmian in his approach to the interpretation of prophetic
literature.

But the most outstanding commentator following the general
alternative espoused by Erasmus is John Calvin. In an age suffused
with apocalypticism, and in the light of the rush to apocalypticism
by later Calvinists, Calvin's distrust stands out as exceptional.[15]

As we have already seen, Calvin did not entirely spiritualize
apocalyptic, but refused to historicize it in the way common to the

---

[13] *(continued)* writings were taken with full seriousness well into the
eighteenth century. In the second decade of the seventeenth century there
was a strong move by orthodox Lutherans to circumscribe the limits of
legitimate prophetic faith, but until then the boundaries of toleration were
elastic. See, R.B. Barnes, *Prophecy and Gnosis*, 141, 217 ff., 228–60.

[14] Firth, *Apocalyptic Tradition*, 2, 14 f.

[15] Daniel, 'The Spread of Apocalypticism', 61.

emerging Protestant apocalyptic tradition. Secular history and apocalyptic history were inseparable because they witnessed to the same reality, which was the march of the kingdom of Christ through time. Yet they remained distinct, and in that distinction allowed comparison in the way they spoke of the same truth. In the interpretation of apocalyptic symbolism, although avoiding de-tailed historicization, Calvin firmly rejected allegorization in favour of metaphorical explanations which must conform to both salvific and secular history, and natural reality. The ultimate principle for interpreting apocalyptic symbolism was the 'purpose' of history, that is, the dramatic unveiling of God's will towards us in the first advent of Jesus Christ. Thus Calvin interpreted the four ages of Daniel as symbolic of the progressive spiritual degeneration of God's people until Christ came, and thus as symbolic of our state if we are in some sense also 'BC'. Hence, the Antichrist of the New Testament is a type of a violently anti-Christian outlook, and in that activity the Antichrist does not have a history as such, but outstanding examples of its class appear in history.

In chapter seven we noted that on Isaiah 2:4 Calvin comments, 'when the gospel shall be published, it will be an excellent remedy for putting an end to quarrels; and not only so, but that, when resentments have been laid aside, men will be disposed to assist each other'. Calvin expects this to happen where Christ reigns by Word and Spirit in the preaching of the gospel. For secular political life this is an application of Isaiah's promise about 'swords into ploughshares'. This expectation will have its fulfil-ment at the last day, but it begins wherever Christ is honoured. 'The fulfilment of this prophecy in its full extent must not be looked for on earth. It is enough if we experience the beginning, and if, being reconciled to God through Christ, we cultivate mutual friendship, and abstain from doing harm to anyone.' But, as we have already noted, this optimism does not at all approach the structural and programmatic proportions it will attain in later Calvinism.

John Owen: 'Eschatological Hopes on British Soil'

In the next century, John Owen (1616–83), an outstanding scho-lastic Calvinist and Puritan, develops the evangelical optimism of Calvin to explicitly include life in the world, as do other scholastics.

What we see in general among many theologians is a shift of the hope and optimism about God's final purposes for Israel (in the Old Testament) to the nations of Britain. Outwardly, the distinction the earlier Reformers made between grace and nature, God's two ways of ruling in his kingdoms (church and state), seems to be preserved because the church alone is under the rule of Jesus Christ. But the two reigns of God become confused as the fate of England and Scotland and their national churches becomes inextricably linked. There is a subtle transfer of Christian hope to civil society, although reason is outwardly said to rule in one, and Word and Spirit in the other.

The same sort of transfer can be identified in the writings of John Owen, a leading English federal theologian and adviser to Oliver Cromwell and the godly Commonwealth. However, Owen, as an Independent, along with the Commonwealth, rejected Presbyterianism's use of secular power to punish heresy. John Owen not only used the Old Testament's description of the office of judge to give detailed advice on the administration of civil justice (with appropriate adjustments to preserve a certain liberty of religious practice),[16] but he especially used prophecy to show how a godly government was involved in bringing to fruition God's latter reign in contemporary history. In his study on Owen's influence on English religion and politics, Peter Toon notes the strong strain of realized eschatology in his outlook. Toon points out that although Owen did not explicitly apply a literal understanding of the thousand years of Revelation 20, nevertheless he often spoke of the latter-day glory of the church of Christ on earth, which would follow the abolition of the power of both the Turks and the papacy.[17] This latter-day glory would be marked by the defeat of

---

[16] 'Although the institutions and examples of the Old Testament, of the duty of magistrates in the things and about the worship of God, are not, in their whole latitude and extent, to be drawn into rules that should be obligatory to all magistrates now, under the administration of the gospel . . . yet, doubtless, there is something moral in those institutions, which, being unclothed of their Judaical form, is still binding to all in the like kind, as to some analogy and proportion', *Christ's Kingdom and the Magistrates Power* (October, 1652), *Works of John Owen* (London: Banner of Truth, 1967) 8.392.

[17] Peter Toon, *God's Statesman* (Exeter: Paternoster, 1971) 30. See also, Christopher R. Smith, ' "Up and Doing": The Pragmatic Puritan Eschatology of John Owen', *Evangelical Quarterly* 61 (1989) 335–49.

anti-Christian political forces and large-scale response to the preaching of the gospel, especially among the Jews,[18] with a consequent numerical enlargement and wide spiritual fellowship in the church, enjoyed under conditions of peace and quietness.

A summary of Owen's views on the future of the church on earth is found in the *Savoy Declaration of Faith* (1658), which he helped draft:

> As the Lord in His care and love towards His Church, hath in His infinite, wise providence exercised it with great variety in all ages, for the good of them that love Him, and His own glory; so according to His promises, we expect that in the latter days, Antichrist being destroyed, the Jews called and the adversaries of His Son broken, the churches of Christ being enlarged and edified through a free and plentiful communication of light and grace, shall enjoy in this world a more quiet, peaceable and glorious condition than they have enjoyed.[19]

More specifically, he discerned the realization of this on British soil through the activity of the English government. On 24 October 1651, which was a day of thanksgiving for Cromwell's victory over the Scots after their invasion of England, in a sermon for the occasion[20] Owen described the Lord General's 'crowning mercy' as one of the most outstanding manifestations of the power of Christ in the Christian era. This event was the third of 'three principle seasons of the Lord's eminent appearances to carry on the kingdom of Christ and the Gospel'. The first was the preaching of the gospel to the Jews, followed by the destruction of Jerusalem in AD 70. The second was the preaching of the gospel to the Gentiles, followed by

---

[18] Renewed Christian interest and hope for the Jews extended beyond the merely speculative to attempts at personal and political amelioration of their contemporary situation in both Europe and in Jerusalem. See David S. Katz, 'Henry Jessey and Conservative Millenarianism in Seventeenth-Century England and Holland' in J. Michman (ed.), *Dutch Jewish History*, vol. 2 (Hebrew University of Jerusalem, 1989 and Maastricht, Netherlands: Van Gorcum, Assen 1989) 75–93. See also N.I. Matar, 'The Idea of the Restoration of the Jews in English Protestant Thought, 1661–1701', *Harvard Theological Review* 78 (1985) 115–48, where Matar also summarizes an earlier paper on the idea of restoration from the Reformation to 1660.

[19] Cited from Toon, *God's Statesman*, 81.

[20] *The Advantage of the Kingdom of Christ*, Works 8.312–39. Citations are from Toon, *God's Statesman*, 81–2.

the destruction of Rome. This third and greatest was 'the coming of the Lord to recover His people from antichristian idolatry and oppression', prophesied in Revelation 17:15 and 19:11–21. The victories over Charles I and over the Scots who had supported his son were seen as part of God's removal of those barriers which prevented the dawn of the latter-day glory of the church.

Many of Owen's sermons evince[21] this sort of identification between the right exercise of government and the coming of spiritual prosperity for the earthly church. His transfer of eschatological expectations to civil order remained constant from about the mid-1640s.[22] From his earliest sermons explicating the role of civil government (for example, *Christ's Kingdom and the Magistrates Power* October, 1652),[23] Owen grounds his understanding in a realized eschatology. Even after the Restoration, with its blighting of Puritan hopes, he remained optimistic. Since God had promised that biblical religion would finally triumph in the latter days, the imperfectly reformed Church of England had only a limited life, and the saints should continue to look to God as their Deliverer. However, we now note in tracts on church-state relations[24] not only the old emphasis on the difference in the role of magistrates in the New Testament era in contrast to the Old, but more appeal to sound reason, secular history and the laws of England. The result is a less-realized eschatology.

What we have then in Owen is the associating of proper Christian government with the eschatological purposes of God for the good of the church, an association which becomes more and more explicitly discernible in contemporary historical processes. There is a concomitant shift in focus from heaven to earth as the locus of true blessing. If they take a certain covenanted shape, civic societies with their governments are both agents and beneficiaries of eschatological blessings.

---

[21] For example, *Righteous Zeal Encouraged by Divine Protection* (Jan 1649), *Works* 8.128–62; *The Shaking and Translating of Heaven and Earth* (April 1649), *Works* 8.244–79; *The Church of Rome No Safe Guide* (1679), *Works* 14.482–516; *A Brief and Impartial Account of the Nature of the Protestant Religion* (1682), *Works* 14.530–55.

[22] Toon, *God's Statesman*, 142.

[23] *Works* 8.367–95.

[24] E.g. *Truth and Innocence Vindicated . . . The Authority of the Magistrate over the Conscience of Subjects in Matters of Religion* (1669), *Works* 13.343–506.

The social and intellectual pressures on Owen to come to these conclusions ought not be underestimated. As Katharine Firth's work on the role of apocalyptic in sixteenth- and seventeenth-century Britain amply demonstrates, 'the need to see in history the fulfilment of prophecies has been an enduring and recurrent theme in western civilization'.[25] During the early modern period there was a growing, public interplay between such streams of thought as Christian Cabala, Hermeticism, angelology, and alchemy, which 'drove an engine of thought'.[26] The direction of this engine can be seen in the changed approach by Protestant apologists. The major-ity of sixteenth-century apologists looked to the past to justify the present, a past often interpreted in terms of fulfilled New Testament prophecies. But in Owen's century, apologists increasingly looked to the future to vindicate the promises of renewal that the Refor-mation intrinsically offered in its stance against the old Catholic Church.

Three influential writers contributed to this development. By the end of the sixteenth century, the Scottish mathematician credited with the invention of logarithms, John Napier (1550–1617), had set the standard in a commentary on the Apocalypse[27] that offered demonstrative proof, consistent with Scripture and history, that the fulfilment of prophecy was a regular, observable, and thus normal process. He thus opened up the possibility that, within limits, future events of certain kinds could be predicted. Between 1609 and 1616 the country parson Thomas Brightman published commentaries on Revelation, Daniel, and the Canticles proving the imminence of a joyous new age. In the context of widespread fear by orthodox theologians and conservative social leaders of radical dreams of a golden age before the day of judgment, Brightman cautiously sug-gested the transfer of the 'millennium' of Revelation 20 from the past to the future.[28] In 1627, Joseph Mede (1586–1638), a student, amongst other interests, of philology, history, mathematics, physics,

---

[25] *Apocalyptic Tradition*, 247.

[26] Firth, *Apocalyptic Tradition*, 204; and 204–54 passim for what follows.

[27] *A Plaine Discovery of the Whole Revelation of Saint John* (Edinburgh: Walde-grave, 1593). See Firth's discussion of its background, method and contents, *Apocalyptic Tradition*, 132–49.

[28] See J.F. Maclear, 'New England and the Fifth Monarchy: The Quest for the Millennium in Early American Puritanism', in Alden T. Vaughan (ed.), *Puritan New England: Essays on Religion, Society, and Culture* (New York: St Martins Press, 1977) 68; Firth, *Apocalyptic Tradition*, 165–79, esp. 174.

and astrology, had his *Clavis Apocalyptica* (Key to the Apocalypse) published for private circulation. It provoked much correspondence and amongst the small but influential circle of critics and admirers of this work was Archbishop Ussher of Ireland. The distinctive feature of this interpretation of the Revelation of John was its studied patterns of 'synchronisms': that is, the correspondence between historical events and the groups of images John so powerfully uses to carry his message, including the millennium of chapter 20. The use of synchrony was hardly new amongst biblical commentators, but Mede's synchronisms were all-encompassing and had an inner rationality which appealed to many of his elite correspondents. After the relaxation of censorship in 1641, apocalyptic ideas, which could presage revolutionary political changes in secular society, were to circulate much more freely. In this environment, after Mede's death, the writings of his admirers and the wider publication of his work were to change Mede's reputation from scholar to prophet.

In summary, in the seventeenth century 'millenarianism' had ceased to look for the end of the world, and instead looked for a millennial kingdom. There were exceptions, like Thomas Hayne,[29] but John Owen is not numbered amongst them. Owen expected in the millennial kingdom, not a radical transformation of the heavens and the earth, but continuity with preceding history.[30]

Seventeenth-Century Context

With the failure of the 'godly commonwealth' and the restoration of the monarchy in 1660, there was in England a distinct move away from historical interpretations of the prophecies of the New Testament and Daniel towards more figurative and universal explanations.[31] Given the social and political links across the Atlantic, it is

---

[29] Firth, *Apocalyptic Tradition*, 237–41.
[30] Smith, 'Eschatology of John Owen', 347.
[31] Firth points out that the process had started with the commonwealth itself, *Apocalyptic Tradition*, 244–7. After all, those interpretations which drove the revolution needed to change so as to forestall further social or political disruption – yesterday's revolutionary, today's conservative. In an earlier study, William Lamont shows that, against the trend, in 1686 we find Richard Baxter actively engaged in millenarian research; 'Richard Baxter, the Apocalypse and the Mad Major', in Charles Webster (ed.), *The Intellectual Revolution of the Seventeenth Century* (London: Routledge & Kegan Paul, 1974) 399–426.

no surprise that in the American colonies, among 'the godly', millennial expectations closely mirrored those of England. New England
was somewhat of an exception; having been founded as a respite from
English religious persecution of the Puritans, it understandably
shows an independent trend.

As sections of the English Commonwealth awaited the imminent
coming of the Fifth Monarchy of Christ (Dan. 2:39–45, Dan.
7:9–14, 23–27), so also sixteenth-century New England had millennial expectations for the coming of spiritual blessings for Christ's
people and triumphant authority for his church. In the New World,
the major features of this expectation were the same as in the Old:

- Eschatological expectation was the arena of the Christian's daily
  battle against the world, the flesh and the devil; Christians were
  not so much spectators of God's remote plans, as participants in
  apocalyptic history.
- They were optimistic about the closeness and certainty of the
  joyous new age.
- A schematic importance was given to the Jews.
- The 'rule of the saints' was expected to be more evident in the
  true church and, by the more radical, in society at large.
- There was a positive expectation for the nation.[32]

The one major trans-Atlantic difference was that New England was
believed to have a special place in the unfolding of these providential
workings: 'by its purity and faithfulness to God's word it was itself
a sign of the approach of the millennium'.[33] John Cotton, Richard
Mather, Thomas Hooker and other members of the emigrant
community tended to see Old England in terms of impending
'desolation', and gospel work in the New as preparing a bastion
against the Antichrist.

But the return of the Stuart's in 1660 saw the end of the high
Puritan profile in English political life, and with it, the destruction of
earlier hope. In London from January 6 to 9, 1661, there occurred
an abortive coup, led by a returned immigrant and radical Fifth
Monarchist, Thomas Venner. This event, and political sympathies
with the English throne, sealed the movement in New England off
from optimistic hopes of an imminent historical millennium. Now
commentary on apocalyptic was characterized by jeremiads.
Attention moved from gospel preaching to bring in a bright new

---

[32] Maclear, 'New England', passim.
[33] Maclear, 'New England', 68.

future, to perfecting existing religious institutions in the light of present corruption, corruption which would end with the return of Christ and the final cataclysm, and after that, the resurrection of the saints.[34]

However, the change did not result in the abandonment of millennial speculation, only a change in its direction.

In the eighteenth century more widely, with its emerging Enlightenment, millennial ways of thinking still characterized secular as well as religious thought. Scholars and scholarly circles of some renown still expected 'the Great Instauration', the great renewal of human thought, knowledge and politics, that Francis Bacon had hoped for at the beginning of the previous century. Pre-eminent physicist Isaac Newton (1642–1727) wrote on the prophecies of Daniel and the Apocalypse. William Whiston (1667–1752), who followed Newton in the chair of mathematics at Cambridge, also wrote on the fulfilment of prophecy, and the unorthodox Presbyterian minister and scientist responsible for the 'discovery' of oxygen, Joseph Priestley (1733–1804), regarded the study of prophecies as both an opportunity for rational men to see how God's plan unfolded in history, and as a worthy pastime for Christians.[35] In the context of his opposition to the idea of a national church and 'so many absurd institutions, by which *the many* are miserably enslaved by the few',[36] Priestly looked for the calamitous downfall of church and state, but with a final, glorious outcome. Consequently, Priestley and others could view the French Revolution with approbation. Later, he held that Napoleon Bonaparte might 'only be the *precursor* to the *great* deliverer'.[37] His millennialism, as religious and literal as it was, and even evangelical in regard to the Jews, was thoroughly integrated with his Enlightenment views on human progress.

This integration of religious millennialism and contemporary secular philosophy and science was common,[38] often moving the

---

[34] See Maclear, 'New England', 82–5.

[35] Clarke Garrett, *Respectable Folly: Millenarians and the French Revolution in France and England* (Baltimore: John Hopkins University Press, 1975), 126; see further 127–43.

[36] Cited from Garrett, *Respectable Folly*, 131.

[37] Cited from Garrett, *Respectable Folly*, 142.

[38] The 'Immortal Dr Cheyne' (1671–1743) is but one example of a genus. Cheyne sought to integrate millennial expectations not only with progressive thought, but also with his special, mystical application of Newtonian mathematics and physics to health. See George S. Rousseau, 'Mysticism and Millenarianism: "Immortal Dr. Cheyne" ', in Popkin, *Millenarianism and Messianism*, 81–126.

focus from God as the active agent in apocalyptic history to natural causes or humankind. Although the scientists William Whiston and Thomas Burnet were happy to interpret biblical events like the creation, flood and final dissolution of the world literally, they did not equate 'literal' with 'supernatural' but natural causes. As early as 1681, Burnet theorized about the literal return of Christ in the context of the tilting of the earth towards the sun, producing worldwide drought and fire, followed by the floods of Noah's deluge breaking through the thin crust, beginning a return to a millennial paradise free from pain or want, sustained by an untilted axis of the earth, as originally the case with Eden.[39] Critics charged that the supernatural had been excluded, but Burnet and Whiston could defend themselves by pointing out that Providence not only lay behind the mechanical working of the universe, but may in fact give events more direct assistance.

On the more strictly evangelical front, Increase and Cotton Mather in New England, who were to some extent archetypical 'premillennialists' of the period before the Great Awakening,[40] not only emphasized that God was *the* Agent of millennial change, and interpreted the prophecies very literally, but also highlighted the cataclysmic nature of events just prior to Christ's return. That is, they were pessimistic about present earthly history. However, they 'waxed ecstatic about the rewards in store for the saints after the conflagration'.[41] The works of the New England theologians, Thomas Foxcroft and Thomas Prince, published in 1730, follow the usual line of presenting New England history within the frame-work of the covenant, the ideal piety of the covenanting fathers, and the mighty acts of God on their behalf, the mighty deliverances. However, both turn into jeremiads, castigating the decline, apostasy and corruption of the present hour.[42]

---

[39] Davidson, Logic of Millennial Thought, 86–93.

[40] Davidson argues that the Mather's were very conscious that their position on a literal return of Christ before the millennium, although undoubtedly right in their own estimation, was not that of a whole lineage of Christian commentators, and somewhat of a novelty amongst at least some of their co-religionists; *Logic of Millennial Thought*, 63 f.

[41] Davidson, *Logic of Millennial Thought*, 61.

[42] M. Darrol Bryant, 'America as God's Kingdom', in Jürgen Moltmann et al., *Religion and Political Society* (New York: Harper & Row, 1974) 49–94. See p. 59 where Bryant cites Perry Miller's influential, *The New England Mind* (1953).

Jonathan Edwards: 'The Eschatological Hope of the New World'

Somewhat of a sea-change came with Jonathan Edwards (1703–58). Edwards stood at the centre of the Great Awakening, and is still with good cause regarded by some as the pre-eminent American theologian and philosopher. Further, he is often claimed as a foundational influence in the formation of the modern idea of progress and the American tradition with its grounding of the American vocation in the divine economy. With respect to millen-nial eschatology, Edwards foresaw a golden age for the church on earth, within history, achieved through the ordinary processes of propagating the gospel in the power of the Holy Spirit. His major writings which evince this position are:

- *History of Redemption*, published in 1774 from sermons given in 1738-9.
- Some Thoughts Concerning the Present Revival of Religion in New England, 1742.
- *A Humble Attempt to Promote Explicit Agreement and Visible Union of God's People in Extraordinary Prayer, for the Revival of Religion and the Advancement of Christ's Kingdom on Earth, Pursuant to Scripture Promises and Prophecies Concerning the Last Time*, 1744.

In modern scholarship, C.C. Goen is credited with articulating the shape of Edwards' eschatological thought and seeing something of its radical significance.[43] Goen's reconstruction has stood the test of time, but the significance he sees in Edwards has been strongly challenged.[44]

In the *History of Redemption*, which he hoped to expand into a *magnum opus*, Edwards tells the story of salvation from its

---

[43] C. C. Goen, 'Jonathan Edwards: A New Departure in Eschatology', *Church History* 28 (1959) 25–40. I am following Goen's reconstruction.
[44] Davidson, *Logic of Millennial Thought*. 29, 31, 35; and Dietrich Buss, 'The Millennial Vision as Motive for Religious Benevolence and Reform: Timothy Dwight and the New England Evangelicals Reconsidered', *Fides et Historia* 16 (1983) 18–34 are amongst many who follow Goen's reconstruction and are in broad agreement with Goen's conclusions about its import. But, while following Goen's description, Bryant is strongly critical of the usual interpretation of Edwards' influence, 'America', passim.

beginning to his own day, and then turns to the biblical prophecies to fill out the remainder of historical time:

1. From Christ's resurrection to the destruction of Jerusalem
2. From the destruction of Jerusalem to Constantine
3. From Constantine to the rise of the Antichrist (the papacy)
4. From the rise of Antichrist to the Reformation
5. From the Reformation to the present time
6. From the present time to the fall of Antichrist
7. From the fall of Antichrist to the Last Judgment (the prosperous state of the church).

This sevenfold periodization and its use of apocalyptic to under-stand the apostasy of the Roman Catholic Church is fairly standard Protestant fare. But the departure from many of his immediate predecessors, and several contemporaries, was to deny that before millennial blessing there had necessarily to be further catastrophic persecution of the church. In his *History of Redemption* and the other writings which came out of his experience of the trans-Atlan-tic Great Awakening, Edwards expressed this in terms of the sequential pouring out of the seven bowls or vials of God's wrath against the beast in Revelation 16. He believed that the process was far advanced. Among commentators on Revelation, a standard marker of the degree of advancement was where one located the synchronism in history of Revelation 11:1–13 with the fifth vial. That is, where one located the work, martyrdom and resurrection of the Two Witnesses. Edwards saw this as already accomplished at the Reformation. Since it was about 220 years after the Refor-mation, 'if the sixth vial has not already begun to be poured out, it may well be speedily expected'.[45] Edwards adduced as evidence the shrinking income and influence of the papacy seen in the political and military reverses of France, one of Rome's mainstays.

Edwards is hardly niggardly in his outline of future prosperity, reminding himself that ultimately no one may make a timetable for God, yet would it not be a wonderful thing if in a half century, Protestantism could be purified and Spirit-filled (i.e. 1750–1800), in the next half century the power of popish abominations broken (1800–50), then the Mohamedans subdued and the Jews converted (1850–1900)? 'And then in the next whole century [1900–2000],

---

[45] *Humble Attempt*, in *The Works of Jonathan Edwards* (Yale University Press, 1957–94) vol. 5 p. 42.

the whole heathen world should be enlightened and converted to the Christian faith, throughout all parts of Africa, Asia, America and Terra Australis, and be thoroughly settled in the Christian faith and order, without any remainders of their old delusions and superstitions, and this attended with an utter extirpation of the remnant of the church of Rome, and all the relics of Mahometanism, heresy, schism and enthusiasm, and a suppression of all remains of open vice and immorality, and every sort of visible enemy to true religion, throughout the whole earth, and bring to an end all the unhappy commotions, tumults, and calamities occasioned by such great changes, and all things so adjusted and settled through the world, that the world thenceforth should enjoy a holy rest of sabbatism?'[46]

Several things need to be said about this fine, gospel-centred vision of human history. In coming to his conclusions, Edwards critically used the commentaries of Daniel Whitby (published 1703), Charles Daubuz (1720), and Moses Lowman (1737), which had in common a 'postmillennial' outlook regarding the return of Christ and a prosperous future for the church in history before that time.[47] Edwards creatively worked with, and within, a history of interpretation, and in a definite social and religious context. Importantly, Edwards was asserting his grand vision in the context of fellow evangelicals who believed that such blessing must be preceded by something of the catastrophe evident in the martyrdom of the Two Witnesses. Edwards was worried that such pessimism over the immediate future would hold them back from the worldwide concert of prayer, and consequent evangelism, that was needed to continue the faltering worldwide spiritual revival and its blessing. He reasoned that people were less likely to pray if they might expect in their own lifetime, not the millennium, but 'only the dismal time that shall precede it'.[48] Thus Edwards insisted that the period of prosperity had already begun, and the moving of revivals from sporadic local events in New England to the sustained and widespread phenomenon of 1740–42, was the sure sign of that fact. Earlier in the century, Samuel Danforth and Thomas Prince had also interpreted the local revivals which they

---

[46] *Humble Attempt, Works* 5.411.
[47] Goen, 'Jonathan Edwards', 37; Davidson, *Logic of Millennialism*, 141–63.
[48] *Humble Attempt, Works* 5.379; cited from Davidson, *Logic of Millennialism*, 150.

experienced as foretastes of the millennial period.[49] What they had seen as foretastes, Edwards made into a definite historical marker.

There has been much interest by historians in the role Edwards gives America, and the impact of that on later secular conceptions of America as 'God's Kingdom' with a special vocation within the divine economy. In *Some Thoughts*, Edwards attempted to show that many things point to the kingdom starting in America. 'This new world is probably now discovered, that the new and most glorious state of God's church on earth might commence here; that God might in it begin a new world in a spiritual respect, when he creates the *new heavens* and *new earth*'.[50] Estimates of the importance of this by secular historians have at times been lavish. But, taken in context and against Edwards' later realism, the reality is more prosaic. It is agreed that millennial expectation of a dawning new age served as the ground for that criticism and innovation which resulted in the American Revolution.[51] The function of a metaphysical vision, such as is found in *History of Redemption*, is to provide orientation or, in societal terms, focus the energies of a people.[52] Edwards' contribution to this process is widely acknowledged, but his concreted focus was on the coming of the new heavens and the new earth, not, perhaps surprisingly, a church triumphant on earth, let alone a scenario for American social and political history. Edwards' vision was intended 'to encourage the faithful to rest in the divine promise'.[53]

For all his emphasis on the positive unfolding of God's millennial plans and our active role in them through prayer and preaching, Edwards did not remove a tenet central to all specifically Christian millennial thinking of the eighteenth century, the afflictive model of progress. Things get better only as things get worse. Christians would only see the success of God's actions in the midst of their experience of trial. This was strongly linked into, even determined by, Edwards' views on salvation. God reclaimed his people the way he reclaimed individuals, through humiliation. Sanctification was thus tied to the path of suffering, ever though in a wider course of progress. In this way, and integral to Edwards' views on anthropology and redemption, the external affliction of

---

[49] Davidson, *Logic of Millennialism*, 149.
[50] *Works* 3.314; cited from Goen, 'Jonathan Edwards', 29.
[51] Bryant, 'America', 58–9, and passim.
[52] Bryant, 'America', 62.
[53] Bryant, 'America', 64.

personal or world events was secondary to the internal psycho-logical state. God could accomplish the proper feelings of abase-ment and awe, of dependence on him, of guilt under law, even in the new millennial era, when a penultimate catastrophe of the sort envisaged under the symbol of the Two Witnesses had already passed.[54]

It is important to appreciate that Edwards' eschatological out-look went through three phases, which were heavily influenced by his experience of revival. In writings from the local revivals of 1734–35, there is no innovative eschatology. But in his *History of Redemption* (sermons from 1738–39), we have the distinctive views on millennial history noted above. At this time local revivals are moving to the wider scene which will earn the title, The Great Awakening. In *Some Thoughts*, 1742, Edwards writes buoyantly: 'The New Jerusalem in this respect (the extraordinary degree of light, love and spiritual joy) has begun to come down from heaven, and perhaps never more of the prelibations of heaven's glory given upon earth'.[55] But in the spring of 1742, the growing anti-revival currents outside and within the movement burst their banks, and Edwards' eschatological views begin the shift to a second phase. An itinerant preacher, James Davenport, was judged by a Con-necticut court 'disturbed in the rational faculties of his mind'. Marches and burnings by his followers of their 'wigs, fine clothes, jewelry, and dangerous books' signalled the unleashing of fanati-cism.[56] Edwards continued to maintain that the Great Awakening was a forerunner of the millennial kingdom, but he was now very critical of both himself and the revival. Pride was the problem; humility and purification were needed. This shift is clearly seen in *Religious Affections*, 1746. The third phase can be dated from his rejection by his Northampton congregation in 1749 for seeking to exclude all 'unconverted' from Communion. Now in the wilder-ness, working amongst Indians, Edwards' pen produces what are considered by some to be his most important works – *Original Sin, Nature of True Virtue, Inquiry into Freedom of the Will*. 'The absence of millennial reflections is conspicuous in these works.'[57] The end of all creation is transhistorical and spiritual: the glory of God. In the tradition of Augustine, the communion of saints

---

[54] Davidson, *Logic of Millennialism*, 146, 151, 156–9.
[55] *Some Thoughts, Works* 4.346.
[56] Bryant, 'America', 74.
[57] Bryant, 'America', 82.

does not have an historical termination, but an eternal one. Edwards had left millennial America.[58]

It is also important to see that at the height of his millennial optimism, Edwards' view is relentlessly God- and gospel-centred. After the church enters the millennial reign of righteousness, divine and human learning will spread over all the world, so that 'the most barbarous nations shall become as the bright and polite as England'! But this is because these lands will bask in gospel truth, where men live as brothers in a world of love. 'They shall all join the facets of their minds in exploring the glories of the Creator, their hearts in loving and adoring Him, their hands in serving Him, and their voices in making the welkin ring with his praises.'[59] Throughout his *History of Redemption*, Edwards emphasizes that it is God's righteousness which will prevail, not man's strivings. It is God who moves history. In the providence of God, so great a part of the world has been discovered, and it is by the gospel that 'Satan's kingdom shall be overthrown throughout the whole habitable globe, on every side, and on all its continents'.[60] After the death of his beloved David Brainerd, who was a missionary to the Indians and died in Edwards' home in 1747 at age 30, Edwards commented in a preface to his *Memoirs of the Rev. David Brainerd* that the exemplary life of this saint was only ever an experience of the cross, not pleasurable self-interest.[61]

Nineteenth- and Twentieth-Century Millennial Belief

Edwards scholars stress the discontinuity between Edwards' millennial view and later millennialism. A substantial explanation for this can be found in the impact of the Enlightenment on both evangelical and secular society. Enlightenment scepticism about the truth status of revealed religion produced a reduction of religious realities to examples of secular humanist realities. In this process, millennial belief moved from well-grounded expectations that God would personally and observably involve himself in history to bring in his own kingdom of righteousness ruled by his Son, to a secularized

---

[58] Bryant, 'America', 81, 85–6.
[59] Cited from Goen, 'Jonathan Edwards', 28. Goen has cited it from, Harvey G. Townsend (ed.), *The Philosophy of Jonathan Edwards from his Private Notebooks* (Eugene: University of Oregon Press, 1955) 207.
[60] *Work of Redemption*, 439.
[61] See Bryant, 'America', 79–81.

optimism about the future under the providence of a generalized Deity. The foci of this postmillennialism are, of course, the nations of the western world, and especially of Northern Europe and North America with their 'manifest destinies'. The details of the biblical vision become but the superstitions which encrust ancient ideals, a primitive way of expressing rational truths of eternal significance.[62]

One of the crucial tools for the rationalistic enterprise of the Enlightenment, as indeed for all rationalism, is the reduction of truth to strict propositional form. By this is meant that truth which cannot be expressed in precise analytical language is essentially unintelligible. As a result, poetic, symbolic, and figurative ways of expressing truth are given little attention and little credence. Partly in reaction to this mood, evangelical understandings of the millennial teaching of the Bible swung towards 'literalism', and because of the obvious interest Revelation has in history, 'historical literalism'. It is in this mood of western culture that what is now in the twentieth century the distinctive shape of millennial belief amongst conservative Christians was hammered out.[63] And as we will see, it is precisely because 'literalism' has been artificially pressed onto the literary modes of the Bible that so much of premillennialism breaks down as a cogent exposition of Scripture.

The differentiation between different contemporary forms of millennialism is founded on their understanding of Revelation 20:1–10. But these forms involve much more than the arrangement of events surrounding the return of Christ.

Premillennialism

The premillennial position can be diagrammed thus:[64]

---

[62] See John F. Wilson, 'History, Redemption, and the Millennium', in N. Hatch and H. Stout, *Jonathan Edwards and the American Experience* (Oxford University Press, 1988) 131–5; cf. Bryant, 'America', 64.

[63] See Wilson, 'History', passim. 'Edward's thought on postmillennialism represented, therefore, nothing remarkably new until the Enlightenment transformed it. That transformation reduced it to literalistic formulations. In consequence, positions that had been much richer, nuanced, and multivalent became expressed in the limited logic of modern propositions', pp. 139–40. Unfortunately, Wilson does not advance or hint at an understanding of religious language which will do justice to the fact that biblical revelation is in propositional form or forms.

[64] Graeme Goldsworthy, *The Gospel in Revelation: Gospel and Apocalypse*, (London: Paternoster, 1984) 20.

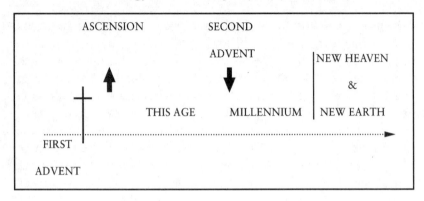

The premillennialist believes that the return of Christ will be preceded by signs including wars, famine, earthquakes, the preach-ing of the gospel to all nations, a great apostasy, the appearance of Antichrist, and the great tribulation. These events will end in the second coming, which will result in a period of peace and righteous-ness when Christ and his saints will control the world. This rule is established suddenly, through supernatural methods, rather than gradually through the conversion of individuals.

The Jews will have a place of prominence in this future age because they will be converted in large numbers and will again have a major role in God's work. Further, most premillennialists hold that during this 1000 years, dead or martyred believers will be resurrected and in their glorified bodies mingle with the other inhabitants of the earth. Nature will have the curse removed from it. The deserts will produce abundant crops. Christ will restrain evil during this age by authoritarian power.

Despite the idyllic conditions of this golden age, there will be a final rebellion against Christ and his saints. This exposure of evil is crushed by God, the non-Christian dead are resurrected, the last judgment conducted, and the eternal states of heaven and hell established.

Historical development[65]
Premillennialism, or a literal millennialism in one form or another, has a long history. In the first three centuries many of the Fathers

---

[65] The historical roots in theology and the society, and contemporary significance of premillennialism have been well researched. For nine-teenth-century origins refer especially to Ernest R. Sandeen, *The Roots of Fundamentalism: British and American Millenarianism, 1800–1930* (Grand Rapids: Baker, 1978, reprint of 1970 original); W.H. Oliver,

espoused a millennial position – Papias, Irenaeus, Justin Martyr, Tertullian, Hippolytus, Methodius, Commodianus, and Lactantius. Especially noteworthy were the Montanists, whose heterodoxy and claims to special prophetic revelation on the matter contributed to a decline in the doctrine's acceptability. Other reasons for the decline were the stress of the influential theologian Origen (185–254) on the kingdom of God as an entity primarily resident in the soul; the coming to power of Constantine, with the subsequent reduction in some of the social conditions favouring millennialism; and the ascent of the church as a European power.

We have already given brief consideration to the doctrine's progress in the Middle Ages and the sixteenth century. In the seventeenth century many of the Puritans took up a millennial outlook, and the Fifth Monarchy Men of the Cromwellian period gave it a direct and radical political expression. Adherence to literal millennialism

---

[65] *(continued) Prophets and Millennialists: The Uses of Biblical Prophecy in England from the 1790s to the 1840s* (Oxford University Press, 1978); David Bebbington, 'The Advent Hope in British Evangelicalism since 1800', *Scottish Journal of Religious Studies* 9 (1988) 103–14; David L. Rowe, *Thunder and Trumpets: Millerites and Dissenting Religion in Upstate New York, 1800–1850* (Chico, California, Scholars Press, 1985). For the wider impact in the nineteenth century, see George M. Marsden, *The Evangelical Mind and the New School Presbyterian Experience* (New Haven: Yale University Press, 1970) 182–98; Dana L. Robert, ' "The Crisis of Missions": Premillennial Mission Theory and the Origins of Independent Evangelical Missions', in Joel A. Carpenter and W.R. Shenk (eds.), *Earthen Vessels: American Evangelicals and Foreign Missions, 1880–1980* (Grand Rapids: Eerdmans, 1990) 29–56. There has been research on the interplay between premillennial ideas and social conservatism in the so-called, 'new Christian right'. See, for example, Larry Jones and Gerald T. Sheppard, 'The Politics of Biblical Eschatology: Ronald Reagan and the Impending Nuclear Armageddon', *TSF Bulletin*, Sept–Oct 1984, 16–19; Robert G. Clouse, 'The New Christian Right, America, and the Kingdom of God', *Christian Scholars Review* 12 (1983) 3–16; Helen Lee Turner and James L. Guth, 'The Politics of Armageddon: Dispensationalism among Southern Baptist Ministers', in Ted G. Jelen (ed.), *Religion and Political Behaviour in the United States* (New York: Praeger, 1989) 187–207; Stephen Kierulff, 'Belief in "Armageddon Theology" and Willingness to Risk Nuclear War', *Journal for the Scientific Study of Religion* 30 (1991) 81–93. Dietrich G. Buss has a useful review article, 'Meeting of Heaven and Earth: A Survey and Analysis of the Literature on Millennialism in America, 1965–1985', *Fides et Historia* 20 (1988) 5–28.

declined somewhat with the collapse of the Cromwellian common-wealth. In the eighteenth century Isaac Newton, Johann Bengel, and Joseph Priestley all evinced a belief in a literal millennium; though once considered to be in a minority, they were part of a wider spectrum of millennial belief in both religion and society.

It is the early decades of the nineteenth century which saw a great rise of interest, and the emergence of new forms with Edward Irving, a Church of Scotland minister in London, and, most influentially, J.N. Darby of the Plymouth Brethren, who is generally credited with founding dispensational millennialism.

Dispensational millennialism

The second coming of Christ is broken up into three stages:

1. a secret rapture or 'snatching away' of the saints which removes the church before
2. a seven-year period of tribulation which devastates the earth, and is followed by
3. the actual visible appearance of Christ with his saints after this tribulation to rule on earth for a 1000 years.

On the question of the tribulation, two further divisions have occurred in the dispensationalist position. The first is over how to conceive of the tribulation. One group, the 'historic premillennial-ists', understands the great tribulation to be a brief but undeter-mined period of trouble. Another, and probably the majority, connects the tribulation with the seventieth week of Daniel 9:27, a period of seven years whose latter half pertains strictly to the great tribulation.

The second major division is over the precise relationship of the rapture to the tribulation. Three views exist:

1. *Pretribulationists* – the rapture is prior to the seventieth week.
2. *Midtribulationists* – the rapture is at the middle of the seventieth week.

   Both of these positions perceive the great tribulation as char-acterized by the apocalyptic wrath of God on the unbelieving world, from which the church is necessarily exempt (1 Thess. 5:9).
3. *Posttribulationists* – the great tribulation is merely an intensifi-cation of the kind of strife the church has suffered throughout history, and through which the church must logically pass.

There are other fine-tunings of this system in evidence.

Further, Darby fitted this understanding of premillennialism into a wider framework, that of dispensationalism. He observed that the church was a mystery of which only Paul wrote. From this sort of observation Darby posited that the purposes of God must be understood as working through a series of periods, or dispensations, in each of which God dealt with people in a unique way. There are seven periods or dispensations:

DARBY'S SEVEN DISPENSATIONS

1. Age of Innocence	pre-law and pre-fall
2. Age of Conscience	pre-law post-fall
3. Age of Human Government	the new economy after the Noahic flood
4. Age of Promise	from the call of Abraham to Moses
5. Age of Law	from Moses to Christ
6. Age of the Church/Grace	post-ascension to second advent
7. Age of the Kingdom/Millennium	from second advent to new creation

This fully developed or dispensationalist form of premillennialism is characterized by distinctive attitudes to two basic Bible passages: Revelation 20:1–10, which speaks of the 1000 years, and Revelation 16 to 20 which depicts the seven bowls of wrath, including the great tribulation and the final battles, and especially Armageddon (Rev. 16:12–16).

Critical evaluation

We can advance three criticisms of premillennialism. First, failure to understand the literary mode of apocalyptic in general, and the literary logic of Revelation in particular.[66] Secondly and relatedly, failure to understand the flow of biblical thought.

For example, the premillennialists point to two future hopes in the Bible: one for Israel, in which Old Testament prophecy is to be fulfilled in terms of the nation of Israel; the other for the gospel, and its future consummation. Now, having marked these off as two different entities, they try to combine them in their appreciation of the New Testament, and do so in literal terms. But the end result is neither fulfilment nor literal. Old Testament expressions of fulfilment are adjusted to include the gospel, such that it involves Christians as well as the Jews, Christ as well as David. But the New

---

[66] Goldsworthy's *Gospel in Revelation* is invaluable on this point.

Testament makes it plain that '*all* the promises of God find their yes and amen in Jesus Christ' (2 Cor. 1:18–20) The davidic hopes are taken up and fulfilled *in Christ* (Rom. 1:1–6; 15:14–19). And, for all their emphasis on the literal as the only proper hermeneutic, their handling of details is only partly literal. For example, the apocalyptic descriptions of the last great battles in both the Old Testament and the New Testament are adjusted to make way for modern technology. Armageddon is not fought with first-century weapons, but atom bombs! In general, there is also poor exegesis of specific passages. The Old Testament prophets speak of an earthly kingdom lasting forever, not 1000 years. Revelation 20 says nothing of a bodily presence of Christ on earth during this period, etc.[67]

What the Bible does with the expectations of the Old Testament for Israel is that at each of the different renewals or reiterations of the covenant, it describes the fulfilment of older expectations in new, expansive, and increasingly spiritual ways. When the pattern of its covenantal interest is taken into account, there are not two hopes in the Bible.[68]

Thirdly, literal premillennialism fails to understand the centrality of the Christ event. The New Testament shows that all the ingredients of the end are in the gospel of the Son of God:

- Humanity's sin has been judged in Christ on Calvary (Rom. 8:3).
- The single, new humanity of Old Testament promise is already resurrected in Christ and ascended to the right hand of the Father (Ephesians 1–2).
- The satan has already been confounded and cast out. His power has been removed by the finger of God. The decisive conflict has taken place, and the kingdom of God is victorious (Lk. 11:20; Col. 1:15–19 f.; 2:8–15).

But is reading Revelation in a christocentric way fair to the book itself? On any view, the book of Revelation is 'a word of encouragement to the churches in the front-line of gospel ministry in a hostile world . . . After the introductory vision, there are six groups of letters and visions which reveal the present age from different perspectives, but always as the age in which the victory of Christ is

---

[67] Graeme Goldsworthy, *Gospel and Kingdom: A Christian Interpretation of the Old Testament* (Exeter: Paternoster, 1981) 127–30.
[68] See Goldsworthy, *Gospel and Kingdom*, passim.

the supreme reality.'[69] These 'six' days lead to the final vision which, fulfilling the expectations of the Old Testament and their treatment in the New, is a vision of the sabbath rest of the people of God. Interspersed at key points among these 'days' are liturgical re-sponses which highlight the gospel victory of Christ (Rev. 4:8,11; 5:9–13; 7:10,12,13–17; 11:15–18; 12:10–12; 15:3–4; 19:1–8; 22:20–1). This structure thus impels us to read the historical drama in which the persecuted churches of Revelation are caught *back-wards* against the birth, life, death, resurrection and heavenly session of Jesus Christ. That is, understanding the experience of the church of all ages past, present and future is dependent in a recursive manner on the complete nature of the Christ event in the first century AD.

Therefore, all history subsequent to the death and resurrection of Christ is history at the end. All history AD is *crisis*, through the operation of the Spirit through the preached Word reapplying the decisive victory of Calvary and the empty tomb. The consummation

---

[69] I am indebted for these insights to my colleague Graeme Goldsworthy who has encapsulated his work on Revelation in the form of a responsive liturgy, Ē LEITOURGEIA TĒS APOKALUYSEŌS, unpublished pamphlet in the library of Moore Theological College, November 1997. Viewed as a liturgy of praise, Revelation may be read along these lines:

Prologue	read 1:1–20 (note esp. vv. 17–18)
	Response: praise of the risen Christ
First Day	read 3:1–6
	Response: 4:8, 11; 5:9–13; prayer for faithfulness and steadfastness in ministry
Second Day	read 6:1–2, 17; 7:9–10a
	Response: 7:10, 12, 13–17; meditation on chapter 7
Third Day	read 8:1–7; 11:15a
	Response: 11:15–18
Fourth Day	read 12:1–10a
	Response: 12:10–12
	read 15:1–3a
	Response: 15:3–4; prayer for mission
Fifth Day	read 17:1–6; 18:1–10
	Response 19:1–8; prayer for the world and the impact of the gospel on our society
Sixth Day	read 20:1–10
	Response: silent prayer
Seventh Day	read 21:1–5, 22–7, 22:1–5
	Response: 22:20–1

at Christ's return will mean that what we actually are in ourselves will finally coincide with what we are in our Head, Representative and Substitute at the right hand of the Father. The 'Day of the Lord' is thus:

- past   Christ has died and risen
- present   Christ reigns on earth through the preached Word
- future   Christ will come again

Thus, understood in the redemptive flow of the Bible, Armageddon is a metaphor for Calvary. Armageddon is every conquest of the gospel in a rebellious world. Armageddon will be a final putting down of the evil age and its deceitful master.[70]

Postmillennialism

Postmillennialism stresses gradual improvement in the human condition, in both spiritual and physical circumstances. It interprets the millennium as symbolic of a period in which the world becomes largely christianized, after which Christ returns:

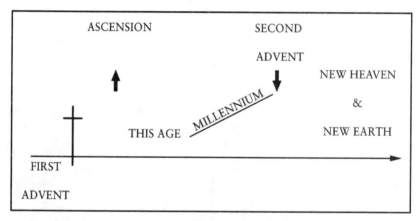

   Historically, it was formally expressed by the Anglican theologian Daniel Whitby (1638–1726), and in a distinctive way by Jonathan Edwards (1703–58). The Enlightenment then produced a paradigm shift which found special expression in the nineteenth-century American writer Hollis Read. In his two-volume *The Hand of God in History*, he celebrated the fact that God's millennial purposes were being fulfilled in civil America. George Marsden

---

[70] Goldsworthy, *Gospel and Kingdom*, 127.

points out that optimistic postmillennialism was 'by far the most prevalent apocalyptic view among American Protestants in the Civil War era'.[71] Millennial ideas seem also to have been appropriated by African Americans at that time, and sustained them in the great assault on their humanity by wider American society.[72] Although by the 1930s postmillennialism had suffered an eclipse,[73] more recently Hendrikus Berkhof in the Reformed tradition has expressed a similar outlook on western culture generally, but in a more evangelical and restrained form:

> So we arrive nevertheless at the conclusion that the Christian ferment has had a decisive role in the origin and evolution of the rules and goals of European-American society. Its characteristics of individualism, humanization, socialization, matter-of-factness, and orientation to the future are to be understood primarily as the penetration of the gospel.[74]

The details of various schemes to one side, postmillennialism fails because the New Testament links the restoration of the world, the removal of creation's futility, to 'the revealing of the children of God', that is, 'the redemption of our bodies' at the resurrection (Rom. 8:18–25). What is promised in the interregnum for the

---

[71] George M. Marsden, *The Evangelical Mind*, 185. Marsden traces some of the interface between postmillennialism and the rising interest in premillennialism.

[72] E.g., Timothy E. Fulop, ' "The Future Golden Day of the Race": Millennialism and Black Americans in the Nadir, 1877–1901', *Harvard Theological Review* 84 (1991) 75–99. Fulop also outlines several premillennial views.

[73] See James H. Moorhead, 'The Erosion of Postmillennialism in American Religious Thought, 1865–1925', *Church History* 53 (1984) 61–77. Moorhead traces the theological and social forces which led to the eclipse, among the latter the growing belief in continuity and efficiency which sat uneasily with the radical dichotomy and the unpredictable movement of the Spirit of God inherent in the biblical presentation of eschatology and evangelism. He concludes: 'In short, experience simply had not sustained postmillennialism. The product of an era when evangelicalism enjoyed cultural dominance, it could not survive when that ascendancy waned. It became a relic of a lost world.'

[74] *Christian Faith: An Introduction to the Study of the Faith* (Grand Rapids: Eerdmans, 1979) 511; for context see pp. 516–18. Earlier, he was even more optimistic; see his *Christ and the Meaning of History* (London: SCM, 1966) 169–78.

children of God is not a sort of prosperity, but suffering as the gospel makes its way in the world (Rom. 8:18–39; Mt. 10:34–9).

Amillennialism

Amillennialism believes that Christ returns after the millennium. The millennium is symbolic of this whole present age in which the gospel is preached. The kingdom of God is now present as the victorious Christ rules his church through Word and Spirit. Revelation 20:1–6 is a description of the souls of dead believers reigning with Christ in heaven, and another metaphor for the day of the Lord and its threefold significance.[75]

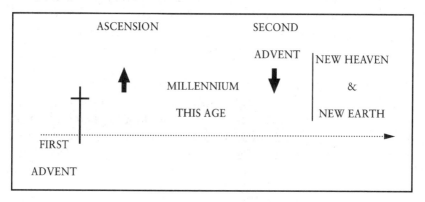

Millennialism Evaluated

P.D. Hanson has criticized modern millennialism, especially in the apocalyptic form it takes in dispensationalism, from the point of view of biblical studies. He argues that the social setting for biblical apocalyptic is alienation, and regards the modern phenomenon as pseudo-apocalyptic. They 'take the symbolic universe of an earlier movement and exploit it programmatically, often for nationalistic, racist, or dogmatic purposes'.[76] While it may be replied that the

---

[75] For a suggestive proposal that the reign of Rev. 20:4–6 should be understood as heavenly, and not earthly, following an earthly-heavenly pattern in John's apocalypse, see M. Gourgues, 'The Thousand-Year Reign (Rev. 20:1–6): Terrestrial or Celestial?', *Catholic Biblical Quarterly* 47(1985) 676–81.

[76] 'Apocalypticism', in *The Interpreters Dictionary of the Bible*, K. Crim (ed.), (Nashville: Abingdon, 1976) supp. vol. p. 33. See also his *The Dawn of Apocalyptic: The Historical and Sociological Roots of Jewish Apocalyptic Eschatology* (Philadelphia: Fortress, 1979) 2–4, 433–34, 442–44.

phenomenon of fundamentalism also springs from alienation, yet on its own terms his criticism may have some application to a resurgent evangelicalism.[77]

Hanson's understanding of apocalyptic as being essentially in tension with, or even contradiction to, the prophetic movement of the Bible has been influential. Apocalyptic tends to show future things as coming down from heaven without involving itself in the connection that these future things have to the present. Prophecy, on the other hand, shows future things as emerging from what already exists on earth. Prophets conserve and nurture mundane institutions by subjecting them to their vision of a cosmic order of justice to which all history is striving. Apocalyptic tends to abdicate social and political responsibility through escape into the timeless security of an alternative symbolic universe, even demonizing mundane institutions.[78] On this count, then, millennialism before the rise of modern premillennialism is more 'prophetic' in outlook, even though freely using the more strictly apocalyptic parts of Scripture to give detail to their historical optimism.

But prophetic and apocalyptic literature in the Bible need not be seen in so sharp a tension if the setting the canon gives it is paramount, and not the sociological reconstruction favoured by Hanson. W.J. Dumbrell has argued that given the unitary covenant structure of the Bible, apocalyptic is another way of depicting the same reality and telos that prophecy depicts, although under circumstances very hostile to the people of God and their aspirations. Apocalyptic claims that it makes plain the hidden meaning behind history, the meaning assumed by the prophets. 'The essential apocalyptic claim comes to be that in the end of days the great Day of the Lord will come. God himself will be enthroned as king.' But instead of acting through human agency, in apocalyptic God directly intervenes to bring in his kingdom and usher in the age to come.[79]

The 'meaning of history' and the fact that 'God directly intervenes to bring in his kingdom' surely give a better stance from which to evaluate millennialism than the social setting of biblical apocalyptic. The New Testament has a clear delineation of these parameters: the cross, the gospel of the cross. The preaching of

---

[77] On the question of the resurgence of evangelicalism, at least in North America, refer to the astute analysis of David F. Wells, *God in the Wasteland* (Grand Rapids: Eerdmans, 1994) 17–31.

[78] See Hanson, 'Apocalypticism', sup. vol. p. 33.

[79] W.J. Dumbrell, 'Apocalyptic Literature', pamphlet in the library of Moore Theological College, April 1991, p. 9.

the gospel is God's direct and personal work to bring about the progress and consummation of the kingdom of his Son, and hence his own kingdom. When evangelists announce the salvation which is in Christ, the Holy Spirit speaks (1 Pet. 1:10–12). That is why the gospel is 'the living and enduring word of God' (1 Pet. 1:23; Heb. 4:12–13; cf. 3:7). The gospel is not only the message of the kingdom, it is the very means by which it advances until the consummation, as the climactic ending of the Acts of the Apostles starkly testifies (Acts 28:30–1; Rom. 1:1–6; 15:14–21; 1 Cor. 15:1–28).

To a great extent, millennialism since the sixteenth century has been a search for certainty in the flow of history. But it is the promises of God which undergird historical flux, and those prom- ises find their fulfilment in Christ: his cross, and its exposition. A general problem with millennialism is that it overestimates particu- lar historical situations, and, it seems to me, does that because it has not made the cross paradigmatic.

In general, the failure has two steps. First, it has not been fully sensitive to the fact that apocalyptic creates a *symbolic* universe. Symbolic of what? The paradigmatic answer must be the cross, and the progress of its gospel to the ends of the earth. To interpret the symbols in terms of secular history is to avoid the intent of those symbols: secular history everywhere and in all cases is under the judgment of God, which he poured out at 'the place of the skull'. The progress and operation of that gospel of judgment (Rom. 2:3–16), as Luther so acutely saw, is always in the context of suffering. The Bible promises not prosperity, but suffering. An earthly kingdom of Christ, a paradisal reign? Yes, but only after *catastrophe*. And that is the second failure of millennialism in the modern period, it is optimistic about the present world order. The place of the Christian community in world history, and world history itself, is affirmed in the eschatological outlook of the Bible, but not quite in the form which millennialism has embraced.

Primary Reading

Jonathan Edwards *History of Redemption*, in *The Works of Jonathan Edwards* vol. 9 (New Haven: Yale University Press, 1989) pp. 127–8, 513–42, 430–41, 471–86.

Hal Lindsey   *The Late Great Planet Earth* (Grand Rapids: Zondervan, 1970) chapters 4 and 12.

OVER COFFEE

- What is Christian about premillennialism?
- How may the history of the Jews be a 'sign of the times'?

9

God and History:
Twentieth-Century Eschatology

The twentieth century marks a great revival in eschatological thought; much of it innovative and concerned to assert the biblical priorities of judgment and the transcendent purposes of God in Christ. In the first half of our century, Protestant theology reacted sharply against the nineteenth-century liberal equation of the kingdom of God and a perfected human world on earth. As Hebblethwaite[1] summarizes this trend, it 'reintroduced the dimension of eternity in religiously powerful ways': realized or existentialist eschatology; the transcendent, sovereign Word which acts now; the eschaton lying essentially outside of time and in eternity; and divine judgment on both individual and social life.

Since the 1950s, eschatology has built on this foundation, and sought to answer questions thrown up by our immediate scientific, philosophical, religious and social contexts.

Evolution has pointed us to a future perfection obtained by degrees. Recent cosmological thought, stimulated by advances in physics, has emphasized the person-producing trend of the universe, the fundamental link between mind and matter, and the fact that progress is by 'quantum' leaps. The theological response to these scientific insights has been various, but overall there is secular and theological interest in predicting the future by extrapolating from present trends, while attempting to recognize that 'quantum' leaps introduce an important element of discontinuity not entirely amenable to prediction.

Secular philosophy has, by and large, continued to be disdainful of any metaphysic, although there is a trend in the opposite

---

[1] Brian Hebblethwaite, *The Christian Hope* (Basingstoke, Harts: Marshall, Morgan & Scott, 1984) 151.

direction from Karl Popper, Michael Polanyi, and the like. Religious philosophy, as it has impinged on eschatology, has focused
on two sets of problems: the question of continuity and individu-
ation raised by life after death; and the relationship between time
and eternity. It has concluded that the concept of God can no
longer be spelled out in purely non-temporal terms, and that thus
the ultimate future of man and of creation cannot possibly take
non-temporal forms.

Our immediate religious context is shaped by the recognition that
other religions evince real experiences of the divine, with appropriate spiritual responses and belief systems. This has focused attention
on the problems inherent in a conception of judgment which fixes
a person's eternal salvation or damnation at death, a death which
most often follows a thwarted and opportunity-deprived life. Must
we not then affirm the possibility of further religious development
after death?

On the social front, eschatological thinking has had to grapple
with the problem of the gross, and seemingly intractable, consequences of world poverty. The fact that Europe was devastated by
World War II, and that the majority of the world's population are
still inescapably caught in a cycle of poverty caused by famine,
overpopulation, underdevelopment, political oppression, ethnic divisions and the like has led to concern about the philosophical
question of hope, and consideration of the concrete possibility of
liberation. What consequences does the Christian conception of the
future have for a human spirit which is at present largely chained
by pessimism and oppression?

In order to understand some of the resurgence in eschatological
thought in the twentieth century, we will concentrate on the contributions of Karl Barth (1886–1968), Liberation Theology, and
Jürgen Moltmann (b. 1926). All three have this in common: they
state, against the idealism of so much liberal theology, that God
actively works in human history.

Karl Barth: 'Let God be God'

Karl Barth is recognized as 'the most influential German-speaking
theologian of the twentieth century'[2], whose work 'is not simply

---

[2] W.A. Elwell (ed.), *Evangelical Dictionary of Theology* (Grand Rapids:
Baker; Carlisle: Paternoster, 1984) 126.

a persuasive restatement of the main lines of the Christian faith; it also constitutes one of the major critical responses to the Enlightenment'.[3] Born into a Swiss theological family, Karl Barth studied at various European universities under the leading teachers of the day, including Adolph Harnack. As a village pastor at Safenwil in Switzerland, he became increasingly dismayed at the hollowness of his liberal theological education, and gradually rediscovered Scripture as revelation – the Word of God and not merely the word of man. From this vantage point Barth was to reject his liberal theological inheritance for what it was, the religion of man. Barth eventually took up important teaching posts, from which he wrote extensively. His major work is the multi-volume *Church Dogmatics*, begun in 1932 and still incomplete at his death in 1968. In the events in Germany leading up to the Second World War, Barth became increasingly involved in opposition to Hitler, and especially Hitler's attempt to baptize Christianity into his pagan Germanic outlook. The result was the Barmen Declaration of 1935 by the Confessing Church which stayed outside the move by the vast majority of Protestant German Christians (including those from pietist backgrounds) into the church structures and beliefs approved by the Nazi state. Barth was then exiled to his native Basle in Switzerland where he taught for the rest of his career.

Barth's theological work is massive and thorough. In the book which launched him into the theological arena in 1920, Barth wrote: 'Christianity that is not entirely and altogether eschatology has entirely and altogether nothing to do with Christ.'[4] Just what is that eschatology? Barth's understanding is best seen against several important emphases in his wider theological enterprise.

Three leading thoughts

There are three leading thoughts in Karl Barth's theological enter-prise. First, that 'God is God', and must be acknowledged as such by theology. God is the transcendent One, and is not reducible to or by any anthropocentric formula. Secondly, 'that God is only known by God'. God is only really known to and by himself, and

---

[3] Sinclair B. Ferguson and D.F. Wright (eds.), *New Dictionary of Theology* (Leicester: Inter-Varsity Press, 1988) 80.
[4] Karl Barth, *Epistle to the Romans* (Oxford: Oxford University Press, [6]1933), 314.

thus God only reveals himself in Jesus Christ, and cannot be known outside of this revelation. Thirdly, in this self-existence, self-knowledge and self-revelation to men, God is the Lord. He alone is sovereign, or free; and in all his works and words, including his self-humiliation in the life and work of Jesus Christ, he remains this free Lord.

We note that Barth has radically answered the theological enter-prise of post-Kantian liberal theology. The Kantian barrier to knowledge of God is breached in that the first thought in theology is not that God is the 'object', and thus limited by man's epistemo-logical *a priori*, but the Subject; the free Lord who reveals himself on his own terms, in Jesus Christ. It is only when we have said that God is the Subject of his own revelation, who has freely in that revelation, as an exercise of his lordship, given himself to human-kind as object, that we can engage in theological discourse about him. We can thus expect that Barth's eschatology will radically deny that the kingdom of God is reducible to a moral experience amongst men.

Further, because Barth takes the Christ event as absolutely normative and all-embracive, we can expect that he will treat salvation history with great seriousness. Thus he insists on the necessity of the historical reality of the miracles of Jesus, and especially on the resurrection and the virgin birth. How then will he handle the promised parousia?

Vertical eschatology of the Word

In his second edition of his *Epistle to the Romans* Barth stated:

> If I have a system, it is limited to a recognition of what Kierkegaard called the 'infinite qualitative distinction' between time and eternity.[5]

What Barth is saying is that God is transcendent, and that there is no bridge from man to God but only a bridge from God to man, Jesus Christ. This emphasis on the absolute distinction between time and eternity, and the only bridge between the transcendent God and us being the short 'visit' amongst us of Jesus Christ, has produced what is often termed a 'vertical eschatology'.[6]

---

[5] *Epistle to the Romans*, 10.
[6] A.A. Hoekema, *The Bible and the Future* (Grand Rapids: Eerdmans, 1978) 306–7.

It is the Word then which has brought God's final purposes to us. Following Calvin at this point, Barth emphasizes that this Word has brought *all* God's purposes to us, and taken them up into heaven, into Godhead, with himself. Thus Barth radically affirms that this eschatological Word is already an absolute Word of *judgment* on man's morality, culture and religion. This Word is also the *nearness* of God to us, and in such absolute terms that it cannot really be thought of as somehow becoming qualitatively greater at a future date. That is, in Jesus Christ, the One who has taken our redeemed humanity up into heaven, we already have the presence of God in our midst, and we are present before him. This approach has produced what is in essence a 'timeless eschatology'.

The point can be illustrated by how Barth viewed the parousia in his commentary on Romans, which marked the public beginning of his theological work. 'Parousia' is a Greek word which means 'presence' as much as 'return', and its use in the New Testament, Barth points out, emphasizes the nearness of Christ, a nearness which has dynamically salvific consequences. Later, Barth will speak of a threefold parousia, a threefold effective presence of Christ as King and Saviour:[7]

- first parousia or coming of Christ – his birth, life, death and most especially, his resurrection: 'the already'
- second parousia or coming of Christ – Pentecost, when he sent his Spirit: 'the even now'
- final parousia or coming of Christ – when he returns as judge of the living and the dead: 'the not yet'

Romans 13:11 states: 'Besides this you know what hour it is, how it is full time now for you to wake from sleep. For salvation is nearer to us now than when we first believed.' In his early commentary on this, Barth denies the chronological aspect apparent in the verse, and instead speaks of a different kind of nearness:

> Standing on the boundary of time, men are confronted by the overhanging, precipitous wall of God, by which all time and everything that is in time are dissolved. There it is that they await the Last Hour, the Parousia of Jesus Christ . . .

---

[7] *Church Dogmatics* (Edinburgh: T. & T. Clark, 1936–77) IV.3.292–6 ff.; 315; 902 ff.

Will there never be an end of all our ceaseless talk about the *delay* of the Parousia? How can the coming of that which doth not *enter in* ever be *delayed*? The end of which the New Testament speaks is no temporal event . . .

What *delays* its coming (the hope of the End) is not the Parousia, but our awakening. Did we but awake; did we but remember; did we but step forth from unqualified time into the time that has been qualified; were we only terrified by the fact that, whether we wish it or not, we so stand at every moment on the frontier of time . . . Then we should await the Parousia . . . and then we should not hesitate to repent, to be converted, to think the thought of eternity, and therefore – to love [8]

Eschatological expectation, then, is not so much a looking forward to certain events which will happen in the future, but rather, apprehending Jesus Christ in repentance and faith at every moment when we confront him. It is in a real sense a timeless eschatology. The eschatological moment is very much *now*, when eternity breaks into time in the Word of judgment and grace, and creates faith and a life centred on God.

Note that Barth does not deny a future parousia of Jesus Christ, but affirms that its real significance is here and now, almost acting as a 'timeless symbol' of the need to respond at once to the Lord. The only new element at the parousia will be the unveiling of Christ's present lordship over what is already, in him, the new creation. The 'last judgment' at that time is just the final recognition by all of the judgment and redemption already completed in Jesus' life and work.

This sort of emphasis flows from Barth's high christology and his careful guarding of God's transcendence from the limitations of time. As a consequence of this transcendence, our resurrection too must be a non-temporal. Resurrection does not mean 'survival' after death, 'more time', a second life beyond the present, but entering into God's eternity where we shall see our whole life and God's creation in relation to what God has already done in Christ. It is in a sense a 'reversal' of how we tend to see things now. Even as Christians we tend to see what God had done in Christ from the perspective of its relation to *us*. This is due to the limitation of living now in time, a time which is of course radically affected by sin. Then, when with the resurrection we are in God's eternity, we will

---

[8] *Epistle to the Romans*, 500–1.

see things as they really are, from the vantage point of their relation to *God*.

In summary then, because of his christology and his under-standing of the transcendence of God, Barth's eschatology is in emphasis 'vertical' and 'timeless'. There is a real end to our present time at the parousia of Jesus,[9] but nothing new will be added then that we do not already have in Christ. The real function of this parousia in the here and now is to motivate us to *wake up*.

What of the future?

This position is not without its critics,[10] who point to the fact that the Christian hope is also for a new *world* beyond death. Jürgen Moltmann is particularly concerned that Barth's position is defi-cient because it not only holds nothing concrete for the historical or worldly *future*, but also, in its emphasis on the already complete nature of God's end purposes in Jesus Christ, lacks the crucial element of a yet-to-be attained and realized promise, which he sees the Bible affirming.[11] We will turn to Moltmann's conception of 'promise' shortly.

Barth himself became unhappy about the treatment he gave the future aspects of eschatology in his earliest work. Later, in *Church Dogmatics*, he reconsidered his exegesis of Romans 13:11: 'But it is also clear that with all this art and eloquence I missed that distinctive feature of the passage, the teleology which it ascribes to time as it moves towards a real end.'[12] Further, he was disturbed by the way Paul Tillich and Rudolf Bultmann welcomed him as a fellow traveller in presenting a conception of God's action in time in which the future hope of the Bible is reduced to the existential 'now', centred not on God but on the passing fancies of human experience. Against that, Barth insists that the eternity of the living God of the Bible encompasses pre-time, time and post-time, and in such a way that God offers us concrete hope and movement towards that which is beyond time.

---

[9] CD, II.1.635.

[10] See Jürgen Moltmann, *Theology of Hope: On the Ground and the Implications of a Christian Eschatology*, trans. James W. Leitch (London: SCM, 1967) 45–58; Hoekema, *Bible and the Future*, 306–8; and Hebblethwaite, *Christian Hope*, 134–9.

[11] *Theology of Hope*, 58.

[12] CD II.1.635.

What more does Barth say about that 'real end'? Barth will not allow us to answer that question without focusing it through Christ, and in this his doctrine of election is most important. Christ is both the Elect One (1 Sam. 10:24; Isa. 42:1; Mt. 12:18; Lk. 9:35), in whom all individual men and women are made elect, are made alive (1 Cor. 15:22), and the Reprobate One, who died so that all might by grace escape death. Jesus' election, unlike ours, is to death, so that we who deserve death might enjoy eternal life. When we speak of Christ's death, we speak of the shadow of predestination. Predestination, then, is double, since Christ is both the elect Man and the reprobate Man. Because Christ has suffered reprobation for us on the cross, we do not need to think of individuals as being eternally destined for reprobation. Further, we may see all humankind as elect in Christ.

Barth can be criticized on two fronts. First, true, the Bible does say that the election of believers is based in the Elect One, Jesus Christ. And it also says that on the last day all will have resurrection bodies because of Christ's resurrection (Jn. 5:25–9; 1 Cor. 15:20–3). But, it does *not* speak of everyone (believers and unbelievers) being elect 'in Christ', *nor* of the dark side of election, reprobation, as also being 'in Christ'. Secondly, what stops this understanding of predestination from falling over into 'apokatastasis', universalism in the sense of every moral creature ultimately being saved? Barth does not answer the first criticism, but he does strongly deny 'universalism', for that would strip God of his freedom. Barth states that we must allow 'the possibility of the impossibly irrational', that there will be men and women who refuse to believe. However, given his understanding of election, it is hard to see how he can maintain his position on predestination without falling into 'universalism'.

More precisely, what does Barth's doctrine of election tell us about his eschatology? First, that like the Reformers, he thinks election and eschatology into each other. Thus, the shape of the future is ineluctably determined by Christ. This is also plainly the point of view of the New Testament, as for example Luke 17:21, Colossians 1:15–23, and Revelation 4 and 5, 21:22–7 show. Also, there will be men and women who will continue to stand outside the city of God in the irrationality of refusal to believe in Christ.

The concern to view the final parousia through the unity given to all God's actions in history by their one Subject or Agent, Jesus Christ, comes out clearly at several points in Barth's writings. In 1946 amid the ruins of the University of Bonn, Barth gave twenty-four lectures on the Apostles' Creed. On the clause, 'from thence he shall come to judge the quick and the dead', he concludes:

> *Venturus judicare:* God knows everything that exists and happens. Then we may well be terrified, and to that extent those visions of the Last Judgment are not simply meaningless. That which is not of God's grace and right cannot exist. Infinitely much human as well as Christian 'greatness' perhaps plunges there into the outermost darkness. That there is such a divine No is indeed included in this *iudicare*. But the moment we grant this we must revert to the truth that the Judge who puts some on the left and others on the right, is in fact He who has yielded Himself to the judgment of God *for me* and has taken away all malediction from me. It is He who died on the cross and rose at Easter. The fear of God in Jesus Christ can be none other than that which stands in the joy and confidence of the question: 'In what doth Christ's coming again comfort thee?' That does not lead to Apokatastasis. There is a decision and a division, but by Him who has interceded for us. Is there to-day a sharper division and a more urgent challenge than the message about this Judge?[13]

Later in 1959 in volume IV of *Church Dogmatics*, Barth devotes a whole section to Christian hope, where he explores the nature of the final parousia as the consummation of the prophetic work of Christ, as his 'not yet uttered Last Word':

> Jesus Christ has spoken in His resurrection. He speaks in the enlight-ening power of His Holy Spirit. And what He has spoken in His resurrection and continually speaks in the enlightening power of His Holy Spirit . . . the one and total and final act of divine reconciliation accomplished in Him, and He Himself as the one and total and unsurpassable Mediator between God and man, was and is the content of this declaration. Nevertheless, He has not yet uttered His last Word in this matter. For He has not yet spoken universally of Himself and the act of reconciliation accomplished in Him. He has not yet spoken of it in such a way that the ears and reason and hearts of all must receive it. He has not yet spoken of it immediately, i.e., in such a way that even those who are awakened by Him to faith and love can hear His voice in perfect purity and to the exclusion of every conceivable contradiction and opposition and above all participation in human falsehood. He has not spoken of it definitively . . . in the final Word of the Judge at which

---

[13] Karl Barth, *Dogmatics in Outline* (London: SCM, 1949) 135 f.

every knee must bow, both of things in heaven and things on earth (Phil. 2:10). He has not yet spoken of it in such sort that for Christians and non-Christians, for the living and dead, there can be no option but 'to live under Him in His kingdom, and to serve Him in eternal righteousness, innocence and blessedness'. This last, comprehensive, immediate and definitive Word has certainly been announced in His resurrection and is declared in the power of His Holy Spirit, but it has not yet been spoken.[14]

On that day, even 'the countless multitudes who either *ante* or *post Christum natum* have had no opportunity to hear' the Christian's witness to Christ, 'will hear His voice, whatever its signification for them (Jn. 5:25).'[15]

That then is the goal of time as it moves purposively towards its end in the future. Here we are not far from Calvin and Luther who conceived of the end as the final conquest of a sinful humanity by the gospel, the consummation of the kingdom of Christ.

Shape of Christian hope: 'striding towards the future'

In his exegetical work, Barth notes how in the New Testament the lines between the Then, the Now and the One Day everywhere intersect. The point being made by Scripture is that because of the person and work of Christ, the Not Yet (the Day) must be viewed in terms of the Already (the Then) and the Even Now (the Now).[16] To be sure, 'there is a plain irremovable distinction' between the three moments, 'but there is no flat contradiction'. From this christological foundation, Barth explores the nature of a Christian's hope.

Our questions about hope are asked in the context of God's judgment on our works as Christians, more specifically, that service of God and the world which the Bible calls 'witness' and which God uses to bring about his purposes. We cannot presume on the final verdict. The very fact that Christians are in a minority, and that our Christian existence and witness is under a double veil of dubiety and frailty, makes the question of hope an acute one. But the Bible only offers hope, not as the vacillating and pragmatic response to changing circumstances we see in pagan thought, the hoped-for

---

[14] *CD* IV.3.903.
[15] *CD* IV.3.918.
[16] *CD* IV.3.911, cf. 908 f.

fulfilment of one's own dreams, but as the sure expectation that *God will keep his promises* about salvation. That is, in contrast to extrabiblical outlooks, Christian hope is not a dialectic between fluctuating experiences. 'The Christian expectation of the future cannot be uncertain, nor unsettled, nor sceptical, but only assured and patient and cheerful expectation.'[17] Further, the Bible makes it clear that hope is a defining characteristic of Christian existence, we exist *in* hope.

Drawing on John Calvin, *Institutes* 3.2.42, Barth notes that Christian hope has real power: hope refreshes faith. Paul says, 'We are saved by hope' (Rom. 8:24). Hope sustains faith in the face of temptation produced by the scoffing of the non-Christian and our own doubts about God keeping his promises. This power though, is not a 'habit', a kind of quality residing in the soul and needing to be practised by the Christian. Hope has power because Christ is not only the object of hope, he is also its subject; it is his power we have, the power of the one who is not absent from this hope but present in it even as its looks and moves towards him:[18]

> Jesus Christ, who does not merely precede and accompany him [the Christian] in time, who also comes to meet him from its end and goal, makes possible and actual his being as a Christian and a witness even in the apparently dark and empty time which is before him, including the hour of death.

Thus, as we ask our question about the nature of hope in the context of conflict, we see that the life of hope is one of 'striding as a Christian into the future' in our witness 'to the Lord who has not only come and is not only present but will come again in the future.'[19] Barth outlines three characteristics of this life of hope, of striding into the future.

First, although we often ask our questions about hope from the point of view of our personal futures, the Bible repeatedly tells us that we do so only from the twin standpoints of being members of the Christian community and of God's purpose to save the cosmos. Thus, 'hope' for a Christian is not for a private end, but in the context of acceptance of our assigned function in God's public ends. Hence the first mark of the life of hope is that we discharge the duty

---

[17] *CD* IV.3.909.
[18] *CD* IV.3.912–5.
[19] *CD* IV.3.929.

of watchmen and women. As eschatological watchpersons we are to be irrepressibly and constantly in a state of unrest, seeking to wake up those who are succumbing to slumber as if 'nothing had happened and nothing out of the ordinary could happen in the future'. 'The Christian now can only wake up others, from the sleeping Church and world around.' Because he is assured that God will keep his promises, 'he can only appear to them from time to time as a watchman'. In this way, the Christian life in hope is 'the seed of eternity already sown in the present world, or rather the seed of the coming salvation of the world'.[20]

Secondly, even though the content of Christian hope is the certainty of final things, because those final things are rooted in the first and second appearances of Christ, Christian hope does not view this life with either resignation or hopelessness. Penultimate developments towards the Not Yet are to be valued. Why? Because in the logic of Christian hope, *this* becomes *that*. Our witness now will be exalted then, even though sifted and purified by judgment. A Christian then must 'look hopefully for the visible signs of His coming, for indications of the impetus or flow of time to its goal and end'. Of course, he knows that 'in these penultimate things he is not dealing with the ultimate, with the judgment and redemption of the world. But he also knows that in them he is dealing with the negative and positive indications of the ultimate.' He hopes with provisional joy for the little lights. Again, Barth is at pains to point out that this 'joy in the penultimate' is not a private feeling but active participation in God's movement in history:

> He hopes that throughout the Christian world and the world at large there will always be relative restraints and restorations and reconstruc-tions as indications of the ultimate new creation to which the whole of creation moves. And as he hopes for these indications, he knows that he has some responsibility for them. He knows that he himself is claimed, not as an idle spectator, but actively . . . In other words, his Christian existence will be a prophetic existence.[21]

What these signs are, Barth does not here elaborate, but from his total repudiation of cultural Protestantism which equated the movement of the Holy Spirit with, first the spirit of western culture, and then in the 1930s the *Volksgeist*, and his stress on the content of hope as the

---

[20]   *CD* IV.3.933 f.
[21]   *CD* IV.3.934–9.

consummation of the prophetic work of Christ, they are the consequences, both positive and negative, of evangelism. This stands in
solidarity with the conception of the present manifestations of the
new creation we saw in Luther and Calvin.

The third characteristic of the life of hope is that is has and seeks
its origin in God and not in man. This obvious point is most
important. 'Hope' most often comes from the false springs of our
intellectual, theological, moral and religious efforts, or in sponta-
neous elevations of our inner or emotional lives. Or, and with
obvious applications in our day to certain hopes that are raised
amongst evangelicals by various church growth movements, 'hope'
may spuriously arise from 'systems' and 'programmes' in the indus-
trial and technological world we live in. Such anthropocentric hopes
cannot have the same clarity and power for Christian life as hopes
grounded in God, in Christ. The former are always exposed to the
possibility of relapse into scepticism or ambivalent obscurity.

It is significant that Barth exegetes the nature of Christian hope in
the context of his extended treatment of the work of the Holy Spirit,
the Spirit who spoke by the prophets and gives life, who brings in the
new creation. This has consequences as Barth goes back to the rise
of hope in God. Real hope gains its power from its origin in God,
and thus is not an idea but a reality, a real change in our beings, which
leads to 'an unbroken series of corresponding acts of human thought,
speech and action'. We *work out* our salvation (in fear and trem-
bling), we *work out* our life in hope, because it is God who works in
us to will and to do his good pleasure. We do not *fear* failure, for God
is the active agent. It is not magic or a trick of the mind. God is *Spirit*,
and therefore he truly brings us life, sets us on our feet as his partners.
'The breath of the living God raises him up a living man.' God as
Spirit works not by removing us ex-statically from ourselves, but
'logically' from within. That is, in the power of his eternal and
incarnate Logos, of his Word spoken in Jesus Christ, the Spirit of
God convicts, persuades and thus converts us to the life of hope. And
because God is the *Holy* Spirit (i.e. self-contained, wholly other) God
is not even bound by the change he has wrought in us, he remains
sovereign. He will have mercy on whom he will have mercy (Rom.
9:14). Therefore, the Christian life of hope is characterized by seeking
afresh each day and hour to be living men and women. 'The Christian
will stride out of the present into the future if according to the last
link in the chain he continues "instant in prayer." ' [22]

---

[22] *CD* IV.3.939–42.

We see then that for Barth eschatological hope is a dynamic, history-oriented concept that gives us an assured expectation of both the acceptance by God of our lives of witness and of the final triumph of the gospel, as the glory of God, the redemption of the world, is finally achieved. While Barth's eschatological outlook is 'vertical', as based in the person and work of Christ and the Spirit he has sent, it is also resolutely horizontal. It is not, therefore, 'timeless', but sees three moments of time as God moves us towards a definite end, a real future in terms of the Already, the Even Now, and the Not Yet.

Liberation Theology: God and the Unjust Society

Liberation theology is a diffuse movement born in Latin America in the late 1960s, and exists mainly within the Roman Catholic tradition. Three of its leading exponents are Gustavo Gutiérrez, Juan Segundo, and José Miranda. Rightly shocked by the massive poverty, injustice and inhumanity in this long Christianized con- tinent, Liberation Theologians ask as their key question, 'Where is the God of righteousness in a world of injustice?' With this question in mind, they turn to the Christian tradition, and find in the Exodus story and the Sermon on the Mount the first plank of their theological system, the priority of 'the poor'.

Theological outlook

We may discern five controlling features in their theological outlook[23]:

1. Goal: the liberation of the oppressed. We ought to start with the suffering of the excluded and the oppressed. Liberation theology represents a theological commitment to the poor, seen not as the objects of gospel charity, but as themselves the artisans of a new humanity – shapers, not shaped. In the revolutionary situation of Latin America, Leonardo Boff can write that 'the executioner shall not triumph over the poor'. Jesus' resurrection guarantees that unsuccessful insurrection

---

[23] In this I am in the main following M.M. Conn's article in S.B. Ferguson and D.F. Wright (eds.), *New Dictionary of Theology*, 389–91.

will triumph by keeping open the vision of the new heavens and the new earth. 'Surely those who have reached the top of the heap, who have a monopoly on power, possessions, or knowledge, may not define the final framework of a person's life, or the final ultimate facts! . . . Those who "rise up" to do battle for justice will rise up to new life as well.'[24]

2. Domain: the concrete social situation. The mission of the church is to be defined in terms of history and historical struggles for liberation. Any theological model that locates the meaning and purpose of history outside the concreteness of the historical 'now' is idealistic. Ideology 'does not offer adequate and scientific knowledge of reality: rather it masks it. Ideology does not rise above the empirical, irrational level. Therefore, it spontaneously fulfils a function of preservation of the established order.'[25] Hence, Liberation theologists have a strongly realized view of eschatological hope.

3. Method: reflection on praxis. 'Praxis' is a term taken from Marxist social theory, which starts with *action* and then moves to *reflection* on what is happening in society. A two-way process or dialectic between action and reflection emerges, whereby action gives insights and keys as we reflect on the Bible, and that reflection in turn gives us pointers to action. Thus, theology is to be *done*, not just learned. Theology as such must follow praxis, which is the precondition for knowledge, as people seek not merely to understand the world but to change it.

4. Use of the Bible. Biblical study is approached from the perspective of the oppressed. The biblical accounts, such as the Exodus, become not so much the *source* of theological norms when interpreted within the whole context of the Bible but *models* feeding the action–reflection cycle.

5. Reinterpretation of traditional Christian doctrines. The same question is applied to traditional Christian teachings as to the Bible: what is the meaning and significance of this truth for the oppressed of our continent? Leonardo Boff sees three main

---

[24] Leonardo Boff, 'How Ought We To Preach the Resurrection in a World Under Threat of Collective Death?,' in *When Theology Listens to the Poor* (San Francisco: Harper & Row, 1988) 135–6.

[25] Gustavo Gutiérrez, *A Theology of Liberation: History, Politics and Salvation*, trans. Sister Caridad Inda and John Eagleson (London: SCM, 1974) 235.

emphases emerging when the person and work of Christ is reflected on:

(i)   The incarnation and the social conditions in which Jesus worked show him to be the supreme model of a poor person who surrounded himself with the poor and identified with them.

(ii) Jesus' message of the kingdom of God involved 'integral liberation – spiritual, yes, but material as well.'

(iii) Jesus' redemptive death shows him to be 'the victim of a plot laid by the mighty of his time'.[26]

Eschatology

We may now make several more specific observations about the eschatological outlook of liberation theology.

1. It is a full-blown Kantian enterprise in that these theologians affirm that the revelation of God is to be found in the matrix of human interaction with history and culture. Segundo argues that whereas the traditional order of knowing is revelation, then faith, then signs of the times, the order of pedagogical value is the reverse, for since history is an open promise, we must expect God to communicate truth about himself and humanity in the challenges of history, the 'signs of the times'.[27]

Within this order of knowing, the historically appropriate inter-pretative tool to understand the oppressive culture within which

---

[26] 'But the One who has been raised was one of these crushed and crucified ones – Jesus, the Suffering Servant. It was not a Caesar at the peak of his glory, or a general at the apogee of his armed might, or a sage at the height of his reputation who inherited the first fruits of life. No, it was One committed to justice, especially to justice for the poor, and before he was raised his life was taken from him in a barbarous fashion.'; Boff, 'How Ought We To Preach the Resurrection', 134.

[27] Jan Luis Segundo, 'Revelation, Faith, Signs of the Times' (1988), in *Signs of the Times: Theological Reflections*, ed. A.T. Hennelly (Maryknoll, New York: Orbis, 1983) 128–48. 'We have shown that, in its very definition, there is no such thing as divine revelation (although there is such a thing as the "word of God" in the Bible) unless there is a human quest that converges with this word, a quest for which the word of God signifies a liberation of human potential and human values: the making of human beings "better that they were." This is the game God agrees to play in the divine self-communication to the human being' (p. 135).

they stand is Marxism. For Marxism argues that man's wholeness can be realized only through overcoming the alienating political and economic structures of society. Marxist class analysis divides a society into oppressors and oppressed. This conflictual sociological analysis identifies the injustices and exploitation within the histori-cal situation. Both Marxism and liberation theology condemn religion for supporting the status quo and legitimating the power of the oppressor. Because of its appeal to a metaphysical foundation beyond present historical experience, traditional Christian religion is lumped with political philosophies other than Marxism as 'ide-ology', which 'masks' the real exploitative situation.[28] However, unlike Marxism, liberation theology turns to the Christian faith as a means for bringing about liberation.

2.   In analysing society and the Bible, the important hermeneutical key is 'the epistemological privilege of the poor'. In the context of a continent which is seen in Roman Catholic terms to be over-whelmingly Christian, and is oppressively poor, liberation theology claims that the struggle is with man's inhumanity to man and not with unbelief. Gutiérrez stresses 'conversion to the neighbour', for 'the poor man, the other, reveals the totally Other to us'. Jesus 'secularizes the means of salvation, making the sacrament of the "other" a determining element of entry into the Kingdom of God' (Leonardo Boff). 'The poor are the epiphany of the Kingdom or of the infinite exteriority of God' (Enrique Dussel).[29]

3.   It follows then that eschatology, especially the biblical descrip-tion of the kingdom of God, is very much to be realized here and now, and in political terms. Gutiérrez thus reads the eschatological promises of salvation – in the Exodus material, the Old Testament prophets, and the subversive gospel message of the Magnificat – in terms of social and political 'praxis'. Yet, unlike Miranda, who insists that the eschaton is not beyond history but already present, Gutiérrez refuses to identify the kingdom with a just society on earth. What happens on Gutiérrez' view is that the announcement of the kingdom brings a realization of brotherhood and justice pointing to the future hope of a complete communion of all men with God. That is the political or temporal is grafted into the

---

[28] Gutiérrez, *Theology of Liberation*, 235.
[29] Cited from Hebblethwaite, *Christian Hope*, 166, and Webster, *Evangelical Dictionary*, 636.

eternal.[30] What happens now in political terms assumes the sort of eternal significance which we usually have only assigned to personal manifestations of the new creation, like 'the fruits of the Spirit'.

4. The concept of 'utopia' is important in understanding the realization now in political terms of the kingdom of God. Boff can refer to the resurrection of the earthly Jesus as 'a utopia come to life'. 'Jesus' message sums up the utopian dream of every heart: the overcoming, for good, of this alienated, subjected world.' 'With the Resurrection, the truth about utopia has come to light: not death, but life is the last word pronounced by God on human destiny.'[31]

In sociological terms, utopian thought refers to a historical plan for a qualitatively different society and expresses the aspiration to establish new types of social relations. It is a dynamic element in the historical 'becoming' of humanity, for its subversiveness means that it can become a driving force in history. In using this concept, Gutiérrez eschews all utopian thought which may be illusory, unrealistic or irrational.[32] He argues that while ideology by its very nature stands over, and thus against, history, utopia is characterized by its relationship to present historical reality. For Christian faith, utopia is ineluctably theocentric, for God calls us to believe that the justice and brotherhood of his kingdom are 'something possible, that efforts to bring it about are not in vain'. As the converse of the fact that all injustice is a breach with God, 'faith teaches that every human act which is orientated towards the construction of a more just society has value in terms of communion with God'.[33]

But, Gutiérrez insists, utopia ought not be confused with the kingdom of God itself. 'The gospel does not provide a utopia for us; this is a human work.' Utopian thought functions as a kind of stimulus to human imagination and action. It is not remote from the gospel, for the gospel is not alien to an historical plan. The Word is the foundation and the meaning of all human existence, including new existence, because – and the long-standing assumption in Roman Catholic natural theology that man encounters God in human love is foundational here – as utopia humanizes economic, social, and political liberation, it reveals God.[34] Liberation theology thus claims

---

[30] Gutiérrez, *Theology of Liberation*, 231–2.
[31] Boff, 'How Ought We To Preach the Resurrection', 127–30.
[32] Gutiérrez, *Theology of Liberation*, 232–9.
[33] Gutiérrez, *Theology of Liberation*, 237–8.
[34] Gutiérrez, *Theology of Liberation*, 237–9.

three functions for 'utopia': a stimulus to imagination and action, a revealer of God, and a mediation God has selected to raise this world from old to new.[35] Because the socialist left is sensitive to utopian thought, Segundo demands that in the Latin American context socialist thought must be an intrinsic element, rather than merely an object of study, in any authentic Christian theology.[36]

5. The relationship liberation theology posits between human history and the kingdom of God gives it the potential to be, at least in its embrace of the secular, a 'big picture' eschatology. Eschatol-ogy determines human history now. 'The commitment to the creation of a just society and, ultimately, to a new man, presupposes confidence in the future.' 'History is no longer as it was for the Greeks, an *anamnesis* a remembrance. It is rather a thrust into the future. The world is full of latent possibilities and expectations'.[37] This is not just an observation by Gutiérrez on contemporary thought, but has an important correlation with how he understands the working of the eschatological promise given to Abraham and fulfilled in Christ, the Lord of history and of the cosmos. That promise becomes richer and more definite in the promises made by God throughout history. 'The Promise is gradually revealed in all its universality and concrete expression: it is *already* fulfilled in historical events, but *not yet* completely; it incessantly projects itself into the future, creating a permanent historical mobility.' Because the Promise is the self-communication of God which dominates history, 'it illuminates and fructifies the future of humanity and leads it through incipient realizations towards its fulness'.[38]

Thus four foundational perspectives enable liberation theology to take up secular history as part of the coming of the kingdom of God: its order of knowing, its understanding of the kingdom of God in concrete political terms, the important role it gives to utopia, and the way it sees the future determining history now. This 'history', though, is progressive, either in actual change for the good or in the crushing of opposition to progress towards justice and humanization. It is a 'whiggish' or progessive view of history.

---

[35] Boff, 'How Ought We To Preach the Resurrection', 124–36; Gutiérrez, *Theology of Liberation*, 128, 238.

[36] Segundo, 'Capitalism-Socialism: A Theological Crux' (1974), in *Signs of the Times*, 18–33. Note especially his conclusions on pp. 31–3.

[37] Gutiérrez, *Theology of Liberation*, 213.

[38] Gutiérrez, *Theology of Liberation*, 160–1.

Critical questioning

More traditional theologians in both Roman Catholicism and evangelicalism have raised a number of questions about important issues in liberation theology.

1. Does the enterprise pay enough attention to the Godward and spiritual nature of the Christian faith? To say that 'God is on the side of the oppressed' does not mean that 'the oppressed are on the side of God'. Although liberation theology has rightly stressed the social aspects of sin, does it still take sin seriously enough? The biblical witness is that sin is personal and deliber-ate revolt against God, it provokes the wrath of God, it is slavery to satan, it is a state of spiritual death, it is a disease of the whole person and of the whole of society and of the whole cosmos. Elimination of poverty, oppression and the like is not the elimination of sin. As the existence of heaven and hell and the fact that Christ is also head over the angels show, the Bible's depiction of the new creation is somewhat larger than the earthly and political sphere (Eph. 1:10; 18–23; Col. 1:15–20).

2. It appears that its view of the atonement is one of moral influence only. Boff's meditations on the cross and resurrection are quite powerful and moving, but one is left wondering about the objective nature of the atonement. This is compounded by Segundo's repudiation of justification by faith alone without works as 'the key to all biblical exegesis, particularly in so far as cosmic and ecclesiological themes are concerned'.[39] Segundo repudiates the eschatology deeply embedded in the Reformation recovery of this doctrine: that God *himself* performs the revo-lutionary action that is decisive for the coming of the kingdom.[40] He argues that it is too one-sided; it evacuates the action of men and history of eschatological content. But justification by faith alone is not just a part of the gospel, an expression of one side of it, it is the gospel, a theological shorthand which invokes all the gospel and thus all of God's action in the world. That, arguably, is how Paul portrays it in Romans 5 to 16.

3. Does the Marxist understanding of class struggle really serve as an adequate understanding of oppression? Events at the end of

---

[39] Segundo, 'Capitalism–Socialism', 32.
[40] Segundo, 'Capitalism–Socialism', 24; where Segundo is citing Rudolf Weth.

the twentieth century place a very big question mark over this axiom of liberation theology.

4. Exegetically, 'the poor' in the Psalms and Jesus' teachings are 'the poor in spirit', that is, the righteous who are oppressed by the godless for their continued faith in God's promises. They may or may not also be materially disadvantaged. Jesus' priority in his ministry was to declare God's saving grace to the godless, 'the sick in need of a physician', including both the oppressor and the oppressed.

5. Liberation theology restricts God and his self-revelation in the Bible to the second stage of theological reflection. Like liberalism, it starts with humanity, not God. It is thus in danger of losing the great insight of Athanasius, Calvin and Barth, that 'God can only be known by God'. God must be understood on his own terms.

6. Are the future and the present linked in quite the way that liberation theology suggests in stressing the importance of utopia and embracing all progressive history as mediations of the kingdom of God? Luther's insight from the little apocalypses of the synoptic gospels gnaws at this whiggish view: the coming of the kingdom of God only brings upset among humanity outside the church. Does God promise progress towards a-kind-of peace and perfection now? Or does he promise suffering as we desperately hold on in faith, awaiting the return of the only true Reformer?

7. Finally, with Jürgen Moltmann, liberation theology has made some very important observations from the Bible about the nature of promise, how the Promise changes and unfolds in history, and the 'openness' of the promise to history. As Moltmann has asked this question more acutely, we will defer comment on this until the next section.

For all these criticisms, liberation theology poses an important question to traditional theology: How is theology to be orientated to the *practice* of justice and compassion towards the marginalized? That is, how may we speak biblically of commitment to the poor?

Jürgen Moltmann: 'The History of God'

Jürgen Moltmann, a theologian in the Reformed tradition, has been professor of systematic theology at Tübingen since 1967. As a prisoner of war in Britain, he reflected on the deep suffering that had been inflicted on humanity, not only in the previous decade in Europe, but also from other causes in other parts of the world. From this experience, Moltmann proceeded to write many articles and two series of books which, although not systematic theologies in the all-encompassing sense of the *Church Dogmatics* of Karl Barth, have progressively centred on certain key issues: suffering, God's involvement in Christ with this world of suffering, the true nature of Christian hope (eschatology), the church, and the Trinity.

FIRST SERIES	SECOND SERIES
Theology of Hope, 1967	*The Trinity and the Kingdom of God*, 1981
The Crucified God, 1974	*God in Creation*, 1985
The Church in the Power of the	*The Way of Jesus Christ*, 1990
Spirit, 1977	*The Spirit of Life*, 1992
	The Coming of God, 1996

His method has been to reflect in each area on the historical progress of Christian thinking, contemporary secular thought and the Bible. Especially, Moltmann has tried to think deeply about the cross, eschatological hope, and the fundamentally trinitarian structure of the New Testament itself. However, he has a core emphasis: history and the future.

We have already noted that Moltmann criticizes Barth's view of the eschaton for being merely the transcendent 'present of eternity', without a real interest in the historical future. Barth, he says, makes the history of Jesus Christ a revelation of eternity instead of a revelation of the future, and in that lies Barth's fundamental mistake. What does Moltmann mean by this fundamental emphasis on history and the future?

Revelation as promise and history

Moltmann's eschatological outlook is determined by his understanding of the nature of revelation. *Promise* is the category which determines revelation. All the revelations of God are promises. Both Old Testament and New Testament revelation is primarily in terms of promise. However, these promises were not completely resolved in any event – there remained an 'overspill', or 'incompleteness' that points to the future. God, Moltmann affirms,

'reveals himself in the form of promise *and in the history that is
marked by promise*'.[41]

What he is affirming here is that the revelation of God, following
the pattern discerned in his promises, does not belong to the
traditional doctrine of God as eternally complete in himself, nor to
anthropology in the Kantian mode, but to eschatology. Revelation
is an expectation of the future of the truth.[42]

Looking at the biblical data on eschatology and promise,
Moltmann notes that:

1.   God reveals himself in the arena of history. In the light of Paul's
words about 'the earnest expectation of the creature' (Rom. 8:19–
22), theology must attain to a *new way of thinking about history* –
a way which is oriented to God's future for the world.[43]

2.   From the 'overspill' nature of these promises we note that they
are open-ended to a future which is unpredictable from our point
of view.

3.   In this series of revelatory promises in history, God himself
freely, out of his love, opens himself up to change and suffering.
That is, God subjects *himself* to change, for us and his creation. The
Christ event is the determinative model. Understood against the
biblical pattern of promise, the resurrection of Jesus is an *anticipation* of the future of creation, which will be a *new* creation. In the
same way that it is possible to say that God in Jesus Christ now has
humanity as the mode of his being, God also has future as the mode
of his being.

4.   God is open to the future, and we in our history must be too.
Our future is the future of God, which is tied to time and history
because that is where God has chosen to reveal himself and realize
his potentiality which is centred on us. Taking points 2 and 3
together, we can see that Moltmann's eschatology is, in its foundation, much more theocentric than the rather secular outlook of
liberation theology, a God-centredness which ties us directly into
active fellowship with God.

The history of God with the world is not merely a manifestation
of what God is already in himself in eternity. God really has opened

---

[41]   Moltmann, *Theology of Hope*, emphasis mine.
[42]   *Theology of Hope*, 42–3.
[43]   *Theology of Hope*, 35.

himself to experience in history. There is therefore an important element of historical 'becoming' in God in his history with men. But, and this is an important caveat in Moltmann's theology, this God is always trinitarian.

This 'element of becoming in God' is illustrated in Moltmann's sensitive exposition of the meaning of the cross in *The Crucified God* (1974).[44] Reviewing the history of Christian thinking about the meaning of the cross, Moltmann endorses the Reformation breakthrough of Martin Luther, that God cannot be known from the point of view of natural theology, but only on the cross: *CRUX est sola nostra theologia* (the CROSS alone is our theology). God reveals himself on the cross. Whom do we expect to meet on the cross? The traditional answer (including to some extent Luther and Calvin) is 'the man Jesus Christ'. The Bible points us in a different direction, 'God'. The cross is a trinitarian event, for the Christ who dies there is both God and man. How then are the Father and the Spirit involved in the cross? If God died on the cross in the person of Jesus Christ, what does this death mean for the God who is trinitarian? Moltmann argues in quite unexceptional fashion that although all of God is involved in his works, the participation of the Persons is different. On the cross, the Son dies, the Father suffers and the Spirit is the mutual bond of love between them who is released into the world to continue God's end time purposes.

Now, because of the eschatological shape of all theology, and because of the nature of the cross event itself, the effect of the cross continues in our present history, and is full of eschatological promise for the future history of God, and therefore his world. In the terms of the Bible's portrayal of the end in 1 Corinthians 15:20–8, the potential of the 'crucified God' which will be then be revealed is the 'consummation of the Fatherhood of the Father'.[45] This is the Scripture's promise of the 'element of becoming in God' which will happen in future history. But why must we speak in these terms of that time when 'the Son will hand over the Kingdom to God the Father', and the Son will be subject to him 'so that God may be all in all'? Not only because of the trinitarian nature of God, but because that is the outworking of the cross and resurrection of Jesus Christ, which is where the passage begins.

---

[44] See especially chapter 6.

[45] *The Crucified God: The Cross of Christ as the Foundation and Criticism of Christian Theology*, trans. R.A. Wilson and John Bowden, (London: SCM, 1974) 266.

Through the consummation of the history of the message of the cross working in our history, we are being remade in the image of his Son. That is, we, his redeemed creation, are being brought into a filial relationship with God, and at the same time the Son shows his subordination to the Father, so that truly the promised end is the 'consummation of the Father'.

Thus the revelation of God's divinity entirely depends on the fulfilment of his promise for the future transformation of reality. We, for our part, can apprehend the truth of revelation 'only by confidently *waiting* for it and wholeheartedly *seeking* it'.[46]

5.   Further, it follows that if the experience of history is real for God, the eschatological Trinity will not be the same as the 'Trinity in the origin'. The Christ event has an eschatological goal, or end. This goal Moltmann calls the 'Trinity in the glorification'. 'Glory' is the biblical term for the divine splendour in which the whole creation is to participate in the End. We know that the history of Christ and the history of the Spirit are movements of the glorifica - tion of God: the glorification of the Father by the Son and the glorification of the Father and the Son by the Spirit. The Bible tells us that this glorification of God is also the glorification of people, since God is glorified only in the liberation of his creation. The liberation of his creation takes place by the inclusion of creation within the divine life. Unlike the more traditional outlook which does not expect the eschatological restoration of creation until the parousia, that is, after an apocalyptic judgment, Moltmann keeps the eschatological renewal of the human individual in synchrony with the renewal of creation conceived of as both culture and environment.[47] His insistence on a theocentric and sacral view of creation, as opposed to a secular or anthropocentric view, makes this all but inevitable in his eschatology. 'All things are created in order that the "common home" of all creatures shall become the "house of God".'[48] In this way, through the work of the Spirit of the Son, God gathers the whole creation into union with himself:

---

[46] *Theology of Hope*, 326; Moltmann's emphasis.
[47] Moltmann, *The Way of Jesus Christ: Christology in Messianic Dimension*, trans. Margaret Kohl (San Francisco: Harper, 1990) 45.
[48] 'Come Holy Spirit – Renew the Whole of Creation' (1990), in *History and the Triune God: Contributions to Trinitarian Theology* (New York: Crossroad, 1992) 74–6.

God experiences history in order to create history. He goes out of himself in order to gather things to himself.

Consequently, God's experience of history results in an enrichment of his own trinitarian being. As seen in Moltmann's exposition of the cross, the Fatherhood of the Father is consummated. 'In respect of the inner relationship of the Son to the Father, the consummation of the salvation of the world lies in the consummation of the history of God within the Trinity.'[49] This is basic to the theological structure he gives to history in *The Crucified God*, where he does not speak of the Spirit in personal terms. Later criticized for this, Moltmann replied, quite correctly, that the key to the personality of the Spirit is to recognize the Spirit's activity in relation to the Father and the Son: that of glorification. But, he goes further than this Athanasian answer: the trinitarian history of God is a history of changing trinitarian relationships, in which the Trinity has no fixed order as an essential Trinity must, but is a living history of changing trinitarian patterns – a view expounded at more length in *The Church in the Power of the Spirit*,[50] and in *The Spirit of Life*.[51]

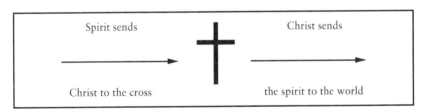

Already though, in *The Crucified God*, the Spirit replaces Christ in justification. This is not without precedence in eastern Orthodoxy, and perhaps in 1 Corinthians 6:11. But the New Testament strongly states that it is God (the Father) who justifies in and through Christ (e.g. Rom. 3:21–6; 4:24–5; 5:1; 8:28–39); and the reference to the Spirit in 1 Corinthians 6:11 is 'in the Spirit', *en tō pneumati tou theou hēmōn*.

We may diagram Moltmann's understanding of eschatology thus:

---

[49] *Crucified God*, 266.
[50] See the discussion of this in Richard Bauckham, *Moltmann: Messianic Theology in the Making* (Basingstoke: Marshall Pickering, 1987) 110.
[51] Jürgen Moltmann, *The Spirit of Life: A Universal Affirmation* (London; SCM, 1992), 268–309.

ORIGIN	GLORIFICATION / END
CROSS, RESURRECTION, PENTECOST	
CREATION	NEW CREATION
Trinitarian God	Trinitarian God +

Although Moltmann's speaks of the enrichment of God in terms of God's trinitarian nature and eschatological purposes, he quite consciously draws on Hegel in articulating his dialectical under-standing of the 'history of God'.[52] Moltmann rejects Hegel's dehis-toricizing of the historical features of the Christ event. Further, he is critical of the way Hegel's notion that the world is already objectively reconciled denies an eschatological future which is somehow *new*. He is also critical of the modalism in Hegel's understanding of the Trinity. But for all that, Moltmann adapts Hegel's dialectic.[53] In *The Crucified God*, Moltmann describes his theology of the cross as a dialectical panentheism: 'a trinitarian theology of the cross perceives God in the negative element and therefore the negative element in God, and in this dialectical way is panentheistic'.[54]

6. Because of the importance of history to God's freely willed revelation and self-realization, Moltmann rejects a non-temporal conception of the eternal, an absence of time in the new creation at the end. 'If the process of creation is to be completed through God's indwelling, then the unlimited fulness of divine *potentiality* (empha-sis mine) dwells in the new creation.'[55] Life systems remain open, even when glorified: 'there will be time and history, future and possibility in the Kingdom of glory as well . . . they will be present

---

[52] *Crucified God*, cf. 217, 246.

[53] See *The Coming of God: Christian Eschatology* (London: SCM, 1996) 326–30; and Bauckham, *Moltmann: Messianic Theology*, 36. On pp. 106–10 Bauckham has a useful, critical discussion of Moltmann's debt to, and differences with, Hegel. See also Richard Bauckham's *The Theology of Jürgen Moltmann* (Edinburgh: T. & T. Clark, 1995) 154–5.

[54] Moltmann, *Crucified God*, 277.

[55] *The Future of Creation* (London: SCM, 1979) 126.

in unimpeded measure and in a way that is no longer ambivalent.'
'We must . . . think of change without transience, time without the
past, and life without death.'[56]

Kingdom of God

Hope and activity now

For Moltmann the kingdom of God is not present but only future.
Christianity is to be understood as the community of those who
wait for the kingdom of God. In *The Theology of Hope*, he states
that the only sense in which the kingdom is present is 'as promise
and hope for the future horizon of all things'.[57] In *The Way of Jesus
Christ* this is viewed in terms of Jesus' gospel, in which the kingdom
of God '*is at hand*', or '*near*'. That is, it is 'close', and if close, 'then
it is already present, but *present* only as the *coming* kingdom'. What
we actually experience now is the immediate lordship of God 'in
the liberating of those who have been bound, and the healing of the
sick, in the expulsion of devils and the raising up of the humiliated.
But the conquest of death's power, and the experience of eternal
life, are undoubtedly future.'[58]

The fact that the kingdom is, in terms of the conquest of death's
power and of eternal life, only future implies that our present
existence stands in contradiction to what shall be:

> Hope's statements of promise, however, must stand in contradiction to
> the reality which can at present be experienced . . . Hence eschatology,
> too, is forbidden to ramble, and must formulate its statements of hope
> in contradiction to our present experience of suffering, evil and death.[59]

Because hope stands in contradiction to present reality, and because the revelation of God's purposes is historically dynamic,
hope may not be a mere passive anticipation of future blessings,
but must be a ferment in our thinking, summoned to the creative
transformation of reality. Christian hope may never rest content
with the status quo but must take up within itself all 'movements
of historic change' which aim at a better world.[60] 'This hope . . .
makes the church the source of continual new impulses towards

---

[56] Ibid.
[57] *Theology of Hope*, 223.
[58] *Way of Jesus Christ*, 97–8.
[59] *Theology of Hope*, 18–19.
[60] *Theology of Hope*, 34.

the realization of righteousness, freedom and humanity here in the light of the promised future that is to come.'[61]

Moltmann asks rhetorically, What does the gospel which announces the coming of God's justice and righteousness bring the poor now? Not the end of hunger, but '*a new dignity*. The poor, the slaves and the prostitutes are no longer the passive objects of oppression and humiliation; they are now their own conscious subjects, with all the dignity of God's first children . . . With this awareness, the poor, slaves and prostitutes can get up out of the dust and help themselves.' As they realize that '*God* is on their side and *God's future* belongs to them', they are on the way to the promised community which is determined by 'the culture of sharing'. But more than this, because Jesus promises that God is already present among the poor and the sick (Mt. 25), and Jesus brings the gospel to the poor and discovers the kingdom of God among them, the poor are the key to both Jesus' messiahship and to entrance into the kingdom of God for the rest of us.[62]

But we need to note that in spite of the fact that this activity is grounded in the never-ending historicity of the kingdom of God, it is not of the same genre as that espoused by liberation theology. The kingdom remains essentially a future entity; radical social activity – the 'commitment to justice and peace in this world' – is not the means by which we know God, but a response to that knowledge, a '*life in anticipation* of the coming One, life in "expectant creativity".'[63] Moltmann's stress on righteousness-producing activity is more akin to Luther's view of good works as the obverse of the Christian's experience of justification, by faith. However, unlike Luther, Moltmann sees Christian social activity as not only springing from our vision of the End, from eschatological hope, but also as having an ongoing eschatological significance because it is taken up into God and continued in God, in his own future. Thus a theology of hope must also embody a political theology, not as a mere ethical appendage, but as a means of talking about God's present revelatory, eschatological activity.

Israel

Moltmann's emphasis on the importance of history in understanding God's eschatological purposes leads him to take very

---

[61] *Theology of Hope*, 22.
[62] *Way of Jesus Christ*, 101–2.
[63] *Way of Jesus Christ*, 340–1.

seriously the hope of Joachim of Fiore and others for the future salvation of Israel. He uses the experience of Paul to expand on Joachim's recognition of the inadequacy of a church without Israel. Moltmann posits that it will be the appearing in glory of the Messiah, the universal appearance of Christ, which will redeem Israel. Both the church and Israel hope for the messianic kingdom which will combine both. Neither the church nor Israel will be triumphant, only Christ, who is the hope of both.[64] Moreover, the dawn of the messianic kingdom on earth will be preceded by the proclamation of a *new* gospel to all nations, the 'eternal gospel' of Revelation 14:6. This gospel is 'the universal preaching of the kingdom': 'a preaching which calls people, no longer to the church but to the kingdom – converts no longer to the Christian faith but to hope for the kingdom.'[65]

Parousia: history and judgment

Moltmann asks whether the parousia refers to an earthly future or a heavenly future. In discussing the earthly future, he uses the Greek term 'chiliasm', where we have used the Latin term 'millennialism'. Both refer to the same concept. Moltmann argues that chiliasm, with its earthly focus, needs eschatology, which is the transcendent side of chiliasm. As the history of Christianity shows, one without the other produces distortion. Chiliasm without eschatology has produced political chiliasm, which has had such disastrous effects in European history. And eschatology without chiliasm dissolves Christian hope into mere transcendent longing.[66]

Moltmann laments that for modern theology the early Christian expectation of the parousia is an embarrassment to be avoided by not mentioning it or by demythologization. Also regrettable are the fantasies woven around it by many Christian sects. Against this Moltmann asserts that Christ's parousia is 'the keystone supporting the whole of christology . . . the key to the understanding of the history of Christ'. Christ's messianic mission, the events of his life and death, 'would remain incomprehensible fragments if we were

---

[64] Moltmann, 'Christian Hope – Messianic or Transcendent? A Theological Conversation with Joachim of Fiore and Thomas Aquinas,' in *History and the Triune God*, 106–8.

[65] Moltmann, *The Coming of God*, 199; emphasis mine.

[66] 'Christian Hope – Messianic or Transcendent', *History and the Triune God*, 108–9.

not to take into account the future "Day of the Messiah" . . . Jesus' parousia in the universal glory of God.'[67]

What then does Moltmann make of it? Christ's parousia ought not be identified with either the temporal future or to be treated as supra-temporal and identical with eternity. How may we legiti-mately think about the fact that Christ's parousia and his kingdom can be thought of simultaneously as the end of time and the beginning of eternity? Following the lead of the word studies done by A. Oepke in *Theological Dictionary of the New Testament*, and by Paul Minear, Moltmann will not allow that 'parousia' can be used for the coming of Christ in the flesh, nor mean 'return'. In the tradition of Luther and Paul Gerhardt, Moltmann translates 'parousia' as 'future', and speaks of 'the future of Christ'.[68] We ought to see parousia as an 'End-time process, which the resurrec-tion of the crucified One has irrevocably set going'. It is a process which unveils *and* brings fulfilment. We cannot talk about this in the mode of *logos*, but only in the mode of promise. The very nature of the biblical statements show that to be the case. So the content must come from the gospel. We must then expect the parousia to 'bring the fulfilment of the history of salvation and the termination of the history of affliction and disaster'.[69]

Beyond that, Moltmann is reluctant to go, except to safeguard the notion of the eternity of God's kingdom from being understood as 'timelessness'. Because the eternity of the new creation is 'a *communicated eternity*, which consists in participation in God's essential eternity', eternity is best seen as 'one of life's dimensions: it is life in depth. It means the intensity of the lived life, not its endless extension.'[70]

What then of the judgment which the New Testament associates so closely with the parousia of Christ? Moltmann sees two strands in the Bible. The one, rooted in prophecy, is the righteousness of God which creates justice. This 'Day of the Messiah' is ultimately not a day of wrath, but the day on which peace begins when judgment is passed on injustice and enmity. The other, which is linked in Jewish apocalyptic to the coming of the Son of Man, is the apocalyptic law of retaliation, the punishment imposed on individual evildoers. There is clear conflict between these two

---

[67] *Way of Jesus Christ*, 316.
[68] *Way of Jesus Christ*, 318 and f.n. 10, 379–80.
[69] *Way of Jesus Christ*, 318–21.
[70] *Way of Jesus Christ*, 326–31.

notions of justice, one which creates and the other which establishes facts and rewards accordingly.

The Christian dilemma is heightened by the fact that the New Testament so clearly links the apocalyptic expectation of judgment with the Son of Man motif (e.g. Mt. 25:32–46; Rom. 8:33 f.; 2 Cor. 5:10). The conflict is heightened by the fact that the love of God which Jesus proclaimed and embodied is not love in mutuality; it is prevenient and unconditional love, whose 'most perfect form is the love of one's enemies'. Further, reconciliation is also seen as having already taken place on the cross (Col. 1:19–23; Eph. 2:16). Will Jesus at the parousia contradict this, by judging according to the penal law of retribution? The answer must be 'no'. Here Moltmann quite consciously falls back on the tradition of interpretation prominent in Origen which sees the law that the judge will apply as being for rehabilitation. Moltmann, however, eschews having to either affirm universal redemption and the redemption of the devil in order to promote confidence about the judgment, or affirm a double outcome for believers and the godless in order to emphasize the seriousness of the human situation. Whether all will be saved or only a few is *Jesus'* judgment. Confidence comes for Christians because 'this Jesus does not come to judge. He comes to raise up. This is the messianic interpretation of the expectation of Christ's judgment.'[71]

Thought through theologically, it becomes a question of whose will prevails.

> The doctrine of universal salvation is the expression of a boundless confidence in God: what God wants to do he can do, and will do. If he wants to help all human beings he will ultimately help all human beings. The doctrine of a double outcome of Judgment is the expression of a tremendous self-confidence on the part of human beings: if the decision "faith or disbelief" has eternal significance, then eternal destiny, salvation or damnation, lies in the hands of human beings.[72]

Against an appeal to both election and reprobation ultimately being the decision of God in predestination, Moltmann urges a universal election.[73]

---

[71] *Way of Jesus Christ*, 334–8; he treats of this at more length in *Coming of God*, 235–55.

[72] *Coming of God*, 244.

[73] Op. cit. 246–9.

Assessment

As we critically assess Moltmann's position we must acknowledge that much of his work on the biblical text rightly challenges some of the tenets of traditional theism which were grounded in pagan Greek philosophy. Further, Moltmann continues to write and refine previous statements. You need to follow his arguments closely, for it is too easy on first appearances to accuse him of heterodoxy. For our more limited purposes, four criticisms need to be made:

1. His stress on the kingdom of God as being only future, except for its role as a ferment in our thinking, is too one-sided. Present experience is not entirely contradictory to what is hoped for. Paul tells us that we have already been raised with Christ (Col. 3:1), that we already sit with him in the heavenly places (Eph. 2:6), and that we already possess 'the first fruits of the Spirit' (Rom. 8:23). We not only await God, but he is already present to us by his Spirit (Rom. 8:9). If the apotheosis of the coming kingdom is 'the con-summation of the Fatherhood of the Father',[74] then our calling on God as *Abba* now is already a real participation in what is yet to come (Rom. 8:14–17). Part of Moltmann's problem here is that he mostly characterizes the coming of the kingdom as liberation from injustice, whereas the New Testament views that as the penultimate of that kingdom in which righteousness is communion or fellowship or participation in the trinitarian life of God himself (Jn. 17 passim; cf. Rev. 21:1–4, 22–22:5).

2. The central problem of his doctrine of God, the meaning of temporality for God and God's relationship to the world is unsat-isfactorily handled in that it tends to picture God himself as open, and somehow 'at risk' as far as the future is concerned. The Bible does indeed see the future as open and in principle not amenable to our prediction, or extrapolation from our present – consider the weight of the apocalyptic images of the end. But as far as God is concerned, the taking up of temporality or history into himself in the person of Jesus Christ, who continues to reign in his humanity for and over us (especially in his high-priestly work depicted in Hebrews), is an event which is timeless from God's point of view, in that it is part of God's purposes 'before the foundation of the world' (Eph. 1:4; 1 Pet. 1:20; Rev. 13:8; Jn. 17:24). The Reformers

---

[74] *Crucified God*, 266.

emphasis on seeing election as the prior point and eschatology as the result does justice to the biblical material. The importance of election (and election which can only be 'read off' in Christ) to biblical eschatology shows us that the cross and its consummation is indeed timeless from God's point of view.

Moltmann's statement about 'the unlimited fulness of divine potentiality' raises the question of his ontological or metaphysical assumptions. His view of the effect on God himself of his involvement in our history and future is distinct from that posited by classical theism. There, God's essence is immutable in such a way that he cannot be changed by his involvement with us in creation and redemption. We have already noted Moltmann's conscious use of Hegel in his earlier work. Even in his more recent work, it is hard to see how the argument that 'the cosmic sufferings of this ecological end-time also become "sufferings of Christ" ', in the ongoing way Moltmann understands it, can work without Hegelian assumptions.[75]

When Moltmann implies ongoing ontological development in God, then surely we need to fall back on an older, traditional ontology or metaphysics which more keenly understood God's essential aseity, (i.e. self-existence) and that creation is *ex nihilo*. In this God, the Creator of heaven and earth who is the Father, there is no unrealized potential, for he is *purus actus*. Finally, Moltmann's estimate of God's being strongly suggests that God's present situation is *not* one of joy and fulfilment in the relationships between the Father, Son and Holy Spirit, and his people. The Bible's emphasis is on the fulfilment of our joy, not God's. God's joy is already complete because joy comes through service, and God's serving of us in Jesus Christ is perfect.

3. Revelation cannot be understood exclusively in terms of promise, let alone the open and historicized form that Moltmann will allow. Moltmann insists that God not only reveals himself in the form of promise, but also in *the history that is marked by promise*. So present history must also reveal God, and Moltmann stresses, from the point of view of the past encompassed by the Bible, the future of the promise must be seen as *open*. It is difficult to see how this does not spill over into a form of historicism, according to which each society produces its own distinctive values in the course of history, and thus reveals 'God' or 'Ultimate Concern', to use Paul

---

[75] *Way of Jesus Christ*, 151–9.

Tillich's phrase. Moltmann strives to understand the trinitarian and christological underpinnings of eschatology from the Bible, which is undoubtedly one of his great contributions to Christian thought. But that effort is undercut by the determinative role he gives to present and future history in the unveiling of an open promise.

Yes, the Bible does stress the element of promise, promises spoken from the mouth of God, and such promises contain 'over-spill', but it also stresses the past, and the present we already have in Jesus Christ. In understanding the present and the future, the Bible has an extraordinary emphasis on the revelatory and definitive nature of the saving deeds of God in the *past*, which are of eternal value at *this* time. We not only await the full revelation of the truth, we already know the truth, believe the truth, and obey the truth, because God has spoken to us by his Son (Jn. 8:32; Gal. 5:7; 2 Thess. 2:13; Heb. 10:26).

It is interesting, is it not, that in defining who we are and who we will become, the Bible uses the term 'remembering' (see Deut. 4:9–20). Such remembering does not seek to bring the past into the present, as in the myth and ritual of traditional religions, but takes *us* back to that act or acts which for-all-time have changed the shape of reality. The present and the future are determined by the past, not for antiquarian reasons, but because *God* has acted there to bring in the new creation. We are told in Romans 6 that 'we have died with Christ' (aorist tense), have been 'buried with him' (aorist), and thus enjoy all his benefits. The events of the death and resur-rection of Jesus Christ have permanently changed the structure of the universe, such that even unbelievers will be clothed with resur-rection bodies and enter judgment in that state (Col. 1:15–20, 2:14–19; Jn. 5:29, 1 Cor. 15:20–6). Thus we are saved as we are incorporated by faith into the living Christ of those past events and the benefits they bring now and in the future.

In terms of systematic theology, our understanding or recogni-tion of the content of revelation is controlled not just by the form of promise in which revelation so often comes, but by both the acts and person of God. The decisions that Moltmann has made about the aseity and potentiality of God, and about God and history, have predetermined his understanding of revelation.

4. It follows fairly closely from the definitive role the Bible assigns God's acts in his Son that christology is the integrating and inter-pretative key which we must apply in order to understand present reality and eschatological hope. The present is not only determined

by the future, but also by the past. The creation 'groans in eager expectation' (Rom. 8:19–22) because of a past event, the Fall of humankind, and will *continue* in that state until all humankind is gathered into the experience of somatic restoration, that is, resurrection. This event does not come until Jesus returns from heaven, where he presently rules for us, and hands the kingdom over to the Father (1 Cor. 15:23–8). Until that time, our relationship to the creation remains under the cloud of 'futility'. Our present experience and response to the kingdom, which is focused in heaven because of Jesus' ascension and present session there, is one of evangelism and suffering in that movement of the gospel not only in our own lives, but also throughout the world (Col. 1:24–9; 2 Cor. 1:5–7; Phil. 3:10; 2 Tim. 3:11). We repent, and point all persons in that direction and to a hope which for the present can only be characterized as 'heavenly'.

From the New Testament's point of view, evangelism and faith in Jesus Christ is the appropriate response to the kingdom of God, whether we view it as already present or to come. Evangelism is the way we are to express both our present dissatisfaction with the status quo and our hope. Mere 'protest' at the ills of a sorry world is not a sign of the life of God,[76] but evangelism is: whether men and women say 'yes', or even 'no' to it. Contrary to Moltmann's view of the coming judgment, where Jesus does not come to judge but only to raise up, evangelism is done in the face of the need 'to flee from the wrath to come' (Mt. 3:7). Paul's gospel is a gospel of judgment, for God will judge the secrets of men by Christ Jesus (Rom. 2:3–16). To the Athenians, Paul announces that the assurance of this is to be found in Jesus' resurrection (Acts 17:30–1). There *is* a conflict between the 'day of wrath' and the 'raising up'. But we are not left at the crossroads, unable to affirm or deny either in the light of the other. The Bible itself gives ample clues to the integration of these strands, and they turn on Christ – on the Christ who reconciles by conquest and humiliation of his enemies as well as by receiving those who flee from darkness to the light (Col. 2:15; Jn. 3:16–21). The evangelical promise of God for the future does not just bring ferment but works *now* to produce *faith* in Jesus Christ.

In this way, Jesus Christ does not just provide us with a paradigm of revelation as promise, but is also the content of that paradigm. In Jesus Christ, God's future is already present to us. The difference between the present and the future is the mode of that presence (cf.

---

[76] 'Come Holy Spirit', *History and the Triune God*, 79.

Calvin), but the content is the same. Moltmann does not appear to have given the weight he should to christology. The biblical witness is uncompromising, '*all* the promises of God find their "Yes" in Jesus Christ' (2 Cor. 1:18–22). Moltmann is undoubtedly correct in sharply drawing our attention to the Father-centred nature of Christ's ministry and person, and of our salvation, but our under-standing of this Father-centredness and its consequences for Chris-tian eschatology must be controlled by the truth that the Father's purposes *have been* fulfilled in his Son.

Following Joachim of Fiore,[77] Moltmann understands history in a linear fashion, in a sense giving the same weight to each era in the revelation of the Father, Son and Holy Spirit who are revealed in the coming of the Messiah, his cross, resurrection and Pentecost. Certainly, alongside the diachronic sequence, both Joachim and Moltmann insist on the three ages being viewed 'synchronously as the one working of the triune God'.[78] But, without denying either the importance of history, or its linear progress through time, or the theological synchrony involved in this, the Bible moves from Creation to New Creation, with Jesus Christ at the centre, the One whose earthly manifestation and present heavenly session encom-pass and control past and future. It is perhaps no surprise that, as with the eastern fathers, the role of the Spirit replaces the present role of Christ in Moltmann's doctrine of justification. One wonders if he has not preserved the place of history in eschatology at the expense of christology.

5.   Moltmann's handling of the details of eschatology leaves one wondering whether he has escaped the very process he abhors, 'dehistoricization'. In blunting the historical and theological par-ticularity of those details, are we not left with just transcendent truths, just mere religion?

This blunting is apparent in Moltmann's treatment of 'the day of wrath' which is hardly a comfortable concept for anyone, but especially modern man, as Moltmann acknowledges. It also shows in his limiting of 'parousia' to the 'future', and shunning any notion of the coming of Christ in the flesh, or 'return'. All this sounds like a concession to the very embarrassment he eschews.

---

[77] 'Christian Hope – Messianic or Transcendent', *History and the Triune God*, 91–109.
[78] 'Christian Hope – Messianic or Transcendent', *History and the Triune God*, 103.

Two exegetical objections may be raised against his treatment of 'parousia'. First, to limit the search for understanding of the nature of Christ's 'return', the immanency of the coming kingdom of God, to one word, *parousia*, somewhat overlooks the fact that parousia is only one of a wider number of words describing the same notion: *hemera* (the day), *apokalypsis* (revelation), *epiphaneia* (appearance, coming). Secondly, to say that *parousia* is never used for the coming of Christ in the flesh is an assumption based not on the way the New Testament can use the word to refer to the coming variously of Stephanus, Titus and Paul, as well as Jesus, but on a reconstructed history of religious ideas.

Moltmann also limits the reality of the disciples' seeing Jesus' resurrection body to 'visions of a supernatural sight', to inner experiences, akin to his understanding of Paul's vision of Christ on the road to Damascus.[79] In this way he does the very thing he does not want to do, he denies the historical reality of Christian hope: 'Christ's resurrection is bodily resurrection, or it is not a resurrection at all . . . The expectation of the parousia is a bodily, earthly, "natural" or material expectation. Unless it is this it can provide no foundation for the hope of the new creation.'[80] Indeed, the New Testament depicts Christ's resurrection body as physical enough to be experienced with the outer senses of sight and touch and hearing (1 Jn. 1:1–4), not as some sort of inner event.

Moltmann's move away from the embarrassing particularity of bodily and historical change in the resurrection of Christ and his return is further evidenced by his preference for the language of 'transfiguration' to describe the coming kingdom of God.[81] 'Transfiguration' is the language of the transcendent, ahistorical eschatology of Thomas Aquinas. Under the impact of the Bible's depiction of the living God who acts and judges in history, although sometimes using the language of 'transfiguration', the Reformers more tellingly used the concept of 'reformation', 're-creation'. 'Transfiguration' speaks of a move from an earthly to an ideal state. 'Reformation' speaks not only of a move from one earthly state to another earthly state, but involves the process of a fiery tearing down of the old and rebuilding of the new, and an abrupt and observable disjunction. Further, the resurrection of Jesus Christ, and the

---

[79] *Way of Jesus Christ*, 216.
[80] *Way of Jesus Christ*, 256–7.
[81] *Way of Jesus Christ*, 253–6; also, 'Come Holy Spirit', *History and the Triune God*, 78.

consequent nature of our resurrection, means that in our thinking about 'the fiery tearing down' we must also affirm a real continuity between what is sown a physical body and what is raised a spiritual body (1 Cor. 15:42–9). This may, with Calvin, make the 'dissolving of the elements' (2 Pet. 3:10) a metaphor, but the same christological control must also make it a metaphor for an abrupt and radical disjunction which comes through judgment.

'Transfiguration' may seem a strange charge to bring against Moltmann, since he also uses the language of 'transformation', and in his appreciation of the Lutheran, Reformed and Eastern Orthodox traditions insists that the transformation promised at the End must not only be of the world of sin and death, but also penetrate 'the first, temporal creation too. The substantial conditions of creaturely existence itself must be changed.' The 'eschatological transformation of the world means a *fundamental transformation*'.[82] But, in his commendation of the position of his predecessor at Tübingen, Johann Tobias Beck, Moltmann reveals his unease with real historical change which would involve a dramatic intervention from outside present human existence and which in turn would bring with it a radical upset of the present world order, such that the operation of the last judgment has a dual outcome, saving transformation and its self-inflicted shadow, perdition. Having posed the question in terms of 'from above and outside' or 'from within', or from 'whence comes the eternal life characteristic of the new heavens and the new earth', Moltmann endorses Beck. Heaven and earth 'will work together for the future Shalom world'. 'If this potency is inherent in the earth, if there is a hidden presence of Christ in the earth of this kind, then in looking for the coming of Christ in glory our gaze cannot be directed merely to heaven, as is generally thought . . . Christoph Blumhardt could be right: "Nature is the womb of God" . . . Out of the earth God will come to meet us again.' Moltmann accepts the consequences of the earth's becoming the bearer or vehicle of both Christ's and our future: 'there is no fellowship with Christ without fellowship with the earth.'[83]

Although there is a real danger of over-exegeting the biblical depictions of the coming of the eschaton in a literal and even speculative direction, these depictions, even when they function as metaphors, speak clearly of two things: a massive disjunction

---

[82] *Coming of God*, 272.
[83] *Coming of God*, 278–9.

between now and then, which is experienced in real space and time as destruction and reconstruction.

The ultimate problem with these tendencies in Moltmann is that his eschatology is moving us towards 'just religion'; a way of embracing trends in the world using religious language and attitudes which the world can recognize on its own terms: 'protest' instead of 'evangelism'. I do not think he really wants to do this; but it is hard to escape the impression that he dissolves the really heavenly and transcendent pole of biblical eschatology into the earthly and immanent perhaps in parallel to his tendency to reduce the essential Trinity to the economic.

Gains in the Twentieth-Century Development

We may summarize a number of gains in the development of Christian eschatology in the twentieth century from the work of Karl Barth, Liberation theologians and Jürgen Moltmann. Karl Barth has focused four things for us:

1. The gap between eternity and time, earth and heaven, the phenomenal and noumenal so devastatingly exposed by Kant, is shown by Barth to be healed by eternity entering time in the person and work of Jesus Christ. Against Kant, who demonstrated that on the basis of our earthly experience we cannot know God, Barth powerfully asserted from the gospel that God can only be known by God,[84] and that God has revealed himself in Jesus Christ.

2. Not since the work of John Calvin has any theologian so clearly established from Holy Scripture that eschatology is grounded in Jesus Christ. Jesus Christ is not only the promise of the future, but he has already fulfilled that future promise in himself.

3. Judgment and parousia are neither obsolete ways of speaking about God's activity in the world nor are they far distant events. Barth has shown how judgment and parousia are immediate as well as future.

4. Eschatological hope is a dynamic movement of God himself which changes us, and it is history oriented, such that it gives

---

[84] 'Let us then willingly leave to God the knowledge of himself. For, as Hilary says, he is the one fit witness to himself, and is not known except through himself', John Calvin, *Institutes*, 1.13.21.

us an assured expectation of both the acceptance by God of our lives of witness and of the final triumph of the gospel as the glory of God, the redemption of the world, is finally achieved.

Liberation theology has acutely brought into focus questions which are often underplayed:

1. Where is the God of righteousness in a world of injustice? This question has been posed implicitly or explicitly throughout the Christian history of the last two millenia. To have it reposed in the way that Liberation theology does at the end of the twenti-eth century ought to discomfort the comfortable and raise the eyes of those suffering to the righteousness of God revealed in Jesus Christ.

2. Their central observation about how the concrete human con-text moulds eschatology makes us aware again of the need both to safeguard the objectivity of God's enscriptured revelation of Jesus Christ and to allow Christian expectation to do its own proper work as we seek, in Luther's powerful phrase, 'to live in God by faith and in our neighbour by love'. It is empirically demonstrable from Christian history that the 'utopias' con-structed from eschatological expectations do influence individ-ual and social behaviour. Liberation theology has reminded us of this, and of the need to ensure that we do not confuse such human 'utopias' with the kingdom of God. Done well, Christian eschatology both stimulates and marks the boundaries of our imagination on behalf of our neighbour.

Moltmann has also contributed much:

1. The notion of 'promise'; God's promise of a good, historical future which is not in principle able to be extrapolated from our present experience is central to Christian hope.

2. Most helpfully, Moltmann has reasserted the trinitarian foun-dation of eschatology, and the fact that Jesus has come from the bosom of the Father to lead us back to that bosom. Eschatology is indeed knowledge of God, who is Father, Son and Holy Spirit. Christian eschatological thought must give the same priority to the Father as trinitarian theology does.

3. Moltmann has creatively stressed the universal aspect of es-chatology through exploring the fact that the cross is an

eschatological event in which God has truly suffered for us. [85] From this he has posited an answer to the problem of evil and suffering in the world. Whatever qualifications one would like to make to that answer, in giving it he has at least exposed from Holy Scripture an eschatological framework for Christians to live by as Christians, and for a Christian appraisal of the non-Christian world.

4. Finally, not since the medieval period has anyone tried to paint a 'big picture' encompassing all reality – material and spiritual, physical and religious, economic and social, time and eternity – under the umbrella of eschatology, as Moltmann has done. Further, he has done it an age of scientific empiricism which no longer allows us to comfortably conceive of a chain of being holding the noumenal and phenomenal together in one whole. And, most especially, he has done so by working with the categories and motifs fundamental to biblical revelation: promise, *Deus adventurus* (the God who comes to us), salvation history, apocalyptic, and trinitarianism. Whether he has succeeded or not, you must judge.

Primary Reading

Karl Barth	'The Coming of Jesus Christ the Judge', in *Dogmatics in Outline* (London: SCM, 1949) pp. 129–36.
Karl Barth	'The Holy Spirit and Christian Hope', in *Church Dogmatics* (Edinburgh: T. & T. Clark, 1962) 4.3.902–42.
Jürgen Moltmann	'Methods in Eschatology', in *The Future of Creation* (London: SCM, 1979) 41–8.
Jürgen Moltmann	'The Hope of Resurrection and the Practice of Liberation', in *The Future of Creation* (London: SCM, 1979) pp. 97–114.

OVER COFFEE

- What may a Christian hope for in this life?
- What does our history mean for God?
- How, if at all, can we give the place to eschatology that the Middle Ages did?

---

[85] Refer especially to *Crucified God*, 200–90.

10

Christian Hope

History of the Doctrine of Hope

In a useful article[1], Jürgen Moltmann points to the underlying tension between Greek philosophical understandings of hope and that of the Bible. Even at their most positive, philosophical conceptions of hope retain undercurrents of uncertainty and unease. In sharp contrast, biblical thought always understands hope as the expectation of a good future which rests on God's promise. 'Because hope is moulded by the way in which God is understood, and determined by a relationship with God, it is unambiguous.'[2] The goal of hope is the eternal presence of God himself in the kingdom of glory which renews heaven and earth. The structure of hope in the Old and New Testaments is characterized by God's promise, fulfilment, and then promise of a sure and radical change of our existence into something which can only be understood as the formation of a new heavens and a new earth. This stands in sharp contrast to extra-biblical expectations which see hope as an extrapolation of the present into an expected future. Christian hope is not extrapolation, but anticipation of the promised future itself. 'This future is already at work in the present in hope for the future of God.'[3]

Moltmann points out that in many of the patristic writers the theme of hope is subordinate to their concentration on what happens to the human soul in salvation. But as we have seen, the apocalyptic strand stood somewhat as a protest against this. Importantly for the development of the theology of the Middle Ages, even

---

[1] Jürgen Moltmann, 'Hope', A. Richardson and J. Bowden (eds.), *A New Dictionary of Christian Theology* (London: SCM, 1983) 270–2.
[2] Moltmann, 'Hope', 271.
[3] Op. cit.

though he conceives of the final state as *societas angelorum* (a society of angels engaged in endless praise), Augustine's Neopla-tonic emphasis on the individual soul or mind as a 'microcosm' individualizes hope. Hope is the expectation of the individual soul for happiness hereafter (*vita beata*) in the vision (*visio*) and enjoy-ment (*fruitio*) of God. The apocalyptic elements of hope in the New Testament become domesticated by being made to speak of a thousand-year rule of the Roman state church. Even Joachim of Fiore's more radical use of apocalyptic is essentially church-centred, and so fails to affirm the renewal of creation. Thomas Aquinas does further work in this vein, and not only makes creaturely change a transfiguration instead of a recreation, but also makes hope one of the cardinal virtues alongside of faith and love. That is, not only is hope an expectation of what God will do for the soul and its body in the future, it is also a habit a Christian cultivates. Consequently, in western catholic theology hope has only a limited certainty.

This limited certainty is roundly demolished by Luther's recog-nition, through his theology of the cross, that justification is a thoroughly forensic event already done outside of us, for us, by Christ. In the present fallen state of the world, where God is hidden, hidden in and behind the cross, this justification is grasped by faith; not *merely* by faith, but by faith alone. Given the utter completeness and decisiveness of what God has done on the cross, faith is the only possible response from our side. Further, from the nature of the cross itself as God's redemptive judgment on the present age, faith is also an eschatological event. An *eschatological* event which, because it can only be understood as rooted and grounded *in Christ*, must in Pauline terms be a full and sure hope. That is, this hope is certain, not wavering, because it depends not on man but on God, the promise of God in Christ. Hence, faith in Christ must carry with it a sure hope, because faith depends on God's word of promise in the cross. Faith and hope cannot be split.

Luther's great contribution, as he thought the New Testament's teaching on 'faith' and 'hope' into each other in the light of the promise of God once given to Abraham and his descendants (Gen. 12:1–3) and now fulfilled on Golgotha, was to tie hope and faith together in a new way which redefined our understanding of both. On the one hand, because God's promise to save his rebellious creation is eschatological, faith is no longer just the start to the Christian life, as it is in the medieval understanding of the way of salvation derived from Augustine, but, because it is faith in an eschatological promise, is properly understood as a sufficient description of *all* of the Christian life. It covers the past when we began the Christian life, it covers the present, and it covers the future, because all are undergirded by the promise of God given in the cross. So, Luther pointed out, we are saved by faith, faith alone. On the other hand, because hope is a constituent part of the promise of salvation which as a promise demands belief as its appropriate response, hope cannot be understood as an uncertain, internal habit whose wavering nature we strengthen through certain religious exercises. Because faith sees that the promise of God has already been fulfilled outside of us, for us, in Christ Jesus, hope must now be affirmed as also outside of us, in Christ. Faith, then, teaches Christian hope that it must look outward and forward to the final fulfilment of God's promises with joyful and self-abandoned certainty.

In the light of those great gains it may be somewhat churlish to point out that Luther concentrated almost exclusively on the hope of the individual believer. But in John Calvin's rethinking of eschatology back into its christological base, and especially in his focus on the dynamic kingship of Christ and God, he emphasized that hope meant the restoration to order, to righteousness, of the whole heavens and earth, including even angels!

But these sixteenth-century reassertions of the distinctives in the biblical doctrine of hope were short-lived, for modern rationalism, whose beginnings lie in the seventeenth century, concentrated on the individual aspects of hope, thus escaping the embarrassment which comes with the way historical particulars are witnessed to by the New Testament. The eternal worth of the 'inner life of the believer', becomes the invisible, spiritual or mental part of man whose very hiddenness allows it to be rationally analysed without the nasty contradiction of normal historical processes posed by an alleged and promised overturn of physical decay in one person, Jesus of Nazareth, let alone the fantastical notion of a whole creation being renewed in the same way. The historical in biblical eschatology is replaced by a timeless idea. The resurrection is replaced by the immortality of the soul. The outcome was not altogether surprising. Descartes, Hobbes and Spinoza categorized hope as illusory, disruptive and dubious. Kant, Kierkegaard, Heidegger and Bultmann affirmed hope once again, but reduced its content to the *act* of hope. Which is as self- or human-centred as was the prevailing medieval notion of hope as a human habit.

Karl Barth marks a powerful turnaround. His christological understanding of eschatology reasserted in powerful ways the nature of Christian hope as the assured presence and expectation of a renewed humanity and cosmos because the promises of God have been fulfilled in Jesus Christ.

Jürgen Moltmann's *Theology of Hope* (1964) marks another powerful reassertion of the biblical vision for a good future resting on the promises of God. Moltmann's work brought into Christian theology the anthropological and social aspects of hope in Ernst Bloch's thinking. Through Marxist and biblical analysis of the concept of hope, Bloch shows that hope is part of what it means to be human. Bloch's 'ontology of not-yet-being' seeks to overcome the alienation of man and nature. Self-consciously working within a biblical and trinitarian perspective, Moltmann stresses the future-related and all-embracing character of the whole of Christian faith and action. His emphasis is very much centred on the fact that the hope which springs from faith in the all-embracing future of the risen Christ produces eschatologically conditioned *love*. This love draws us into acceptance and solidarity with the whole of suffering creation.

Moltmann's challenge goes further: He divides the development of Christian doctrine into three phases, each taking up and express-ing what was lacking in the other; 'A theology of love was developed in the Middle Ages and a theology of faith at the time of the Reformation; now it is important to develop a universal theology of hope which directs the church and humankind, humankind and nature, towards the kingdom of God and prepares them for it.'[4] But, is this in fact the case? Were Calvin and Luther wrong in identifying the life of faith as a sufficient description of Christian, eschatological existence? We need now to examine the relationship between faith, love and hope in the New Testament before we can offer some response to Moltmann's challenge.

Nature of Hope

Faith, hope and love

The occurrence in the New Testament of the trilogy, 'faith, hope and love' (1 Cor. 13:13), elsewhere expressed in the order 'hope . . . faith . . . love' (1 Pet. 1:3–9), and 'faith . . . love . . . hope' (Col. 1:4–5), is such that these three act as a suitable summary of

---

[4] 'Hope', 272.

Christian existence: 'remembering before our God and Father your work of faith and labour of love and steadfastness of hope in our Lord Jesus Christ' (1 Thess. 1:3). How are they related?

There is no insurmountable difficulty in seeing them related progressively as faith, love, hope, referring to past, present, future. Faith is in the promises of God given and fulfilled in the history of salvation unfolded for us in the Bible; love describes an appropriate form of relationship to One who very much deals with us now, who by his Spirit is present to us now; hope looks to the future fulfilment of what is inherent in the promise. But the progression is not chronological in the sense that one moves from one state or experience to another, however one may define the order of the three. 1 Thessalonians 1:3 shows us that they stand in a parallel relationship to one another, and can almost act as synonyms, even while we acknowledge the different content of each. This is so because all three are grounded in God, 'in our Lord Jesus Christ'. That is, each is a way of exegeting the other. There can therefore be no Christian faith which does not hope and love, no love which . . .

Are the three 'equal'? That is, must they continue to so coexist that to diminish one is to misunderstand the mind of God? Yes, but more, thus explained, they *must* be equal. Following Augustine's Neoplatonic outlook, medieval theology challenged this. On the basis of 'the greatest of these is love' (1 Cor. 13:13), and 'now we see in a mirror, darkly, but then face to face' (1 Cor. 13:12) taken with 'for we walk by faith, not by sight' (2 Cor. 5:7), 'faith' was seen as the earthly and inferior starting point for the Christian life of pilgrimage which sought to move on to the superior and other-worldly 'sight'. This 'sight', which one not only moved towards but tried as much as possible to realize now, was as Thomas Aquinas expressed it, the beatific vision, the enraptured gaze of one intellec-tual substance (the human soul) on another (God). That is, it was 'love'.

This, as the Reformation showed, was patent misexegesis due to reading the data of the Bible in a foreign (philosophical) framework instead of in accord with its immediate and ultimate context (the passage, and the history of God's promise). So, the 'sight' of 2 Corinthians 5:7 is not a description of the ultimate goal, but the 'appearance', the fact of our outer decay in the face of which faith continues to cling to the promises of God about ultimate resurrec-tion glory. 1 Corinthians 13 does not say that 'faith' and 'hope' give way to 'love', which remains alone at the end, but that love must be considered the greatest of these. Why? In the context of Paul's argument the answer is clear. Love makes the gifts, even the powerfully mysterious 'gifts of healings', subservient to the needs of the neighbour, that is, to their edification in the faith and hope of Jesus Christ. What does 'the greatest' mean on the wider stage? It is the greatest because God – who is the ground of this 'faith, hope, love' – can be characterized as 'love' in himself, but not as 'faith' and 'hope' in himself. God is love (1 John 4:8).

In the thirteenth century, against the individualism and rationalism of Boethius' understanding of God, Duns Scotus emphasizes the primacy of love and the freedom of the will in God and humanity. There are not three 'individuals of a rational nature' in God (along the Boethian line) but three Persons in one, who have their true Being-in-communion as Father, Son and Holy Spirit in the freedom of love. In God, his being and his love are identical. The unity of the Father and the Son and the Holy Spirit is not a mere numerical unity but the dynamic relational unity of love. The nature of the relationship between the members of the Trinity is love. And because of the love of God in sending his Son to die for us, through *faith* in that death, in *hope*, we have been brought to share in the life, the inner *love* of God who is Trinity. As Scotus puts it, the church as the first fruits of Christ's redemptive work and of the new creation is a communion of saints, a fellowship of *condiligentes*, fellow-lovers.

All of present Christian existence then must always be describable as faith, hope and love. And when it is thus described, when for example we understand that faith is always eschatological, and that hope springs from faith because hope is the promise that future realities have already been fulfilled outside of us in Jesus Christ and thus are assured for us, we may say 'love' and mean 'faith, hope and love'. Faced with the great promise of God to justify us in the death of his Son, we see that real life is living by every word which proceeds from the mouth of God, words which make up the promise, so that *the* characteristic way of describing the Christian life which embraces all aspects is 'faith', the life of faith. What content then, does 'hope' give to this 'faith'?

Hope is in Christ

Our hope is the promise of the resurrection of the dead (Acts 23: 6), eternal life (Tit. 1:2), the crown of righteousness (2 Tim. 4:8). This hope we must describe as an 'inheritance incorruptible and undefiled, and that does not fade', 'a living hope' (1 Pet. 1:3–4), a new creation

(1 Pet. 1:3; 2 Cor. 5:14–17), which God promised 'before times eternal' (Tit. 1:2), because we have been born into it, firmly implanted in it, by the resurrection of Jesus Christ from the dead (1 Pet. 1:3–4; 1 Cor. 15:12–23; Rom. 6:1–14). Our hope therefore is both grounded in Jesus Christ, and is in Jesus Christ, in God fulfilling his promises in his Son. Because of what he has already done, that is, justified us (which is testified to by his resurrection – Romans 4:25, 'was raised because of our justification'), we must also confess two further things. First, that this hope is a present as well as a future reality; by faith in Christ we are already made alive in him (Jn. 11:25–6; Rom. 6:1–14). Secondly, this resurrection hope encompasses all of the created order, even though it still groans under the weight of our disobedience (1 Cor. 15:20–2; Gal. 5:5–7; Eph. 2:5–7, 11–19; Col. 1:19–23; Rom. 8:18–25).

A movement of the ground of 'hope' needs to parallel what Martin Luther did for the ground of 'faith'. In the medieval schema, the faith which accessed justification was *fides charitate formata*, faith formed by love, faith active in love. When Luther saw that the righteousness of God, which is the righteousness of Christ revealed at the cross, is given to the faithful through faith (*per fidem*), he replaced the older understanding of *fides charitate formata*, with *fides Christo formata*: faith formed in Christ, faith living in Christ. We can state Luther's understanding of saving faith as:

> fides Christo *pro nobis* formata *extra nos*
> *(faith formed [i.e. living] in Christ who is for us outside of us)*

Thus, justification by faith is at once God's deed and God's word, *really* granted and really *granted*.[5]

When we likewise ground hope in Christ, we both remove it from the realm of human desire (the *spes passio*) and from merely being a comforting narrative by which the community sustains itself – we grasp it as *real* as it grasps us. Barth has put his finger on it: Christian hope has real power; hope refreshes faith, not because it is a habit, but because hope is *in* Christ. Christ is not only the object of hope, he is also its subject; it is his power we have.

---

[5] Heiko A. Oberman, ' "*Iustitia Christi*" and "*Iustitia Dei*": Luther and the Scholastic Doctrines of Justification', in *The Dawn of the Reformation: Essays in Late Medieval and Early Reformation Thought* (Edinburgh: T. & T. Clark, 1986) 120–5.

Hope has a goal

The blessed hope of the resurrection of the dead which embraces both creation in general and humanity in particular is not only a goal, it also has a goal, or rather, two goals. First, that we may have untrammelled fellowship with God our Father. He who is the resurrection and the life raises Lazarus to reverse the unnatural rupture to loving relationships which sin and death had imposed (Jn. 11:25–44; Rev. 20:11–21:5). Secondly, and consequently, be-cause God's glory is his redeemed children (Eph. 1:14 [cf. Deut. 32:9], 17–18; Col. 1:27 [cf. 1 Thess. 2:20]; 2 Cor. 8:23; Rom. 5:2), the goal of our resurrection is the consummation of the Fatherhood of God (1 Cor. 15:20–8).

Hope is heavenly

Because our hope is in Christ who is now seated in the heavenlies at the right hand of the Father, it is no surprise to note that hope is heavenly, 'kept in heaven for us' (1 Pet. 1:4) and will be revealed on the last day (2 Tim. 4:8; Rom. 8:18–25). As the third petition of the Lord's Prayer shows us ('your will be done on earth as in heaven'), heaven is the place where God's will is done unopposed. 'Heaven', then, is a metaphor for the untrammelled rule of God over us and for us. It is we, in the rebellion of Adam and Eve, who have created the need for heaven. 'Heaven', as the special sphere of God, is not needed in Genesis 1 and 2. God walks in the garden in the cool of the evening, directly and personally ruling his people, exercising his fatherly love of them. After Genesis 3:6, heaven is needed. The 'hope of heaven' reminds us that this untrammelled rule, fully displayed in the life, death and resurrection of Jesus Christ, yet waits to be fully revealed. Nonetheless, because of Jesus' resurrection and ascension, we already sit in the heavenlies where Christ is (Eph. 2:6), while we await the full revelation of this rule in our daily struggle. We await heaven with patience and pride (Heb. 3:6). Our pride, our boasting, is in and of Christ. At the consummation, when the Holy City comes down from heaven and the dwelling place of God is amongst his people, at the time of the new heaven and the new earth, where is heaven? After the coming of this City, in Revelations 21–22, there is no more description of heaven, or earth, for at that time the distinction is abolished, God rules his people directly.

Hope and faith and love

Hope, then, because it is a promise about things yet unseen, requires commitment. It requires our prayers, our patience, our perseverance (Heb. 3:6, 14; 6:11). It must become our goal, the determinant of Christian living (Col. 3:1–4; 1 Pet. 2:11–12). We must live in the hope of heaven, with the blessed hope of the resurrection before our eyes, we must not, in oft-quoted words, 'live like dead men on furlough', but like dead men who are alive in Christ. Hope requires faith as much as faith requires hope.

> The Christian hope is not only the last chapter of theological doctrine; it is itself the goal to which the Christian faith reaches forward. It is what faith intends, what is at stake in faith. But this is nothing else than the full revelation of what is already given to us in faith in Jesus as the true Word of God: that the love of God is the first and last thing, through which we and the world were created. That this love will be manifest without concealment by the world and that God 'will be all in all': this is the meaning of the gospel.[6]

Hope and the Shape of the Christian Life

Graveyards, or rather the inscriptions on their tombstones, yield material for social history. The inscriptions speak of ultimate aspirations and thus reveal the structures of thought with which we undergird life. It is interesting to note the shift from 'in the blessed hope of the resurrection', to 'in loving memory of'. A shift, which although it may in one locality distinguish an earlier generation from a later one, or even the other way round, never-theless reflects a pre- and post-enlightenment view of the last things.

In the eschatology of the Bible, promise is foundational and determinative of our final expectations (Gen. 12:1–3; Rom. 4:16–21; Heb. 12; Rom. 8:18–25). In our contemporary context, we may note four shifts, even denials of the 'the blessed hope of the resurrection', or rather, four lifestyles whose underlying nakedness and corruption are stripped bare by that blessed hope.

---

[6] Emil Brunner, *The Christian Doctrine of the Church, Faith and the Consummation* (Philadelphia: Westminster Press, 1962) 346.

1. Materialism

Materialism in its Marxist form, which is now capitulating to its other form, capitalism, defines the *summum bonum* ('the ultimate good', that is, 'the good life') as being brought about by and enjoyed as material plenty in this life. This is the goal of the debilitating struggle between humanity and nature – humanity and their personal, social and physical environment – and it will be achieved in this age through our collective effort.

It is a nonsensical idea. Corrupt humanity cannot resolve the corruption of this world which flows from its own corruption (Rom. 8:18–25), that is, its own hatred of God and therefore of each other. Even the theoretical materialism of Marxism recognized this and was forced to posit a perfectible humanity free from original sin. The failure of the Marxist hypothesis now lies open on the world stage.

It is even more nonsensical in its capitalist form. The stock exchange has screamed, 'greed is good', or rather, 'greed is god', and our taxes now apply Band-Aids to the consequences of this idolatry. Western materialism in its suburban form affirms that life is a race against one's neighbours. The winner is the one who has the most material goods before he goes up the crematorium chimney in a puff of smoke.

Jesus says,

> Do not lay up for yourselves treasures on earth, where moth and rust consume and where thieves break in and steal, but lay up for yourselves treasure in heaven, where neither moth nor rust consumes and where thieves do not break in or steal. For where your treasure is, there will be your heart be also (Mt. 6:19–21).

2. Hedonism

Sensate person, 'testicular man',[7] Sexual Person, the product of the sensual libertarianism so peculiar to the West, sniffs the air like a donkey on heat for experiences to attain the goal of fully gratified senses.[8] It is now clear that the sexual revolution contained within it the seeds of its own downfall. It has produced hundreds of thousands, millions in large western nations, of deserted children

---

[7] Carl F. Henry, 'The New Image of Man', sermon in Moore Theological College chapel, 1975.

[8] Jer. 2:24.

living below the poverty line in single (overwhelmingly female) parent families, the self-recriminating dissolution of personality we witness in the once or now promiscuous, and the AIDS pandemic. To say the last is to shudder, and respond to the cry with a massive outpouring of selfless compassion, not to believe the lie that AIDS is accidental to the eschatology which produced it, or that God does not exist in this situation.

In Samuel Beckett's play *Waiting for Godot*, hedonism exposes its impossible and self-centred hope as characters discuss self-realization through death by hanging in order to achieve the ultimate orgasm.

Against the background of the heavenly Jerusalem, the writer of Hebrews declares: 'Let marriage be held in honour among all, and let the marriage bed be undefiled; for God will judge the immoral and adulterous' (13:4).

3. The openness of hope

Jürgen Moltmann has powerfully argued for the essential openness of hope, an openness which must be conceived of not in terms of eternity, but in terms of an historical future. This future is so open-ended that is not only unpredictable from our point of view, but present experience, even Christian experience, can only be entirely contradictory to what is hoped for. Within this framework Jesus' resurrection is an anticipation of the future of creation, not the new creation itself.[9]

But Christ's resurrection is already our resurrection, and our future resurrection is in his resurrection: 'we shall certainly be united in a resurrection like his' (Rom. 6:5), 'in Christ shall all be made alive' (1 Cor. 15:22). Because we are united to Christ by faith, the resurrection of Jesus Christ cannot be a metaphor, even a model, of our future hope but is the harbinger in present history which continues through into future history and takes us with it.

Without repeating my earlier criticisms of Moltmann's monu-mental and stimulating reinvestigation of the biblical material, the root of the failure of his conception of the nature of future hope as entirely open lies in his treatment of the place of Jesus Christ.

Jesus Christ does not just provide us with a paradigm of revelation as promise, but is also the content of that paradigm. In Jesus Christ,

---

[9] See Moltmann, *The Way of Jesus Christ: Christology in Messianic Dimension*, trans. Margaret Kohl (San Francisco: Harper, 1990) 223, 236 ff., 240 ff.

God's future is already present to us. The difference between present and future is the mode of that presence (cf. Calvin), but the content is the same. Moltmann does not appear to have given the weight he should to christology. The biblical witness is uncompromising, '*all* the promises of God find their "Yes" in Jesus Christ' (2 Cor. 1:18–22). Moltmann is undoubtedly correct in sharply drawing our attention to the Father-centred nature of Christ's ministry and person and of our salvation, but our understanding of this Father-centredness and its consequences for Christian eschatology must be controlled by the truth that the Father's purposes *have been* fulfilled in his Son.

Christian hope then, will *not* take up within itself all 'movements of historic change' which aim at a better world.[10] Rather, as we die in the service of our neighbours in whatever state we find them, we will utter the gospel of the resurrection which creates faith, and thus repentance and life.

4. *Signs and Wonders*

The root sadness in the quest for affirmation through being enveloped in 'spiritual' phenomena is that it denies the cross, and thus Christian hope. The power of the weakness of the cross has been replaced by the power of signs and wonders. The blessed hope of the resurrection has been replaced by the hope of dying well, innate to the search for physical and psychological healing. The expectation is that one will die comfortably at a great age, surrounded by prosperity, firm friends and extended family who are likewise prosperous and faithful Christians. In the light of Jesus' promise of the gospel bringing not peace, but a sword to every level of our social relations (Mt. 10:34–6; Mk. 13:9–13), the hope of dying well domesticates and individualizes heaven, making it the mere continuation of victorious Christian living now.

The ground may shift, but the charismatic hope, and its means, remains the same. As actual organic healings evaporate before open medical investigation in Sydney and London,[11] John Wimber's signs

---

[10] Jürgen Moltmann, *Theology of Hope: On the Ground and the Implications of a Christian Eschatology*, trans. James W. Leitch (London: SCM, 1967) 34.

[11] In 1984 a Signs and Wonders Conference was conducted by John Wimber in London. On behalf of the conference a report was produced by two of its delegates, C.E. Fryer of Ilfracombe, Devon and D.G.T. McBain of Manna Ministries Trust. They reported that total attendance

and wonders movement may privately admit changes in theological understanding, but nothing is definitely withdrawn in public. [12] Like the inrush and exit of a fifteen-metre tide, the major emphasis moves to prophecy, and then on to the Toronto Blessing, but the old

---

[11] *(continued)* was 3,600 and that 645 completed and returned detailed questionnaires. 'Of the 645 delegates, 74 report full physical healing.' After further analysis they state, p. 3: 'There are no definite medical verifications for healings, though a few have since consulted a doctor. There are reports of improvements to sight and hearing disorders and to lameness. We have heard news of healings from major organic conditions, but have to say there are no such reports in the data to hand.'

For a very critical analysis by Professor Verna Wright, a leading English rheumatologist, of a meeting held by John Wimber in St George's church, Leeds, refer to Tony Payne (ed.), *The Briefing* Issue 33, Sept 15, 1989.

Within the context of widespread involvement by English evangelicals in various signs and wonders and healing ministries, in 1989 Inter-Varsity Press published a book in which seven prominent Christians debated both sides of the issue. Dr Peter May, who has spent 20 years investigating claims of healings, including prominent ones concerning people with Down's Syndrome, peptic ulcers and terminal renal disease, has found that in each case the claim collapsed in the face of medical evidence. See, *Signs and Wonders and Healing* (Leicester: Inter-Varsity Press, 1989) pp. 27–81. The editor, John Goldingay, an Old Testament scholar and Principal of St John's College Nottingham, who movingly tells of the positive ministry charismatic renewal has had to him in sad circumstances (pp. 11–15), at the end of the book concludes, 'I myself would like to believe that lots of miracles are happening, but like Peter May find hard evidence difficult to come by' (p. 181).

In 1990, a Spiritual Warfare Conference was conducted by John Wimber in Sydney. Three leading evangelicals in Sydney met with John Wimber and his team before the conference, with his agreement that the contents of the conversations would be made public. From these conversations, and attendance at the conference itself by other concerned evangelicals, a wide-ranging report was published in T. Payne (ed.), *The Briefing* Issue 45/46 April 24 1990. As part of this process, John Wimber agreed to a request from the Anglican Archbishop of Sydney that a panel of four doctors be given cases of healing from the Sydney conference so that they might verify them. There was much emphasis on healing at the conference. Many hundreds went forward for healing. By July 1991, not a single case has been referred to the panel for verification.

[12] See T. Payne (ed.), *The Briefing* Issue 45/46 April 24 1990. Phillip Jensen reported, p. 4: 'Given the very low percentage of healings, we asked John Wimber if he considered that his healings were like Jesus' or the Apostles. He quickly and rightly saw that they were quite radically

remains, and the new move is but another place on a spectrum refracted not from heaven, but earth.

It is the triviality of it all which is blasphemous, if not its contents.

Once, it was sufficient for friends to pray for each other during sickness so that with divine support for failing bodies, like Job, they might remain faithful (Jas. 5:1–18). Prayer for healing was once seen as a mere compassionate event; mere, because the main event which dominated evangelical thinking and activity was the life, death, resurrection and present heavenly session of Jesus Christ. Now, whole conferences, congregations, and denominations focus on charismatic phenomena because to do otherwise is to have a deficient gospel and an immature and ineffective Christian life. But the cross defines becoming and remaining a Christian, believing and living in the forgiveness of sins and the blessed hope of the resurrection, as the main event.

Prophecy stirs excitement and creates eager followers. Such is the force of the Kansas City Prophets and the Vineyard network of churches that even well-researched critical analyses by charismatic co-religionists may be deemed by an evangelical outsider, friendly to the movement, 'torment', almost amounting to 'persecution'.[13] But it is not so much the crude mind reading of these prophecies, an activity well known on the American carnival circuit, which takes the Lord's name in vain, so much as the double shift from his death and resurrection. All the promises of God, the law and the prophets are fulfilled in Christ (2 Cor. 1:19–20). The current imperative to search for further prophecies, unlike those of the Apostolic period, is a denial of the sufficiency of the promises and

---

[12] *(continued)* different . . . thanks to the advice of Jack Deere he has come to understand that the current miracles fit into the New Testament not at the point of Jesus and the Apostles and the coming of the Kingdom, but in 1 Cor. 12–14 and the gifts of healing . . . He was asked if he would be explaining this change of mind to the Sydney conference, but declined. (As it turned out, both views were expressed during the course of the week.)' Dr Philip Selden reported on the conference itself, p. 19: 'Earlier reading had suggested that Mr Wimber had been teaching that we were still in the New Testament age of signs and wonders. At this conference, the message seemed to be that we are yet to enter into the apostolic age again, when healing will again be given to the church in large measure. What we are seeing now, they argued, are just tokens.'

[13] So Michael G. Maudlin, 'Seers in the Heartland: Hot on the Trail of the Kansas City Prophets', *Christianity Today*, Jan. 14, 1991, pp. 18–22.

prophecies of God which he has fulfilled in his Son. The Corinthians are commanded to desire prophecy for edification (1 Cor. 12:1–14:40). The content of Christian edification, as Paul has argued extensively throughout his letter, is the gospel, the message of the cross.[14] Our contemporary need to guide and direct life, to remove obstacles and overcome doubt of God's love towards us when Christ can no longer be physically seen, by resorting to prophecies is to place our hope and expectation elsewhere than in the coming resurrection (Rom. 8:18–25).

What contribution does the 'signs and wonders' movement make to the church? What contribution does 'laughing in the Spirit' make to the Christian ecclesia?

In Romans 8, as in his first and second letter to the Corinthians, Paul addresses the whole church, including those who place special emphasis on physical manifestations of the Spirit, especially sighing or groaning in prayer (*stenagmos alalētos*, Rom. 8:26; cf. 1 Cor. 14:15; 13:1; 2 Cor. 12:4; Eph. 6:18; Jude 20; Rev. 22:17). What is the meaning of this activity? Within the structure of his argument in Romans 8, with its focus on present eschatological suffering and the future hope of the resurrection (vv. 18–25), Paul describes this prayer in the Spirit in the same terms as he does the utterance of creation (*sustenazō*), 'groaning'. While some may well believe that in their ecstatic praying they have victoriously and wonderfully tapped into the power of the Spirit, the Spirit knows otherwise, for as their intercessor (in exact parallel to Christ who as our Mediator intercedes for us with the Father, Rom. 8:34; Heb. 7:25), he cries, rather he groans with the same groans, with which creation signals its weakness and futility to the Heavenly Father: 'In accordance with your will these Christians too are weak and broken, even if they do not see it, and also need to await the blessed hope of the resurrection with patience (vv. 18–27).' Their ecstasy signals not

---

[14] Surely (true) prophecy is defined by its content, not its form. The current interest in New Testament prophecy seems mostly to be concerned with its form, as if, by finding this, we might have its benefits. But clearly the New Testament does not define its form, or even show an interest in it, as the myriad of conflicting answers by scholars show. As with other eye-catching phenomena, Paul is concerned not with form, but content. Edification is the issue. What edifies is the gospel of the cross. If we have that, then that is sufficient. We might even have 'prophecy' without knowing it! The Spirit is sovereign, his presence and activity is not measured by form, but by content (1 Cor. 12:1–5, 11; 14:1–3; cf. Jn. 16:13–14).

strength, but weakness and powerlessness, along with the rest of Christendom.[15]

What contribution does the signs and wonders movement make to the church? It brings us its hurts and suffering, its lack of assurance and passion for comfort. How should it be met? Untruth does not help. On the contrary, it fans pride and hides the truth. The Christian life is summed up in faith, hope and love. All Christians need to be led by the gospel to Jesus Christ, who is the object and ground of these three. In him, through our shared tears, we may confess: 'We know that in everything God works for good with those who love him, who are called according to his purpose . . . I am sure that nothing in all of creation will be able to separate us from the love of God in Christ Jesus our Lord' (Rom. 8:28–39).

* * *

Christian eschatology is about hope.

God does not promise that we shall die well, but that we shall share the sufferings of Christ (Phil. 1:29; 1 Pet. 2:21; Rom. 8:17–18; 2 Cor. 1:5–7; Phil. 3:10), and that he has a crown, 'an inheritance which is imperishable, undefiled, and unfading, kept in heaven for you' (1 Pet. 1:4), which is our living hope. We will, in God's time, live as renewed people in God's new creation because all is grounded and determined in Jesus Christ, as Calvin so clearly perceived.

What shape should this hope give to our lives? That has been the subject of this book. We see this shape reflected for us in the face of our mediatorial king. That is, we should be conformed to the image of God's Son – Romans 8:29. The contents of this shape are well defined by Paul in the surrounding chapter and chapters. Here, this shape is explicitly commended in the context of suffering, under the promise of God's mighty act of justification already completed in Christ.

What *present* expectation for this shape may we have? Much, for the same thing which promises and determines the shape also operates now to inaugurate it, the gospel. The gospel, not signs and wonders, historical movements of liberation, let alone hedonism and materialism, produces faith in the promises of God (Rom. 10:17). And that faith, of men and women who believe in Jesus

---

[15] See Ernst Käsemann, *Commentary on Romans* (London: SCM 1980) 229–45.

Christ, who eagerly await his return, is not only itself the great sign and wonder of the kingdom of God in the world, it *is* that kingdom (1 Cor. 1:18–2:5; 1 Thess. 1:2–10). Faith is the shape God wants for the Christian life, that is, to be like his Son, the man of faith (Mt. 27:43; cf. Rom. 4). That faith will believe that the message of the cross itself creates faith in the promises of God.

The Preacher – Kibeho Massacre Series, Rwanda

George Gittoes described the events behind his painting which won the 1995 Blake Prize for Religious Art. Under the auspices of the United Nations, Gittoes and a medical team were visiting the village of Kibeho when suddenly they found themselves in the midst of a massacre.

> It was horrific, we saw children killed before our eyes. We were going in and getting the wounded out as the people were macheting and shooting and killing.
>
> Suddenly, there was this guy standing in the middle of the people who were dying all around him. He just began to give this sermon in one of those beautiful melodious African voices, mingling English and French and Rwandan and quoting those sections of the New Testament to them, those bits which give hope and tell us about the possibility of an afterlife.
>
> I thought it took tremendous courage, because he exposed himself, yet he had the presence of mind to know that other people needed some kind of reassurance. He gave it to them.

Gittoes said he began to sketch him very quickly, and then he photographed the preacher standing in among the people.

> Then the killing closed in. I don't know if he survived or whether the people around survived. As we began pulling the bodies out, I looked for him, I looked for the distinctive yellow coat he was wearing, but I could not see it.

(*Sydney Morning Herald*, December 15, 1995, p. 14)

Because He Lives

'Because I live, you also will live' (John 14:19 NIV)

God sent His Son, they called him Jesus;
He came to love, heal, and forgive;
He lived and died to buy my pardon,
An empty grave is there to prove my Saviour lives.

Because He lives I can face tomorrow;
Because He lives all fear is gone;
Because I know He holds the future,
And life is worth the living just because He lives.

How sweet to hold a new-born baby;
And feel the pride, and joy he gives;
But greater still the calm assurance,
This child can face uncertain days because He lives.

And then one day I'll cross the river;
I'll fight life's final war with pain;
And then as death gives way to victr'y,
I'll see the lights of glory and I'll know he lives.

WORDS: Gloria Gaither, 1942–; William J. Gaither, 1936–
MUSIC: William J. Gaither, 1936–   RESURRECTION irregular
Copyright 1971 by William J. Gaither

Bibliography

Authors before the Twentieth Century

Athanasius, *Life of Antony*, The Nicene and Post-Nicene Fathers, second series (Grand Rapids: Eerdmans, 1978) vol. 4 pp. 195–221

Augustine, *Answer to Skeptics,* in *Writings of Saint Augustine, volume 1.* The Fathers of the Church, a new translation (New York: CIMA, 1948) vol. 5 pp. 85–225

———, *Augustine: De Doctrina Christiana*, trans. and ed. R.P.H. Green, Oxford Early Christian Texts (Oxford: Clarendon, 1995)

———, *The City of God by St Augustine*, trans. Marcus Dods two vols. (New York: Hafner Publishing Company, 1948)

———, *Confessions*, ed. A.C. Outler, *Augustine: Confessions and Enchiridion*, Library of Christian Classics (Philadelphia: Westminster, 1955) pp. 13–333

———, *Enchiridion*, ed. A.C. Outler, *Augustine: Confessions and Enchiridion*, Library of Christian Classics (Philadelphia: Westminster, 1955) pp. 337–412

———, *Faith and the Creed*, trans. J.H.S. Burleigh, *Augustine: Earlier Writings*, Library of Christian Classics (London: SCM, 1953) pp. 349–69

———, *Homilies on the Gospel of John*, 'Tractate IX', The Nicene and Post-Nicene Fathers, first series (Grand Rapids: Eerdmans, 1978) vol. 7 pp. 63–8

———, *Homilies on the Gospel of John*, 'Tractate XXIII', The Nicene and Post-Nicene Fathers, first series (Grand Rapids: Eerdmans, 1978) vol. 7 pp. 150–7

———, *The Magnitude of the Soul,* in *Writings of Saint Augustine*, The Fathers of the Church, a new translation (New York: CIMA, 1947) vol. 4 pp. 51–149

———, *On the Good of Marriage*, The Nicene and Post- Nicene Fathers, first series (Grand Rapids: Eerdmans, 1978) vol. 3 pp. 400–13

————, *On the Profit of Believing*, The Nicene and Post- Nicene Fathers, first series (Grand Rapids: Eerdmans, 1978) vol. 3. pp. 347–66

————, *On the Trinity*, The Nicene and Post-Nicene Fathers, first series (Grand Rapids: Eerdmans, 1978) vol. 3 pp. 15–228

————, *Saint Augustine: The Retractions*, trans. M.I. Bogan, The Fathers of the Church, a new translation (Washington: The Catholic University of America Press, 1968) vol. 60

————, *The Spirit and the Letter*, ed. J. Burnaby *Augustine: Later Works*, Library of Christian Classics (Philadelphia: Westminster, 1955) pp. 193–250

Calvin, John, *Calvin's Commentaries* (Edinburgh: Calvin Translation Society, 1843–1855)

————, *Calvin's Commentaries*, eds. David W. and Thomas F. Torrance (Edinburgh: Saint Andrew Press, 1959–72)

————, *The Catechism of the Church of Geneva* (1545), in J.K.S. Reid, *Calvin: Theological Treatises*, Library of Christian Classics (Philadelphia: Westminster, 1954) 83–139

————, *Concerning Scandals*, trans. John W. Fraser (Grand Rapids: Eerdmans, 1978)

————, *Concerning the Eternal Predestination of God* 8.6, ed. J.K.S. Reid (Edinburgh: James Clarke, 1961)

————, *Corpus Reformatorum*, vols. 29 to 87 are the *Ioannis Calvini Opera Quae Supersunt Omnia*, eds. G. Baum et al. (Brunsvigae: Schwetschke et Filium, 1865–1897)

————, *Institutes of the Christian Religion*, trans. F.L. Battles (London: SCM, 1961; Philadelphia: Westminster, 1960)

————, *Ioannis Calvini Opera Selecta*, 5 vols., eds. Peter Barth and William Niesel (Munich: Chr. Kaiser, 1926–36)

————, *Letters*, last 4 volumes, eds. Henry Beveridge and Jules Bonnet, in *Selected Works of John Calvin: Tracts and Letters*, 7 vols. (Grand Rapids: Baker, 1983)

————, *Psychopannychia*, eds. Henry Beveridge and Jules Bonnet in *Selected Works of John Calvin: Tracts and Letters*, 7 vols. (Grand Rapids: Baker, 1983) vol. 3 pp. 413–90

————, *Sermons from Job*, selected and trans. L. Nixon (Grand Rapids: Baker, 1952)

————, *Sermons of M. Iohn Calvin upon the Epistle of Saincte Paule to the Galatians*, trans. A. Golding (London: Lucas Harison & George Bishop, 1574).

————, *The Sermons of M. Iohn Calvin upon the Epistles of S. Paule to the Timothe and Titus*, trans. L. T[omson] (London: G. Bishop & T. Woodcoke, 1579)

————, *The Sermons of M. Iohn Calvin upon the fifth Booke of Moses called Deuteronomie*, trans. Arthur Golding (London: Henry Middleton for Thomas Woodcock, 1583)

————, *Sermons on the Epistle to the Ephesians* (London: Banner of Truth, 1973)

Chrysostom, *Homilies on the Gospel of Matthew*, 'Homily XIII on Matt. IV.i', The Nicene and Post-Nicene Fathers, first series (Grand Rapids: Eerdmans, 1978) vol. 10 pp. 80–6

Cyprian, *Address to Demetrianus*, The Ante-Nicene Fathers (Grand Rapids: Eerdmans, 1986) vol. 5 pp. 457–65

————, *Epistle 62*, The Ante-Nicene Fathers (Grand Rapids: Eerdmans, 1986) vol. 5 pp. 358–64

————, *Treatise 4: On the Lord's Supper*, The Ante-Nicene Fathers (Grand Rapids: Eerdmans, 1986) vol. 5 pp. 447–57

Cyril of Jerusalem, *Catechetical Lecture 22: On the Body and Blood of Christ*, The Nicene and Post-Nicene Fathers, second series (Grand Rapids: Eerdmans, 1978) vol. 7 pp. 151–2

————, *Catechetical Lecture 23: On the Sacred Liturgy and Communion*, The Nicene and Post-Nicene Fathers, second series (Grand Rapids: Eerdmans, 1978) vol. 7 pp. 153–7

Dante Alighieri, *Dante, The Divine Comedy*, 3 vols., ed. and trans. Mark Musa et al. (New York: Penguin Books, 1984–86)

Dante, *The Divine Comedy 3, Paradise*, trans. Dorothy L. Sayers and Barbara Reynolds (London: Penguin Books, 1962)

Edwards, Jonathan, *The Works of Jonathan Edwards*, 14 vols. (Yale University Press, 1957–1994)

Gregory of Nazianzus, *Faith Gives Fullness to Reasoning: The Five Theological Orations of Gregory of Nazianzen*; ed. F.W. Norris, trans. L. Wickham and F. Williams (Leiden: E.J. Brill, 1991)

————, *Oration 5: On the Holy Spirit*, The Nicene and Post-Nicene Fathers, second series (Grand Rapids: Eerdmans, 1978) vol. 7 pp. 318–328

————, *The Five Theological Orations of Gregory of Nazianzus*, ed. A.J. Mason (Cambridge: Cambridge University Press, 1899)

————, *Oration 7: Panegyric on Brother S. Caesarius*, The Nicene and Post-Nicene Fathers, second series (Grand Rapids: Eerdmans, 1978) vol. 7 pp. 229–38

————, *Oration 34: On the Arrival of the Egyptians*, The Nicene and Post-Nicene Fathers, second series (Grand Rapids: Eerdmans, 1978) vol. 7 pp. 334–8

————, *Oration 38: On the Theophany, or Birthday of Christ*, The Nicene and Post-Nicene Fathers, second series (Grand Rapids: Eerdmans, 1978) vol. 7 pp. 345–51

Hilary of Poitiers, *On the Trinity*, The Nicene and Post-Nicene Fathers, second series (Grand Rapids: Eerdmans, 1983) vol. 9 pp. 40–233

Hume, David, *Enquiries Concerning the Human Understanding and Concerning the Principles of Morals* (Oxford: Clarendon, [2]1902)

———, *A Treatise of Human Nature*, vol. 1 (London: J.M. Dent & Sons, 1911)

Ignatius of Antioch, *Epistle to the Ephesians*, The Ante-Nicene Fathers (Grand Rapids: Eerdmans, 1987) vol. 1 pp. 49–58

Irenaeus, *Against Heresies*, The Ante-Nicene Fathers (Grand Rapids: Eerdmans, 1987) vol. 1 pp. 315–578

Justin Martyr, *First Apology*, The Ante-Nicene Fathers (Grand Rapids: Eerdmans, 1987) vol. 1 pp. 163–87

Kierkegaard, Søren, *Philosophical Fragments or A Fragment of Philosophy by Johannes Climacus: Is an historical point of departure possible for an eternal consciousness; How can such a point of departure have any other than a mere historical interest; Is it possible to base an eternal happiness upon historical knowledge?* trans. H.V. Hong et al., comm. N. Thulstrup (Princeton: Princeton University Press, 1962)

Luther, Martin, *Lectures on Romans*, trans. and ed. W. Pauck, Library of Christian Classics (Philadelphia: Westminster Press, 1961)

———, *Luther's Works*, ed. Jaroslav Pelikan et al., 56 vols., American Edition (St. Louis: Concordia Publishing House, 1955–86)

Napier, John, *A Plaine Discovery of the Whole Revelation of Saint John* (Edinburgh: R. Walde-grave, 1593)

Origen, *The Commentary of Origen on S. John's Gospel*, ed. A.E. Brooke (Cambridge University Press, 1896) vol. 2

———, *De Principiis*, The Ante-Nicene Fathers (Grand Rapids: Eerdmans, 1989) vol. 4 pp. 237–384

———, 'Documents: The Commentary of Origen on the Epistle to the Romans', A. Ramsbotham, *Journal of Theological Studies* 13 (1912) 209–24, 357–68

———, *Origen: Commentary on the Gospel According to Saint John, books 1–10*, ed. R.E. Heine (Washington: Catholic University of America, 1989)

———, *Origene: Homelies sur Josue*, ed. A Jaubert, Sources Chretiénnes, (Paris: Cerf, 1960) vol. 71

Owen, John, *Works of John Owen*, 16 vols. (London: Banner of Truth, 1967)

Thomas Aquinas, *On the Truth of the Catholic Faith: Summa Contra Gentiles*, trans. A.C. Pegis et al., 4 vols. (New York: University of Notre Dame Press, 1955–6)

———, *Summa Theologiae: Latin Text and English Translation, Introductions, Notes, Appendices and Glossaries*, 61 vols. (Blackfriars,

Cambridge in conjunction with McGraw-Hill, New York et al., 1964–80)

Twentieth-Century Authors

Aulén, Gusta, *Christus Victor: An Historical Study of the Three Main Types of the Idea of the Atonement* (London: SPCK, 1931)

Ball, Bryan W., *A Great Expectation: Eschatological Thought in English Protestantism to 1660* (Leiden: E.J. Brill, 1975)

Barnes, Robin Bruce, *Prophecy and Gnosis: Apocalypticism in the Wake of the Lutheran Reformation* (Stanford University Press, 1988)

Barrett, C.K., *The Epistle to the Romans* (London: A. & C. Black, 1973)

Barth, Karl, *Church Dogmatics* (Edinburgh: T. & T. Clark, 1936–77)

——, *Dogmatics in Outline* (London: SCM, 1949)

——, *Epistle to the Romans* (Oxford University Press, [6]1933)

Bauckham, Richard, *Moltmann: Messianic Theology in the Making* (Basingstoke: Marshall Pickering, 1987)

——, *The Theology of Jürgen Moltmann* (Edinburgh: T. & T. Clark, 1995)

——, *Tudor Apocalypse* (Appleford, Oxford: Sutton Courtenay Press, 1978)

Bebbington, David, 'The Advent Hope in British Evangelicalism since 1800', *Scottish Journal of Religious Studies* 9 (1988) 103–14

Berkhof, Hendrikus, *Christ and the Meaning of History* (London: SCM, 1966)

——, *Christian Faith: An Introduction to the Study of the Faith* (Grand Rapids: Eerdmans, 1979)

Berkower, G.C., *The Return of Christ* (Grand Rapids: Eerdmans, 1972)

Bickersteth, Geoffrey L. (trans.), *The Paradiso of Dante Alighieri* (Cambridge University Press, 1932)

Bloesch, Donald G., *Essentials of Evangelical Theology*, vol. 2, *Life, Ministry, and Hope* (New York: Harper & Row, 1982)

Bloomfield, Morton W., 'Joachim of Fiore: A Critical Survey of his Canon, Teachings, Sources, Biography and Influence', *Traditio: Studies in Ancient and Medieval History, Thought and Religion* (New York: Fordham Press, 1957) 249–311

Boff, Leonardo, *When Theology Listens to the Poor* (San Francisco: Harper & Row, 1988)

Booth, E.G.T., 'St Augustine's *De Trinitate* and Aristotelian and neo-Platonist Noetic', in E. Livingstone (ed.), *Studia Patristica* 16/2 (1985) 487–90

Bouwsma, William, J., *John Calvin: A Sixteenth Century Portrait* (Oxford University Press, 1988)

Brown, Colin and Coenen, Lothar, 'Resurrection' in C. Brown (ed.), *The New International Dictionary of New Testament Theology*, vol 3. (Exeter: Paternoster, 1978) 259–309

Brunner, Emil, *The Christian Doctrine of the Church, Faith and the Consummation* (Philadelphia: Westminster Press, 1962)

Bryant, Darrol M., 'America as God's Kingdom', in Jürgen Moltmann et al., *Religion and Political Society* (New York: Harper & Row, 1974) 49–94

Burrell, David B., 'Aquinas and Scotus: Contrary Patterns for Philosophical Theology', in Bruce D. Marshall (ed.), *Theology in Dialogue: Essays in Conversation with George Lindbeck* (Indiana: Notre Dame University Press, 1990) 109–11

Buss, Dietrich G., 'Meeting of Heaven and Earth: A Survey and Analysis of the Literature on Millennialism in America, 1965–1985', *Fides et Historia* 20 (1988) 5–28

————, 'The Millennial Vision as Motive for Religious Benevolence and Reform: Timothy Dwight and the New England Evangelicals Reconsidered', *Fides et Historia* 16 (1983) 18–34

Carnley, Peter, *The Structure of Resurrection Belief* (Oxford: Clarendon, 1993)

Chenu, M.-D., *Toward Understanding St Thomas* (Chicago: Henry Regnery, 1964)

Clark, Mary T., 'Augustine's Theology of the Trinity: Its Relevance', *Dionysius* 13 (1989) 69–84

Clouse, Robert G., 'Millennium, views of the', in W.A. Elwell (ed.) *Evangelical Dictionary of Theology* (Grand Rapids: Baker, 1984) 714–18

————, 'The New Christian Right, America, and the Kingdom of God', *Christian Scholars Review* 12 (1983) 3–16

Cohn, Norman, *The Pursuit of the Millennium*, rev. ed. (New York: Oxford University Press, 1970)

Conn, M.M., 'Liberation Theology', in S.B. Ferguson and D.F. Wright (eds.) *New Dictionary of Theology* (Leicester: Inter-Varsity Press, 1988) 389–91

Copleston, Frederick, *A History of Philosophy*, vol. 2 (Westminster, Maryland: Newman, 1950)

Cranfield, C.E.B., *The Epistle to the Romans* (Edinburgh: T. & T. Clark, 1975)

Crouse, R.D., 'St Augustine's *De Trinitate*: Philosophical Method', in E. Livingstone ed., *Studia Patristica* 16/2 (1985) 501–1

Cunliffe-Jones, H. (ed.), *A History of Christian Doctrine* (Edinburgh: T. & T. Clark, 1978)

Daley, Brian E., *The Hope of the Early Church: A Handbook of Patristic Eschatology* (Cambridge University Press, 1991)

Daniel, E. Randolph, 'The Spread of Apocalypticism, 1100–1500: Why Calvin could not Reject It', in J. H. Leith (ed.), Calvin Studies V: *Presented at a Colloquium on Calvin Studies at Davidson College, North Carolina*, (Calvin Studies Society, 1990) 61–66

Davidson, James West, *The Logic of Millennial Thought: Eighteenth-century* New England (New Haven: Yale University Press, 1977)

Davies, Paul, *The Mind of God: Science and the Search for Ultimate Meaning* (London: Penguin, 1992)

Dodd, C.H., *The Apostolic Preaching and its Developments* (London: Hodder and Stoughton, 1944 rev. ed. ; original 1936)

———, *History of the Gospel* (London: Nisbet, 1938)

———, *The Parables of the Kingdom* (London: Nisbet, 1935)

Doull, James, 'What is Augustinian "Sapientia"?', *Dionysius* 12 (1988) 61–7

Doyle, Robert C., 'The Context of Moral Decision Making in the Writings of John Calvin: The Christological Ethics of Eschatological Order', unpublished PhD thesis, University of Aberdeen, 1981

———, 'The Search for Theological Models: The Christian in His Society in the Sixteenth, Seventeenth and Nineteenth Centuries', in B. Webb (ed.) *Explorations 3: Christians in Society* (Sydney: Lancer, 1988) 27–72

———, *Signs and Wonders and Evangelicals: A Response to the Teaching of John Wimber* (Sydney: Lancer, 1987)

Du Roy, O.J.-B., 'Augustine, St.', *New Catholic Encyclopedia*, vol. 1 (Washington: Catholic University of America, 1967) 1041–58

Dumbrell, W.J., 'Apocalyptic Literature', pamphlet in the library of Moore Theological College, April 1991, 9

———, *Covenant and Creation: An Old Testament Covenantal Theology* (Exeter: Paternoster Press, 1984)

Dyer, George J., *Limbo: Unsettled Question* (New York: Sheed & Ward, 1964)

Edwards, D.L. and Stott, J.R.W., *Essentials: A Liberal–Evangelical Dialogue* (London: Hodder & Stoughton, 1988)

Ellingsen, Mark, 'Luther as Narrative Exegete', *Journal of Religion* 63 (1983) 394–413.

Elwell, W.A. (ed.), *Evangelical Dictionary of Theology* (Grand Rapids: Baker; Carlisle: Paternoster, 1984)

Evangeliou, Christos, 'Porphyry's Criticism of Christianity and the Problem of Augustine's Platonism', *Dionysius* 13 (1989) 51–70

Evans, G.R., *The Mind of St. Bernard of Clairvaux* (Oxford: Clarendon Press, 1983)

Fabro, Cornelio, 'The Overcoming of the Neoplatonic Triad of Being, Life, and Intellect by Saint Thomas Aquinas', in Dominic J. O'Meara (ed.), *Neoplatonism and Christian Thought* (Norfolk, Virginia: International Society for Neoplatonic Studies, 1982) 97–108

Ferguson, Sinclair B. and Wright, D.F. (eds.), *New Dictionary of Theology* (Leicester: Inter-Varsity Press, 1988)

Firth, Katharine R., *The Apocalyptic Tradition in Reformation Britain, 1530–1645* (Oxford University Press, 1979)

Forde, Gerhard O., 'When the Old God's Fail: Martin Luther's Critique of Mysticism', in C. Lindberg (ed.) *Piety, Politics, and Ethics: Reformation Studies in Honor of George Wolfgang Forell* (Kirksville, Missouri: Sixteenth Century Journal & Northeast Missouri State University, 1984) 15–26

Fulop, Timothy E., ' "The Future Golden Day of the Race": Millennialism and Black Americans in the Nadir, 1877–1901', *Harvard Theological Review* 84 (1991) 75–99

Garrett, Clarke, *Respectable Folly: Millenarians and the French Revolution in France and England* (Baltimore: John Hopkins University Press, 1975)

Goen, C.C., 'Jonathan Edwards: A New Departure in Eschatology', *Church History* 28 (1959) 25–40

Goldingay, John (ed.), *Signs and Wonders and Healing* (Leicester: Inter-Varsity Press, 1989)

Goldsworthy, Graeme, *Gospel and Kingdom: A Christian Interpretation of the Old Testament* (Exeter: Paternoster, 1981)

———, Ē LEITOURGIA TĒS APOKALYPSEŌS, unpublished pamphlet in the library of Moore Theological College, November 1997

———, *The Gospel in Revelation: Gospel and Apocalypse* (London: Paternoster, 1984)

Gourgues, M., 'The Thousand-Year Reign (Rev 20:1–6): Terrestrial or Celestial?', *Catholic Biblical Quarterly* 47 (1985) 676–81

Gutiérrez, Gustavo, *A Theology of Liberation: History, Politics and Salvation*, trans. Sister Caridad Inda and John Eagleson (London: SCM, 1974)

Hankey, W.J., *God in Himself: Aquinas' Doctrine of God as Expounded in the Summa Theologiae* (Oxford University Press, 1987)

Hanson, Paul D., 'Apocalypticism', in *The Interpreters Dictionary of the Bible*, K. Crim (ed.) (Nashville: Abingdon, 1976) supp. vol.

———, *The Dawn of Apocalyptic: The Historical and Sociological Roots of Jewish Apocalyptic Eschatology* (Philadelphia: Fortress Press, 1975)

Harris, Murray J., *Raised Immortal: Resurrection and Immortality in the New Testament* (London: Marshall, Morgan & Scott, 1983).

———, 'Resurrection and Immortality: Eight Theses', *Themelios* 1 (1976) 50–5

Hatch, N. and Stout, H., *Jonathan Edwards and the American Experience* (Oxford University Press, 1988)

Hebblethwaite, Brian, *The Christian Hope* (Basingstoke: Marshall, Morgan & Scott; Grand Rapids: Eerdmans, 1984)

Henry, Carl F., 'The New Image of Man', sermon in Moore Theological College chapel, 1975.

Hill, Charles E., *Regnum Caelorum: Patterns of Future Hope in Early Christianity* (Oxford: Clarendon, 1992)

Hoekema, A.A., *The Bible and the Future* (Grand Rapids: Eerdmans, 1978)

Iserloh, Erwin, 'Luther's Christ-Mysticism', in J. Wicks (ed.) *Catholic Scholars Dialogue with Luther* (Chicago: Loyola University Press, 1970) 37–58, 173–81

Jones, Larry and Sheppard, Gerald T., 'The Politics of Biblical Eschatology: Ronald Reagan and the Impending Nuclear Armageddon', *TSF Bulletin* (Sept–Oct 1984) 16–19

Käsemann, Ernst, *Commentary on Romans* (London: SCM, 1980)

Katz, David S., 'Henry Jessey and Conservative Millenarianism in Seventeenth-Century England and Holland' in J. Michman (ed.), *Dutch Jewish History*, vol. 2 (Hebrew University of Jerusalem, 1989 and Maastricht, Netherlands: Van Gorcum, Assen 1989) 75–93

Kelly, J.N.D., *Early Christian Doctrines* (London: A. & C. Black, 1965)

Kerr, H.T., *A Compend of Luther's Theology* (Philadelphia: Westminster, 1943)

Kierulff, Stephen, 'Belief in "Armageddon Theology" and Willingness to Risk Nuclear War', *Journal for the Scientific Study of Religion* 30 (1991) 81–93

Kittel, G. (ed.), *Theological Dictionary of the New Testament* (Grand Rapids: Eerdmans, 1964)

Knox, D.B., 'The Five Comings of Jesus: Matthew 24 and 25', *Reformed Theological Review* 34 (1975) 44–54

Kreeft, Peter, *A Summa of the Summa* (San Francisco: Ignatius Press, 1990)

Ladd, George Eldon, *A Theology of the New Testament* (London: Lutterworth Press, 1974)

Lamont, William, 'Richard Baxter, the Apocalypse and the Mad Major', in Charles Webster (ed.), *The Intellectual Revolution of the Seventeenth Century* (London: Routledge & Kegan Paul, 1974) 399–426

Lewis, C.S., *Fern-seed and Elephants, and Other Essays on Christianity* (Glasgow: Fontana, 1975)

Lincoln, A.T., *Paradise Now and Not Yet* (Cambridge University Press, 1981)

Lindsey, Hal, *The Late Great Planet Earth* (Grand Rapids: Zondervan, 1970)

Lohse, B., *Martin Luther: An Introduction to His Life and Work* (Edinburgh: T. & T. Clark, 1986)

Maclear, J.F., 'New England and the Fifth Monarchy: the Quest for the Millennium in Early American Puritanism', in Alden T. Vaughan (ed.), *Puritan New England: Essays on Religion, Society, and Culture* (New York: St Martins Press, 1977) 66–91

Marsden, George M., *The Evangelical Mind and the New School Presbyterian Experience* (New Haven: Yale University Press, 1970)

Matar, N.I., 'The Idea of the Restoration of the Jews in English Protestant Thought, 1661–1701', *Harvard Theological Review* 78 (1985) 115–48

Maudlin, Michael G., 'Seers in the Heartland: Hot on the Trail of the Kansas City Prophets', *Christianity Today* (Jan 14, 1991), 18–22

McDermott, Timothy, *Summa Theologiae: A Concise Translation* (Westminster, Maryland: Christian Classics, 1989)

McGinn, Bernard, *The Calabrian Abbot: Joachim of Fiore in the History of Western Thought* (New York: Macmillan, 1985)

———, *Visions of the End: Apocalyptic Traditions in the Middle Ages* (New York: Columbia University Press, 1979)

McGrath, Alister E., 'Divine Justice and Divine Equity in the Controversy between Augustine and Julian of Eclanum', *Downside Review* 345 (1983) 312–19

———, *Iustitia Dei: A History of the Christian Doctrine of Justification*, 2 vols. (Cambridge University Press, 1986)

———, *Luther's Theology of the Cross* (Oxford: Blackwell, 1985)

Merkt, Joseph T., 'The Discovery of the Genetic Development of Thomas Aquinas' Theology of Hope and its Relevance for a Theology of the Future', in Robert J. Daly (ed.), *Rising from History: U.S. Catholic Theology Looks to the Future*, The Annual Publication of the College Theology Society, 1984 (New York: University Press of America, 1987) 104–23

Moltmann, Jürgen, *The Coming of God: Christian Eschatology*, trans. Margaret Kohl (London: SCM, 1996)

———, *The Crucified God: The Cross of Christ as the Foundation and Criticism of Christian Theology*, trans. R.A. Wilson and John Bowden (London: SCM, 1974)

———, *The Future of Creation* (London: SCM, 1979)

———, *History and the Triune God: Contributions to Trinitarian Theology* (New York: Crossroad, 1992)

————, 'Hope', in A. Richardson and J. Bowden (eds.), *A New Dictionary of Christian Theology* (London: SCM, 1983) 270–2

————, *Theology of Hope: On the Ground and the Implications of a Christian Eschatology*, trans. James W. Leitch (London: SCM, 1967)

————, *The Way of Jesus Christ: Christology in Messianic Dimension*, trans. Margaret Kohl (San Francisco: Harper, 1990)

Moorhead, James H., 'The Erosion of Postmillennialism in American Religious Thought, 1865–1925', *Church History* 53 (1984) 61–77

Musa, Mark (trans. & comm.), *Dante, The Divine Comedy*, vol. 1: *Inferno* (New York: Penguin Books, 1984)

————, *Dante, The Divine Comedy*, vol. 2: *Purgatory* (New York: Penguin Books, 1985)

Niebuhr, Helmut Richard, *Christ and Culture* (London: Faber, 1952)

————, *The Kingdom of God in America* (New York: Harper & Row, 1956)

O'Daly, G.J.P., '*Sensus interior* in St Augustine, *De libero arbitrio* 2.3.25–6.51', E. Livingstone (ed.), Studia Patristica 16/2 (1985) 528–32

O'Meara, John J., 'The Neoplatonism of Saint Augustine', in Dominic J. O'Meara (ed.), *Neoplatonism and Christian Thought* (Norfolk, Virginia: International Society for Neoplatonic Studies, 1982) 34–41

Oberman, Heiko A., '*Facientibus Quod in Se Est Deus Non Denegrat Gratiam*: Robert Holcot, O.P. and the Beginnings of Luther's Theology', *Harvard Theological Review* 55 (1962) 317–42

————, ' "*Iustitia Christi*" and "*Iustitia Dei*": Luther and the Scholastic Doctrines of Justification', in *The Dawn of the Reformation: Essays in Late Medieval and Early Reformation Thought* (Edinburgh: T. & T. Clark, 1986) 104–25

————, *Luther: Man between God and the Devil* (New Haven: Yale University Press, 1989)

Oliver, W.H., *Prophets and Millennialists: The Uses of Biblical Prophecy in England from the 1790s to the 1840s* (Auckland University Press and Oxford University Press, 1978)

Ozment, Steven, *Age of Reform 1250–1550: An Intellectual and Religious History of Late Medieval and Reformation Europe* (New Haven: Yale University Press, 1980)

Pannenberg, Wolfhardt, *Basic Questions in Theology* vol. 1 (London: SCM, 1970)

————, *Systematic Theology* vol. 2 (Grand Rapids: Eerdmans, 1994)

Parker, T.H.L., *Calvin's New Testament Commentaries* (London: SCM Press, 1971)

Patrides, C.A. and Wittreich, Joseph (eds.), *The Apocalypse in English Renaissance Thought and Literature* (Ithaca, New York: Cornell University Press, 1984)

Payne, Tony (ed.), *The Briefing*, PO Box 225 Kingsford 2032, Australia

Pelikan, Jaroslav, *The Christian Tradition: A History of the Development of Doctrine* vol. 1 (University of Chicago Press, 1971)

Polkinghorne, John, *Science and Providence: God's Interaction with the World* (London: SPCK, 1989)

Popkin, Richard H. (ed.), *Millenarianism and Messianism in English Literature and Thought 1650–1800* (Leiden: E.J. Brill, 1988)

Prenter, Regin, 'Metaphysics and Eschatology in St Augustine', *Studia Theologica* 1 (1947) 5–26

——, *Spiritus Creator: Luther's concept of the Holy Spirit* (Philadelphia: Fortress, 1953)

Rahner, Karl, 'The Hermeneutics of Eschatological Assertions', in *Theological Investigations*, vol. 4 (Baltimore: Helicon, 1966) 344–46

Ramirez, S.M., 'Hope', *New Catholic Encyclopedia* (New York: McGraw-Hill, 1967) 7.133–41

Ramm, Bernard, *The Witness of the Spirit* (Grand Rapids: Eerdmans, 1959)

Reeves, Marjorie, 'The Originality and Influence of Joachim of Fiore', *Traditio* 36 (1980) 269–316

——, *The Influence of Prophecy in the Later Middle Ages: A Study in Joachimism* (Oxford: Clarendon, 1969)

Reinke, D.R., 'From Allegory to Metaphor: More Notes on Luther's Hermeneutical Shift', *Harvard Theological Review* 65 (1973) 386–96

Richardson, A. and Bowden, J. (eds.), *A New Dictionary of Christian Theology* (London: SCM, 1983)

Robert, Dana L., ' "The Crisis of Missions": Premillennial Mission Theory and the Origins of Independent Evangelical Missions', in Joel A. Carpenter and W. R. Shenk (eds.), *Earthen Vessels: American Evangelicals and Foreign Missions, 1880–1980* (Grand Rapids: Eerdmans, 1990) 29–56

Robinson, James M. (ed.), *The Nag Hammadi Library in English* (San Francisco: Harper and Row, [3]1988).

Rousseau, George S., 'Mysticism and Millenarianism: "Immortal Dr. Cheyne"', in R.H. Popkin (ed.), *Millenarianism and Messianism in English Literature and Thought 1650–1800* (Leiden: E.J. Brill, 1988) 81–112.

Rowe, David L., *Thunder and Trumpets: Millerites and Dissenting Religion in Upstate New York, 1800–1850* (Chico, Calif.: Scholars Press, 1985)

Russell, Robert,,'The Role of Neoplatonism in St Augustine's *De Civitate Dei*' in H.J. Blumenthal and R.A. Markus (eds.), *Neoplatonism and Early Christian Thought: Essays in Honor of A.H. Armstrong* (London: Variorum Publications, 1981) 160–70

Sanday W. and Headlam, A.C., *A Critical and Exegetical Commentary on the Epistle to the Romans* (Edinburgh: T. & T. Clark, 1902)

Sandeen, Ernest R., *The Roots of Fundamentalism: British and American Millenarianism, 1800–1930* (Grand Rapids: Baker, 1970)

Sayers, Dorothy L. and Reynolds, Barbara (trans.), *Dante, The Divine Comedy 3, Paradise* (London: Penguin Books, 1962)

Schmiel, David G., 'Martin Luther's Relationship to the Mystical Tradition', *Concordia Journal* March 1983, 45–9

Segundo, Jan Luis, *Signs of the Times: Theological Reflections*, A.T. Hennelly (ed.) (Maryknoll, New York: Orbis, 1983)

Siggins, I.D.K., *Luther* (Edinburgh: Oliver & Boyd, 1972)

Smith, Christopher R., 'Up and Doing': The Pragmatic Puritan Eschatology of John Owen', *Evangelical Quarterly* 61 (1989) 335–49.

Steinmetz, David C., 'Calvin and Abraham: The Interpretation of Romans 4 in the Sixteenth Century', *Church History* 57 (1988) 443–55

———, 'Calvin and the Absolute Power of God', *Journal of Medieval and Renaissance Studies* 18 (1988) 65–79

———, 'Luther and the Ascent of Jacob's Ladder', *Church History* 55 (1986) 179–92

———, *Luther in Context* (Bloomington: Indiana University Press, 1986)

Tapia, R.J., 'Habit (In Theology)', *New Catholic Encyclopedia* (New York: McGraw-Hill, 1967) 6.884–5

Toon, Peter, *God's Statesman* (Exeter: Paternoster, 1971)

Torrance, T.F., 'The Eschatology of the Reformation', in W. Manson (ed.), *Eschatology: Four Papers Read to the Society for the Study of Theology*, Scottish Journal of Theology Occasional Paper No. 2 (Edinburgh: Oliver & Boyd, 1952) 36–62

———, *The Hermeneutics of John Calvin* (Edinburgh: Scottish Academic Press, 1988)

———, *Kingdom and Church: A Study in the Theology of the Reformation* (Edinburgh: Oliver and Boyd, 1956)

———, 'Knowledge of God and Speech about Him according to John Calvin', *Theology in Reconstruction* (Grand Rapids: Eerdmans, 1975) 76–98

Townsend, Harvey G. (ed.), *The Philosophy of Jonathan Edwards from his Private Notebooks* (Eugene: University of Oregon Press, 1955)

Trompf, G.W., *Melanesian Religion* (Cambridge University Press, 1991)

Turner, Helen Lee and Guth, James L., 'The Politics of Armageddon: Dispensationalism among Southern Baptist Ministers', in Ted G. Jelen (ed.), *Religion and Political Behaviour in the United States* (New York: Praeger, 1989) 187–207

Wallace, W.A.and Weisheipl, J.A., 'Thomas Aquinas, St.', *New Catholic Encyclopedia* (New York: McGraw-Hill, 1967) 1.102–15

Webster, D.D., 'Liberation Theology', in W.A. Elwell (ed.) *Evangelical Dictionary of Theology* (Grand Rapids: Baker; Carlisle: Paternoster, 1984) 714–18

Weinstein, Donald, 'Savonarola, Florence and the Millenarian Tradition', *Church History*, 27 (1958) 291–305

Wells, David F., *God in the Wasteland* (Grand Rapids: Eerdmans, 1994)

West, Delno C. & Zimdars-Swartz, Sandra, *Joachim of Fiore: A Study in Spiritual Perception and History* (Bloomington: Indiana University Press, 1983)

Williams, Ramon, *'Sapientia and the Trinity: Reflections on the De Trinitate'*, in *Collectanea Augustiniana: Melages T.J. Van Bavel*, 2 vols. (Leuven University Press, 1990) 317–22

Wilson, John F., 'History, Redemption, and the Millennium', in N. Hatch and H. Stout (eds.), *Jonathan Edwards and the American Experience* (Oxford University Press, 1988) 131–41

Wimber, John, *Power Evangelism: Signs and Wonders Today* (London: Hodder & Stoughton, 1985)

Subject Index

Name Index